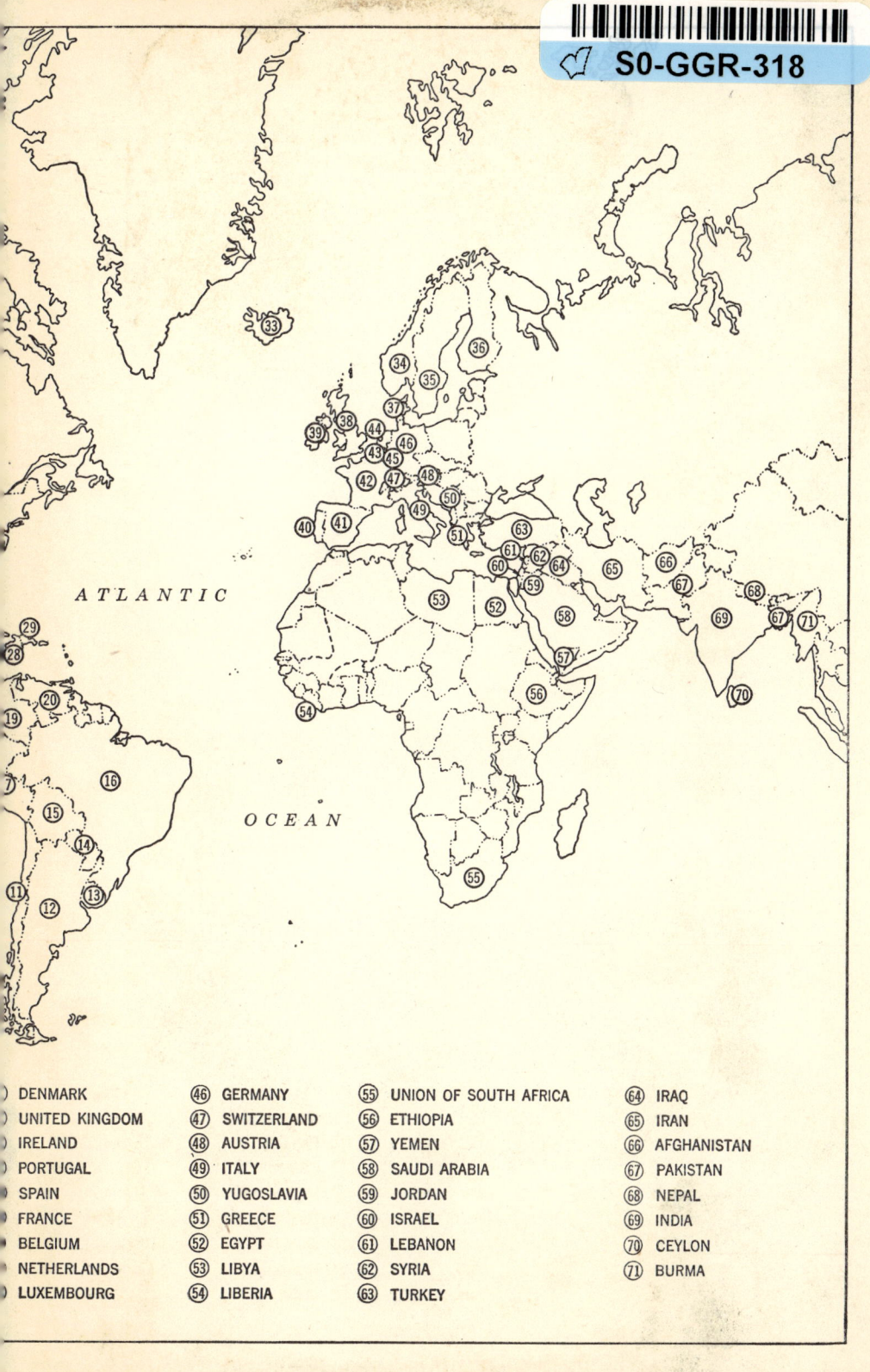

The Story of
F A O

GOVE HAMBIDGE
*North American Regional Representative
Food and Agriculture Organization
of the United Nations*

D. VAN NOSTRAND COMPANY, INC.

TORONTO　　　　NEW YORK　　　　LONDON

NEW YORK
D. Van Nostrand Company, Inc., 250 Fourth Avenue, New York 3

TORONTO
D. Van Nostrand Company (Canada), Ltd., 25 Hollinger Road, Toronto

LONDON
Macmillan & Company, Ltd., St. Martin's Street, London, W.C. 2

Copyright, 1955, by
D. VAN NOSTRAND COMPANY, INC.

Published simultaneously in Canada by
D. Van Nostrand Company (Canada), Ltd.

All rights reserved. This book, or any parts thereof, may not be reproduced in any form without written permission from the author and the publishers.

Library of Congress Catalog Card No. 55-6256

All royalties from the publication of this book are paid to FAO.

PRINTED IN THE UNITED STATES OF AMERICA

Preface

I HAVE BEEN closely associated with so much of the story told in this book that reading it seems almost like reading a chapter of my own life.

When I think back over the long, eventful period that life has spanned, it seems to me the years during which I was privileged to participate in the work of FAO were the best and most significant.

They have been years rich with the friendship of a host of men and women, partners in a struggle which surely is one of the most remarkable manifestations of these challenging times. I speak not only of the FAO staff but of the delegates and advisers who gather at our Conference sessions and Council meetings, and the many members of our technical advisory committees, and the government officials with whom we work in so many countries, and the research men and college professors, and the students who come to our training courses.

These people are from all parts of the world. They have profoundly different ethnic, cultural, religious, social, political, and economic backgrounds. They speak many different languages. But also they all speak the same language of science and technology and share the same dream of human advancement. They are a gallant company, growing in numbers and influence.

Some readers may think this book makes the struggle seem too easy. I can assure them it is not easy. Back of every effort and every success described in these pages lie hardships, disappointments, and delays which at times are so irksome as to wreck the health of individuals not fitted to cope with them. This will continue to be true for a long time, though conditions should gradually improve. I have a feeling that the kind of international teamwork described here is creating a new breed of explorers on the frontiers of social advance, one tough-minded and patient enough to stand persistent frustration without giving up.

But I do not mean to overemphasize this because the work is deeply rewarding.

Again, some readers may feel that the field operations of FAO, as this book describes them, consist too much of unrelated projects not coordinated in a general plan of development for each country and region. In a sense this is true, though I think there is more co-ordination and general planning than the author indicates. On the other hand, the reader must keep in mind that effective economic planning is a product of a rather high degree of development, whether the organization concerned is an industry or a government department. FAO deals in the main with the problems of countries that have not reached a high degree of economic development. In most cases, probably, they are planning and co-ordinating and integrating, to use the jargon of modern bureaucrats, as much as they are able to with the technical experience and material facilities they have available. They will do more as they develop further. Nor can FAO or any other international agency step in and do their planning for them. In the first place, no agency has enough staff or enough wisdom to plan the economic development of several score countries. In the second place, plans superimposed from outside could not be made to stick except by a world dictatorship, and probably not even then. These things have to grow from within, like the ability of a human being to creep, to stand, to walk, to run.

Governments created FAO to foster that growth. Impatience will not help, but it can hinder. This book tells about the first phase. It is a remarkable beginning.

NORRIS E. DODD

Baker, Oregon
September, 1954

Foreword

I HAVE TALKED about FAO with many people, individuals and groups, in a great many different places. Invariably I have sensed an immediate favorable response. Never have I seen an adverse reaction to the basic purpose, the major objectives of this organization.

But all too often I have been asked why *more people* do not know about FAO, why so many thousands who share a belief in its objectives have no understanding of its activities, or are unaware of its existence.

It is no simple task to tell the world about the job of FAO, especially when its limited resources are of necessity largely consumed in doing that job. Yet it is of the utmost importance that the world know FAO—what it is, what it does, and how it does it.

Now, at last, here is a book from the heart of FAO—an interesting, satisfying, and hope-inspiring presentation of a truly great international cooperative endeavor to promote peace and welfare in a troubled world.

The task of FAO is broad in scope and extremely difficult. Perhaps this *Story of FAO* is, if anything, too prone to stress achievements rather than obstacles. We are keenly aware of the impediments we face, the barriers we have to surmount, the disappointments we must encounter every day, and the failures we have at times been forced to acknowledge. But in spite of all this, we try always to see the horizon toward which we struggle, and we have a heartening feeling that we are making steady progress, as I believe this book shows. What we need is clear and sympathetic understanding and the moral as well as material support that such understanding brings.

P. V. CARDON

Rome
July, 1954

The Author to the Reader

YOU WILL REALIZE that having finished this book, I find myself in that humble and somewhat depressed state of mind in which an author realizes how much better any one of a number of other people could have done the work and deludes himself into thinking how much better even he could have done it if only he had had more time. In this mood he is strongly moved to indulge in a public avowal of faults and sins, which would be a waste of time because you will find them out soon enough.

A few explanations are in order nevertheless.

First I want to say that the book is in a sense a product of dual authorship. My assistant, Mrs. Frances Wyatt Rodgers, did so much of the work that her name might well be on the title page as a co-author. Without her capable, painstaking attention to the multitudinous details and the research attendant on such an undertaking, it could not have been carried through. Her direct contributions to the text are considerable, and the appendix and index are hers. Perhaps few people who do not write books realize how much labor they involve. For better or worse, for example, all of these chapters have been redone from three to six times, so that to produce a book of some 100,000 words meant dictating 500,000.

The book is mainly about FAO. It is not the story of world agricultural co-operation as a whole. I have tried, however, to sketch in a little of the background of earlier work by religious missions and other groups, indicate some of the current operations of national agencies and foundations, and show how FAO joins forces with United Nations organizations and others in many projects and programs. These references to various agencies are very incomplete indeed, but they may help you to see the work of FAO in its proper setting. I can only hope that other organizations and individuals will forgive the manifest failure to do justice to their efforts and realize that it was because I had to stick close to FAO's own story.

Necessarily, too, the story of FAO is a continued story, changing from day to day as the work goes on. New things are happening all the time, and in a book it is not possible to keep the account up to date as it is in a newspaper or journal. All the current projects discussed in this book will have undergone some change by the time it gets into type, and some will have been finished, and new ones will have started. But this does not matter; a book has functions different from those of a newspaper. I hope this one may contribute something to your understanding of some of the things that happen every day.

FAO has so far had some 800 technical experts in the field. I could not give all their names without making the book a directory; I could not omit all their names without being artificial and stilted. So I named some and did not name some. The choice, I fear, was decidedly hit-or-miss. The mention of a name does not mean that that particular man or woman was more important or meritorious than a dozen others not named; in some cases he or she may be less so. To the many not mentioned by name I tender my regrets.

For the same reason I tender regrets to most of my fellow workers on the FAO permanent staff. All of them deserve to be named in this story, which is essentially their story, but that was not feasible. To avoid any feeling of invidious comparisons, I finally decided that it would be best to name no one unless it could hardly be avoided, usually for historical reasons, or because of authorship of a book mentioned, or something of the sort. You will understand, however, that *The Story of FAO* is fundamentally a product of the thought and effort of the whole staff. I wrote the chronicle. They did the work. Some of them also read the manuscript, pinpointed mistakes and weaknesses, and suggested valuable improvements. I am deeply grateful. For any errors that remain I am responsible.

Acknowledgments are due to several outside the staff who also read the manuscript and suggested corrections and emendations, including particularly Dr. Frank G. Boudreau, F. F. Elliott, Reverend William J. Gibbons, S.J., Wylie Goodsell, John Reisner, Hazel K. Stiebeling, Conrad Taeuber.

Norris E. Dodd was godfather to the project during the latter part of his service as Director-General of FAO, and I am greatly indebted to his understanding and interest.

I have eliminated footnotes and tried to avoid cluttering the text with long lists. If the reader wants to know what people were on a certain committee or what countries were represented at a certain meeting, he will find them in the appendix, under the proper page number. The appendix also contains some other reference data.

GOVE HAMBIDGE

Washington
January, 1955

Contents

	PAGE
Preface	iii
Foreword	v
The Author to the Reader	vii
List of Illustrations	xi

Part I. The Background

CHAPTER
1	ABU LIBDA	3
2	JIM BARTON	18
3	NARROW THE GAP	28

Part II. FAO: Genesis and Development

4	CONCEPTION	39
5	BIRTH	50
6	GROWTH	61
7	NEW DIRECTIONS	82

Part III. Technical Co-operation

8	NEAR EAST AND AFRICA	101
	Regional Projects	101
	Work with Individual Countries	114

9	FAR EAST	145
	Regional Projects	145
	Work with Individual Countries	163
10	LATIN AMERICA	179
	Regional Projects	179
	Work with Individual Countries	194
11	EUROPE	216
	Regional Projects	217
	Work with Individual Countries	228
	APPENDIX	239
	SOME SOURCE MATERIAL	264
	INDEX	279

List of Illustrations

FOLLOWING PAGE 20

Preparing food in an Indian village
Ethiopian woman spinning her own cotton thread
Peruvian woman and girls doing their laundry
Fetching water in East Bengal
A nomad home in Afghanistan
Children working in Peru
An Afghan boy bringing home firewood
Woman and child learn about food and health in Thailand
High-school boy studying chemistry in India
Schoolgirls in a chemical laboratory in Ceylon
A growing hunger for education

FOLLOWING PAGE 84

Young men in Pakistan using primitive hoes
Afghan farmer with a broad-bladed mattock
Javanese women harvesting rice
Farmer in Ceylon threshing grain
Afghan farmer and the hand sickles used to harvest crops
Small-tools expert displaying better hand tools on an FAO mission in Afghanistan
Afghan farmer with his new scythe
The water buffalo, one of the world's most useful creatures
The camel, another hard and faithful worker
Donkey and camel carrying firewood in Libya
Elephant at work in Thailand

FOLLOWING PAGE 148

Afghan farmer using a team of bullocks for plowing
Afghan farmer learning about tractors
Irrigating land by a slow backbreaking method
Modern tractor clearing an area in northern Ceylon
Farmers cultivating rice fields in the Gal Oya area
Workers hauling dirt on an irrigation project in Java
Log being split at a plywood factory in India
Truck trailer replaces the elephant in Thailand
Boatbuilder using primitive tools on a beach in Pakistan
Worker running a wood-molding machine in Ceylon
Hybrid corn breeder in Italy
Indian scientist and his microscope in the rice field
Ethiopian farmer admires the quality of flax fiber

FOLLOWING PAGE 212

Ethiopian technicians inoculating an animal against rinderpest
Afghan army officer sterilizing needles in the field
Clearing a road in Afghanistan
Sanitary inspector examining cows in Ecuador
Afghan boy getting his birds inoculated
Swarms of desert locusts in flight
Laboratory worker in Nicaragua prepares locust specimens
Marketplace in Guatemala
Cotton grading in Afghanistan
Fishermen and their sailboats in Ceylon
Fishermen and their motor-powered boats in Ceylon
Javanese inland fish culture
Thai women fishing

PART ONE

The Background

CHAPTER ONE

Abu Libda

We went to the village where Abu Libda lives. Abu is one of millions of fellaheen, the peasants of Egypt, tillers of the soil. This was in the days before the new land reforms were made. Some people think the land reform in Egypt will prove in the long run to be one of the great advances of modern times. In any case, it will eventually change some of the conditions we saw on that journey. It is the more important, then, to describe these conditions because they were part of the reason for the land reform.

Like most villages in the Nile Delta, Abu's village was a collection of one- and two-story dwellings made of clay plastered over a framework of cornstalks or reeds or palm leaves. The houses were not separated from each other but were built in rows. They seemed to be part of the earth and to have risen out of it.

Abu's House

Each house had a doorway and perhaps two small openings in the thick walls for windows. In the center was a small courtyard, essentially a room without a roof, where daylight entered from above. Here Abu kept his animals—a *gamoosa,* or female water buffalo; some chickens; and several rabbits, so clean they looked freshly laundered, in a round basket made of clay and straw.

Abu's wife and two other women sat on the earthen steps leading up to the roof. Four small children played on the floor. A baby lay on his stomach on a piece of burlap. Every inch of his body not covered by a little shirt was covered by flies. Through the dirt and the sores on their faces, the children smiled at us shyly and sweetly.

A doorway from the courtyard led to a small dim bedroom or sleeping place. It consisted of a raised platform made of clay which filled the whole room except for a narrow passage. This platform served as the family bed and also as an oven, since the space underneath was used for baking. Straw was spread over the platform for bedding. The bedroom passageway was occupied by a calf.

Egyptian families are large, often consisting of parents, married children, small children, and a relative or two. Most of the family apparently slept on this bed except in summer, when they slept on the roof or, some of them, in the fields.

The other room was a living room. It contained a dilapidated couch, two or three battered chairs, a table on which stood unglazed water jugs cooled by evaporation of moisture from the clay surface, and a kerosene lamp. These, plus a few cooking utensils, were all the household possessions. They were more than most families had. In fact, not many could afford a *gamoosa;* they had to be satisfied with a donkey.

On the whitewashed walls of the living room inscriptions from the Koran had been painted, since Abu Libda's father was one of those pious persons who had made a pilgrimage to Mecca—a memorable thing, for hardly ever does a man or woman go away from the village, and those who do go are likely not to stay long because of the homesickness. (Abu's father could not read the inscriptions on the wall. None of the adults could read or write, and the news they got came mainly by word of mouth.)

The house had a strong animal-and-manure smell. The children hardly bothered to brush the flies, which buzzed everywhere, off their faces.

On the roof was the fuel for the under-bed stove—dry cotton stalks and cornstalks for quick fires and flat dried cakes of dung and chopped straw, made by the women and children, for long-lasting fires. Also on the roof were a pigeon house and a small, dome-shaped clay storage place for grain.

We walked along the village streets—narrow alleys where children, donkeys, goats, and chickens wandered. Now and again a woman passed, balancing on her head a big water jug tilted jauntily sidewise. There was one tiny store, probably owned by a Greek who was also the village moneylender.

The poverty and squalor, the dust, dirt, sores, flies seem to a Westerner almost unbearable. But the fellaheen live so day after day and year after year and generation after generation. They do not know anything better. They do not live long.

It was threshing time, and to the big flat threshing area by the bank of the canal wheat had been brought from the fields. Abu Libda and some of his neighbors forked it from the piles and spread it on the earthen floor in three or four big circles. In each circle the grain was trampled and cut by a *norag,* a sort of sled of heavy planks fitted with sharp steel disks turning on three axles and drawn slowly by a pair of water buffaloes or cows or donkeys or camels or a mixed team of two kinds of animals. The driver sat on a high seat, and as the *norag* was dragged monotonously round and round, the animals trampled out the grain and the steel disks chopped the stalks into small pieces. Children love to ride on the *norags,* and sometimes small children drive them.

The *norags* made a gentle creaking sound. Golden dust rose endlessly from the threshing floor into the soft Egyptian sunlight. The whole scene—the sleepy village street on one side, the slow-flowing canal on the other, the women, many of them young and beautiful, balancing their water jugs with such graceful dignity, the slender white egrets or herons by the canal bank—looked just as it might have in the days of the Pharaoh whose grain storage problems Joseph tried to solve. On the walls of pyramids and temples thousands of years old scenes exactly like this are painted.

After the *norags* have done their work, the villagers winnow the grain by tossing the chopped straw into the wind with four-tined wooden forks. The straw blows to one side, and the heavier grain falls straight to the ground; the women then sift out the chaff in large flat basketlike containers and put the grain in sacks for market. Only city people eat wheat. Country folk like Abu Libda live on corn, which is cheaper because an acre of land yields twice as much corn as wheat.

The Imam's House

In another village we visited a much better house. It was owned by an *Imam,* a religious leader. The *Imam* and his wife had no children, so it cost them less to live than the average family. He was a retired craftsman who owned two acres of land which he rented at a good price—45 Egyptian pounds, or nearly $130, an acre. His income was therefore generous compared with that of most fellaheen, and this was reflected in much better living conditions.

The *Imam's* only animals, a few chickens and rabbits, were kept on the roof and not allowed to run loose in the house, so there were practically no flies. The dirt floors were so carefully made that they looked almost like concrete. The inside walls were whitewashed in bright colors, and everything looked clean and neat. Clean mats instead of straw covered the bedstove, and for summer use there was a metal bed on the roof. The *Imam* could afford the luxury of a pump, so built as to be free from contamination, and the house had a latrine in a tiny room off the courtyard. The *Imam* was ingeniously making a small radio out of odds and ends, including an inductance coil and a crystal. On a little patch of ground in the square courtyard behind the house he had an orange tree, a guava tree, a grape arbor, and a few vegetables.

The chief landlord of this village of 4000 people owned some 800 acres which he rented to the fellaheen at the equivalent of some $100 an acre a year. Only about half the fellaheen in Egypt's 4000 villages owned any land themselves; the rest were sharecroppers and wage laborers. Of the landowners, about five out of six had less than an acre apiece—not enough, even with Egypt's high yields and low living standards, to support a family. Half of one per cent of all the landowners owned 40 per cent of all the arable land, in big estates. These were mostly absentee landlords.

Workers were plentiful. A wage laborer made perhaps 40 cents a day; a woman, 25 cents; a boy, 20 cents. Abu was always in debt.

Not Pyramids but People

In Cairo you can look across the Nile from the hotel and see two ghostly stone pyramids in the distance. These are at Giza. They are reminders of the ancient glory of Egypt, one of the great builders of civilization thousands of years before any European set foot on America.

Egyptian architecture, sculpture, painting, mathematics, religion, philosophy—these were unique. In originality and vigor ancient Egyptian art compares favorably with that of any civilization. The feats of construction of ancient Egypt seem almost superhuman to anyone who has seen the massive pyramids, built with no mechanical equipment, merely by making long runways of earth up which thousands of slaves, under the overseer's whip, dragged huge squared stones to make dwelling places for the souls and possessions of dead kings.

The tombs were elaborate houses for the *Ka,* or spirit, which when it left the body must have food and drink and be able to return to the body. So that each *Ka* might be sure to find the right body, the Egyptian sculptors and painters developed extraordinary skill in realistic portrayal. This art and architecture is itself the *Ka* of ancient Egypt. For that Egypt is as dead as the old Pharaohs.

Tourists come from all over the world, and rightly, to admire its achievements. Most of them, however, see little of the life and problems of Egypt today. When they are not looking at ruins, they spend their time in the great cities, especially Cairo. There they see magnificent mosques with graceful minarets like spears striving to pierce the blue heavens. They see the bazaars, where narrow streets zigzag in a tangled maze, filled with people on foot, on donkeyback, on camelback, driving carts, shouting their wares, laughing, singing, and bargaining over every purchase, big or little, in the open stalls. A bazaar is a warmly human, colorful place, a place where you are close to human beings in their most lively companionable mood. But the life of most of the people of Egypt is in the villages and fields, not in the cities.

Erosion for Life

Across the Delta country we journeyed from Cairo north and west to Alexandria. This is the lower end of the Nile, toward the sea, where the river fans out into a great triangular estuary.

This river is the life of Egypt. Flying over the country, you see a meandering narrow green strip abruptly flanked on both sides by pale desert sand. There is no intermediate stage; it is desert or crops. Southward, in Upper Egypt, the green strip is often no more than 2 miles wide. Northward from Cairo, in the Delta, the land is crisscrossed with irrigation and drainage canals.

More than 90 per cent of the people are crowded along this narrow cultivated band which covers only one-thirtieth of the land area. It is not unlike California's San Joaquin Valley. Egypt has practically no rain of its own; it has to get its rain second hand, via the Nile, from Ethiopia, Kenya, Uganda, Tanganyika. During the rainy season the water that pours in torrents into the streams in these countries carries with it enormous masses of soil from the eroding hills. Heavily charged with this silt, collected in a journey of 3000 miles, two great rivers, the White Nile and the Blue Nile, join at Khartoum, in the Sudan, to become the Nile. The Aswan Dam, at Egypt's border, impounds the flood waters and carefully bestows their fertility upon Egypt.

Erosion created Egypt's civilization and sustains its people. About 110 million tons of silt come down every year from Ethiopia and the other lands to the south to be spread thinly over the Nile Valley lands. But this has been going on so long that even though only $4\frac{1}{2}$ inches are deposited in a hundred years, the depth of the rich soil is between 50 and 70 feet.

In the Upper Nile region great dams now spread the water over a wider area than in ancient times. Ridges and dikes make rectangular basins into which the water is led in floodtime, about the middle of August. From then until October the water flows gently over the land and lays down the lifegiving silt. Then it is run off and the crop is planted.

This basin irrigation, which goes far back in the history of Egypt, supplies water for only one crop a year. Not enough moisture is left in the soil after harvest for another crop. Only in limited areas where there are canals or pumps can more than one crop a year be grown in Upper Egypt on the same land.

But in the Delta region, Lower Egypt, irrigation water is available the year round through an elaborate system of canals and drainage ditches completed in about 1840. The land is never idle, and its 12,000 square miles, an oasis in 400,000 square miles of desert, is the most productive and most crowded part of Egypt. But year-round irrigation has not been without its penalties. It has raised the water table to dangerous levels, increased the salt content of the soil, and spread malaria and parasitic diseases.

Good Farmers

Practically every foot of Delta land is cultivated except where villages squat or there are roads and canals. The villages are not far apart. From a distance along the road they look like brown earth mounds, with a few graceful palms and a minaret breaking the skyline. In the occasional larger towns are busy markets and places where you can sit down to enjoy a cup or two of thick Turkish coffee.

Everywhere, people like Abu Libda are working at a steady, unhurried pace which seems to be timed to the deliberate strides of the camel and *gamoosa*. These, with the donkey, are the constant companions of the fellah, almost members of the family as well as almost his sole capital wealth. The donkey is the animal most commonly used for hauling loads and riding. As for the *gamoosa*, it is one of the world's most remarkable animals. A man is lucky indeed if he owns one, since it is worth about 100 Egyptian pounds (nearly $300). Most of the male water buffaloes, which have the reputation of being bad-tempered, are killed young and sold for veal; usually only one or two are saved for breeding in each village. The females are not dual-purpose but quadruple-purpose animals, providing labor, food, fertilizer, and fuel, besides companionship for the children. Healthy, strong, patient, the *gamoosa* not only does the field work but produces more milk than the average Egyptian cow, and milk with much more butterfat. Along any canal toward the end of the day you can see *gamoosas* submerged so that only horns, eyes, and nose show above the water. Food and a muddy bath to soak in—these are the only rewards they ask.

We passed groups of chattering women, on their way to market, with bundles and baskets and jars on their heads. (Sometimes a woman leads one child, carries another in her arms, has a third in the womb.) Market day, about once a week, is a big event. The marketplace is the center for exchanging news and gossip. Little heaps of grain and other products are placed on the ground, each seller squatting beside his little pile.

Abu Libda's wife was in one of the groups along the road. She lifted the basket down from her head and showed us what it contained—a dozen hens' eggs, not much bigger than pullets' eggs; a bit of cheese and a bit of butter, both white because the fat of buffalo milk is white; some fenugreek —all to be sold in the marketplace for a few piastres; and a little corn, to be ground at the mill for the family. They cannot afford to keep such good foods as milk and eggs to eat themselves; these must be sold to buy other necessities. The basket also contained three or four large flat cakes of crisp bread made of cornmeal mixed with fenugreek. These Abu Libda's wife would have for her noon meal. (Fenugreek is a leguminous plant with oily seeds that have an odd, rather agreeable taste and so strong an odor that it may dominate whole sections of a marketplace. The seeds are reputed to be rich in pellagra-preventing B vitamins, and they have a glutinous quality which binds the dough better than when it is made of corn alone.)

Abu Libda could not live without corn. Half the cultivated land in Egypt is used to grow grains, yet it has been necessary since the war to import half a million tons every year. Cornbread, the Egyptian equivalent of tortillas, supplies about three-fourths of the fellah's energy. When did this crop come from the Americas to Africa? It has long been grown in Egypt, where its name is *dura,* but it was certainly not known to the ancient Egyptians. Its introduction must have meant a revolutionary change in the food habits of almost a whole country. Yet people say food habits cannot be changed.

Beans are the other principal food, again as in most of Latin America, and among poor people in all countries where meat is scarce. They are cooked in many ways, often in the form of a dish called *bisara,* made of dried broad-beans pounded, boiled to a sort of mush, and mixed with jute leaves. Sometimes the *bisara* contains fried onion or garlic and a bit of *samn,* liquid butter. On rare occasions a little meat may be added, but Abu Libda's family seldom has meat except when an animal has to be slaughtered for some reason or someone holds a feast. Another common dish is *kushr,* made of lentils and rice. Various kinds of squashes are eaten cooked, and onions, turnips, green peppers, cucumbers, usually raw, are also eaten. Most people also are able to get fruit, especially dates.

Abu's food provides barely enough energy for the work he does. But he is not starving; there are no famines, as there used to be. The nature of the irrigated agriculture in Egypt makes it possible to bank on a sure crop every year. (But infant mortality is high, and this is usually an indicator of poor nutrition.)

These people are skilled farmers. The big crops are corn and wheat for food, berseem clover for the work animals, cotton for sale. The average corn production per acre, 33 bushels (1952), is 20 per cent less than the average in the United States. Wheat production averages 28 bushels to the acre (1952), compared with 18 in the USA (but all Egyptian wheat is grown on irrigated land, which boosts yields tremendously, as it does in the case of other crops). Rice production also is high, 65 bushels per acre in 1952 compared with 99 for Italy, 82 for Japan, 54 for the USA. Cotton yields top those of all other countries; in 1952 the average was 481 pounds per acre compared with 276 in the USA.

Though these yields are good, they could be increased with certain improvements in farming methods. The trouble in Egypt, however, is not low yields but too little arable land for the number of people who have to live on it. In some countries the opposite is true; there are too few people to make full use of the land.

Straws and Camels

Abu Libda works hard. His principal tool, the universal tool, is a *fass,* a heavy mattock with a broad iron head and short handle, stumpy as a sawed-off shotgun, which is used as a spade to break up and turn the soil and to dig and clean ditches, and as a hoe for weeding and tillage. A man or woman wielding a *fass* has to bend double, and it must take a lot of energy in a day's work.

Abu's plow is primitive too. Essentially it is a piece of tree branch, sharpened at one end, which is tipped with an iron point, and fitted with a handle to hold on to at the other end. This implement weighs about 100 pounds and has a shaft 10 feet or more long to which draft animals are attached, the yoke pressing on their withers. They are guided by hand and voice without reins or bridle. With this plow, which breaks up but does not turn the soil, Abu can scratch about three-fourths of an acre a day.

For harrowing he uses a drag made of a tree trunk or beam of wood to level the furrows and break up clods. He also uses an animal-drawn scoop, the *cassabia,* to scrape down hummocks and fill hollows. In this irrigated country all the land must be as flat as possible. A bit of leveling here and there may add a few precious feet to the crop area.

Animals and people, not machines, do practically all the farm work. Along the road you constantly pass animals and people carrying all kinds of loads. Camels plod by, swaying like boats in a groundswell, carrying big flat baskets of humus scraped up from somewhere (the fellah needs more commercial fertilizer than he can afford, so he uses whatever else he can find) and manure (which is animal urine mixed with straw and earth, since much of the dung is used for fuel), to be placed carefully by hand around each plant; or loads of berseem to feed livestock; or square stacks of straw that look as if they would be a load for a half-ton truck. A camel on his knees under this load is completely out of sight except for his head sticking out of the bottom of the pile; he wears an expression of combined scorn and boredom that may or may not represent his true feelings. You understand then the proverb about the straw that broke the camel's back; it looks as if one more would. The cheerful little donkeys are similarly loaded, and often a woman goes by carrying, it seems, as much straw on her head as half a camel load. No one made a proverb about her.

Water

Always on the canals and river are boats. The heavy broad-beamed feluccas ride high at prow and stern, but when they are loaded, the gunwales amidships are almost at water level. Each boat is rigged with a triangular lateen sail, graceful as a heron's wing. Occasionally one sees a motor-driven barge, or a string of barges towed by a tug. The boats carry cotton to the great cotton trading center, Alexandria, and bricks and sand and all kinds of goods. To pass under the low Nile bridges, the boatmen furl the felucca's sail and take down the mast, neatly and expeditiously, like a heron folding its wing.

The canals are the main water supply, for irrigation and every other need. At the canal's edge, men strip, walk into the water, and bathe. Women go in waist-deep with their clothes on, taking a bath fully dressed and doing the family washing. From the canal, too, they fill the jars with water for drinking and cooking. Animals bathe in the canal. The desire for cleanliness is not accompanied by knowledge of the nature of sanitation such as has gradually become widespread in the West. There are places where the canals have to be drained for cleaning once a year. Here for a couple of months there may be no water at all for drinking or cooking or bathing except what can be dipped from stagnant scum-covered pools.

The thousands of miles of canals and ditches are the veins, arteries, capillaries carrying the lifeblood of the Delta. Life centers around water. As in all irrigated country, there must be strict laws to insure that every man has his just share of the precious fluid and does nothing that might deprive his neighbor of a just share. So the water is carefully rationed (though some experts think it is used more liberally than necessary for economical crop production). Abu is allowed to spread water on his land for so many days during flood time and so many days when the Nile is low. The law prescribes the kinds of crops he can grow, the quantities, when he must plant, and many other things. Keeping the water channels clear takes a good deal of his time.

Again and again along the road we saw people working at the endless task of getting water onto the fields. In the Delta country four principal devices are used. The first and simplest is a big tin or leather bucket which is dipped into the water, lifted, poured out, dipped, lifted, poured out, rhythmically for hours under the hot sun, usually by two men standing face to face. It is a very slow, laborious way to irrigate.

Then there is the *shaduf,* also a bucket but this time hung by a rope from the end of a 10-foot pole, which has a counterweight of rock or a lump of dried clay at the other end and is balanced on a crossbar. Essentially, the *shaduf* is a wellsweep. With it, too, the work of lowering, lifting, emptying goes on all day, but it is less strenuous.

The *tambour,* or screw of Archimedes, is a wooden cylinder 6 to 10 feet long with a spiral inside which is turned by a crank. The lower end of the cylinder is held under the water, and as the spiral turns it lifts the water up the sloping cylinder and empties it steadily out of the upper end. Two men turn the screw, and this too is hard, monotonous work, but faster than a bucket.

Finally there is the *saqia,* a big horizontal wheel with cogs that engage the cogs on a vertical wheel. The lower edge of the vertical wheel is below water level and pots are fastened close together around its circumference. As they dip under the surface the pots fill with water which they spill out when they reach the top, much as a mechanical ditch digger scoops up and dumps out dirt. The heavy *saqia* is turned by a donkey, *gamoosa,* or camel hitched to the horizontal wheel which it turns by plodding in a circle, eyes blindfolded with a thick pad to keep it from getting dizzy. Usually a child is in charge to keep the animal moving. The wheels make a perpetual groaning, creaking lament, and this sound is very characteristic of the Egyptian countryside.

All four of these methods were in use in the days of the Pharaohs. They are wasteful of time and labor; none will irrigate more than an acre a day; small pumps would be far more efficient. But Abu has muscle; he has time; he does not have money; so he does the best he can. Seeing him, you appreciate what a blessing it is to have water just drop down from the sky.

The main impressions you get traveling over the Delta are these: the endless hard labor of the fellaheen, for so little return; the wretchedness of the places in which they live; the lack of possessions, things they can use and enjoy and call their own; the competence of their farm work with very primitive equipment; the immense fertility and tranquil loveliness of this countryside.

But the surrounding desert, from which came this rich Delta garden, is harsh and cruel. One evening we were to drive back from Alexandria to Cairo by the desert road. All afternoon it had been oppressively hot, and the wind blew, and overhead drifted an ominous yellowish-gray dust cloud. This was the *Khamsin,* the wind that ushers in summer and stirs up desert sandstorms. We did not come back by the desert road that day. When this wind blows, visibility in the desert is zero. Driving sand blots out roads, chokes motors, scours cars of enamel. You wait respectfully wherever you happen to be until the raging desert is calm again.

Big Farm

We visited the estate of a wealthy landowner, a pasha (before that traditional title was abolished), one of the few who owned so much of Egypt. We crossed the canal on a barge and entered the grounds through a gate in a wall blazing with bougainvillea blossoms. On the other side lay 600 acres of the richest greenery one could see anywhere.

This land had been newly reclaimed not many years before. Practically all of it was a vast grove of fruit trees and vines, including citrus, mangoes, grapes, all thriving wonderfully. At least 300 fellaheen were employed on the estate, which was skilfully managed. The income from the fruit was said to be equivalent to about a quarter million US dollars a year.

At the time of our visit the owner was abroad, but we were guests at a luncheon in his luxuriously furnished house. The meal was sumptuous, starting with huge casseroles of squabs cooked with rice, baked to a crusty brown, and going on and on through one delicious dish after another until we were stuffed with food and ready for a siesta. Instead we mounted donkeys and ambled along the broad shady avenues to inspect groves of fruit trees.

At one point were a dozen or so big Egyptian pigeon cotes. These are of whitewashed clay, gleaming in the sun and looking like gigantic old-fashioned cone-shaped beehives, perhaps 20 feet high, raised on stilts. All around the cones were holes for the pigeons to enter, with a perch below each hole. Great numbers of pigeons flew and fluttered around the towers.

Abu Libda

One of these structures may house as many as 60,000 birds, 30,000 pairs. The cotes provide not only squabs but large quantities of much needed manure, rather like the guano islands off Peru.

At the end of an avenue we came to a high fence. On our side was lush greenery; on the other, bleak desert stretching away to the horizon; and far off across the sands, a camel caravan silhouetted sharp against the sky. A little water made this difference; but it did not account for the difference between this estate and Abu Libda's acre.

The Welfare Centers

The government has village welfare centers throughout Egypt, and at one we saw some of the work being done to improve agriculture and village life. A ferment of change is under way to better Abu Libda's lot and solve some of Egypt's difficult economic and social problems.

The houses in the welfare-center village were of better quality and were better cared for than those in other villages. Some were neatly square instead of random-shaped, and were painted on the outside.

In the main building we were met by a buxom, healthy, intelligent young woman who served as village nurse and midwife, ran the day nursery, and taught domestic science and needlecraft. In the nursery lunchroom 50 little girls and boys, bright, clean, and dressed in pink smocks, were sitting at a big oblong table getting a noonday meal of eggs, cheese, beans, honey, and bread. At ten that morning they had each had a glass of tomato juice or milk. The young woman gives the children a bath when they arrive in the morning, and they are taught to wash their hands before meals and at other times. Several girls about fifteen years old help in the nursery, which includes a simply-equipped play yard.

This is much better for the small children of the village than being left all day in the streets while their mothers work in the fields.

There were rooms at the social center which the village women could use, instead of the canal, for bathing themselves and their babies or for doing the family laundry. The nurse taught sewing, mending, and embroidery at the center, and she went to the women's homes to teach cookery and child care. The center also had a boys' club, a medical clinic, and an outpatient clinic. Attendance at the public school was compulsory. (Many people report a growing hunger for education in Egypt, even in the rural areas where children are often needed to work on the farms. A rural school has been established in each village where there is a welfare center.)

So that all the families would feel they had a stake in the work of the center, each paid 12 piastres (about 35 cents USA) a year toward its expenses. Committees of villagers took part in the work. The agriculture committee was concerned with such things as distributing seed of improved varieties of crop plants, teaching the villagers how to use fertilizer and control plant diseases and insects, obtaining veterinary services, providing improved sires on government loan for better livestock breeding, improving poultry through the distribution of good-quality chicks free or at low cost, substituting modern movable-frame beehives for antiquated skeps, and rearing of silkworms.

The village welfare centers were started in 1941, and by 1950, 136 were in existence. The plan of the government has been to extend them gradually to all the villages in Egypt. They are under the supervision of the Fellah Department, a branch of the Ministry of Social Affairs.

These centers foster home industries and small rural industries using raw materials available locally—for instance, rug and carpet weaving, spinning, weaving cloth and matting (of which large amounts are used in Egypt), and knitting shawls and stockings and *libdas* (skull caps, worn by Abu Libda and practically every other fellah). The centers are active in setting up co-operative societies; they hold evening classes to reduce adult illiteracy; they conduct lectures and discussions, establish rural libraries, operate village radios, show educational films, give theatrical plays.

Nine out of Ten

At another village we visited a health center which served several villages, including Abu Libda's. There were then 170 such centers in Egypt. This one served about 30,000 people. Nine out of ten of those who came to the clinic had internal parasites, the most common being bilharzia, a minute, bloodsucking fluke. The bilharzia egg is carried by human urine into the irrigation canals or onto damp ground. The parasite lives for a while in a snail, returns to the water, and then enters the human body. Since practically everyone walks barefoot on irrigated land or bathes in the canals, there is plenty of opportunity for the flukes to penetrate the skin. Once inside, the parasites may reach the bladder, kidneys, liver, even the eyes, producing dysentery, hemorrhages, sometimes tumors. The disease may persist for 20 years. No one afflicted with it ever feels entirely well.

Hookworm was common, too, and so was the amoeba which is the source of amoebic dysentery. We saw patients with asthma, jaundice, pellagra, anemia. Malaria was widespread, and more than half the people had eye diseases, including trachoma; throughout Egypt you see many who are blind or have lost the sight of one eye.

The maternity clinic at the center was the one that helped Abu Libda's wife when she had trouble with her last baby. When we visited it, there were several women and children (the clinic takes care of children up to a year old) in the waiting room, most of them sitting on the floor instead of the benches. All the women wore the usual dark shawl that covers them from head to feet. The babies hardly moved; none of them cried; even the older children seemed subdued. Maybe they were awed by this unusual place. Only one little girl was playing, trying to walk around the room in her mother's shoes.

The indispensable need of every family is to have sons who can help with the farm work. If a woman bears eight children, three or four are likely to die in their first year. Since some of the children will be girls, it is necessary to have a considerable number to make sure there will be a surviving boy or two.

The health centers have paid major attention to the fly problem. We were told that they have used all the modern fly killers in succession, beginning with DDT. A few flies were resistant enough to each of the chemicals in turn to survive, and the survivors quickly built up large resistant fly populations. So the flies won in that phase of the battle and continued to spread diseases. Perhaps the problem will not be fully solved until some age-old customs are changed, particularly the custom of keeping farm animals in the house, and the habit of using any convenient spot outdoors as a toilet. Some health authorities are now drilling latrines at intervals, but it will be some time before enough are available for general use. This problem is more difficult in farm areas than in factories.

So the average man in Egypt cannot count on living beyond the age of thirty-six, or the average woman beyond forty-two, and the infant mortality rate is one of the highest in the world.

Too Few Too Much—Too Many Too Little

Nevertheless the population has grown faster than production has increased, even with additions brought by new irrigation and drainage works. In that direction, much more work is now under way or planned.

According to an official report in 1950, it is calculated that the electrification of Aswan Dam and new irrigation programs will increase the cultivable land by about 40 per cent, to 7 million feddans. The Aswan Dam electrification project would provide current for deep-well irrigation pumps in Upper Egypt, which in turn would make it possible to grow more than one crop a year and to diversify agricultural production considerably. Power from Aswan would also be used for nitrate manufacture; in fact it would lead to a good deal of industrial development. A start has been made on much more extensive (and costly) long-term engineering projects beyond the borders of Egypt, near the headwaters of the Nile in the Sudan and Ethiopia.

Before the land decree of the new government went into effect, the children divided the land they inherited on the death of the head of a family, the sons receiving twice as much as the daughters. "It is by no means unusual," said Father Ayrout in his perceptive book, *The Fellaheen,* "to find the grandson of a man who had forty feddans [a feddan is a little over an acre] inheriting no more than one, so that he falls back to the level of the fellaheen." In extreme cases, several families might own one date palm. Father Ayrout went on to say that the small holdings resulting from this continual subdivision through inheritance accentuated the very conditions that caused them. Help was wanted as cheap as possible; children could provide it; so Abu Libda was forced to have as many children as possible. In fact, wife, children, *gamoosa,* and donkey constituted his capital and production equipment.

Too few people owned too much land, and too many owned too little. The contrast between the luxury of the pasha's estate we visited and the misery of the villages was stamped on the whole countryside. "The economic progress of Egypt," Father Ayrout noted, "is as striking as its political development. . . . But this progress has resulted in no increased well being for the fellah. His standards of life and his methods of work have remained unchanged. . . . Neither capital nor industry has helped the fellaheen." Economic development, in other words, resulted in a highly profitable agriculture supported by modern engineering works, but it did not lower the fellah's rent or raise his wages.

There were many signs of revolt against these conditions at the time when the new land reform law was promulgated on September 9, 1952, and there had long been evidence of a growing social consciousness. Progressive Egyptians, including some high army officers and government officials, some large landlords, some members of the middle class, had become increasingly aware of the nature of the situation and its dangers. Something had to be done to bring a genuine improvement in the lot of the fellaheen. One manifestation of this concern was the comprehensive plan for the development of such welfare and health centers as those already described. But these did not, by themselves, go to the heart of the problem. "The almost unanimous expert opinion," Hedley V. Cooke noted, "is that the breaking up of the great estates into small but viable holdings, together with an alteration of the inheritance laws and a consolidation of holdings which are too small to be economic, would constitute the most important step in the right direction which the government could take." The aim would be to end absentee landlordism by redistributing land among the fellaheen in holdings of about 5 acres per family—a size generally regarded as sufficient under conditions of year-round irrigation such as prevail in Lower Egypt.

The New Land Laws

Thus there was a marked consensus of opinion among various groups within Egypt and friendly observers outside about the nature of the reforms needed to remedy conditions that had become almost intolerable for Abu Libda and his kind. These changes were started in the sweeping 1952 land decree. The new law was sudden only in the manner of its making. It had behind it a long background of thoughtful analysis.

Shortly after this law went into effect the government published an explanatory note which brings out with great frankness many of the conditions already discussed in this chapter.

For example, the note points out that in Egypt people tend to invest their savings in agricultural land. This raises the price of land and forces landowners to try to get as large a return as they can from the soil, which they do by reducing expenses—that is, paying as little as possible to agricultural labor.

The bad distribution of land wealth has resulted in social evils which came to an end in civilized countries with the end of feudalism, but persist in this country up to our time.

Among the worst consequences of this state of affairs is that a class of a few big landowners has held in slavery an immense number of agriculturists. . . . Land reform was the basis of all subsequent social reforms in Western Europe in the 19th century, and in Eastern Europe and the Near East in the 20th century. The time has come to carry out this reform in Egypt as a preliminary step to building Egyptian society on new bases, ensuring free life and dignity to each and all . . . and removing an important cause of social unrest and political troubles.

Under the new law, the main points of which are summarized in the Appendix to this book, ownership of agricultural land is in general limited to 200 feddans. Over a 5-year period and beginning with the largest estates, the government is to expropriate land above that limit, compensating the owners. The expropriated land is to be redistributed to the fellaheen, each receiving not less than 2 feddans or more than 5. The new owners are to pay for the land over a period of 30 years. The fellah must farm the land himself and cannot dispose of it until the price has been fully paid. Strict limits are placed on the inheritance, sale, and exchange of land to prevent its being broken up into plots of uneconomic size. Agricultural co-operatives are to be set up in each village to handle farm loans, purchase equipment, sell produce, and in fact to undertake all kinds of agricultural services. This provision is designed to make it possible for the Egyptian fellaheen to do a businesslike job of production as quickly as possible under the new system.

The land rental system is also reformed under the new law, and one chapter relates to agricultural labor, providing that wages are to be fixed annually by district committees representing owners, tenants, and workers. It has been estimated that a million peasant farmers in Egypt rent land and that the landless labor force includes a half million persons. The new regulations could bring about great improvements in both cases.

Land reform properly carried out should accomplish a great deal, but only further agricultural developments such as those mentioned earlier in this chapter can add to the area under cultivation. It has been variously estimated that the cultivated area could be increased by 40 to 100 per cent. Industrial development employing sizable numbers of new workers would of course reduce the number who must subsist on the land.

So Abu Libda is now caught up in the great movement, which is spreading so widely in his part of the world, to break the grip of feudalism, broken long ago in the West. It looks as if his village will change its ways in the next 50 years more than it has in the last 3000.

CHAPTER TWO

Jim Barton

LIKE Abu Libda, Jim Barton lives in the valley of one of the world's greatest rivers. His is the Mississippi, flowing down the middle of the United States as the Nile flows down the middle of Egypt.

Both men are farmers. Both are good farmers. Both have lived all their lives in the same place. Both have that instinctive understanding and deep love of soil, plants, and animals which bespeak long familiarity with earth, sky, living things, rural ways of life. Both are happily married. Both love their children and want to do well for them. Both want to get ahead.

There likenesses end and differences begin.

Until recently, when history started pushing him, unknowing, out of the Middle Ages, Abu Libda had seen little change in his lifetime, except that farms for people like him kept getting smaller and even an inconspicuous livelihood was harder to make. Changes there were, of course—a world depression, a world war, trouble with foreign powers—but on the whole they were rather remote disturbances about which he really knew little. They did not make him worse off or better off as far as he could tell. *Insha Allah*, all is as God wills.

As for Jim Barton and his wife Sarah, they do live on the same 160 acres in northeast Iowa that Jim inherited from his father Sam Barton. They do carry on much the same kind of farming as Sam and his neighbors did in that corner of Iowa—corn, hogs, dairy cows, chickens. They do live in the same two-story, six-room frame house, with clapboard siding and shingle roof, that Sam built, and it is still painted white. The barn is the same, too, though a bit larger and more modern. But Jim and Sarah live in a world in which there have been continuous changes that affect their lives directly; and they know there will be other changes that will affect the lives of their children.

Between Old and New

Jim Barton was born in 1910. When he was a small boy, the Barton place was on a winding narrow dirt road. You knew the nearest town was a long way off because it took so long to get there with a horse and buggy, or a horse and sleigh in winter. There was free postal delivery, but you had to go a mile and a half to the postbox at the crossroads to get your mail. The Sam Bartons had no telephone or electricity; Jim's mother had the endless job of cleaning and trimming and filling the oil lamps. In the barn on winter evenings you used lanterns, which gave a dim light for milking and chores. You carried a lantern if you had to make the long trip after dark to the little "back house," the outdoor toilet. Jim well remembers the stilty shadows of his legs moving jerkily in the lantern's eerie halo.

All the work was done by hands and horses. Sam Barton, a good farmer, taught his boy to handle a team hitched to plow or harrow or mower, to pitch hay, to fork manure off the tail of a wagon, to pick and shell corn by hand, to milk by hand, to pump water and fetch it to the animals, to chop wood with ax and hatchet for the cooking stove in the kitchen and the pot-bellied heating stove in the parlor.

One of the regular winter jobs was to cut ice on the pond and store it in the straw-insulated icehouse for milk cooling and for the kitchen icebox in summer. Sam eventually got a cream separator, which was turned with a hand crank, but before that Jim's mother used to "set" the milk in big round pans, then skim off the thick cream, let it sour naturally, and churn it into farm butter, to sell and use at home. The skim milk was fed to the pigs and chickens.

Doubtless the bacterial count of the milk was high. Arrangements for sanitation, and ideas about it, were crude in those days. The same was true, in general, of methods for combatting diseases and pests. There was no tuberculin testing of cows, no way to fight hog cholera. If cows lost their calves before birth, it was just nature's way; Bruce had not yet invented Brucellosis. Paris green and nicotine sulphate were almost the only insecticides for plants. Sam used no commercial fertilizer. He had a good bull, but milk production was not high by present standards. Nor was egg production. He was proud of his heavy Duroc Jersey hogs which yielded fat bacon and plenty of lard.

Sam by no means got rich. But the family produced practically all their food, and all their fuel and fence posts, most of their building lumber, and all the manure they used; and the cash income was enough so they were not behind with debts and could live comfortably. It meant constant hard work and long hours; there is never any letup in dairy farming—milking and feeding come with deadly regularity 365 days a year (366 every fourth year). In winter you hopped out of bed in a shivery room long before daylight, and long after dark you finished work and came into the warm lamplighted kitchen, stamping the snow off your boots.

It was no easier for the womenfolk. There was the cooking to do on the woodburning stove, the bread to bake, great quantities of vegetables and fruits to be put up in glass jars in summer and fall, water to be fetched from the pump and heated on the stove, the family washing to be done, the ironing with heavy sad-irons, the making of sausage and smoking of hams and sides of bacon, the sewing, knitting, quilting, mending, the sweeping and dusting and scrubbing, the children to be got off to school with their lunchboxes, the baby to be taken care of. "Man may work from sun to sun, but woman's work is never done," Jim's mother used to say, cheerfully.

Sam Barton's generation was in an intermediate stage between the primitive farming of Abu Libda and the modern farming of Jim Barton. It might be better to say, an advanced intermediate stage; for though Sam, who was born in 1875, had as a boy used scythe and cradle for cutting grain, even those tools were well ahead of Abu's sickle. But the agricultural revolution was under way, and Sam not only accepted it but helped it along, so that in due course his equipment included steel moldboard plows, springtooth and disk harrows, cutter-bar mower, horse-drawn hayrake, thresher—all far beyond the reach of Abu and his neighbors, for the present. And if the hard work of Sam's womenfolk was fundamentally like that of Abu's womenfolk, it was done with better tools, and the house was far more substantial, roomy, comfortable, attractive, and livable. To Abu's folk it would seem like a palace.

Inventions and Ideas

The most significant thing about the modernization of agriculture that began before Sam's time was that it was a meshing of agriculture and industry new in the world.

Around 1800, when the United States of America was a narrow strip along the Atlantic seaboard, nine out of ten people were farmers because they had to be. With the simple hand tools of those days, it was all a farm family could do to produce their own food plus a little to sell. Each farm was self-sufficient. The family not only grew its food but carded and spun, wove cloth, made its clothing, and in fact got practically everything it needed off the place. What was left over to be sold helped to feed the town folk, who were not numerous. With almost all the population tied to the soil to subsist, industry could not move ahead fast for lack of workers.

In 1822 50 to 60 hours of work were required to produce 20 bushels of wheat on an acre of land. The farmer walked behind the plow, harrowed with a bundle of brush, broadcast the seed by hand, harvested with a sickle, threshed with a flail. Most of the wheat in Egypt is produced in much the same manner today.

In an Indian village. Dough for *chappatis*, thin flat cakes of unleavened bread, is mixed in a bowl with a big stick like a pestle. There is goats' milk in the urn at the left. In much the same way did many American housewives two or three generations ago prepare food before the open fireplace. Outside the USA and a few other countries, most of the world's people are poor. Most of them live in rural villages. Most of them have homes no better than this.

Modern industry has not yet reached out to meet even the most basic needs of millions. The home is still the factory. This Ethiopian woman is spinning her own cotton thread, drawing the fiber from her left hand, twisting it with the simplest of spindles in her right. Later she or someone else in her family will use a primitive hand loom to weave from the thread a voluminous cotton robe, or *shamma,* like the one she is wearing.

The nearest pool or lake, river or canal is the laundry where most women do the family wash, without soap, using stones as washboards. This is one of the women's never-ending chores. The woman and girls here are from a fishing village in Peru.

Another perpetual chore is fetching water for the family, usually in huge jars carried by the women on their heads from the village well or wherever water is to be found. Life is especially hard for this family in their bleak home in East Bengal, in an area hit by famine.

The nomads take their homes with them on the backs of camels. This tent of black goats' hair erected on a stony desert in Afghanistan is typical of Bedouin homes in many parts of the Near East. The wandering tribes must be perpetually on the move seeking grass and water for their flocks and herds. Overgrazing of the sparse vegetation is a serious problem. Better grasslands, better water supplies, homesteading in new irrigated areas are all getting attention in this region.

Children in many countries commonly go to work in the fields about as young as these little fellows on a mountainside in Peru. Under such conditions, large families are an economic asset. Besides, when so many die in childhood, large families are necessary to make sure a few will survive.

Life is a very serious business for this Afghan boy, bringing a load of firewood down from the mountain top to his father's home in the village. He will probably never learn to read or write. He will not have very much time for playing. He very early has to take on many adult responsibilities.

Nevertheless, the hope for a better future lies with the young generation—and their mothers. This intent woman with the small intent child is learning new things at a meeting in Thailand concerned with questions of food and health.

So are these schoolgirls in a laboratory in Ceylon, typical of women in many parts of the world who are breaking away from tradition and doing more than their share to change conditions that perpetuate poverty and ignorance.

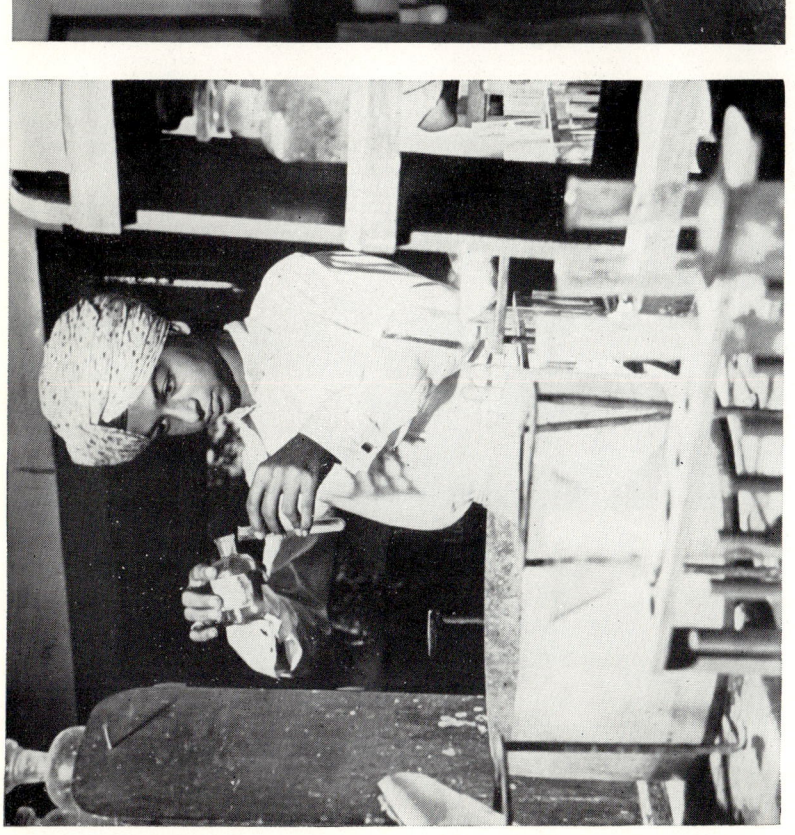

This high-school boy studying chemistry in India is getting the kind of technical knowledge that will help him to play a part in the drive for economic development and better living standards which is sweeping over his country.

It will take a vast spread of knowledge and understanding if peoples are to together to remedy the world's worst ills. There is a growing hunger for education among groups who never before realized the need.

During the next few years changes came rather rapidly. With better equipment, farmers could produce a little more, so they could sell more to the towns and buy more of the things they needed from the towns. Good land was being settled westward, too, and that increased production; in 1830 the USA extended as far as the Mississippi River.

By 1834 steel plows and reapers were being made. When Jim Barton's great-grandfather was a boy in 1840, so many improvements had come along that only about three out of every four people were needed in farming. A fourth of the population could work in industry.

New inventions and ideas kept appearing. Before 1860 there were mowing machines, kerosene lamps to replace candles and whale oil, two-row cultivators; and a few years later, gang plows and sulky plows. In 1862 came the epoch-making Homestead Act, under which any American could get free land in the West; the creation of the US Department of Agriculture; the Morrill Land-Grant College Act, providing for agricultural colleges in the states. By 1870, five years before Sam Barton was born, less than half the working people were farmers; each farm family could feed a city family and have enough to eat at home. From then on, the proportion of people in farming declined steadily.

The Hatch Act of 1887, providing for agricultural experiment stations in all the states, was a big forward step in applying science to farming.

By 1890 a man could produce 20 bushels of wheat on an acre of land with only 10 to 15 hours of work, using a horse-drawn gang plow, harrow, seeder, binder, thresher. Thirty years later, in 1910, the year Jim Barton was born, the proportion of farmers was down to one out of three working people. By that time many new and better roads were being built because automobiles began to appear in the early 1900's, and they needed good roads. In 1906 the first county extension agent was appointed in Texas; eight years later, in 1914, came the Smith-Lever Act, providing for extension agents in every rural county in the country, and also for 4-H clubs for farm boys and girls, under the leadership of the land-grant college extension service and the US Department of Agriculture.

Jim was seven years old when, in 1917, the USA was getting into World War I. In the same year the Smith-Hughes Act provided for agricultural and home economics education in all the rural public schools.

So, gradually, an educational underpinning for American agriculture, perhaps unique in the world in its completeness and directness, was built up. The agricultural experiment stations, the teaching of agriculture in the rural public schools, the 4-H clubs involving young people in agricultural and household projects, the agricultural colleges training scientists and farm leaders and farm youth, the county and home demonstration agents, the "short courses" in the colleges giving a few weeks of instruction and demonstration, the later system of "supervised" credit—together, these new institutions gradually played an increasingly important part in making it possible for Jim Barton, and farmers like him, to attain rather high levels of productive efficiency.

During the decade following 1910, many more people were able to quit farming for other occupations, so that in 1920 when Jim was ten years old only one person out of every four was a farmer; one farm family provided enough food for four families in town, plus enough for itself and some to ship abroad.

The Commingling of Country and City

There were hard times for farmers in the postwar depression early in the 1920's. Prices of farm products dropped disastrously; land values declined. Long before this, however, farmers in Sam's part of the country, and elsewhere, had come to feel that they were at a disadvantage compared with workers in business and industry, and through their farm organizations such as the National Grange, the Farm Bureau Federation, the Farmers' Union, the farm co-operatives, they were trying to strengthen agriculture in the national economy. During the depression of the 1920's this movement went further. Legislators from rural areas got together to form a farm bloc in Congress which for the next 10 years carried on an active fight for laws to protect agriculture against economic stresses to which it was peculiarly vulnerable. For with the bottom knocked out of the market, many farmers could hardly meet costs of production. Surpluses began to appear. The agricultural problem was becoming a national headache.

Meanwhile, technical progress continued. The first successful light tractor appeared in 1926 when Jim Barton was sixteen years old; hitherto there had been only big costly machines suited to very large farms. The new development was destined to make mechanization far more widespread. It meant that horses and mules were used less and less, and this in turn freed more land for the production of human food instead of animal feed.

So Jim, like other American farm boys, was brought up to be machine-minded. He had attended one of the consolidated country schools not far from his home—several scattered local schools combined into one at a central location for the sake of better facilities and greater economy. The youngsters went off to school in the morning and came back in the evening. By the time he was in high school, Jim knew as much as his father about tractors and automobiles. He had made up his mind that he wanted to be a farmer. His two older brothers had left the farm, one, who had been a flier in the war, going into the new industry of commercial aviation, one to a farm machinery manufacturing company. Jim's sisters were married, one to a farmer over the line in Illinois, the other to a drugstore owner.

In high school Jim took all the subjects he could related to farming, and in the autumn of 1928 he entered the agricultural college with high hopes.

JIM BARTON

Things looked interesting. The proportion of people in farming in the USA had by now dropped to one in five. More than half the farms had automobiles and about a third had telephones. Multiple-row cultivators were widely used; corn planters and corn pickers were becoming fairly common; experiments were being made with hybrid corn. Farther west, a man could produce 20 bushels of wheat on an acre with only 3 to 4 hours of work, using a tractor, three-bottom gang plow, 10-foot tandem disk harrow, 12-foot combine, and trucks for hauling.

But Jim was not destined to finish college. By 1930 farmers were in really serious trouble as a result of the stock market crash of 1929; and in addition, Sam Barton's health was failing and Jim was needed on the farm.

Three years later, in 1933, he married Sarah Leigh, a neighbor's daughter who also had expected to go to college but could not afford it because of the depression. The following year Sam died, leaving the place to Jim and Sarah. Their first child, Tom, was born in 1935.

During the early 1930's farmers were in desperate circumstances; in some places they seemed almost ready to revolt. Fortunately the Barton farm was clear of mortgage debts so Jim was in a little better shape financially than a good many others. He figured the total investment in the farm at about $13,000, of which $10,000 represented the value of land and buildings, $1,100 equipment and machinery, and $1,700 livestock. In spite of his comparatively favorable position, he was, like other farmers, operating at a loss every year between 1930 and 1934.

Some people thought agriculture had become too efficient and farmers were producing too much, flooding the market with products that could not be sold at any price. Actually, the whole world was going through a severe depression, of which both the 1929 stock market crash and the plight of farmers were symptoms. There was as much physical need for food as ever; in fact, more people were hungry because so many were out of work or on drastically reduced earnings.

Something had to be done to prevent serious crippling of American agriculture. Thus the decade of the 1930's saw much farm legislation, including price supports, marketing quotas, production adjustments, improvements in farm credit, payments to farmers for soil conservation practices, a school lunch system, and the Food Stamp Plan to sell "surplus" foods to needy people at low prices and make up the loss to the producer by a government subsidy. Some of these measures lasted beyond the emergency as economic devices to reduce major risks in agriculture.

This was the layout of Jim Barton's 160-acre farm in 1952: 100 acres was in crops for harvesting (corn 40, oats 30, hay 30); 15 acres in pasture; 6 acres in pastured woodlands; and the garden, orchard, house, barns, and some rough land took up 39 acres. The farm was typical for that part of the country, a beautiful, rolling part of northeast Iowa not (like most of the state) devoted to the raising of hogs, corn, and the fattening of beef cattle but mainly to a combination of dairying and hog production.

Jim's livestock included 30 head of cattle (16 being milk cows), 65 pigs and hogs, 150 chickens. Something more than half of his 1952 cash income ($10,700) came from the sale of dairy products, cattle and calves, poultry and eggs; another 40 per cent came from hogs; and about 5 per cent came from the sale of corn. In addition, the family figured that the food they produced for themselves and the rental value of their home added up to about $750. That included over 2600 pounds of milk, 100 dozen eggs, 200 pounds of beef, 350 pounds of pork, 150 pounds of poultry, $75 worth of vegetables. They were not undernourished.

Jim had a tractor and a full set of implements. His corn production was so completely mechanized that machines did everything from planting through harvest.

There had been many changes since the depression of the 1930's, particularly during the war, when manpower shortages made it more necessary than ever before for American farmers to step up their efficiency by more intensive use of improved techniques and machines. Under this stimulus they produced about 30 per cent more than in the years 1935-39 on almost the same amount of land and with five million fewer people on farms by the end of the war. Production per man hour increased so rapidly throughout the 1940's that by 1951 only one worker out of nine in the USA was engaged in farming.

Back of this increased efficiency were such factors as hybrid corn, better varieties of other crops, disease and pest control, and mechanization that made more timely operations possible. In 1938, too, the average Iowa farmer was using 1 pound of fertilizer per acre for all crops; in 1948, he was using 28 pounds. In 1934, only 15 out of every hundred Iowa farms had central station electric service; by 1951, 95 out of every hundred had it.

Jim's high school and college training served him in good stead. He was alert to take advantage of improved methods; he studied government bulletins and articles in farm journals for worth-while ideas; he got a great deal of information from the radio—which also brought market news—and from demonstrations put on by the county extension agent and other Federal and State experts who worked in this area. The result was that his crop yields in 1952 were up about 28 per cent over the prewar period, to 70 bushels an acre for corn and 45 for oats. Both were the best available products of scientific breeding. In the management of his soil, too, he followed conservation practices designed to build up and maintain fertility.

The changes in Jim's farm operations during this period were reflected in changes in his home and in the family living. Some of the old furniture was replaced by new, and the Bartons gradually acquired quite a bit of electrical equipment, including a refrigerator, vacuum cleaner, washing machine, and such smaller conveniences as an electric iron and a toaster. They expected to have an electric cookstove before too long, though it was a temptation to get a television set first. They did not own a quick-freezer for food storage because they belonged to a co-operative that ran a community frozen-food locker in the town near by.

Meanwhile the family had grown larger. Tom was sixteen years old and in high school, Jane twelve, Ned nine. Tom and Jane belonged to the 4-H club (there were some 85,000 of these clubs in the United States at that time, with close to two million members) and were deeply involved in its projects—Tom with a heifer he was raising and hoped would be a prize winner, Jane with a flock of chickens. The Bartons expected to send the youngsters to college.

Both Jim and Sarah were active in local church and school affairs and in the work of the local farm organization. The county extension agent sometimes used their place for demonstrations, as did the young woman who was serving as home demonstration agent in the area.

Jim and Sarah lived in some ways very much like city or suburban folk. With excellent roads spreading in almost every direction, they got around a good deal in their car for business and pleasure. They enjoyed a rather full community life, and though the farm work was exacting, it was interspersed with trips to the motion picture theaters, shops, picnics, dances, church socials, civic meetings, vacation spots in late summer. A local group put on amateur plays, and the town even boasted an annual exhibition of paintings by artists in the state, of whom two or three were near-by farmers or their wives. To the Bartons' living room the radio brought news of the world, good music, talks by people who were making history. A daily newspaper was put in the rural free delivery box every morning. The Bartons took an intelligent interest in current affairs, national and international as well as local, and had a sense of participation in what was going on in the world.

Jim and his wife thought the farm was a far better place to live than any city or town, however. They were able to have many of the advantages of the city without its disadvantages, and they had a deep love of the country.

Life was quite different from what it had been in the days when Jim was a boy, walking to the outhouse with a lantern, jogging to town in the buggy or sleigh.

In a sense, Jim Barton had become a big businessman. The farm that was worth some $13,000 when he inherited it was valued by 1952 at nearly $43,500—about $25,000 for land and buildings, $5,500 for machinery and equipment, $8,500 for livestock, $4,500 for feed and supplies. No wonder youngsters were having a hard time getting started in farming. How could any young person save up enough for that?

Income had risen in proportion. Jim's net earnings in 1952 were around $6,200 compared with $1,600 ten to twelve years earlier. In spite of increased living costs, he was better off than he had ever been, except maybe in the peak years.

Agriculture Industrializes

It has been said that there has been more progress in food production in the last 50 years than in the previous 3000. The evolution in the USA and other highly developed countries might be thought of in a sense as an industrialization of agriculture. The plain fact is that twice as much power is now used to run the tractors, trucks, and engines on farms in the United States as is used to run all the factories put together. By the same token, enormous quantities of steel, chemicals, crude petroleum, rubber, and electrical power are now required in carrying out farming operations in the United States. The city has come to the country; or rather, the country and the city have mingled, like the blood of two people in a transfusion. The figures we have quoted for the small proportion of workers engaged in farming in the United States are deceptive. They do not tell the true story. For when Jim Barton plants and cultivates and stores and sells his crops, or breeds and feeds and milks his cows and markets his dairy products, or raises pigs and chickens, he does not work all by himself in the field and barn, the hog lot and chicken house, as his forebears did. He has invisible hands and brains working with him—factory workers, scientists, engineers, miners, and employees on railways, ships, and planes, in warehouses, offices, stores, in telephone and radio companies—whose knowledge and inventions and services and products he uses 24 hours every day, sleeping and waking.

Out of a total working population of 61 million in the USA in 1951 only 7 million were working on farms. But millions more were processing and distributing farm products, and other millions were producing for farmers and providing them with services. A much higher percentage than one worker out of nine, therefore, was directly involved in the complex processes associated with modern agriculture. Together, these workers accomplished disproportionately more than the nine out of ten who were exclusively farmers in 1800.

The hours that somebody puts into supplying Jim with gasoline and electricity, making and repairing his tractor and milking machine, producing the fertilizer he uses, carrying on the research that gives him better plants and animals, processing and handling and advertising and delivering and selling his products after they leave the farm—these in effect substantially reduce the hours Jim himself would have had to put in had he been farming under the same conditions as his ancestors. This close division of labor, this splitting up of the total process of production and distribution into many intricately related parts, and in particular this handing over of many operations to machines make it possible for Jim to accomplish far more than he could if he had to do everything for himself by himself, as Abu Libda has to do in Egypt. Jim's efficiency, in turn, makes it possible for a great many people to be doctors, teachers, merchants, factory workers, who, back in 1800, would have had to be producing their own food. Basic resources can be used more effectively and with far greater latitude for expanding and varying production than is possible with simpler, more primitive methods and types of economic organization. A pair of hands can produce more; standards of living can be more generous; life can encompass a wider range of interest and activities.

This meshing of city and country to form an efficient producing unit, which is the main characteristic of agriculture in a modernized economy, has two implications of great importance for Jim Barton.

One is that Jim's fixed expenses are much higher than those of a farmer in the days of self-sufficiency. He is more vulnerable to declining prices and can "go broke" more quickly. In other words, he must have prices for his products sufficiently high so he can afford to use the equipment, materials, and services that make it possible for him to continue producing at high levels—and, in fact, to raise the levels when necessary to meet expanding consumer needs and demands. If the prices of the products he sells fall too low to make this possible, his efficiency and the production of his farm suffer. Then the city workers who provide him with these things also suffer.

The other big implication is that for Jim land is no longer the most important factor in increasing farm production. He farms the same piece of land his father farmed, no more, no less. But his production is very much greater, though he and his family put in fewer hours of work, and the work is less exhausting. How is this possible? Because Jim Barton has at his disposal the same resources—machinery, materials, skilled labor, brains—that industry has. These are the capital that a modernized economy uses to enlarge the productive capacity of the land.

The same principle is true elsewhere. If Abu Libda is to be able to produce much more than he is now producing, industry in Egypt, too, needs to develop further, make new resources available for its farmers, and provide opportunities for many of those now on the land to find profitable employment elsewhere.

CHAPTER
THREE

Narrow the Gap

I‍T WOULD NOT BE ACCURATE to leave an impression that the conditions described in the chapter about Abu Libda apply to everyone in Egypt's villages. Besides the big landowners at the top and the fellaheen at the bottom, there is a middle group which has given the country some of its outstanding leaders in education, economic and social affairs, politics, science, and other professions. In spite of age-old tradition, too, an increasing number of the young women of Egypt are getting a higher education, and they are as alert and forward-looking as young women anywhere. Abu Libda and his family are nevertheless typical of the overwhelming majority of the rural people.

On the other side of the picture, farming conditions in the USA are not so favorable everywhere as they are in Jim Barton's community. There is a wide range of types and sizes of farms, incomes, living conditions. A sizable number of farms—well over a half million—do not turn out more than $250 worth of produce a year; and some 77,000 of them are 3 acres or less in size compared with the nationwide average of about 216 acres. Many of the little places are run by people who have other work from which they get part of their income.

In the Cotton Belt, where nearly a third of the farm people live, the average value of farm products tends to be especially low. Work on the cotton plantations is done largely by sharecroppers and hired labor. About half the farmers are tenants who do not own their land, and two out of five of the tenants are sharecroppers. The standard of living is on the average considerably below that of USA farmers as a whole.

Midway between the Cotton Belt farmer and people like the Bartons is a group, not very large, who farm on a strictly self-sufficing basis. They live in certain highland areas, especially the Appalachians and the Ozarks. They grow their own food, and each farm is likely to have its springhouse to keep butter and milk cool, smokehouse to cure meat, root cellar to store vegetables. They make their own clothing, furniture, blankets, baskets, and many other things. Some are expert craftsmen. They sing old songs, play old tunes, dance old dances; even their language has the flavor of earlier days. Mostly, these farms lie in the back country, a long way from good roads. The average cash income, not counting the rather meager value of home-grown and homemade products, is the lowest in the country. About a million of these low-income farm families have had effective help in the form of government loans accompanied by the technical assistance commonly known in the USA as "extension services."

In spite of such variations as these, the Mississippi Valley, and Iowa in particular, are about as typical of USA farming as anything you will find in such a big country; and Jim Barton is perhaps as near to an "average" USA farmer as you will find.

The gap between Jim and Abu is a wide one, but it is not owing to differences in innate ability so much as to conditions that are capable of change. Anyone who has lived long enough must in fact be keenly aware from personal experience how much conditions have changed within the USA—how many major economic, scientific, and technological developments are of quite recent origin. The author of this book is old enough to have lived under conditions like those that existed in the days of Jim Barton's father Sam. There were no automobiles, no telephones, no electric lights, no airplanes—or at least none that I saw. In the cities, people rode in carriages and horsecars; in the country, on horseback and in carriages and coaches. Little progress had been made with farm machinery; practically all the work was still done by hand and horse. Sanitation was not quite so primitive as in parts of Egypt, but it was crude enough—no running water in the house, no bathroom, no central heating, milk unpasteurized and often not too clean, typhoid common, malaria widespread. To cure a sore throat we used an onion poultice, and to "purify the blood" we were dosed with sulphur and molasses each spring. Most people did not live past forty—little longer than the average Egyptian today. Infant mortality was high, as it is now in Egypt. Women were not allowed to vote. Labor unions were not considered respectable.

In fact, when I realize how wide is the gap between conditions when I was young and conditions today, and how much things have changed, I cannot doubt the possibility of narrowing the gap between Abu Libda and Jim Barton. And narrowing it much faster than the time-gap between *then* and *now* in the USA: for the knowledge that underlay this change is now, or can be, the possession of all countries; and they can help one another to speed the change, find short cuts, avoid mistakes. On the other hand, I did not contrast Jim's situation and Abu's to convey an impression that any country should try to imitate the way things have been done in the USA. There are basic principles that underlie development in both cases, but the development process in any country must be in accord with its own cultural backgrounds and values and its own native genius.

Poverty

Abu's poverty and hardship are not, of course, peculiarly Egyptian. Most people at present are farmers, and most farmers are about as badly off as he. This is one of the things drastically wrong with the world; one of the direct and indirect causes of the unrest, violence, revolt so common beyond the bounds of the stabilized well-to-do countries; one of the conditions that many men and women are trying hard to change.

To crack world poverty is at least as massive and difficult an undertaking as cracking the atom. All the brains and resources that can be spared for it will not be too much. To glimpse the size of the task, let us look around the world a bit.

It is hard for the average person in the USA or other highly developed countries to realize how very poor most of their fellow human beings are; how little they have to eat, to wear, to own, to work with; how limited are their lives and opportunities.

Food is of first importance. The first *World Food Survey* made by the Food and Agriculture Organization covered 70 countries and about nine-tenths of the world's people. It provided a more comprehensive and detailed picture of the food situation than anything that had been done before. The survey showed that in areas where over half the people live (Far East, Near East, Africa, Latin America), there was only enough food for each person to have some 2250 calories a day at the retail level (the usual starting-point for figures of this kind), which means about 1900 at the actual consumption level, after deducting losses in preparation, cooking, and so on. Many people, of course, were well below this average, down to 1500 and 1600 calories. At the other end of the scale, about a third of the world's people (in Western Europe, Australia, New Zealand, Canada, the USA) were able to average more than 2750 calories a person a day at the retail level, or, say, 2350 at the consumption level; and considerable numbers were well above this, up to 3200 calories or more (retail). The remaining sixth of the population was between these levels.

A committee of nutrition experts brought together by FAO agreed that in the temperate zones 1900 calories a day (consumption) is the minimum needed by most people to prevent serious undernutrition. In warmer climates, particularly in Eastern and tropical areas, the "minimum subsistence" level would be 1500-1600 calories. These minimum allowances are so low, the committee warned, that they would not be safe for any length of time.

But a considerable part of mankind before the war did subsist throughout life (a short life) at such levels. According to the later *Second World Food Survey* and other FAO studies, world food supplies per person were still below the prewar levels until the beginning of the 1950's. Since then steady progress has been made in world food production, perhaps because the international and national efforts of recent years are beginning to bear fruit. But though the situation is improving it is still far from satisfactory. In many places levels of consumption are incredibly low even where they may be somewhat above those before the war. There are also signs that even such modest increases as these are beginning to outrun the purchasing power of consumers, so that more attention from now on will have to be given to the economic problem of improving the market for food as well as expanding production.

In the Far East most people still have less food than they had before the war because production has not increased as fast as population. Hunger in this region, where so much of the human race lives, has been advancing like a slow insidious plague while in the Western Hemisphere it has been retreating. (See Appendix, Table 1.)

Calories measure only the fuel or energy value that foods supply for body functions and muscular movement; even while we sleep we must have a certain minimum quantity of fuel, which can come only from food, to keep the life-fire burning, and every move from winking an eye to digging a ditch demands additional quantities. If calories were all that mattered, the food problem would be relatively simple; we could live on pure starch and refined sugar. But to keep that intricate and wonderful organism, the body, in life and health we must also have a complicated array of minerals, vitamins, amino acids. The cereal grains, legumes, starchy roots in general contain relatively small amounts of these vital substances. To provide the full quota required to encourage good physical growth, build vigorous bodies, and make the life-fire blaze instead of smoldering, we should also have a variety of vegetables, fruits, meat, fish, eggs, milk, fats. It is unfortunate for most of mankind that these foods are the most expensive, because they take more land and labor to produce and more trouble to store and ship and process and market than does grain, for example. So poor people cannot afford to eat enough of them—or, frequently, even enough grain.

In many countries of the Far East, the Near East, Africa, and Latin America, most people get as much as 70 to 80 per cent, or even more, of their total energy from cereals, starchy roots (manioc, taro, yams, potatoes), beans, sugar. People in Canada and the USA, on the other hand, get less than half their fuel from these sources and the other half from foods richer in the nutrients that add dividends to living. (Appendix, Table 2.)

And More Poverty

Food is not the only thing that measures standards of living, though it is the one about which there is the most information. The amount of clothing and household textiles—sheets, towels, rugs—that people can afford is another measure, since it has a good deal to do with health and cleanliness.

Information recently collected by FAO tells approximately the same story as the data for food consumption. Ill-fed people are ill-clothed people. In 1952, for instance, the average Indonesian used less than 2½ pounds of textiles a year; the Thailander, about 3; the Egyptian, about 8; the Cuban, 10½; whereas the Australian used 28; the American, more than 37. (Appendix, Table 3.) It is true that many of these people live in the tropics and have no need for heavy clothing, but this fact does not fully account for the enormous differences. The Cuban lives in a warm climate, yet he uses more than four times as much in the way of textiles as the Indonesian.

Again, a high standard of living goes with fairly generous use of paper for newspapers, journals, books, boxes and cartons, wallpaper, wrapping, toilet tissue. If we consider wood pulp and pulp products as a convenient measure, the contrasts in consumption are enormous. Thailand and Iraq, for instance, each has a little more than 2 pounds a person a year; Japan has 22; whereas Sweden has 187 pounds, Canada has 176, and the USA has something more than 281.

So much for food and some of the other things people use in daily living. If we look at the resources available to different populations for the production of these things, we find similar sharp divisions. For example, at the low end of the scale about one-seventh of an acre of arable land per person is available in Japan to grow food and other products for her people; in Egypt, less than a third of an acre; in Ceylon, something less than half an acre; in Italy, eight-tenths; in Brazil, about nine-tenths of an acre. At the upper end, the USA has about 3 acres of arable land per person, Australia, nearly 6, Canada, 9½. In between, Denmark has 1½ acres. (These figures are calculated by multiplying the total land area per person by the percentage that is arable. Appendix, Table 4.) The proportions vary a great deal; for instance, Italy has only 1.6 acres of land per person, but more than 51 per cent is arable, whereas in Australia, with 247 acres per person, only 2.3 per cent is arable.

Such figures give a rough, though on the whole valid, idea of the basic production resource of a country. But much depends on how the arable land is handled. In Egypt it is all irrigated; an acre along a canal in the Delta produces more than do several acres dry-farmed in Syria. Similarly, an acre in Denmark planted to some high-yielding variety of crop plant, well fertilized, tilled and weeded with adequate tools, and kept free of major diseases and insects, yields more than would several acres farmed without these advantages in, say, a village in India. Nor, of course, is food production confined to arable land. Range and pasture yield livestock products; and here too there are great differences, in both extent and quality, in the available resources. In Mexico half the country is counted as grazing land; in Denmark, only about one tenth; but one lush acre of Danish pastureland produces more milk and meat than do many acres of dry Mexican range.

The fact that some peoples seem to be badly skimped on land resources is not the only reason for their poverty. The crowding of the land may be owing less to the smallness of the soil resources than to the dearth of opportunities for work other than farming. People have to stay on the land even when it is overcrowded if they have nowhere else to go to earn a livelihood. They farm because they have to produce their own food. As this population glued to the land increases with each generation, the land is divided into smaller and smaller pieces, as we have seen in the case of Egypt. There are also a good many countries, notably in Latin America, Africa, and parts of the Near East, with low production and low standards of living in spite of the fact that they have comparatively large amounts of potentially productive land in relation to the number of people. Land alone does not tell the whole story. The comparatively prosperous countries of Western Europe are among the most crowded, with the least land per person; but a large part of the population can make a livelihood in pursuits other than agriculture. In practically all highly developed countries, in fact, a relatively small proportion of the people are farmers. (Appendix, Table 5.) In the USA, as we have seen, only 11 of every 100 working people are on farms; the other 89 are in industry, trade, and the professions. In Thailand the situation is almost exactly the reverse; 85 are farmers and only 15 are in other occupations.

It is clear from the story of Jim Barton that land is actually the smaller, though an indispensable, part of the resources for modern agricultural production. The larger part consists of equipment, materials, knowledge, and services applied to the land and its products and to human labor, to magnify their productiveness, usefulness, and value.

Some of the most important factors in this complex interplay are summed up in the term "energy." The more energy a country uses to supplement muscle, the more highly developed the country is likely to be. If for the purpose of ready comparison we express this mechanical energy in terms of coal, we find that each person in the USA has the equivalent of 8 tons a year to do work for him—400 times as much as the Thailander, with the equivalent of a fiftieth of a ton a year. (Appendix, Table 6.)

Animals still provide 85 per cent of the power needed to do the farm work of the world. But even animal muscle and human muscle can be used more efficiently or less efficiently, depending on the tools they have to work with. Vastly more sickles than scythes cut the world's grain, and the fact that so many millions of farmers have only the most primitive tools and materials, like those of Abu, is probably as important as lack of land in holding down production.

Vicious Circles

Here we come upon some well-known vicious circles.

In general, the degree of industrialization of a country is reflected in average annual income per person. In terms of US dollars, the average income in Denmark is about $689; in Canada, $870; in the USA, $1453; but in agricultural Indonesia, Thailand, Ethiopia, Afghanistan it is $50 or less. (Appendix, Table 7.) When almost no one has more than $50 to $100 a year to spend, people cannot buy much. When they cannot buy, industry does not develop. When industry does not develop, earnings and purchasing power are low. And so on around.

The vicious circle is conspicuous in the case of health. People who are ill-nourished, badly housed, without sufficient clothing, lacking even elementary sanitation, succumb readily to diseases. Many children die in infancy. Though infant mortality rates even among some of the poorest people have been strikingly reduced in recent years because of the widespread application of public health measures, they are still much higher in some countries than in others—for example, Egypt, 130 per 1000 live births; India, 116; Mexico, 100. In contrast, the infant mortality rate for the USA is 29 per 1000 live births; the Netherlands, 23; Australia, 24; Iceland, 26. (Appendix, Table 8.) In the same countries where infant mortality is high, average life expectancy at birth is low—in India 32 or 33 years, in Mexico about 40, but in the USA about 68, and in Australia and England over 70.

People who are not well and who die young do not work as hard or produce as much as those who are well and long-lived, nor can society afford to spend much giving them an education so they might be better producers. Because they cannot produce enough, they do not have enough food and other things needed to keep them well and enable them to live to an advanced age. And so around another vicious circle.

Where disease is widespread and death snatches most men and women before the prime of life, the aggregate loss in productiveness is incalculably great. "Today the death rate is the decisive factor in Indian demography," said Dr. S. Chandresekhar, Director of the India Institute of Population Studies, at the first All-India Conference of the Family Planning Association of India. "No comment is necessary on this inordinate and tragic loss of human life. Nor is this all. There are many who do not die but who cannot be counted among the truly living, healthy, active, and gainfully employed because of the shocking nature of Indian morbidity."

Is Progress Possible?

In this world of deep and bitter contrasts in the opportunities, life, death, and fate of immense numbers of human beings, it is obviously not a simple business for a large part of humanity to produce enough to be adequately fed and attain better standards of living. Indeed it is an extremely complex problem.

A good many people have grave doubts about the possibility of achieving anything of the sort. The theory of the eighteenth-century clergyman Thomas Robert Malthus, that population always tends to increase faster than food supplies and is held down only by famine, disease, and war, was in disrepute for some time following scientific developments and the opening up of new lands which together greatly expanded food production. Today the ideas of Malthus are again gaining wide acceptance in a somewhat modified form, mainly because world population has been increasing at an unusually rapid rate now that medical science is checking the depredations of so many deadly infectious diseases.

I shall not go into the neo-Malthusian argument here because a large number of recent books, pamphlets, and articles about it are readily available. (Most of the material has been summarized in detail in a study published by the United Nations, *The Determinants and Consequences of Population Trends;* and in September 1954 an international conference on world population problems convened at FAO headquarters in Rome in which many organizations and individuals co-operated.) It will suffice here to mention the main viewpoints in current thinking. At one extreme, it is argued that the resources of soil and sea are and always will be insufficient, even with the wisest use, to feed a population much larger than the world now has, and that they are certainly insufficient to improve living standards materially for most of mankind. The opposing view is that there is no physical barrier to indefinite expansion of the food supply in advance of population growth. There are various gradations between these two.

Those who argue that there are definite physical limits to expanding production differ in their views on what should or can be done to achieve a reasonable balance between the quantity of food and the number of human beings.

Some believe the problem will solve itself. As people attain better standards of living they will voluntarily limit the size of families, just as they have already done in every highly industrialized country. Meanwhile, improvements in production and distribution will also increase the food supply, even though there may be limits to the possible increase.

Others say this process is too slow to cope with the rapid expansion in numbers of people that will occur in some countries before industrialization can proceed far enough to have any great influence. If the world is to avoid a dangerous situation, this group believes, there is urgent need to speed up family limitation as a deliberate social policy.

A third view, the most pessimistic one, is that self-interest will always lead the more aggressive nations to build up populations as large as possible. Others will have to follow suit in self-defense. Since there will not be enough food for everyone, and since disease is being conquered more and more, starvation and war will continue to be the final arbiters controlling the size of the world population.

All the views mentioned and gradations not mentioned are being ably, persuasively, and in some cases heatedly defended by various experts. But almost all of them agree on one point, whatever they may think about the ultimate bounds of production or about the need for limiting the size of populations. They agree that by means within reach, men can make the earth's resources much more productive. An FAO study prepared for the Rome conference on world population problems concluded that world production of cereals and many other crops can be at least doubled without assuming anything like the full application of technical knowledge; or alternatively, current production could be obtained from half or less than half of the present area. In the case of livestock, the study concluded that the resources and technical basis exist for a level of production of animal products not less than five times the present world output. Fish production could be increased two or three fold without using more than a small fraction of the productivity of the seas and inland waters. The bleak winter of universal starvation is not upon us yet.

As the United Nations study summarizes the situation:

> The danger of world population reaching the maximum that could be supported by the earth's resources seems remote. . . . All except the most pessimistic estimates of the amounts of land and other sources of food which could be brought into use, and of the possible increases in agricultural yields, imply that it would be technically possible to feed a very much larger population than the world now holds. Studies of the sources of energy and essential raw materials likewise imply that, with prudence in the use and conservation of these resources and ingenuity in devising substitutes for those which are in shortest supply, they could be made to meet the needs of a growing population for a long time to come.
>
> The increases in production that are actually likely to be achieved within the foreseeable future, however, are much smaller than those which are technically possible. Ignorance, greed, strife, superstition, and blind adherence to tradition prevent men from accomplishing the works which are in their power, even though the alternative may be misery and starvation. It is, therefore, easily possible that the means of producing the necessities of life will not be increased as rapidly as population grows, and that the level of living of the world's peoples will be depressed as their numbers increase. Moreover, it is not sufficient to match population growth with an equal increase in the means of subsistence. Progress demands an expansion of production greater than the increase of world population, so that all nations can achieve a better living standard.

To overcome obstacles on the scale needed for substantial progress in narrowing the gap between an Abu Libda and a Jim Barton will take all the wisdom, good will, and persistence humanity can muster. No one country or people can hope to do it alone, least of all those in greatest need.

PART TWO

FAO: Genesis and Development

CHAPTER FOUR

Conception

SEVERAL DEVELOPMENTS of recent decades have created the possibility, and determined the nature, of international collaboration to narrow the gap, chief among them being • the new science of nutrition • the great depression of the 1930's • the breakup of the League of Nations • World War II • the widespread want and suffering that followed that war.

Food and Life

Few of those who today almost unconsciously use the modern science of nutrition in their daily lives realize how new most of this knowledge is. We take it for granted, but it developed a step at a time during a few recent decades of exciting and important research.

Even in ancient times, however, some facts were known empirically that are in line with these discoveries. As Louise Stanley noted, in the thirteenth century burned sponges were administered for goiter, although nobody knew why until a chemist in 1819 found iodine in the ash. Cod-liver oil was used for rickets long before anyone knew anything about vitamin D. Medieval pharmacists in Florence sold lemonade to cure scurvy hundreds of years before vitamin C was discovered. In 1720 a physician wrote: "If you can prepare a sufficient quantity of fresh antiscorbutic juices, if you have oranges, lemons, citrons, or their pulp and juice preserved with whey in cask, so that you can make a lemonade or rather give to the quantity of 3 or 4 ounces of their juice in whey, you will, without other assistance, cure this dreadful evil." Another physician, Lind, on the British ship *Salisbury*, proved by a controlled experiment that he could cure sailors of scurvy with oranges and lemons. Thereafter a regular ration of lemon juice was issued in the British navy.

These were isolated cases. It was not until after 1900 that an integrated body of knowledge was built up which explained these and many other phenomena. Until then, foods were believed to consist of water, fat, carbohydrate, protein, and "salts," or minerals—the ash left when the foods were burned. The function of the minerals was not understood. All one needed to be well nourished was enough carbohydrate, fat, and protein. Even this was comparatively new knowledge; and information about the energy needs of the body supplied by foods was also new. If you are near the age of the author of this book, you will remember the gush of popular writing some decades ago about calories, as though they summed up the whole of nutrition.

One of a number of pioneers in this research was W. O. Atwater, who headed the first agricultural experiment station in the United States (in Connecticut) and also became the first Director of the Office of Experiment Stations in the US Department of Agriculture. In the latter post he had a unique opportunity to stimulate and co-ordinate research relating to food and nutrition in all the young agricultural colleges and experiment stations throughout the country. He used the opportunity to excellent advantage, starting a program which during the next decades resulted in a vast amount of more or less correlated work of world-wide significance in these public institutions.

It was appropriate that this work should be associated closely with agriculture. The growing knowledge of animal nutrition was important to farmers because it helped them in the production of livestock and livestock products. This led naturally to research on human nutrition. As Atwater wrote in 1890: "It has been urged by not a few of the best thinkers and wisest agriculturists and economists that in studying the food of animals we have no right to neglect the food of man. The principles involved are essentially the same. The majority of our people and practically all wage-workers spend and must spend at least half the money they earn for food."

Atwater's work on human energy requirements (based on such fundamental discoveries as those of Lavoisier) was carried out with an ingenious device called a respiration calorimeter, a big box in which a human being could live for several days, under observation through a window. Food was passed in through an opening, and air was pumped in and out through tubes. By measuring the amount of heat and moisture given off by the subject it was possible to calculate the energy he used asleep and awake, lying down, sitting, exercising. Studies of this sort gradually built up accurate knowledge about the energy needs of human beings as related to age, size, sex, and physical activity. Meanwhile accurate determinations were also being made of the energy supplied by foods of all kinds, which under Atwater's leadership were systematically analyzed for their content of fat, carbohydrate, protein, ash, crude fiber, and water. The tables containing this information were first published in a US Office of Experiment Stations bulletin in 1896. So basic were they that almost 50 years later, in 1940, a revision of the same bulletin appeared.

Even in those early days, Atwater had an exceptional grasp of the broad implications of the new science. "As he saw it," his daughter Helen Atwater wrote, "the problems of human nutrition included what the body needs in its food, what nutrients different foods supply, how the nutrients are utilized by the body, what diets are actually used in different regions, and what foods and methods of food preparation will furnish the most economical and healthful diet—*all leading back to the fundamental question of how national food production can be made to yield the best returns in economic progress and social welfare.* [My italics.] Though work since Atwater's day has introduced new elements and changed the emphasis on old ones, research in human nutrition still follows the general pattern he laid down."

Even more striking developments in the new science came with the unfolding discovery of the part played by vitamins and minerals in preventing certain diseases.

Beriberi has long been common in the Orient. Its victims often suffer profound damage to the nervous system or heart. Around 1897 the Dutch physician Eijkman cured a similar nerve disease in pigeons by feeding them rice polishings that had been discarded in milling the grain. Even a water extract of raw grain effected cures. Eijkman erroneously thought this counteracted a toxin, or poison, in the starch of highly milled rice. His coworker Grijns proved that the toxin hypothesis was wrong and theorized that the rice polishings contained a "protective" substance (now known to be thiamine, vitamin B_1). Most of the people who get beriberi live mainly on a diet of polished rice from which the outer coat has been removed. A few years later, around 1905, a physician in the University of Utrecht, Dr. Pekelharing, substantiated the work of Eijkman and Grijns in experiments with mice which demonstrated that animals can starve to death even when they have plenty of food if the food does not include some substance, then unknown, essential to life.

In 1911 the Polish-born American nutrition worker, Casimir Funk, coined the word *vitamine,* meaning *vital amine*—the amines being a class of chemicals related to ammonia—for "the chemical that cures polyneuritis in birds induced by a diet of polished rice." Later, when more was known about these disease-preventing substances, it was found that they are not all amines. The term was so apt, however, that with the final *e* left off it became the now universally used *vitamin.*

A long series of important discoveries developed from the work of these early days. Beginning with vitamin B_1, a dozen B vitamins have been found, and it is not unlikely that there are still more. The substance that prevented and cured scurvy was named vitamin C. Another, named vitamin A, prevented a serious eye disease, xerophthalmia. Vitamin D prevented rickets and some other crippling or deforming bone ailments and played an essential part in the body's use of calcium and phosphorus for bonemaking. And so on; a growing list of diseases were found to be caused, primarily, by lack of one or another of these mysterious vitamins. But for a long time no one ever saw a vitamin; their discovery, like that of molecules, atoms, genes, was a triumph of deduction from indirect evidence. Today, not only are vitamins seen and touched, but many of them are produced synthetically.

Meanwhile the role of minerals in the body was also intensively studied. In 1925 John Orr told how the brilliant work of a number of scientists had shown that "those inorganic elements play a vitally important part in all physiological processes, and that the hidden mysteries of cell life which are slowly being unraveled are intimately connected with their activities." All life is based on protoplasm, and "in a real sense protoplasmic activity is regulated by the action of the mineral elements in solution in the protoplasm or attached to its colloids," or gelatinous particles. For example, "All the organs regulated by the central nervous system depend for the integrity of their functions upon the maintenance of definite ratios of calcium, potassium, and sodium in the fluids within the nerve tissues."

Knowledge was also being built up during this period about the amino acids, the substances that living organisms can combine in various proportions to make the complex proteins of which all the tissues of the body are composed. To support life and health, it was found, the body requires a considerable number of amino acids, all of which can be obtained from foods.

In this work, it might be said in passing, man owes a debt to hosts of laboratory animals—rats, mice, guinea pigs, rabbits, dogs, monkeys, pigeons. Because of the shortness of their life span, because they can be so accurately controlled and observed, because some of them are peculiarly sensitive to certain nutrient deficiencies, these animals have made possible in a few years discoveries that would have taken decades, sometimes centuries, if the experiments that were performed on them had had to be carried out through direct observation of human beings. Though the rat is an enemy of man, it also deserves a monument for its contributions to human well-being.

Like all science, this modern knowledge of nutrition is the work of men and women of many nations. A scientist in Germany makes a discovery; a scientist in England learns about it and gets a clue that enables him to make another discovery; a scientist in the USA learns about that and carries the process a step further with a third discovery. And the people of all countries can make use of these discoveries to better their lives.

Knowledge of the part played by vitamins, minerals, and amino acids in life processes has gone far beyond the early work related to the prevention or cure of a few nutritional diseases. As scientists now see it, these chemical substances are intimately related, in complex interactions, to the whole functioning of the body from conception to death. Since the developing organism, once ovum and sperm have united, is built entirely from the food it obtains, and food is essential for all its functions, the quantity and character of the food must obviously be matters of the utmost import.

We know now that, other things being equal, good nutrition makes it possible for human beings on the average to attain higher levels of health and physical well-being, to live longer, to keep young and remain in full possession of their faculties to a later period in life, and even to grow faster and taller than had been thought possible before. This does not mean that good nutrition prevents infectious diseases or improves genetic inheritance; but it helps the body to resist and recover from the diseases and provides conditions favorable for attaining the full possibilities of one's inheritance.

As the new knowledge grew, it gradually provided information about the quantities of various nutrients that individuals need for good health. In the USA, the generally accepted figures are those published by the Food and Nutrition Board, which was established in 1940 as part of the National Research Council. The "recommended allowances" of the Board include specific figures for energy (calories), protein, and a number of the minerals and vitamins—calcium, iron, vitamin A, thiamine, riboflavin, niacin, ascorbic acid, vitamin D. Recommendations are also given for fat, iodine, water, salt, phosphorus, copper, vitamin K, folic acid. The figures, representing carefully considered conclusions from the knowledge of today (subject to change in the light of new knowledge), take into account sex, age, size, degree of physical activity, and the special requirements of pregnancy and lactation.

It is not possible for the average person to make practical use of such recommendations as these unless calories, minerals, and vitamins can be readily translated into terms of bread, meat, vegetables. One method of insuring that meals and food supplies meet the requirements of good nutrition was worked out in the early 1930's by Hazel K. Stiebeling of the US Department of Agriculture. She divided the common foods into several groups according to their special nutritive values. Then she calculated what quantities and proportions of each group would be needed in diets at four levels of cost. The cheapest was made up of combinations that would provide the necessary nutrients at low cost. The more expensive included more of the foods that improve flavor and variety as well as nutritive value.

By classifying foods in groups according to their main nutritive values, Stiebeling simplified the selection and analysis of diets, whether of an individual, a family, or a population. This is extremely important in food management and in planning adequate production. The method provides maximum flexibility in the choice of foods because each group includes several foods that are about equally good nutritionally. This classification takes the emphasis off particular foods, which may not be available, or which the individual may not be able to afford or may not like, and puts it on achieving the right proportions among the groups.

Stiebeling's studies of food consumption at various economic levels in the USA in the 1930's showed that a third of the population at that time was poorly fed. (On the basis of the same standards, the figure today would probably be not more than 10 per cent, thanks largely to the rapid progress made possible by this new science.) Similar studies were made in other countries, notably in the United Kingdom, where Dr. John Orr of Aberdeen, a physician who had come to specialize in nutrition because as a young man he was so deeply moved by the sufferings of the people he saw in the slums of Glasgow, published a small book called *Food, Health, and Income* in which he analyzed the food consumption of people at different income levels and showed how poverty means poor diets and poor diets mean poor health. But instead of dealing only with small samples of the population, Orr showed the whole national income distribution, which gave a startling picture of the extent of poverty and malnutrition.

Techniques for putting nutrition science to practical use came at the right time, for the depression of the 1930's was under way, great numbers of people were out of work, and incomes were in general so drastically cut that almost everyone had to economize on food and try to get the most for his money.

Agriculture suffered badly. Farmers could not meet costs of production. Many lost their farms, and many more could not afford to take proper care of their soil, buildings, and equipment. Meantime, food sometimes piled up and rotted or had to be destroyed because people could not afford to buy, though hunger stalked the great cities. The story of Jim Barton describes some of the things that were done in the United States at that time to save agriculture from ruin. The emergency brought government action, at the demand of farmers and with their participation, to an extent that would hardly have been conceivable in the USA before the great depression. Perhaps the chief lesson learned was that maintaining a healthy agriculture is as much a matter of public concern as maintaining an adequate educational system, and that a great deal can be done to keep it healthy.

Proposal for Marriage

The development of new knowledge about foods and new interest in the welfare of agriculture resulted during this period in a movement concerned with both in the League of Nations. Many people realized around the mid-1930's—as Walters puts it in his history of the League—that the whole complicated network of high tariffs, quotas, prohibitions, exchange restrictions, and so on, which had gradually been created in an effort to solve depression problems was strangling trade and making the situation worse. There was a growing conviction

. . . that untold possibilities of material advance were being neglected, and that opportunities which might never recur were being allowed to pass. Never perhaps in history had there been so wide a gap between the actual and the possible conditions of human life. New discoveries and new methods made it easy to raise to new heights the production of all that men needed for a decent standard of living for themselves and their families. Yet in actual fact the standard of living of the workers, and of the poorer sections of the community, was, on a wide view, falling rather than rising. . . . Though perhaps only a few experts realized the true extent of the gap between what men's lives might be made and what they actually were, none but the most benighted could fail to realize that big changes were necessary.

Against this background a World Monetary and Economic Conference was held in London in 1932-33. Stanley Bruce, at that time Australian High Commissioner in London and previously Prime Minister of Australia, represented his government at the meeting. When it seemed that the conference would disagree about almost everything except the need to restrict production, Bruce bluntly said that if this was the best that could be done for a poverty-stricken world by a meeting so carefully prepared and with such high-level representation, the only result would be to strengthen the forces tending toward fascism and communism.

Later, when the shadows of coming war were beginning to darken and the League of Nations was dying as a political organization, a number of people got together to try to salvage some measure of international co-operation by enlarging action in such practical spheres as food, agriculture, housing, child welfare, education. The foundation for this effort had been laid in earlier studies by the League secretariat—for example, by its Health Section, at one time directed by Dr. Frank G. Boudreau (USA). Two physicians, Dr. Wallace Aykroyd and Dr. Etienne Burnet of the Health Section, made studies of conditions in several countries and prepared a report, *Nutrition and Public Health,* which was published by the League and attracted a great deal of attention. The Health Committee, an outside advisory group not on the League staff, then prepared a notable document, *The Physiological Bases of Nutrition,* which pioneered in defining dietary requirements for health, stressing especially optimal allowances rather than (as hitherto) the minimum needs of the body. (This, incidentally, set the example which was later followed by the USA Food and Nutrition Board.)

With these studies as a springboard, a small group that included Bruce, his economic adviser F. L. McDougall (also from Australia), and John Boyd Orr of Scotland argued: Mankind needs food. Farmers want to produce as much food as possible as efficiently as possible. If these two drives can be effectively linked, the world can start on the road to an economy of abundance instead of the economy of scarcity that seems to obsess men's minds.

Bruce and McDougall decided that the time was ripe to bring these ideas to the attention of the League Assembly. Bruce made a speech proposing a "marriage of health and agriculture"—vigorous revival of trade between the industrialized and the agricultural countries which would make it possible for immense numbers of people to get more of the foods they needed for health. The Assembly was impressed. In a formal resolution it recognized that "the relation of nutrition to the health of the people has become a social and economic problem of widely accepted significance and . . . that this subject has an important bearing on world agricultural problems."

After that meeting Bruce, McDougall, and Lord de la Warr sent a jubilant telegram to Orr in Aberdeen saying, "Brother Orr, we have this day lighted such a candle, by God's grace, in Geneva, as we trust shall never be put out." (There is a story that in 1555, when Hugh Latimer and Nicholas Ridley were burned at the stake for heresy, Latimer said, "Be of good comfort, Master Ridley, and play the man; we shall this day light such a candle, by God's grace, in England, as I trust shall never be put out.")

Subsequently the Assembly set up a Mixed Committee on the Problem of Nutrition, headed by Lord Astor, to study this idea that governments might build healthier populations, stimulate increased production, and deal effectively with the problem of agricultural surpluses and depressed prices by extending their work in the comparatively new field of nutrition. The expert members of the committee brought in outside authorities as consultants and worked for two years on a series of reports. The final document, *The Relation of Nutrition to Health, Agriculture, and Economic Policy,* was published in 1937. Walters writes:

This famous Report showed the real character of the connections, hitherto ignored or misunderstood, save by a few pioneers, between food and health. It explained the function of the different kinds of food, and drew up tables indicating the diets needed for health at various ages and in various types of occupation. It discussed recent scientific developments in agriculture and the enormously increased production which they made possible. It described the various ways in which governments could help to improve the nutrition of town and country dwellers alike; it described also the various ways in which they were in fact preventing such improvement.

The nutrition report was an immediate success and became a best-seller among League of Nations documents; the New York *Times* had a leading editorial about it and called it the book of the year; its recommendations were studied (and carried out) by a number of governments. When Bruce made his first statement in the League Assembly, only three countries had national nutrition committees. Within four years, the number grew to 30. These committees aroused public interest in nutrition and got work started in this field by governments. Before the war broke out they held two international conferences, in 1937 and 1938, in Geneva; and in 1939 a third conference was held in Latin America.

Thus by the end of the 1930's a world food movement had started and plans had been made for additional regional meetings in the Far East and Africa. These the war prevented. Ironically, Walters notes, "the scientific

Conception 47

standards of diets drawn up by the League were used first by Germany, then by other governments, as a basis for their rationing systems." But the idea had put down deep roots in various countries. For example, the recommendations made by the 900 delegates of the 1941 US Nutrition Conference for Defense ended on this ambitious note:

There seems no reason to doubt, on the basis of present evidence, that just as, by the use of modern medical science, we have conquered diseases that took an enormous toll of life in the past, so by the use of the modern knowledge of nutrition we can build a better and a stronger race. . . .

This can be done by the conquest of hunger—not only the obvious hunger man has always known, but the hidden hunger revealed by the modern knowledge of nutrition. . . .

No nation, certainly no large nation, has ever truly conquered hunger, the oldest enemy of man. Such an aim is not too high, such a goal is not too difficult. . . . It is a particularly fitting task for us in this day when democracy should point the way to a new and better civilization for oppressed peoples all over the earth.

If the League of Nations was dead as a political organization, the work in food and agriculture was to survive and emerge again as the basis for a stronger movement. "In turning their attention to the problems of the individual rather than of his government," according to Walters, "the League's institutions had been, in a sense, retreating against their will from the positions they had originally occupied. But in their second line they had found elements of strength which had never been fully available in the first. They had opened up new springs of popular interest and support. . . . They had at least drawn the outline of a common front against poverty, ignorance, and disease. Their new enterprises transcended all differences of nationality, race, religion, continent, or color. There remained one boundary which they could not cross. None of the authoritarian States would participate, although it was always open to them to do so."

Acid Test

The war destroyed resources needed for production and transport and violently dislocated normal channels of trade. It also brought dramatic developments in food and agriculture. Every country did everything possible to stimulate production. Almost every country had to institute a system of food management for all its citizens, including rationing and control of prices which would otherwise have skyrocketed. Every country at war also had the gigantic task of feeding its armed forces.

In the case of agricultural production the whole range of recent developments in applied science and technology was drawn on more intensively than ever to increase the output of food and fiber. In Jim Barton's story we saw the striking results in the USA. The same kind of results occurred in the United Kingdom, Canada, and other countries. The newer knowledge of nutrition also made it possible to do things that had never been done before in periods of great crisis. The outstanding example, perhaps, was in Great Britain. That country developed a rationing system, based on the nutritional needs of the whole population and of particular groups—children, pregnant and nursing women, workers in war industries—which was so effective that in spite of food shortages, bombing, difficulties of transport, and the monotony of the wartime diet, the poorer people were better fed than they had ever been. The food supply was tailored as well as possible under the circumstances to people's real needs, and under the rationing system everyone was able to get his fair share; if the well-to-do had to give up luxuries, the poor got more necessities. Vital statistics showed an upward curve in national health in the midst of the most terrible war in history. In Switzerland, isolated by war from the outside world, F. T. Wahlen directed a production and rationing system which also achieved remarkable results. In the USA conditions were less stringent and there was less hardship, but here too it was necessary to institute a nationwide rationing system which, as in England, was based in part on nutritional science, and which safeguarded the health of people who would otherwise have suffered most from food shortages. Similarly, in the feeding of the armed forces the new knowledge of nutrition was pressed into service as it could not have been hitherto because it did not exist.

In other words, three great developments—scientific agriculture, the techniques of economic adjustment learned in the depression years, the new knowledge of nutrition—tested in the most destructive of wars, achieved near-miracles.

An Idea Takes Form

The preoccupation with food created a favorable atmosphere for keeping alive the beginnings of the international approach to food problems which had been made in the latter days of the League of Nations.

Some of the individuals directly involved in the League developments helped during the war in the food management work of their own countries. Boudreau, for example, became head of the Food and Nutrition Board in the United States. McDougall came to the USA as representative of Australia in the negotiations for international wheat agreements in 1941 and 1942. Orr visited the United States at about the same time.

During the wheat discussions a small group of people, most of them in the US Department of Agriculture, met occasionally with McDougall to discuss international food problems. This group worked out a memorandum, known as "the McDougall memorandum," which outlined proposals for establishing an international organization concerned with food and agriculture as soon as the war ended. These ideas were set out in an article written by McDougall late in 1942 for *The Annals of the American Academy of Political and Social Science*. He wrote:

CONCEPTION

The exigencies of war and of the relief period will in the next few years render almost all men everywhere in the world highly food conscious. . . . Psychological reasons may therefore lead us to anticipate that in the United Nations plans for world reconstruction, action to secure better nutrition and improvements in food production and distribution will be accorded a high priority. . . .

If the United Nations decided to make freedom from want of food the first step towards the attainment of . . . freedom from want, this will require national action in every country and international action to assist countries lacking technical knowledge and financial means to secure improvements in food production.

McDougall pointed out that at least 60 per cent of the world's workers are engaged in farming and that therefore on the basis of numbers the welfare of farmers is "the outstanding social problem of the world." He then went on to propose a "United Nations Organization for Food and Agriculture" as the first step in the creation of a world-wide agency for the preservation of peace and the attainment of full employment and rising standards of living. This organization would have three broad functions: to collect, compile, and interpret statistics relating to agriculture and food consumption; to organize a world service around the sciences affecting agriculture; and to provide technical guidance and help for the less developed countries by recruiting groups of agricultural experts who would be "available to be sent to any part of the world to assist in improving agricultural methods, securing better land tenure systems, bringing about more effective marketing, or promoting agricultural education."

A copy of the McDougall memorandum got into the hands of Mrs. Eleanor Roosevelt, and in September 1942 she invited McDougall to have luncheon with her. As she later told the story to the author of this book, she regarded it as her duty to see people who seemed to have interesting ideas or important proposals and decide whether it would be worth while for the President to talk to them. She thought McDougall's ideas were worth bringing to the President's attention, and it was not long before McDougall was invited to dinner with a small group at the White House. The President talked about the thing nearest his heart, the establishment of the United Nations. McDougall suggested that since food would be the first preoccupation of the whole of mankind after the war, this would be a good starting place for the work of the new international agency, and he brought into the conversation some of the ideas in the memorandum. The President was responsive, but he gave no indication that he favored the proposals.

McDougall heard nothing more until he read a newspaper announcement that the President was going to invite the allied governments to send representatives to a conference on food and agriculture, to be held at Hot Springs, Virginia, in May 1943.

CHAPTER
FIVE

Birth

THOUGH THE Hot Springs Conference came in the midst of the war (it was fitting that the USA wartime Food Administrator, Judge Marvin H. Jones, should be elected chairman) it was concerned with peace. The fact that it dealt with the most basic of the biological, social, and economic problems of mankind—the provision of food for life and health—augured well; this was a practical start for international co-operation. The delegates of 45 countries who attended, many of them traveling with great difficulty since it was hard even to get space on a plane, train, or boat because of military priorities, had a sense of participation in a world event of unusual significance. They hoped to contribute something vital to future friendly relations among governments.

There were a few conflicting views and interests, mainly in the realm of economics. Some food-importing countries, for example, were highly dubious about the possibility of international action to protect producers if unmarketable surpluses should develop, because this might tend to raise prices. Some big-production countries, on the other hand, were not cordially disposed toward the possibility of establishing international food reserves (buffer stocks) to protect consumers against shortages, because the practice might tend to depress prices. The delegates nevertheless found more areas of agreement than disagreement. The fact that so many were technical people—experts in nutrition, in agricultural sciences, in fisheries, in statistics—rather than diplomats or politicians perhaps helped to make this agreement possible; for in the language of science, hunger and its effects are the same everywhere, and so is animal disease, and so is the breeding of better varieties of plants.

The discussions focused on three main subjects—actual food consumption levels compared with food requirements, increased production to meet consumer needs, and better distribution—which were broken down into subtopics handled by 11 committees. The Final Act of the conference, with its 33 recommendations and three discursive reports—on production, consumption, distribution—is a basic and statesmanlike document. Some of the recommendations were rooted in the prewar work of the League, with new contributions from the extensive documentation prepared by the USA for the conference, but they had a new energy and drive resulting in part from the sense of urgency inevitable in wartime.

As in all such conferences, no recommendation was binding; a recommendation has a certain moral force, but only one resolution emerged that bound the participating governments. This was to make a further study of the problem and, more specifically, to prepare plans for a permanent international organization concerned with food and agriculture. What the delegates had agreed upon, in essence, were these points:

- Food production must be greatly expanded.
- The necessary technical knowledge is available.
- To produce more food is useless unless markets are created to absorb it by a widespread increase in consumer purchasing power.
- Each nation is responsible for seeing that its own people have the food they need, but no nation can fully achieve this objective without the co-operation of others.
- A permanent international organization with a wide range of technical functions and duties, concerned with food and agriculture, must be established as quickly as possible.

This bare outline of the Hot Springs conclusions does not convey the spirit of the conference or the feeling the delegates had of breaking new ground and coming to grips with problems of tremendous import to all nations. In the end this feeling was shared even by those who at the start were lukewarm. But to describe the results achieved at Hot Springs in greater detail would involve repetition of material that will appear in other ways later in this book, since those results permeated the subsequent work of the Interim Commission, the Quebec conference, and the early work of FAO.

Laying Plans

Shortly after Hot Springs an Interim Commission on Food and Agriculture was organized to work out plans for the permanent organization, with all the countries represented there as members. L. B. Pearson of Canada was elected chairman. "Mike" Pearson, young, modest, responsive, intelligent, and possessed of a quick sense of humor and a flair for working out effective compromises between opposing viewpoints, had made an excellent impression at the Hot Springs Conference, which he attended as Minister-Counselor of the Canadian Legation in Washington. (Later he was to become Ambassador to the USA, Minister of External Affairs in Canada, and Chairman of the General Assembly of the United Nations.) More than any other one person he was responsible for steering the Interim Commission through two years of successful work.

The government representatives included many other outstanding individuals. A small technical secretariat was brought together to service the commission, and a private house on McGill Terrace in Washington was rented as headquarters. There the commission and its committees and advisory panels met in the dining room around a huge oak table, the other rooms being turned into offices.

The commission organized its work in three committees: one, headed by Sir Girja Bajpai (India), to draft the constitution; another, headed by Eurico Penteado (Brazil), to prepare a declaration which eventually took the form of a preamble to the constitution; the third, headed by Darwish Haidari (Iraq), to help work out the technical functions and duties of FAO. Haidari's committee had five subcommittees dealing with agriculture, nutrition, forestry, fisheries, and economics and statistics. In addition three panels of experts—science, economics, and a reviewing and co-ordinating body—were appointed.

It would be hard to find an organization more carefully and painstakingly prepared for than FAO. The work of the commission was permeated by a sense of high purpose which was part of the atmosphere of the time. The world was then still caught in the most destructive of all wars, to be marked in its last phase by the explosion of an atomic bomb at Hiroshima which would send shivers up man's spine and bring an unprecedented awareness of the deadly threat to civilization implicit in war from now on. How well that sense of foreboding has since been justified! As President Truman said in his State of the Union message to Congress in January 1953, "Atomic science is in the full tide of development; the unfolding of the innermost secrets of matter is uninterrupted and irresistible. . . . From now on, man moves into a new era of destructive power. . . . The war of the future would be one in which man could extinguish millions of lives at one blow, demolish the great cities of the world, wipe out the cultural achievements of the past—and destroy the very structure of a civilization that has been slowly and painfully built up through hundreds of generations. Such a war is not a possible policy for rational men."

In 1943 the feeling that nations must and could get together to prevent further conflicts was becoming nearly universal. Though by no means everyone in the USA was in favor of the projected United Nations, it had widespread support. About that time Wendell Willkie's book *One World* appeared, expressing the belief of millions of people that there would indeed be one world or none. This kind of conviction was part of the background of the Interim Commission's work. The group also shared the conviction that humanity can achieve a new era of abundance by bringing the beneficent powers of science into much wider use. And they had a keen sense of the need to move quickly because food shortages after the war would be so acute as to bring widespread suffering and violence.

"The nations accepting this Constitution," said the Preamble submitted by these constitution-makers,

... being determined to promote the common welfare by furthering separate and collective action on their part for the purposes of

> raising levels of nutrition and standards of living of the peoples under their respective jurisdictions,
>
> securing improvements in the efficiency of the production and distribution of all food and agricultural products,
>
> bettering the condition of rural populations,
>
> and thus contributing toward an expanding world economy,

hereby establish the Food and Agriculture Organization of the United Nations ... through which the Members will report to one another on the measures taken and the progress achieved.

In spite of these large areas of agreement there were also, as at Hot Springs, differences of opinion. In particular, two viewpoints soon developed about the fundamental nature of the proposed agency. One group favored establishing a strong food and agriculture organization which could take positive steps to foster economic expansion and help prevent disastrous crises, the recent depression being still much in men's minds. The other group wanted a rather narrowly limited fact-gathering and advisory agency which would be carefully insulated from positive action. The organization that gradually took shape, with the functions outlined in Article I of the draft constitution (Appendix), was a compromise, more on the advisory than the action side but with the way open, constitutionally, to develop in whatever direction the member nations might find most useful.

The views on the size of the budget reflected the same difference. The group that conceived of the agency as a sort of world department of agriculture favored a rather liberal budget, say of the order of ten million dollars a year (small, of course, compared with the billion-dollar budget of the US Department of Agriculture, which deals with the farm problems of a single country). The group that believed the organization should be limited to gathering and disseminating statistics and other information felt that a modest sum such as a million or a million and a half dollars a year would be all that could be used. Again the outcome was a compromise—an annual budget of five million dollars, of which it was agreed in the course of considerable negotiation that the United States of America would contribute 25 per cent, the United Kingdom 15, the Union of Soviet Socialist Republics 8, China 6.5, France 5.69, Canada 5.06, India 4.25, Brazil 3.46, Australia 3.33, and the remaining countries smaller percentages—several, a nominal one-half of 1 per cent each. (The 1953 conference raised the budget ceiling for the regular program to six million dollars. For the 1955 scale of contributions, see the Appendix.)

Deciding on a name also involved a good deal of discussion. Some wanted to call the agency the United Nations Organization for Food and Agriculture or the United Nations Food and Agriculture Organization, which would emphasize the United Nations by putting it first; some, the World Food and Agriculture Organization, with no reference to the United Nations. The name finally decided on, the Food and Agriculture Organization of the United Nations, or FAO for short, emphasized the agency's independent functions, though it was to be "related" to the United Nations when the latter was established.

The original members, according to the constitution, were to be the 45 countries represented on the Interim Commission. Additional members might be admitted by two-thirds vote. The governing body would be a conference meeting at least once a year (later changed to once every 2 years). The conference would determine policy, approve the budget, appoint committees, and appoint the Director-General who, in turn, would select the staff.

The constitution appeared in the Interim Commission's first report to governments. Its second report recommended that the prewar International Institute of Agriculture should be merged with FAO in due course. The third report dealt with the functions of FAO in connection with forestry and forest products, a field included after the Hot Springs Conference. In addition, the commission published five detailed technical reports, on nutrition and food management, agricultural production, fisheries, forestry and primary forest products, and statistics, prepared by the subcommittees previously mentioned.

The Reviewing Panel prepared a general report on *The Work of FAO*. This panel, headed by McDougall, coordinated the work of the technical committees and in addition laid out the broad plan for the operations of the future organization as a basis for discussion at the first conference. The group met intermittently for many months around the big table in the dining room on McGill Terrace, exploring ideas and proposals. Its 20 sessions were a high-level discussion or debate on the world's food and agricultural problems and what nations could do through the proposed new agency toward solving them.

There is more than historical interest in looking back at the deliberations of this group. Their report built much of the philosophical base for the organization's work and was prophetic of what was to come in the development, not only of FAO but of the subsequent even broader technical cooperation programs of various agencies. For that reason I shall quote from this first *Work of FAO* at some length, taking the liberty of telescoping the text at several points without indicating omissions.

*

The Work of FAO

The Food and Agriculture Organization is born out of the idea of freedom from want. This is not one man's fortunate phrase; it expresses an aspiration as old as mankind. Whenever primitive men tried to imagine paradise in concrete terms, they pictured it as a place where food was plentiful and want no longer existed. Every utopia man has conceived has been such a place. But in this generation freedom from want has come to have a different meaning. It has been taken out of the realm of utopian ideas. The conviction has spread that it can be achieved; indeed, this is one of the convictions most characteristic of the thinking and the mood of this generation.

The Food and Agriculture Organization is born out of the need for peace as well as the need for freedom from want. The two are interdependent. Peace is essential if there is to be progress toward freedom from want, for the insatiable demands of modern war will in the end take all men can produce [and, it might have been added, destroy the means of production]. Progress toward freedom from want is essential to lasting peace; for it is a condition of freedom from the tensions, arising out of economic maladjustment, profound discontent, and a sense of injustice, which are so dangerous in the close community of modern nations.

If there is any one fundamental principle on which FAO is based, it is that the welfare of producers and the welfare of consumers are in the final analysis identical.

For a vast majority of people, this is self-evident; they are the farmers, hundreds of millions of them, outnumbering all the other people, who produce the food they themselves consume and little or nothing besides.

But in the case of the two other great groups—the consumers who live in towns and work in industry and trade, and the farmers who sell a sizable proportion of their produce to this group—the identity of producer welfare and consumer welfare is by no means always self-evident. On the contrary, the interests of the two often apparently conflict.

But the conflict is only apparent. The exploitation of producers as a group will not in the long run benefit consumers, nor, in the long run, will it benefit producers if consumers as a group are put at a disadvantage. Wherever the contrary seems to be true, it is because all of the factors have not been taken into account, including the risk of social upheavals and wars.

There is always a larger framework in which producer and consumer interests are seen to be the same.

It will be the business of FAO to seek and to emphasize this larger framework, this whole view.

*

It is not possible to wave a scientific wand and make production efficient and people healthy and well-nourished.

Knowledge about better production methods, better processing and distribution, and better use of foods is available and can be spread fairly readily. How to get it put into practice on the necessary scale is the problem.

The barriers that stand in the way of the needed improvements are many and difficult: deep-rooted customs and traditions, lack of education, rigid economic and social institutions, vested interests, lack of money, lack of international collaboration.

To surmount these difficulties will call for all the wisdom and will that nations, acting by themselves as well as through FAO and other international organizations, can muster.

Fortunately, there is no need to think in terms of the millennium—that is, in terms of achieving freedom from want everywhere equally and quickly.

*

Surpluses were the nightmare of most of the highly developed countries during the inter-war depression. The word *surplus* bit deep into the consciousness of farmers in particular. They still have a wholesome dread of it, knowing that if the same forces are again allowed to operate, agricultural producers may again come uncomfortably near to fulfilling Shakespeare's prediction about the farmer who hanged himself in the expectation of plenty.

The only possible basis for a program of expanding production is to enlarge effective demand so that it will equal and even outstrip production, and organizations concerned with international economic problems, including FAO, will be expected to work toward this end.

The possibilities for enlarging effective demand by building up and maintaining full employment and high purchasing power are enormous, for it could be made coextensive with human needs, which themselves enlarge as the more elementary ones are satisfied.

*

In some ways the development of the less advanced countries may be regarded as the major need of the decades following the war.

In an age of increasing agricultural efficiency and industrial mass production, it is little less than suicidal to leave two-thirds of the world's people in a state of chronic poverty and undernourishment. Here lies the greatest opportunity not only for improving human welfare but for expanding the demand for agricultural and industrial products.

The most significant fact in the less advanced countries is that in this the twentieth century, out of every ten people seldom less than seven are farmers; in some areas, where the proportion has changed little in a thousand years, the number is as high as eight or nine out of ten. The industrial revolution and its accompanying agricultural changes have not yet reached these people.

In the technically advanced countries a vast amount is known that can be adapted and applied to revolutionize production in the less developed regions.

There is no reason why a country should not be able, through FAO, to have its whole agricultural system, or any segment of it, surveyed by some of the world's outstanding experts with a view to working out comprehensive plans for improvements and new developments.

There is no reason why it should not be able, through FAO, to obtain the services of experts for temporary periods to get new developments started; arrange to send many more students abroad for study; start new research, co-ordinated with that in other countries; get in touch with sources of breeding material for improved crops and livestock; obtain help in co-ordinating its commercial production with world market needs; and do many other things that would be much more difficult to do without the aid of an international organization.

This is not to say that the task will be easy. A country with a relatively primitive agriculture, poor, and perhaps with far too many people on the land, faces years of struggle to bring about extensive improvements.

The simplest beginnings should not be despised; indeed, they should sometimes be especially sought.

A steel hoe can make a great difference to a man who has never had one. The use of a little insecticide dust may double or triple the quantity of food obtained from a patch of land. A village incubator can furnish better bred poultry that will make it possible for small farmers to increase their meager cash income by many dollars a year besides getting more eggs to eat.

Just such improvements as these, elementary yet vastly important to people who have almost nothing to work with, should be developed on a wide scale. They can be the basis for local industries which would use materials largely of local origin to make needed equipment, quickly paying their own way and taking up some of the slack of underemployment on the land. Through FAO, the possibilities for such developments can be systematically surveyed, and agricultural engineers, agronomists, and others can be made available to get them started and to instruct local leaders.

This work is analogous to that of the Extension Service in the United States and similar services in other countries.

Such a service is the intermediary between the scientist and the farmer, translating the findings of science into terms the producer can understand and showing him how they can be applied under his conditions.

*

There is a vast amount to be done of a larger sort.

In some countries farmers stagger under a perennial burden of debt at usurious rates. The load must be taken off their backs and an adequate credit system set up if agriculture is to progress very far.

Tenure systems that force a continual reduction in the size of holdings as farms are divided among the heirs from generation to generation may make it impossible ultimately for anyone to get a decent living from the land. Feudal types of landholding, or the exploitation of producers by absentee landlords controlling large areas, are sometimes the major obstacles that stand in the way of improving rural welfare and the economic status of farmers.

*

Of a different kind are large-scale development projects.

Many million more acres of land could be irrigated in China, India, South America, Africa, the Middle East. Though the initial installation is costly, the public investment can pay large dividends in the form of increased agricultural production and opportunities for many people to make a better livelihood not only within the irrigated areas but in others adjacent to or dependent upon them.

Similarly, considerable areas of land can be made productive by clearing and drainage.

On a still larger scale are regional or river valley developments that may involve extensive flood-prevention and erosion-control measures, afforestation, the development of hydroelectric power which can be used for new industries, and a well-planned program of agricultural production.

Or a country may wish to improve and build up its livestock or dairy production where suitable areas of land are available.

In all such cases difficult technical problems are involved and mistakes are costly. FAO will be equipped to mobilize up-to-date scientific information, the services of survey parties, and expert assistance in getting projects started.

*

No purely agricultural development, however, will entirely meet the need, particularly in countries in which there is a heavy and increasing pressure of population on the land. Industries must be established which can siphon off the excess rural population and furnish opportunities for work at adequate pay in shops, factories, and offices. The industrialization must eventually be on a large scale if the pressure on the land is to be materially relieved, though the development of small village industries may be the first step and help considerably.

Rapid population growth without adequate means of subsistence is the critical problem in large parts of the Orient, and if nothing is done it will become more and more acute.

The conclusion is inescapable that the sooner industrial development can begin and the more rapidly it can take place, the sooner an important step will have been taken toward solving one of the most dangerous and potentially explosive problems of modern times.

*

There is a still more fundamental aspect of FAO's work.

Over those parts of the earth not covered by water lies a thin crust of soil, perhaps equal by comparison to the thickness of a sheet of tissue paper wrapped around a globe six feet through.

Much of this soil is inaccessible for cultivation, or it is unusable for other reasons. From the rest, the world's growing population, now more than two thousand million, must draw all their sustenance except what they get from the sea; and even the fishes, like all other living things, are fed out of the fertility of the land.

Whether this thin layer of soil is to be a wasting asset or one maintained in perpetuity and made more fruitful for mankind will depend on how it is used and managed.

Nothing more deeply concerns the well-being of men and nations. FAO is dedicated to furthering good use and good management, in all ways and by all peoples, of this most basic of man's resources.

*

Science itself is essentially a pooling of knowledge, each advance becoming part of the common pool on which scientists can draw in order to make further advances.

The time has come when international organization is urgently needed to accelerate throughout the world the advance of scientific knowledge and its application to human affairs. FAO would fulfill such a function in the great and important area represented by food and agriculture.

*

This is the end of the quotations from the *Work of Fao,* which turned out to be a fairly accurate preview.

The Quebec Conference

Because of war conditions, it took longer than had been expected to get the 20 notifications of acceptance of the Constitution required to establish FAO. Finally the date of the first conference was set for October 16, 1945, in Quebec. The Interim Commission prepared the program for the meeting. Arrangements were made for hotel accommodations for some 300 people; for office supplies, typewriters, mimeograph machines, and other equipment; for press and radio representation; for a secretariat, including technical experts of high and low degree, stenographers, clerks, mimeograph operators, messengers; for all the other requirements of a big conference; and for a special train—still difficult to get so soon after the war—to carry delegates and secretariat from Washington to Quebec and return.

At the last minute another coach had to be added to this train for the representatives of the USSR. The Soviet Government had participated in the Hot Springs Conference and in the work of the Interim Commission. Up to a day or two before the departure for Quebec, however, the Russian members of the commission had not had word from Moscow whether they were to attend the conference or whether their government would actually join the new organization. Then they received orders to send a large delegation of more than 30 people, including representatives of the Byelo-Russian and Ukrainian Soviet Socialist Republics, who were named separately from the representatives of the USSR. Later, during the conference, the delegation received instructions from Moscow to participate only as observers, not as voting delegates, and it was announced that the USSR would have to give further consideration to the question whether it would join FAO. It did not.

At Quebec, L. B. Pearson was elected conference chairman. Sir John Orr, who had not been sent by his government to the Hot Springs Conference, did come to Quebec, not as a delegate but as a technical adviser to the United Kingdom delegation. The bushy-browed Scottish nutrition expert and farmer, who had devoted much of his life to preaching the idea that modern civilization must find ways to feed the world adequately or it would be overwhelmed by hungry hordes, gave only one speech. The delegates elected him the first Director-General. At a dinner in the grand ballroom he took the oath of office which made him, as he liked to put it, the first citizen of the world in a new international service, dedicated to working for the whole of mankind. "Here we have in this Organization a most valuable means of bringing about some degree of world unity," he said. "If nations will not agree on a food policy which will benefit them all, they will agree on nothing. At an early date therefore we should go before them and say, 'Here is a food policy; here is a thing you can agree upon and on which action can be taken immediately.' And we can prophesy that if action is taken immediately it will begin to solve some of the apparently unsolvable economic problems of the world of the present day. . . . Then I think you will begin to develop . . . a technique of co-operation in getting this policy applied on a world scale. It should be easier then to develop international cooperation in other fields."

The delegates at Quebec included many able and brilliant minds. Basically, this is what came out of their work:

- Forty-four governments established a co-operative Food and Agriculture Organization as the first of the new United Nations agencies. (ILO was not one of the new agencies; it had continued in existence since the days of the League.)
- They accepted the constitution prepared by the Interim Commission and endorsed the commission's proposals for a program of work.
- They decided to establish the temporary headquarters of FAO in Washington, elected Sir John Orr the first Director-General, and appointed an Executive Committee with Sir Girja Bajpai as chairman, the members being selected for their individual competence and not as representatives of governments.
- The technical people representing agriculture, forestry, fisheries, nutrition, economics, statistics drew up many detailed recommendations for activities to be undertaken by FAO.

The Quebec conference ended on the recurrent theme of our time as L. B. Pearson said in closing: "We at this Conference know, and we have shown, what science could do if harnessed to the chariot of construction. Man's fears have, however, harnessed it also to another chariot—that of atomic obliteration. On that chariot race, with science driven by both contestants, all our hopes and fears and agonies and ecstasies are concentrated. If we lose in that contest anything that we have done here or may do elsewhere in London, or Washington, or San Francisco, or Moscow will have as much consequence as a pebble thrown into the Gulf of St. Lawrence. But if we should acquire some trace of sanity and bring social progress in line with scientific development by subjecting the annihilating forces of science to some sort of social control, which in the last analysis means some sort of international control, then the work we have done at Quebec will have made a worthy and permanent contribution to man's long effort to move upward from the jungle of hatred, suspicion, and death where so many powerful, selfish, and frightening influences even today are working to keep him mired."

CHAPTER SIX

Growth

O<small>N THE WAY BACK</small> from Quebec Sir John discovered that there were well over 250 things he was supposed to do, many of them immediately, if he followed all the recommendations; everyone had ideas and projects in which he was particularly interested. But the staff to carry out all these proposals consisted for a while of two persons—McDougall as Special Adviser and the author of this book as Director of Information. Sir John's immediate concern was to add more people, but he wanted to proceed cautiously. Under the best of circumstances it is much more difficult to build an international staff drawn from many countries than a staff drawn from one country; and in addition, many governments at that time needed their best technical people at home.

Within a few months, however, Sir John had filled a number of top posts, including the appointment of the late S. L. Louwes (the Netherlands) as another special adviser, and of four division directors—W. R. Aykroyd (UK) Nutrition, Howard Tolley (USA) Economics, Marcel Leloup (France) Forestry, D. B. Finn (Canada) Fisheries, the late G. Scott-Robertson (UK), succeeded by F. T. Wahlen (Switzerland), Agriculture. In later developments, Noble Clark (USA), succeeded by Sir Herbert Broadley (UK), became Deputy Director-General, and staff changes brought in three other division directors—Frank Weisl (USA) Administration, Duncan Wall (USA) Information, A. H. Boerma (the Netherlands) Economics, succeeding Tolley—and Marc Veillet-Lavallée as Secretary-General.

In Sir John's view, and also in that of the Quebec Conference, the first urgent need was to get the facts about the world food situation. What he had in mind was the kind of appraisal that would show the quantities of foods available in all countries, compare them with the nutritional needs of the people, and determine what additional production would be needed to bring deficient supplies up to moderately good levels within the next decade or so. (The increases proposed, in world totals, were cereals, 21 per cent; roots and tubers, 27; sugar, 12; fats, 34; pulses, 80; fruits and vegetables, 163; meat, 46; milk, 100.)

To find, assemble, weigh, and interpret such a mass of data was a large undertaking for an infant organization, and it could not possibly have been carried out with the small FAO staff. Early in 1946, therefore, Sir John borrowed experts to form a working party or committee. (This was to become a characteristic FAO technique for getting work done with limited funds. In fact, it is in itself a form of international co-operation which the Interim Commission had foreseen as a development that should be fostered.) The members of this group came from the Combined Food Board, the US Department of Agriculture, the British Ministry of Food, the Emergency Economic Committee for Europe, the United Nations Relief and Rehabilitation Administration, and other agencies; and the group was reinforced when necessary by other special committees of experts who served for short periods.

I have already dealt briefly with the *World Food Survey* in an earlier chapter and shall not go into further detail. With all its unavoidable faults, the survey was so unique and gave so striking and useful a picture that it attracted widespread attention; there had never been anything really like it, nor have the data ever been seriously assailed. As Sir John realized, the undertaking was an extraordinarily apt beginning—in US slang, "a natural"—for the work of an international food and agriculture organization. He had a keen perceptiveness about such things. In these early days, for instance, McDougall was trying to find a suitable motto for FAO. He picked *Ut educas panem de terra,* "That ye may bring forth bread from the earth," suggested by Dr. Russell Wilder of the Mayo Clinic. "Too long and literary," Sir John growled. "We should have something as simple as *Fiat lux.*" Next day he came up with *Fiat panis,* "Let there be bread."

The Food Crisis

In addition to the difficult *World Food Survey* FAO in its first months undertook two other big jobs. One involved setting up an international agency to continue wartime international food allocations during the emergency period just after the war. The other was a survey mission to Greece.

The emergency action on food followed an exchange of transatlantic cables and telephone calls. In London, McDougall was attending the General Assembly of the United Nations. The Assembly was fearful that the imminent demise of the temporary agencies concerned with relief—the Combined Food Board, the Emergency Economic Committee for Europe, the United Nations Relief and Rehabilitation Administration—would leave a hiatus, during the period of acute shortages before food production could be brought back to somewhere near normal, which might result in widespread starvation. Some of the UN delegates suggested setting up a new agency to deal with the situation. When McDougall telephoned this to Sir John, his reaction was that with an international food and agriculture organization already in existence, it would be foolish to create another one. Food allocation had not been envisaged as a function of FAO, but he believed it should take the responsibility of mobilizing the necessary action. This view was accepted, and Sir John promptly issued invitations to a Special Meeting on Urgent Food Problems, to be convened in Washington in May, and set his staff, supplemented by an expert working group, to preparing an *Appraisal of the World Food Situation for 1946–47*.

Twenty-two governments and six international organizations sent representatives to this meeting, which lasted through a week of intensive discussion and had several important results. First, it brought to public attention the fact that the postwar food crisis would not be over in a few months, as many people had optimistically assumed, but would last at least another year and probably longer. The meeting emphasized that in Europe and the Far East during the coming year there would probably be a gap equivalent to some ten million metric tons of wheat between the urgent needs of the importing countries and the supplies that would be available from the chief exporters. Second, the meeting made rather strongly worded recommendations for action by both supplying and receiving countries to reduce this gap and mitigate the hardships of the coming year. Third, the meeting recommended that governments establish an International Emergency Food Council which would replace the wartime Combined Food Board but have far broader representation (only the USA, Canada, and the United Kingdom were represented on the Board) and continue in existence as long as the shortage of basic foods lasted. FAO was to name the Secretary-General of the IEFC and provide the secretariat.

Finally, Sir John was requested to present proposals at the forthcoming session of the FAO Conference, only a few months off, for international machinery of a longer-term nature designed to prevent both shortages and surpluses. He had expected to make such proposals in due course, but this request pushed his plans forward by a year.

Starting with 20 countries, the International Emergency Food Council had 34 members within a few months. Sir John nominated Dennis A. FitzGerald, then Director of the US Office of Foreign Agricultural Relations, as Secretary-General. L. A. H. Peters of the Netherlands was elected to be the first Chairman. The IEFC worked for two years as an independent agency. Then, with improved food supplies, the work tapered off, but the agency continued for a time, incorporated in FAO, under the name of the International Emergency Food Committee.

The council was organized in a number of committees, made up of representatives of governments, each dealing with a single commodity or a group of related commodities—beans and peas, cereals, cocoa, fats and oils, fertilizers, fish, meat and meat products, rice, seeds, sugar, tea. The secretariat kept the supply/demand situation under continuous review, and on the basis of this information the committees recommended the amounts of the products in short supply that each importing country should have from the total available for export. The IEFC had no executive power to carry out these allocations; it could only say, in effect, "This is what we think ought to be done for the good of everyone and these are the reasons." It was then up to the conscience of each government to follow these recommendations or not. Actually there was a high degree of compliance. Between September 1947 and August 1948, for example, the total number of allocations added up to 475. In only 13 cases did the governments concerned refuse to concur; and after concurrence, the allocations were on the whole conscientiously carried out.

Thus the IEFC was able to perform a vital function during the postwar food shortage on a purely voluntary basis. Without some such international agency to parcel out scarce foods, the situation would have been much more critical and the suffering far greater. The IEFC could not increase food supplies, but it could help to assure reasonably fair distribution of available food among countries in need and forestall a scramble for scarce foods in which the highest bidders would have taken all they could get, the devil taking the hindmost.

Program for Greece

The request for a mission to Greece reached FAO about a month before the request for emergency food action. The people of Greece were suffering from drastic food shortages. They needed help in rehabilitating the wreckage of production and transport facilities throughout the country. But beyond that, they also wanted advice in formulating a long-term program that would hold some hope for the future. Sir John agreed to send a group of experts to make a survey. In effect, this was the beginning of the technical assistance which now plays so large a part in the work of FAO.

Fortunately, about that time F. S. Harris, President of the Utah State College of Agriculture, R. E. Buchanan, Director of the Iowa Experiment Station, and Afif I. Tannous, Lebanese-American extension expert in the US Department of Agriculture, were being sent by the US Government to the Near East. They agreed that on their way they would go to Greece for FAO. To this nucleus Sir John added experts in dairy and livestock raising, fruit growing, fruit packing, plant pathology, irrigation engineering, and agricultural economics. He also got the help of a home economist and two fisheries experts already working in Greece for UNRRA.

The members of this mission stayed in Greece from May to September 1946, traveling the length and breadth of that lovely, mountainous, rocky land, frequently under very difficult conditions of transport. (According to the Greeks, legend says that when God created the world, many rocks were left over. They were dumped in a heap in one place. The place was Greece.) In their study of the country's agriculture and general economy, the mission was given every possible assistance by the Greek Agricultural Bank and other government organizations and by the agricultural co-operatives.

Out of the survey came detailed proposals for the development of Greece which began with emergency measures to keep children from starving and went on to recommendations for modernizing agriculture, carrying out extensive irrigation and hydroelectric developments, expanding facilities for agricultural research and education, encouraging the growth of co-operatives, and improving fisheries. Suggestions were included also for industrial development and for changes in the fiscal system and the civil service, since these are intimately related to agricultural production and marketing. Considerable emphasis was given to better processing of such products as raisins, currants, dried fruits, wines, tobacco, olives, olive oil, to improve the competitive position of Greek producers in near-by international markets.

To take a single example: Olive oil is one of the major products of Greece. At that time it provided over 10 per cent of total exports and almost 15 per cent of total production, and olive trees occupied more than a fourth of the agricultural area. There had been much progress in the culture of the olive, but oil mills were in general small and not well equipped. In the belief that olive oil from Greece can achieve a reputation for exceptionally high quality in foreign markets if processing facilities are improved and expanded, the mission made specific recommendations to that end.

The FAO mission calculated that if the whole program it proposed for agricultural development were carried out, Greece could double or even triple production and income within a period of 25 years.

This report was well received in Greece and attracted a good deal of attention elsewhere. But the recommendations were not destined to be carried out with the help of an international agency because the USA early in 1947 undertook an extensive bilateral program of technical, economic, and military assistance in Greece and Turkey, followed in turn by the Marshall Plan. The FAO mission's findings provided the basis for many of the agricultural and food aspects of the Greek-USA program.

Subsequently FAO did some other significant work in Greece. Early in 1947 Sir John sent Andromache Tsongas (now Mrs. Aristotelis Sismanidis), Greek-American expert in nutrition and home economics, to that country. She stayed for about three years, working in many of the villages as well as in Athens and other cities. The food problem was acute, and there was no government agency especially concerned with food management and nutrition. Tsongas planned a nutrition service and drew up the necessary legislation to get it started. She helped to organize a general food program and special programs for milk distribution, school feeding, canteens for undernourished children, nutrition education, the training of nutrition and home economics workers, improvement of diets in public institutions, nutrition work with starving refugees, and the preparation of a cost-of-living index. The impress left by this pioneer FAO technical co-operator will not soon be forgotten in Greece.

Orr's World Food Board

The emergency food meeting in May 1946 asked Sir John to develop definite proposals for a world food policy in accordance with the ideas he had expressed at Quebec. During the summer the main job of the small staff, assisted by advisers and consultants, was to get these proposals into shape for presentation at the Copenhagen Conference, beginning in September.

To the agency embodying his ideas Sir John gave the name World Food Board. It was to be an international organization with power to buy, hold, and sell important agricultural commodities entering world trade, and to set maximum and minimum prices for these commodities in the international market. For producers, the Board would support prices by buying a commodity when the world price fell below an established minimum; for consumers, it would keep them from going too high by selling when the world price exceeded an established maximum. It would have a revolving fund large enough to pay storage costs for about as much of various products as would normally enter international trade during a period of 6 to 12 months. Preferably, though not necessarily, the Board would be under the aegis of FAO, and it would be closely related to the International Bank for Reconstruction and Development, the Economic and Social Council of the United Nations, and the proposed but never consummated International Trade Organization.

These functions and operations were designed to achieve four main objectives. By smoothing out violent price changes through its buying and selling transactions, the World Food Board would assure continued high production—in fact, expanding production—adequate to meet the world's expanding consumption needs. It would build up food reserves big enough for any famine emergency that might arise through crop failures. It would have funds that could be used to relieve the pressure of surplus agricultural products by disposing of them on special terms—below ordinary market prices—to countries where the need was urgent. It would be an important link in a group of international organizations concerned with credit, agricultural and industrial development, and trade and commodity policy.

"This is neither a revolutionary nor a new idea," Sir John said. "The proposal merely synthesizes many national and international measures and brings them together in one organization. . . . It may seem premature to put forth such an ambitious proposal, but we are living in a world which is being driven so fast by the advance of science that bold measures are required if we are to resolve the tremendous social and economic problems that face all countries. . . . There are only two alternatives for the nations today: either co-operation for mutual benefit in a world policy, or a drift back to nationalistic policies leading to economic conflict which may well be the prelude to a third world war that will end our civilization."

Sir John was a passionate and tireless advocate of this approach to the world's food and economic problems—and the problem of peace. "If the nations cannot agree on a food program affecting the welfare of the people everywhere," he had said many times, "there is little hope of their reaching an agreement on anything else." If on the other hand they agree to co-operate in bold measures, "the people will have hope that the resources of the earth will be developed to provide adequate food, clothing, and shelter. . . . Hope for tomorrow will make them better able to bear the hardships of today."

As a student of biology, a farmer, a doctor of medicine, Sir John had become convinced that food must be considered as something much more than a trade commodity alone. Its trade aspects he, being a farmer, appreciated shrewdly enough, as his attention to prices showed. But over and above this, being a medical man, he saw food as the primary necessity of life itself; and he felt that if we bring people into the world, we must find ways to feed them, even if it cannot always be at a profit. In his thinking, civilization has a profound moral obligation to provide food for those who are hungry and in need, just as it has a duty to provide medical care for those who are sick and in need. He believed that the World Food Board, or something like it, was necessary not only to galvanize expanded production and industrial development and start what he liked to refer to as "the upward spiral of prosperity," but also to solve the problem of surpluses, nightmare of agriculture during the depression.

By some miracle the small overworked FAO staff was able to have the proposals ready for discussion at the second FAO conference, held in the quiet, lovely city of Copenhagen in September 1946. The Danes had turned over a large part of the Rigsdagen, that portion of Christiansborg Castle where the Parliament meets, for the conference. In fact so hospitable were they that they urged FAO to make its permanent headquarters forthwith in Copenhagen, where it would be in a setting of some of the world's best-managed farmland (and best fisheries).

At the start the feeling seemed rather on the side of Sir John's proposals. New York's ex-mayor, the late Fiorello H. LaGuardia, then head of UNRRA, made a rousing speech before a plenary session. Statements that were generally favorable came from a number of delegates, including Norris E. Dodd, then US Under Secretary of Agriculture and head of his country's delegation, who served as the chairman of the conference commission that dealt with the broad subject of world food policy. "I believe . . . farmers generally can have fair prices and the world can have better nutrition," he said, "but we will have to devise better methods . . . to make it possible. . . . The solution to this problem will be essential to securing lasting peace and greater well-being. We in the United States therefore strongly favor the general objectives laid down by Sir John Boyd Orr." John Strachey, then British Minister of Food, quoted the epitaph, "Here lies the body of Farmer Pete, who starved from growing too much wheat," and said no one wanted to see that situation occur again. But Herbert Broadley (then a member of the UK delegation), chairman of the committee that actually considered the proposals, summed up the prevailing opinion when he said: "This Conference . . . accepts the general objectives of the proposals. . . . It does not say . . . that a World Food Board shall be set up forthwith. What it does say is that there is a necessity for international machinery for achieving those objectives."

So the World Food Board was turned down when the votes were counted.

There had always been a great deal of opposition to any centralized world food setup. As I noted earlier, the idea of "buffer stocks," designed essentially as a commodity-holding operation to stabilize prices, had come up at the Hot Springs Conference, where it was politely shelved. Though some producer groups strongly favored and still favor this approach, others were fearful of it, and trade interests were in general strongly opposed.

Bruce's World Food Council

The defeat did not mean the death of the basic idea. In fact, it is an idea with remarkable vitality which was to reappear internationally and to be repeatedly incorporated, in one aspect or another, in national programs. In order that the search for an acceptable approach to the problem might continue, the Conference established a Preparatory Commission on World Food Proposals, instructed to examine not only the Director-General's ideas but any others that seemed pertinent. Sixteen governments were to be members and Sir John appointed Stanley Bruce as chairman.

Late in October the representatives of these governments convened in Washington, where the Preparatory Commission continued working until the end of the following January. The group undertook an exhaustive examination of basic questions, economic and technical, connected with the production and distribution of agricultural products. In the end, what it proposed instead of a World Food Board was that FAO establish a World Food Council, or Council of FAO, with a membership of 18 nations, which would replace the original FAO Executive Committee; but its members, unlike those of the Executive Committee, would be official representatives of governments rather than persons chosen solely for their individual competence (the drawback of the latter method being that since the members could not speak officially for their governments, the committee could not provide authoritative direction for FAO). Meeting between sessions of the Conference, this Council would not only be concerned with the work of FAO in general but would especially keep the world food situation under continuous review and promptly call emergency needs to the attention of governments—a matter of considerable importance at that time since the postwar food emergency still continued.

Concerning the threat of possible surpluses of major agricultural products in some of the high-producing countries, the Preparatory Commission had a good deal to say. "Productive capacity has been expanded in many countries outside the combat areas," it noted. "The war-devastated areas are being repaired. The world is being restocked and re-equipped. What are we going to do when these tasks are accomplished? If nothing is done to absorb the much greater production which our efforts in World War II have stimulated, we may find ourselves heading for a greater disaster than in 1929." The preventives proposed were on the one hand to speed up development and modernization of agriculture and industry in the countries where this was needed, which would increase purchasing power and stimulate international trade; and on the other, to work out intergovernmental commodity arrangements designed to keep the prices of agricultural products sufficiently stable to assure continued production. These arrangements, the commission thought, should include limited reserves (buffer stocks) of certain commodities that are especially subject to extreme price fluctuations.

But whereas Sir John thought production and trade logically belonged together in the same organization since they interact (successful efforts to stimulate production can in fact result in embarrassing market surpluses), the Preparatory Commission separated them. FAO was to be the production stimulator; trade arrangements were to be in the hands of separate commodity organizations (like the International Wheat Council), with which FAO might be rather loosely related, at least pending the establishment of the proposed International Trade Organization. Like Sir John, the commission emphasized, however, that "the basis of all intergovernmental arrangements should be an expansion of consumption and not restriction of production"; and it vigorously endorsed the idea of making surpluses available to needy countries "at special prices for approved nutritional programs."

The commission proposed that the FAO Conference undertake a more elaborate annual review of the world food and agriculture situation than had hitherto been envisaged. The Conference should become, in fact, a sort of world food parliament through which governments would co-operate in shaping policies, plans, and programs. The Bruce report also advocated larger investments, national and international, in agricultural development and urged much more active work by other United Nations agencies, particularly the Economic and Social Council, in stimulating the development of industries.

Finally, the commission undertook a number of studies of commodity situations—wheat, sugar, rice, livestock products, oils and fats, fish, fruits and vegetables, tea, cocoa, cotton, wool, timber—and made some recommendations. In the case of wheat in particular it outlined guiding principles for an international agreement which were useful later when the first postwar international wheat agreement was being negotiated. In the case of rice the commission recommended an international conference in Southeast Asia in the near future—the first move toward setting up the International Rice Commission, to be discussed later in this book.

Just before the work of the Preparatory Commission ended, Bruce had word from London that the King had elevated him to the peerage as Viscount Bruce of Melbourne.

Sir John made the best of the commission's recommendations, and he certainly hoped that the proposed World Food Council would become a dynamic and influential body. Inwardly, however, he was bitterly disappointed over the failure of his original proposals to win endorsement. By the time the Preparatory Commission had its report ready he had made up his mind that he would not be a candidate for re-election as Director-General of FAO. He believed strongly in the technical assistance work of the organization; he had said many times that even if a moratorium were declared on agricultural research for several years, it would be possible for the world to increase production enormously if farmers could only apply on a wide enough scale what is already known. But he was impatient when "people ask for bread and we give them pamphlets." Crusader, slayer of dragons, seeker after the Holy Grail—driven by an intense desire to right wrongs and help make this world a better place to live in—he thought in terms of a big plan to solve the food problem. When it did not work out that way, his interests and energies turned more and more to the cause of world government.

In recognition of his contributions to world peace through FAO and in other ways, Sir John was awarded the Nobel Peace Prize in 1949. In the same year he too was elevated to the British peerage as Lord Boyd-Orr.

The third session of the FAO Conference, held in Geneva in September 1947, accepted the report of the Preparatory Commission and established the Council of FAO. Ordinarily such a body would elect its own chairman from among its members, but many people were in favor of having Lord Bruce appointed to head the Council. That could be done only if the chairman did not represent a government, as did each of the council members, but was instead considered to be independent. This proposal was accepted and the Conference appointed Lord Bruce the first Council chairman.

In 1951 Dr. Josué de Castro (Brazil) was elected to succeed Bruce, and in 1953 the number of Council members was increased from 18 to 24 in view of the enlarged membership of FAO by that time.

Dodd's International Commodity Clearing House

While I am on the subject, it might be well to deal here with subsequent efforts to develop positive FAO functions in the commodity field, although it means jumping a year ahead in the story of FAO. In 1949, after Norris E. Dodd had become Director-General, the World Food Board idea was again revived in the considerably modified form of an International Commodity Clearing House.

The Clearing House proposals, presented at the 1949 conference held in Washington in November, stemmed from a meeting of the FAO Council in Paris in June. The Council expressed a good deal of apprehension about the current drop in agricultural prices, which seemed to portend a renewal of serious surpluses in some areas. Accordingly, it asked the Director-General to have a group of experts study the commodity question once again. He therefore organized a small committee, with John B. Condliffe of the University of California as chairman. This group met for five weeks at FAO headquarters, obtaining evidence from many organizations and individuals.

Lack of hard currency (chiefly dollars) was the greatest obstacle to purchases of food from high-producing countries by countries in need. One of the principal objectives of the Condliffe committee was to meet this problem. It proposed that an operating organization, the International Commodity Clearing House, be set up as an action arm of FAO. It would start with a revolving fund equivalent to a billion dollars, contributed by member countries in proportion to national income, each country contributing in its own currency. Additional sums could be called up for specific transactions, these sums being earmarked for use in the contributing countries to buy commodities declared surplus.

The Clearing House could use either of two methods to dispose of surpluses. Suppose S is a selling (exporting) hard-currency country with, say, surplus wheat, and P a purchasing (importing) soft-currency country. Under one method, P would buy wheat from S, through the Clearing House, with the soft currency, paying the full market price. S would use this currency to buy products in country P; or, alternatively, the money would be held to the credit of country S until world economic conditions improved enough to convert it into hard currency. Under the other method, P would pay for the wheat in hard currency but would buy it for less than the market value. These cut-price sales could be made only under special circumstances—to countries in need and for strictly defined uses such as relief, nutrition programs, or the feeding of workers employed on development projects.

Such arrangements were considered by the Condliffe committee to be of a temporary nature, to help countries during the period of economic distress pending wider economic expansion and improvement in world trade. There were also to be longer-term functions of the Clearing House. To prevent extreme price declines, the organization could buy and store certain commodities when the price on the world market fell below an agreed level and, in turn, sell these buffer stocks in periods of rising prices to protect consumers against extreme increases. Pending the setting up of an International Trade Organization, the Clearing House might even negotiate and administer international commodity agreements.

The Dodd proposals were turned down by the 1949 FAO Conference as decisively as had been the Orr proposals three years earlier. Four main objections were raised: The accumulated debts in soft currency, which would eventually have to be paid by the food deficit countries in the form of exports, would be a burden that would tend to delay rather than hasten recovery. The payments for foods bought at reduced prices would further reduce the small hard-currency reserves of the deficit countries. The transactions as a whole would tend to interfere with normal trade. The proposed buffer-stock operations were open to the same objections as the similar functions proposed for the World Food Board. A fifth point not raised specifically was that few countries are ready to entrust to an international agency such potent functions as the management of a world food reserve.

Cardon's Consultative Committee on Surplus Disposal

Even after this second rejection of a broad-scale international commodity proposal the member governments were reluctant to close the door entirely. They established a Committee on Commodity Problems which has met periodically since 1949, kept the commodity situation under review, and at one stage directed studies for a different kind of proposal, an Emergency Food Reserve to prevent famine, made in 1951 (Appendix). This was turned down by the 1953 Conference.

Meanwhile in the case of a few products the problem of surpluses was becoming increasingly acute in a number of high-producing countries. Early in 1954, at the time when P. V. Cardon became Director-General, an eight-nation FAO Working Party on Disposal of Agricultural Surpluses met in Washington for several weeks, under the chairmanship of Francis Linville (USA). This group made a systematic classification and analysis of the character of surpluses, the circumstances that produce them, and the known ways of dealing with them. It was particularly concerned with possibilities for surplus disposal, with emphasis on sales on special terms (or outright grants) to countries carrying out development programs in which supplies of food or other consumer goods might help to pay costs, or similar sales or grants for special welfare programs or for emergency relief. The group also worked out a set of principles to insure that such special sales would not damage normal trade interests. Finally, it recommended that FAO establish a permanent Subcommittee on Surplus Disposal in Washington which would help interested governments to keep the situation under constant review and work together rather than at cross purposes. Later, in June 1954, the 20-nation FAO Committee on Commodity Problems accepted this suggestion and the Subcommittee was established in Washington.

Early Technical Assistance Work

Now to return to events at about the time of the Geneva conference, in 1947.

Even before Geneva, FAO had embarked on a program which was to provide valuable experience for later expansion of technical assistance.

The United Nations Relief and Rehabilitation Administration, which was then about to go out of existence, worked out an agreement with FAO whereby the latter assumed responsibility for the agricultural advisory projects of UNRRA in nine countries—Austria, China, Czechoslovakia, Ethiopia, Greece, Hungary, Italy, Poland, Yugoslavia. FAO took over from UNRRA $1,135,000 in residual funds to do this work.

The most extensive and varied operations under these UNRRA-transfer funds were in China, and there rinderpest control was the most important part of the program.

There is no rinderpest on the North American or South American continents, in Europe, or in Oceania, but in the Far East and parts of the Near East and Africa it is the most widespread of all serious animal diseases. When an epidemic—or, more correctly, epizootic—flares up it may kill as much as 90 per cent of the cattle in the affected area.

This is especially serious because cows and water buffaloes not only provide food but furnish the power for farm work throughout this region. When a man loses his buffalo it is almost as bad as losing his right arm, and it may be a long time before he can afford to get another buffalo, if ever.

During the war the United States and Canada had been secretly working on a new anti-rinderpest vaccine—on Grosse Isle in the St. Lawrence—which was to be used in case the Germans or Japanese tried to spread the virus in North America. It was expensive to produce, but after the war FAO helped in developing improved vaccines sufficiently low in cost for extensive rinderpest control operations. For the first time there was hope of eradicating the disease.

I shall have more to say about this in later chapters. It is enough to point out here that the first large-scale testing ground was China, where FAO continued work begun by UNRRA. Chinese technicians were trained in the use of modern equipment for vaccine production, and a large-scale control program got under way. At that time it was reported that rinderpest was killing a million animals a year in China. The program envisaged complete eradication of the disease in the area south of the Yangtze River, which would have involved the vaccination of some 15 million head of cattle.

Many other programs were undertaken by the Chinese Government with UNRRA and FAO help—projects for the control of animal diseases other than rinderpest, big land reclamation and flood prevention projects on the Pearl River, model irrigation projects near Canton and elsewhere, surveys and recommendations for drainage in North China, the introduction and breeding of better crop plants, the manufacture of fertilizers and insecticides and small-scale spraying and dusting equipment, demonstrations of agricultural machinery and the organization of farmer co-operatives to own and operate it, training courses and bulletins on food processing, distribution of processing units to co-operatives and other agencies, help in agricultural extension, rehabilitation of fisheries, the planting of millions of tree seedlings and cuttings, and so on. Most of this work was well under way when the FAO teams had to withdraw from the mainland late in 1948. Subsequently the USA provided technical assistance in agriculture to the Nationalist Government on Taiwan (Formosa). In July 1951 the latter notified FAO of its withdrawal from membership.

In Ethiopia FAO fell heir to an UNRRA program that had exceptional possibilities and that has subsequently broadened and developed, as we shall see in a later chapter. When the Emperor Haile Selassie returned to his country after the Italian occupation, he undertook political unification and economic development. On taking over the UNRRA work there, FAO first sent in a general agricultural adviser to review the whole situation from the standpoint of agricultural improvement and the building up of government services. Particular attention was given to rinderpest control because of the large number of cattle in the country. It was necessary to start practically from scratch, establish a laboratory, train people in laboratory work and field vaccination, and help the government to organize a systematic control program which has greatly expanded since its modest beginnings in February 1948.

Though China and Ethiopia accounted for almost half of the UNRRA-financed programs, a fair amount of work was done in five other countries.
• In Italy a soil conservation expert helped the government to develop its conservation program; a range management specialist worked on the improvement of mountain pastures; two Italian experts visited Spain to select seed of blight-resistant chestnuts for test plantings in Italy; work was done in agricultural extension, forestry, home food preservation. • In Greece, preceding Tsongas, there was work on community canning centers and other aspects of food preservation; land reclamation and drainage; the development of fisheries. • Austria used the services of a livestock specialist and a farm machinery expert. • Czechoslovakia, which later withdrew from membership in FAO, got a good deal of help in the early days in

animal disease control and other livestock operations, control of San José scale, development of plans for refrigerated food storage. • In Poland, which also later withdrew from membership, a good deal of work was done on farm machinery, control of the Colorado potato beetle, animal diseases, forestry.

A different type of operation with UNRRA funds involved organizing and conducting regional training centers and professional meetings, a technique that has since proved to be extremely fruitful. In war-torn countries government services had been disrupted, professional staffs depleted, universities and colleges and libraries badly damaged. The result was a great need not only for scientific literature and for laboratory and other equipment but for some means, such as meetings and refresher courses, by which scientific workers could catch up with recent developments. The most important FAO work of this kind was the hybrid corn program in Europe, which brought plant breeders from various countries together in an organization that developed a carefully prepared co-operative corn-breeding and -testing program about which I shall have more to say in a later chapter. FAO also sponsored demonstration courses or seminars in Milan on artificial insemination of livestock, in Weybridge on new developments in veterinary laboratory techniques, in Florence on control of infestation in stored grains and on soil conservation, in Copenhagen on food freezing and refrigeration, in Warsaw on new developments in the control of animal diseases, in Brussels and The Hague on agricultural extension services, in Zurich on livestock feeding, in Reading on dairy technology.

The hybrid corn work soon led to a broader program for distributing many different kinds of seed—grains, forage crops, oil-bearing and fiber plants, vegetables, tea, tree seeds—for experimental purposes. FAO supplies this seed only when the requesting country has difficulty in obtaining material direct from some other country, and the organization tries to insure receiving full data about the results of the tests, which are often of great interest to other countries. About 50 countries so far have received some 3000 lots of experimental seed. The work costs little except postage since the samples are for the most part contributed free by the seed trade. By providing material so generously, US seed producers have in a sense been repaying some of their debt to parts of the world from which plant explorers gathered the breeding stocks that helped make possible the tremendous production in that country.

Besides the seed distribution, FAO also developed and continues to maintain catalogues of strains and varieties of wheat and rice available for breeding purposes in public institutions throughout the world, with descriptive notes, and also publishes a list of plant breeders.

The meeting in Florence on control of infestation in stored grains was part of a program originated by McDougall, who thought something worth while might be done through international action to lessen the enormous waste of food that has been going on since the days of the Pharaohs. Early in 1946 Sir John gathered a committee of experts to consider the problem. Annual losses due to inadequate storage were then estimated to be possibly as high as 10 per cent of all stored grain—enough to feed millions of human beings. About half the loss is caused by insects, 40 per cent by rats and other rodents, 10 per cent by mold.

Since that time FAO has hammered away persistently at the improvement of grain storage, partly through publicizing losses and sound methods of preventing them, partly by regional and country projects of technical cooperation which involved sending experts to countries in the Far East, the Near East, and Latin America. Frequently the problem is mainly one of holding down moisture content. In the case of corn in Central America, for instance, the rice weevil is the chief enemy. It can penetrate damp corn but cannot break through the hard surface of dry grain. In a bad season practically the whole late crop may go into weevil stomachs instead of human ones. These appalling losses can be prevented by drying the grain with artificial heat to a moisture content at least as low as 12 per cent and providing storage facilities that will keep it dry.

The work on grain storage is rather slow, but results are encouraging. Costa Rica, Venezuela, Guatemala, El Salvador, Nicaragua, Panama, Ecuador, Honduras, Mexico, and Haiti have all undertaken improvement programs or expanded work they had previously started. In other parts of the world, too, the traveler will suddenly come upon a sturdy modern storage building rising beside the railroad track in a place where perhaps grain was formerly kept in ragged burlap sacks open to the depredations of insects, rodents, birds, and weather. That lone structure sharp against the skyline is a monument to the patient, persistent efforts of those who are trying to save food for mankind.

Three Missions

In addition to the work financed by UNRRA funds, FAO undertook three other technical assistance operations in 1947 and 1948.

The Government of Thailand asked Sir John to send a mission to that country to study six problems: technical aspects of crop husbandry, especially rice production; development and control of water supplies; control of rinderpest; forest conservation and management, especially teak and other tropical woods; improvement in the economic status of the farmer, with emphasis on credit facilities, co-operative organization, and marketing; and improvement in statistical services, especially crop reporting.

The Thailand mission was headed by R. H. Walker, then Dean of the School of Agriculture and Director of the Experiment Station at Utah State Agricultural College. Between January and April 1948 Dean Walker's group made a thorough survey of agriculture and forestry in Thailand.

The Thai Government has used the detailed observations and recommendations of the group as the basis for much of its development program and has reported to FAO at intervals on what was being done to carry out the recommendations. The US Government has also made use of the Walker mission findings in its technical assistance work in Thailand.

Thailand now produces a good deal of the export rice of Southeast Asia. Rice covers nine-tenths of the arable land and accounts for more than two-thirds of all exports. Baskets of rice, bags of rice, long slender boats loaded with rice are characteristic features of the country. The acreage has steadily increased, but since total production is about the same as it was 20 years ago, yields per acre must have fallen. The mission made many recommendations regarding rice culture—for improved water control, the use of manures and fertilizers, better cultivation, experiments with machinery, control of pests and diseases. Special emphasis was given to the development of varieties that will produce higher yields.

Since rice and water are inseparable, the mission also made a close study of irrigation. At least 15 irrigation projects covering well over 4 million acres were under construction at that time, though the work had been greatly delayed by the war. A fundamental examination of the whole basis of irrigated agriculture brought many recommendations on the ownership and management of water resources, design and construction, pump irrigation, the training of engineers, and so on.

Similarly, because the plodding wide-horned buffalo is the main source of power for rice cultivation—just as the elephant is the living tractor of the forests—the mission emphasized rinderpest control, which I shall have occasion to discuss later.

Other recommendations concerned the common practice of "shifting cultivation," also discussed in a later chapter, and the production of crops other than rice. In the case of forests, the mission felt that there had been a long period of rather indiscriminate destruction which now requires a compensating program of reforestation and use on a sustained-yield basis. Subsequently, Thailand undertook a program with technical co-operation from FAO.

In the economics of agriculture, special attention was given to policies for the procurement of rice from farmers for sale and export. This is a government monopoly. The mission felt that not enough attention was being given, especially in this time of rising prices, to sharing the profits with producers as a stimulus to greater output. As we shall see later, recent FAO technical projects in Thailand have been concerned with rice marketing.

Some months before this, an FAO mission, headed by Noble Clark, then Associate Director of the Wisconsin Agricultural Experiment Station, went to Poland, in July and August 1947. Its report is now of somewhat academic interest since Poland later withdrew from membership in FAO and little is known officially about agricultural developments there. The mission made a careful comprehensive survey, and its recommendations ranged from emergency measures for meeting the postwar food needs of children to broad-scale changes and innovations in many technical agricultural fields.

A mission to Venezuela early in 1947 had a single objective. In that country, where the chief source of the national income is petroleum, the supply of edible fats and oils was exceptionally low. The FAO group, headed by K. S. Markley (USA), helped the government to formulate a many-sided program for increased production from oil palms and from sesame and other oil-bearing seeds, mechanization of certain farming operations, improvement of oil processing, study of a possible fish oil industry, and the development of farm loans designed to encourage expansion of oilseed crops.

More Foundation Stones

During these early days FAO was strengthening other foundations for its future work. For example, at Sir John's instigation most of the member countries established national FAO committees, made up of representatives of all the government agencies with which the Food and Agriculture Organization deals and in some cases including, as advisers, representatives of nongovernmental agencies interested in FAO—farm organizations, women's organizations, labor unions, religious groups, and so on. • The functions and some of the staff of the old International Institute of Agriculture were absorbed in the far broader operations of FAO. Some years later, after FAO moved its headquarters to Rome, the library of the IIA was merged with that of FAO and dedicated as the David Lubin Memorial Library. • Sir John established a European regional office in Rome, with the late S. L. Louwes as Regional Representative, and appointed three temporary special advisers: M. T. Hefnawy (Egypt) for the Near East, Chien Tien-Ho for China, Sir Pheroz Kharegat for India. (Subsequently, in 1948, the Near East Regional Office was established in Cairo, with Hefnawy as Regional Representative, and the Far East Office in Bangkok, headed by W. H. Cummings [USA]. In Latin America there are at present [1954] three offices— in Rio de Janeiro, in Santiago, Chile, and in Mexico City. There is a North American Regional Office, in Washington.) • In Europe important work was begun in forestry, to be discussed later, and foundations were started for regional forestry operations in Latin America. • A rice study group met in Travancore, India (following the Preparatory Commission's recommendations), and began exploring the possibilities of a co-operative regional approach to the rice problems of the whole of South and East Asia. • Countries in Southeast Asia agreed to organize an Indo-Pacific Fisheries Council. • Plans got under way for a 1950 world census of agriculture, the first in 20 years. • FAO developed a comprehensive series of international publications —statistical yearbooks of agricultural production, agricultural trade, forestry and forest products, fisheries; periodicals in these same fields; and

Growth 79

monographs and studies concerned with practical aspects of agricultural science and of nutrition. • Meanwhile the staff was gradually built up and strengthened and the work was becoming more clearly defined.

From Washington to Rome

In his second annual report, at the Geneva Conference, Sir John announced that he would not be a candidate for re-election. The atmosphere of the conference was therefore rather heavily weighted with politics because of the preoccupation with the business of choosing a successor. Since it would have been difficult to make a wise choice under these circumstances, Sir John was persuaded to remain as Director-General long enough for a committee to seek other possible candidates. The conference agreed that the election should take place at a special session to be called the following spring. In April 1948 this session met in Washington, and Norris E. Dodd, then US Under Secretary of Agriculture, was unanimously elected Director-General.

The next year, 1949, saw the Clearing House proposals, which I have already discussed, and the beginning of a new vigorous expansion of technical co-operation which not only enlarged the work of FAO but brought a number of new agencies into existence. The chapters that follow will be devoted to this work. To avoid interrupting the account later, I shall take up at this point, out of their chronological order, two other major developments.

One was the transfer of FAO headquarters to Rome. At Quebec the question of a permanent site was left open on the assumption that FAO might have its headquarters at the same place as the United Nations. When New York was selected for the United Nations, however, there was a widespread feeling that this was not a very suitable location for a world agricultural agency. The decision was postponed from year to year until the 1949 conference. Then there was a sharp debate, mainly between the proponents of a European site (Italy, Denmark, Switzerland) and those who argued for the location of headquarters in the USA. Five ballots were required for the final decision, and then the vote was close—30 for Italy, 28 for the USA (in or near Washington), with three delegates abstaining.

Moving headquarters to Rome was not easy after the organization had reached the stage of development of FAO in 1950. It meant severing close associations with technical agencies which from the beginning had given an immense amount of help. It also meant losing a considerable part of the professional staff—mainly Americans who for one reason or another could not take their families permanently to Rome—and practically all of the clerical and secretarial employees, who had to be hired in Europe to reduce operating expenses and because knowledge of Italian and other European languages was essential. Secretaries and clerks are always the main storehouse of knowledge of detailed day-to-day operations, and the loss of so large a proportion of this group was a cause of much confusion for a considerable time. The members of the staff who did move had to transfer their families—altogether some 600 men, women, and children (a very sizable overseas migration)—and household goods and settle down in a country where the language, customs, schools, shops, and living conditions were strange. In a little over a year, however, the staff was up to nearly full strength and operations were normal again. The buildings generously provided for FAO by the Italian Government in the Viale delle Terme di Caracalla, in the old part of the city near the Colosseum, are in some ways the best headquarters occupied by any international agency.

Dodd was to head FAO for nearly six years, from the spring of 1948 to March 1954. A native of Iowa, he had gone to Oregon as a young man. Trained as a pharmacist, he became a successful operator of drugstores in a number of towns. Soon he was buying land and livestock and in the course of years built up a large ranch, producing wheat and cattle. He learned farming the hard way, from his mistakes; for he started from scratch. In the early days he and his wife—the Boss, he called her—did all the work themselves, and it was pioneering work at that time in Oregon. Thus his knowledge of the practical side of farming became intimate and detailed.

Dodd's knowledge of the economic and political aspects of agriculture was to become equally detailed. From the beginning of the movement to strengthen the agricultural economy of the US against the inroads of the great depression he played an active part. This movement began in the mid 'twenties and culminated in the establishment of the Agricultural Adjustment Administration in 1933 after President Roosevelt was elected. Dodd worked first at the local and county levels, then at the state level, then at the regional level; and ultimately he wound up in Washington, where he was to become head of the AAA and later Under Secretary of Agriculture. All this gave him a unique experience in dealing with a great range of farm problems and the people concerned with them, from the man on the land up to congressmen, Senators, and the top executives in the world's most complex agricultural agency.

When he became Director-General of FAO, Dodd brought a wealth of experience that would be hard to equal, combined with a homely and earthy quality and a fighting idealism in the cause of farmers. Taking up where the crusader John Orr left off, he carried out the difficult move to Rome, built up a solid organization, and got the technical co-operation program of FAO off to a good start, as we shall see later.

In the USA, Dodd had traveled the entire country many times. He insisted on direct knowledge. In FAO he followed the same course, but with the world as his orbit. Perhaps no other high-level international official has covered so much ground, or covered it under such arduous circumstances, or talked face to face with as many individuals about their problems. With the move to Rome accomplished, the staff at full strength, and the new technical assistance program well under way, he decided at the conference held at headquarters in November–December 1953 to withdraw as a candidate for re-election in favor of P. V. Cardon, scientist, administrator, and former head of the extensive scientific and economic research of the US Department of Agriculture.

Philip Vincent Cardon, who had been intimately associated with FAO's work since the days when he was a member of the US delegation at the Hot Springs Conference, was unanimously elected the third Director-General.

CHAPTER
SEVEN

New Directions

THE IDEA of technical co-operation or technical assistance was in the forefront of the early conceptions of FAO. The article written in 1942 by McDougall, which I have previously quoted, said:

The Food and Agriculture Organization will have special responsibilities towards the less advanced countries. To discharge these duties it will not be enough for arrangements to be made for the provision of agricultural credits. It will be equally necessary to afford technical guidance and help. For this purpose a corps of agricultural technologists may be recruited, drawn from those countries with advanced methods of agriculture and available to be sent to any part of the world to assist in improving agricultural methods. . . . This might well become one of the major purposes of the international organization.

This was a new conception for an international agricultural agency; the International Institute of Agriculture had made many studies and reports but did not provide on-the-spot technical aid. The technical co-operation idea was prominent in the discussions at Hot Springs and in the work of the Interim Commission. In its early years, as we have seen, FAO had a number of technical missions, but up to 1949 it was unable to carry out any extensive field work except that financed by UNRRA, because its funds were too limited.

An address by President Truman at the fourth FAO conference, held in Washington in November 1948, in effect marked the beginning of a sudden new impetus in this kind of work. For the President gave a foreglimpse of what he was to say two months later, on January 20, 1949, when in his inaugural address he launched the proposal for an expanded program of technical co-operation for economic development. In November 1948 he said at the FAO conference:

The world has many food problems ahead of it, and the peoples of the world are counting on FAO for a major part of the work in solving those problems. . . .

Rebuilding countries that were once self-supporting and prosperous is not nearly so difficult as building up the economies of countries where there is comparatively little to build on. Underdeveloped countries offer a challenge to the ingenuity of those nations which have greater resources.

FAO has clearly recognized the importance of this problem and the responsibility of all countries in helping to solve it.

- The United States is happy to join with other countries in FAO in giving freely of our technical experience and knowledge in the job of agricultural improvement. . . . I can promise you that this country will continue to send its experts wherever FAO believes they are needed. . . .

One of the ways to restore stability to the world is to produce plenty of food and see that it is distributed fairly.

Hunger has no nationality.

Abundance should have none, either.

In Point IV of his inaugural address in January Mr. Truman enlarged on this idea and made it more specific:

We must embark on a bold new program for making the benefits of our scientific advances and industrial progress available for the improvement and growth of underdeveloped areas. . . .

I believe that we should make available to peace-loving peoples the benefits of our store of technical knowledge in order to help them realize their aspirations for a better life. And, in co-operation with other nations, we should foster capital investment in areas needing development.

Our aim should be to help the free peoples of the world, through their own efforts, to produce more food, more clothing, more materials for housing, and more mechanical power to lighten their burdens.

We invite other countries to pool their technological resources. . . . This should be a co-operative enterprise in which all nations work together through the United Nations and its specialized agencies wherever practicable. It must be a worldwide effort for the achievement of peace, plenty, and freedom.

Ambassador Austin, then United States delegate to the United Nations, promptly proposed a resolution, which was adopted by the Economic and Social Council at its eighth session, calling for the preparation of a comprehensive plan of expanded technical co-operation to be carried out by the United Nations and the specialized agencies.

Head Start

FAO was in a position to move quickly, since these proposals were an extension of work it was already doing. The staff drafted the outlines of programs in agriculture, forestry, fisheries, nutrition, economics, and statistics which could be quickly begun when funds became available. Subsequently these proposals and those of the other agencies were published by the United Nations in a volume called *Technical Assistance for Economic Development*.

In June 1950 the United Nations held a Technical Assistance Conference at which 50 governments pledged approximately 20 million dollars for the work, the USA agreeing to contribute 60 per cent, or about 12 million dollars. (Appendix.) The first 10 million dollars received was to be allocated to the participating organizations in accordance with a scale worked out by the Economic and Social Council. FAO was to receive the largest single share, 29 per cent, because of the prime importance of food, agriculture, forestry, and fisheries in the countries which the expanded technical assistance program was designed to aid. The United Nations was to get the second largest share, 23 per cent, and the World Health Organization the third largest, 22 per cent. Following these came the United Nations Educational, Scientific, and Cultural Organization with 14 per cent; the International Labour Organisation, 11 per cent; and the International Civil Aviation Organization, 1 per cent. Of the second 10 million dollars, 70 per cent was to be made automatically available in the same way. The remainder was to be set aside for subsequent allocation in accordance with circumstances. All contributions above 20 million dollars were to be similarly set aside.

Actually, no contributions were made until the autumn of 1950, but some United Nations funds were available with which to begin, and FAO drew on these to get a few urgent projects under way.

In the first half of 1949 the Director-General of FAO made an extensive survey throughout much of the Far East, the Near East, and Southern and Eastern Europe to study local conditions and needs and discuss technical assistance possibilities with top officials. To quote (with some minor changes) from his 1949 annual report, the observations on that journey "made me confident that the desperate conditions of hunger and poverty in these countries can be changed. I saw examples of the best modern production practices and the most modern approach to problems of human welfare. These were tokens of what can be done on a far wider scale. Even more important was the spirit so widely evident—an awareness of the nature of the problems and the kinds of solutions needed, a keen interest in science and technology, and a faith in the possibilities of improvement which was the opposite of negation and despair. This spirit was the yeast fermenting throughout the regions I visited. At the same time I was doubly impressed on this journey with the fact that all the efforts of FAO would amount to nothing unless governments themselves took action and unless they would work together for common ends. If the recommendations of FAO were made by the wisest and ablest experts to be found anywhere in the world they would be a waste of breath unless governments carried them out within their own countries."

The food situation in much of these regions was a gloomy one; world production of rice, for example, was 3 million tons below prewar production, and meanwhile the population in Southeast Asia had increased by perhaps

The amount of labor that goes into the production of meager quantities of food is incalculable and unbelievable. These young men in Pakistan are breaking up the soil around corn plants with the most primitive of hoes, a metal blade fastened to a short piece of wood. This implement may well go back to the earliest days of cultivation. No matter how hard a man works, he cannot accomplish much in a day's labor with such tools as these.

A common form of hoe or broad-bladed mattock is the one carried by this Afghan farmer, who is using it to cultivate sugar beets. It takes hard work too, especially when the handle is about half the length of the one shown here, so that a man bends over double all day hoeing or cleaning out ditches.

The Javanese women are harvesting rice, carefully cutting off one head at a time with a small implement about the size of a safety-razor blade. The use of larger, better tools would create problems of unemployment. In other words, as agriculture improves in efficiency, opportunities must be created for people to work in industry and elsewhere.

After harvest the grain is usually threshed by equally primitive methods. This farmer in Ceylon is using a straight stick to whack out the rice—an even simpler implement than the hinged flails once common in Europe and America. Frequently animals are used to thresh the grain, trampling it out with their hoofs as they are driven round and round over the piles of straw.

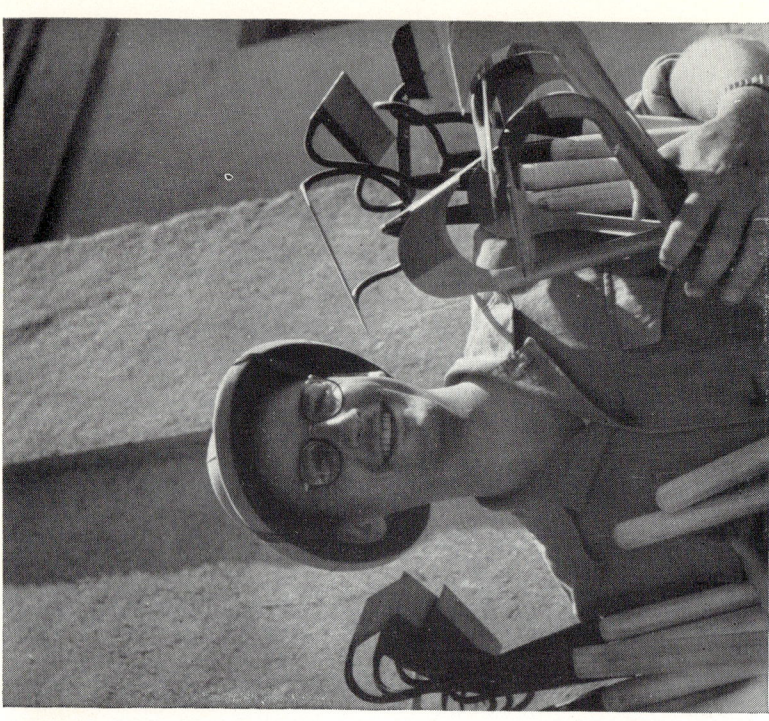

On most of the world's farms grain is harvested not with combines or mowing machines or even scythes but with hand sickles such as the ones displayed by this Afghan farmer. Crowds of men and women go to the fields and toil all day to do less work than one good machine.

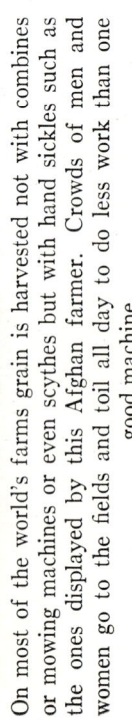

The jump, however, should seldom be from primitive implements to power equipment. Usually the first step is to use better hand tools. This Austrian small-tools expert on an FAO mission in Afghanistan carries two armloads of hoes and hand cultivators that will be eagerly snatched up by local farmers once they have seen with their own eyes and felt with their own hands how efficient these implements are.

As in the case of this farmer in Afghanistan, whose splendid dignity well befits the shiny new scythe, equipped with a grain layer or cradle, which he learned to use from the FAO demonstration team and promptly bought. With the scythe he got a whetstone, an anvil, a hammer. Following the demonstrations in the fields surrounding the villages, there are never enough of these tools to meet the demand. Yet many people believe that farmers are backward.

This lady will not win a beauty contest, but she is one of the world's most useful creatures. In the Far East and Near East the water buffalo does more farm work than any other animal—and in addition, the female yields milk richer than any other in butterfat. Patient, plodding, tractable, she asks no other reward than a bit of feed and a good wallowing bath every day in any convenient stream, pond, or mud hole.

Looking scornful and blasé, and apparently always afflicted with housemaids' knee, the camel too is a hard, faithful worker under trying circumstances. If this picture had been taken in the Andes, the pack animals would have been llamas.

Most powerful of all are the pachyderms. This handsome tusker is moving logs, and big ones, in one of the rich forests of Thailand.

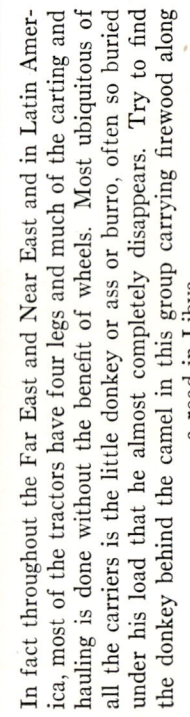

In fact throughout the Far East and Near East and in Latin America, most of the tractors have four legs and much of the carting and hauling is done without the benefit of wheels. Most ubiquitous of all the carriers is the little donkey or ass or burro, often so buried under his load that he almost completely disappears. Try to find the donkey behind the camel in this group carrying firewood along a road in Libya.

as much as 85 million. Distribution in many areas was woefully inadequate, and where guerrilla warfare was going on farmers were frequently unable or afraid to take their products even to the nearest markets. Masses of refugees, destitute of the barest necessities, multiplied the general misery. In spite of this wretched situation, the report went on to say: "I am confident that enough food can be provided for the populations of the Near East and the Far East to more than keep pace with population growth for some time to come. To do that, it will be necessary to concentrate first and immediately on changing primitive and inefficient methods of cultivation. Next, attention will have to be given to large-scale developments, which will require heavy equipment and considerable financial investment. It will also be necessary to improve trade and in particular to do everything possible to overcome currency difficulties."

There were three main ways to expand production: use better practices and better equipment to increase yields on land now cultivated; wherever possible, grow two or more crops a year on the same land; bring new land into cultivation, mainly by irrigation and reclamation. But in many cases these things could not be done unless two other steps were taken. He came back from this journey, Dodd continued, with a strong feeling that in their agricultural planning governments would have to give attention to land tenure conditions which in many parts of the Near East and Asia obviously need to be revised. The land tenure conditions he saw are among the major indirect causes of the low crop yields, bad land use, and widespread economic difficulties of the farmers. Land reform can go a long way to achieve more efficient use of the land and to provide incentives so that farmers can make a decent living by their labor. The other major requirement is to bridge the gap between modern knowledge and the actual practices of the producers. The most urgent need here is to set up agricultural extension advisory services, not to dispense theoretical advice, but to assist farmers effectively. This means expanding training facilities for extension workers and giving special attention to the training of local leaders drawn directly out of the farm communities.

Subsequently, in 1951, following an urgent plea by the Director-General, the FAO conference agreed that progress in increasing food production by 1960, on the basis of existing national programs, would fall short of desirable goals. It recorded its belief "that a well balanced increase of one to two per cent per annum in world production . . . in excess of the rate of population growth . . . is the minimum necessary to achieve some improvement in nutritional standards," and recommended that all member governments co-operate to achieve at least this much during the next five years. Much emphasis was given to the need for strengthening extension services as a basic part of this drive. By 1953, however, the conference noted that supplies in certain areas "have overtaken effective demand for some important commodities so that some surpluses have emerged." But "in spite of the marked progress in production in the last few years . . . [and] the large stocks now accumulating in some areas, a large part of the world's population, especially in the less developed regions . . . still lacks enough to eat." Indeed, "the differences in agricultural production between the more developed and less developed regions of the world have tended to increase. . . . A more selective expansion of production is now necessary . . . with maximum development in areas where additional supplies are most needed."

These comments on the changing world situation bore out not only the aims and philosophy of the expanded technical co-operation program but also the conclusions of those who from the beginning had felt that the surplus problem is intimately related to the production problem in the work of FAO. The 1954 FAO report on *The State of Food and Agriculture* shows that for the world as a whole production is now increasing somewhat faster than population growth and surpluses of some products have been developing in some places. There are large variations in the rate of increase in different regions.

But at this point, the discussion digresses from our main story, to which we now return.

The Director-General's discussions with officials during the 1949 survey were useful in getting technical co-operation projects formulated promptly. By September, only a short time after the expanded program had been officially announced, 22 member governments had submitted requests to FAO. This was long before the pledging conference in June 1950 and more than a year before funds became available, in October of that year. Such a head start was possible only because the new program fitted FAO operations as comfortably as an old shoe. By the first of September 1951 the organization had work under way on more than a hundred projects in 35 countries, involving 213 scientific and professional experts of 32 nationalities, about a third of them from the USA.

Creative War

These events were the early skirmishes in what was to develop into something resembling a world war against want. Is it possible that this is World War III—a creative war instead of the destructive one mankind dreads? In 1945, a month before the Quebec conference that established FAO, the author of this book, then Executive Secretary of the Interim Commission, had occasion to say in a speech in New York: "We have just finished a world war. In about a month from now another one will begin. It too will be waged by the United Nations, standing together. I hope it will be a total war. I hope it will last for decades. I hope all of us here will be enlisted in it, and that it will involve our children, and our children's children. This coming world war will not pit nation against nation. It will pit nations against a dictator who is the enemy of men in every country. His name is Hunger."

Five years after FAO was established, Dodd struck the same note in his 1951 annual report as Director-General: "Grim is still the word for the world food situation. In spite of the dark facts I find myself with a feeling of hope and confidence. This is because nations seem at last to be preparing for a genuinely large-scale world war against want. I am confident that such a war can be won, and that it is a necessary part of the counter-strategy to prevent another war of nations against nations, which none can really win. . . . I believe this movement which FAO helped to foster can effectively counteract the forces that work to undermine freedom and threaten world peace. Those forces operate best in an atmosphere of poverty, frustration, and injustice. They do not thrive in an atmosphere of expanding opportunity for common men. This is essentially a movement to wipe out mass hunger and lift the burden of hopeless poverty from men's shoulders by applying modern scientific knowledge to the development of the earth's resources."

General Operation of the Program

At this point it might be well to outline briefly some of the basic procedures and considerations involved in the expanded technical program.

General policy decisions are made by the Economic and Social Council and the General Assembly on the recommendations of the Technical Assistance Committee (TAC), an arm of the Council. TAC is composed of representatives of governments, who come primarily from ministries of foreign affairs, and therefore the Committee operates more or less at the diplomatic level. But technical assistance, by its name, is in the technical field, not the diplomatic or political or military fields. The organization functioning at the technical level is the Technical Assistance Board (TAB), made up of the heads of the eight participating agencies (or, in practice, their senior representatives). All of these agencies are technical and represent technical interests of their member countries. TAB has an Executive Chairman, appointed by the Secretary-General of the United Nations, and a small staff at UN headquarters. The Executive Chairman also supervises a group of technical assistants, "resident representatives," and liaison officers located in a number of countries. Since the participating agencies have complete responsibility for planning, negotiating, administering, and operating their own projects, the functions of TAB are mainly to help to co-ordinate operations, achieve uniform administrative procedures, solve problems of relationships among agencies, facilitate the programming and review of activities, and prepare periodic reports for TAC and the Economic and Social Council. Recently the responsibility of the technical agencies has been somewhat reduced and more control over programs has been concentrated in the TAB Secretariat and the governments receiving assistance.

It need hardly be said that no United Nations agency can undertake a project in any country or region except on the basis of a specific request from the country or countries concerned; otherwise the agency would be violating national sovereignty. There are also certain general principles adopted by governments to insure that the work will be truly international and non-political. According to the resolution passed by the General Assembly:

The technical assistance furnished shall (i) not be a means of foreign economic and political interference in the internal affairs of the country concerned and shall not be accompanied by any considerations of a political nature; (ii) be given only to or through governments; (iii) be designed to meet the needs of the country concerned; (iv) be provided, as far as possible, in the form which that country desires; (v) be of high quality and technical competence.

The governments as well as the United Nations organizations assume certain responsibilities. For example, a government receiving technical assistance agrees to

... undertake the sustained efforts required for successful development, including the organization and adequate support of administrative services ... ; give full, prompt and sympathetic consideration to the technical advice it receives;

undertake continuing support of the institutions or programs initiated under international auspices;

normally assume responsibility for some part of the costs of the technical assistance with which it is provided, for example for local expenditures.

These provisions are in line with the nature of the international agencies. FAO, for instance, is in effect a co-operative organization of which the members are 71 governments, each with a voice in formulating policies and programs. When a member government undertakes technical co-operation through FAO, therefore, the assistance it receives is free of any suspicion of political influence, economic exploitation, patronage, charity, or ulterior motive. One of the guarantees of co-operative participation in the work is the provision that governments shall normally pay at least part of the internal costs of projects—transportation within the country, housing, office space, secretarial and clerical help, and so on—whereas FAO pays such costs as the salaries of experts and their travel to and from the country.

Within FAO, the work of technical co-operation is closely integrated with the regular program, though the two must be budgeted separately since the funds are separate. A group representing all the technical divisions screens requests from governments for projects and programs, recommends what can be undertaken with the available funds, determines priorities, initiates recruitment of field experts, reviews progress reports, evaluates results.

By now the technical co-operation picture as a whole is a complex one. So much is being done by international and national agencies that one of the big problems is to keep each other informed. This is essential to minimize overlapping and duplication, avoid unwise competition for the limited supply of experts, and insure that various projects supplement one another as much as possible within each country. This is one of the main reasons for getting together in TAB for co-operation and clearance; each year, for instance, all the proposed projects of the United Nations agencies in each country are considered simultaneously by the representatives of the UN agencies in that country and the representatives of the government. Equally important is co-operation and co-ordination with organizations outside UN. It is vital, for instance, that the FAO agricultural program in country X should dovetail as much as possible with any agricultural program the USA might have in that country. The process of co-ordinating these activities, insuring good relationships, and avoiding duplication is not an easy one, but it is succeeding very well ("almost uniformly excellent," according to a US Government report).

Before going on a field assignment, each FAO technical worker is briefed not only on his duties but on conditions in the country or area where he is going and on the attitudes that an international servant must strive to attain as fully as possible if his work is to succeed—attitudes of understanding, patience, fairness, friendship, and respect for ideas and ways that may be alien to his own. Similarly, those going from one country to another on fellowships or scholarships are briefed on the conditions to which they will need to adapt themselves. Aside from any other aspect of the program, this passage of professional workers from one country to another is itself significant; for these men and women return home with a new knowledge and understanding of other people and other places, and those with whom they have come in contact also develop a new understanding, often a lasting friendship, for the people from overseas who came to work with them for a time.

The Temples of Men's Souls

The idea of technical co-operation for economic develpment did not of course spring full-born from the brain of Mr. Truman or the brains of the FAO founding fathers, or from any other one individual or group. In the form of rather scattered and sporadic efforts, it has a long history. The ancient Romans, as M. T. Hefnawy once pointed out, probably had the first international technical assistance program, a far-flung one designed to provide grain for the bread of Rome.

Probably few people realize what deep roots and wide ramifications this modern movement has. Though it means interrupting the story of FAO, I shall digress for a few pages at this point to tell a little about work that has been done and is being done outside FAO; this is necessary, indeed, if the reader is to see FAO in its proper setting. I want to emphasize, however, that the account in these pages is incomplete and in fact consists only of a number of examples about which the author happens to know and which seem pertinent to this story. The most important omission is the technical assistance work of the so-called metropolitan powers—Great Britain, for example, and France and Holland and Belgium—in their overseas possessions and territories, mainly during the second half of the nineteenth century and the early part of the twentieth. Some of these programs have been very extensive—for instance, the fairly recent irrigation works built under British direction in the Punjab, and, currently, the agricultural development program in the Belgian Congo. But to deal at all adequately with this kind of work would take us very far afield. The growing tide of nationalism, too, has eliminated it in the countries that have gained independence. That, in turn, emphasizes the part FAO can play in helping governments to continue and perhaps expand these earlier developments through an agency in which they themselves have a controlling voice.

Religious missionaries have been among the most active pioneers in what we now call technical co-operation. In ministering to the needs of the soul, they found it necessary to minister to those of the body; is not the body the temple of the soul? They cared for the sick; they taught people to read and write and tried to help them produce more food. The missionary was likely to feel a strong moral responsibility for succoring those in need, and to think of even the most primitive people as individual human beings, each capable of better things. As far back as the days of the Spanish conquests in Latin America, some of the priests who accompanied the *conquistadores* condemned the cruel exploitation commonly practiced by the conquerors, who regarded the enslaved Indians as animals, and fought to preserve their rights and dignity and raise their status.

Among these men of courage and compassion were the Jesuits who established the famous "Reductions," or colonies, of Guarani and other Indians near the Parana River in Paraguay and parts of Argentina and Brazil. In these colonies land, livestock, and equipment were communally owned, and agriculture, crafts, industries, and arts, including even printing, reached a high stage of development. At times the thirty-or-so villages in the Guarani Reductions, which Cunningham Grahame called a Vanished Arcadia, housed upwards of 140,000 people.

In more recent times Protestant and Catholic missionaries have done a great deal of work in promoting agricultural development. In discussing the life of Abu Libda, I quoted from *The Fellaheen,* the interesting little book on the Egyptian peasant written by the Syrian Catholic priest, Father Henry Habib-Ayrout. In China during a period of perhaps 75 years Catholic priests carried on work in agriculture, helped farmers to finance the purchase of land, and encouraged the organization of co-operatives. The White Fathers of Africa have worked on that continent for about 85 years. Priests of the Maryknoll Order have long been engaged in activities related to agriculture, health, education, and family and community welfare in Latin America.

Some of the Protestant missionaries have been intensely interested in agriculture and rural welfare. In 1793 William Carey, a missionary in India, wrote: "In one of the finest countries in the world the state of agriculture and horticulture is abject and degraded, and the people's food poor, and their comforts meager. India seems to have almost everything to learn about the clearing of jungles, the tillage of wastes, the draining of marshes, the banking of river-courses, the irrigation of large areas, the mixing of composts and manures, the rotation of crops, the betterment of tools and of transport, the breeding of stocks, the culture of new vegetables and herbs, the planting of orchards, the budding, grafting and pruning of fruit trees, the forestation of timbers." Carey made a livelihood by cultivating indigo. He founded the Agri-horticultural Society for India, still in existence and a forerunner by almost two decades of the famous Royal Agricultural Society of England. Like Thomas Jefferson, Carey corresponded with agricultural experts in many parts of the world, obtaining seeds and plants to try in India.

In 1876 W. S. Clark, one of the first presidents of Massachusetts Agricultural College, established the Imperial Agricultural College in Sapporo, Japan, lecturing on Christian ethics and on agriculture in the same classroom. When William C. Bell, graduate of the Agricultural College of Cornell University, went as a missionary to Africa in 1897, he and his wife persuaded their African neighbors to use plows in place of heavy hoes (wielded by women) and got them interested in growing rice, wheat, flax, cotton, and coffee.

One of the outstanding examples of work of this kind was and is the American Farm School in Salonika, Greece, founded in 1902 by the late John Henry House, a Protestant missionary, who borrowed $500, bought 50 acres of land, and started giving practical courses. The school is now run by Dr. House's son Charles and the latter's wife Ann. Today it covers 450 acres, gives a four-year high school course which includes practical training in every aspect of farming, and graduates some 35 boys each year.

In 1903 Sam Higginbottom was sent to India as an evangelist. His first assignment was to teach economics in the Allahabad Christian College. Finding that the fundamental economic problem was agricultural, he raised a fund of $25,000 through friends, bought a farm of 275 acres, built cattle barns, got some livestock and American implements, and started the Allahabad Agricultural Institute as part of the college. Today this Institute gives two-year courses in general agriculture, dairying, and home economics, a four-year course in agricultural science, a five-year course in agricultural engineering. Much experimental work is done, including the development of improved farm implements adapted to Indian conditions. With funds from the Ford Foundation, the Institute is now operating an extension training and demonstration program.

By 1907 a number of US mission boards had launched agricultural undertakings. In China, for example, the College of Agriculture and Forestry of the University of Nanking was organized in 1914 under the leadership of Presbyterian missionary Joseph Bailie. By 1950 it had graduated 3000 students in agriculture and forestry, including some of the best-trained men in these fields in China. The college organized an extension service, set up a crop-reporting system, published two volumes on the *Chinese Farm Economy* and *Land Utilization in China,* as well as scientific and popular bulletins and a biweekly newspaper, carried on agricultural research, and co-operated with Cornell University (USA) in a plant improvement project which included an active two-way exchange of personnel.

This is only a small part of a distinguished roster that includes Spencer Hatch and Ira W. Moomaw in India, Brayton Case in Burma, the Society of Friends in various countries, and many other groups and individuals.

In 1920 a number of people whose major interest was agriculture formed the International Association of Agricultural Missions (now the Christian Rural Fellowship) to give greater impetus to the rural movement on a world scale. In 1930 Agricultural Missions, Inc., was organized under the chairmanship of John R. Mott, with John H. Reisner—who has spent 20 years in China, most of the time as dean of agriculture and forestry at Nanking —as Executive Secretary (recently succeeded in that post by Ira W. Moomaw). Representing many Protestant denominations, Agricultural Missions reaches out to all parts of the world. It acts as a clearinghouse for agricultural and rural mission activities, keeps in touch with 3500 missionaries and others in this field, provides opportunities for special training, recruits trained men and women for field service, and publishes books, bulletins, and periodicals.

After FAO was established and the expanded technical assistance program got under way, the interest of religious and secular organizations in this kind of work was greatly intensified. Two recent Catholic conferences are significant indicators of this trend. In 1951 the Holy See for the first time sponsored an international meeting on agriculture and rural life, convened in Castel Gandolfo by the National Catholic Rural Life Conference, of which Monsignor Luigi Ligutti of Des Moines, Iowa, is director. The conclusions of this meeting dealt with the rural environment, modernization of agriculture, size of farm, private property, co-operation, professional instruction in agriculture, professional organization, social security, international problems, and religious instruction and education. Early in 1953 Monsignor Ligutti's organization convened a meeting with similar aims at Manizales, Colombia—the first Latin American Catholic Conference on Rural Life Problems, attended by some 600 delegates and observers from 23 countries, including archbishops, bishops, rectors, parish priests, missionaries, and laymen. That conference, too, got down to very practical issues.

In all this work in agriculture there is a great deal of co-operation between Catholic and Protestant groups. Both the Holy See and the Protes-

NEW DIRECTIONS   93

tant Commission of Churches on International Affairs have consultative status with FAO. The commission was established by the World Council of Churches, representing 158 denominational bodies in 43 countries, with a membership of some 150 million people.

Foundations and Endowments

If religious bodies, and lay organizations related to them, pioneered in what we call technical co-operation, others were also involved. As Cornell University worked with China, so did Utah State Agricultural College with Iran and the Oklahoma Agricultural and Mechanical College with Ethiopia.

The Near East Relief, started shortly after World War I and largely backed by Church groups, later became the Near East Foundation, which has carried on technical assistance work in that region for many years.

Other foundations have also in recent years turned to technical assistance in agriculture and other fields as a fruitful activity. During World War II, at about the time of the Hot Springs Conference in 1943, the Rockefeller Foundation started an agricultural program in Mexico, in co-operation with the Mexican Department of Agriculture, concerned with a wide range of scientific and technical work. The biggest achievements so far have been the development of more than a score of improved corn varieties and hybrids, a number of improved varieties of wheat, and several varieties of legumes and sorghums. A government Corn Commission distributes the new corn hybrids and varieties among farmers. The *Escuela Agricola Panamericana* in Honduras is an agricultural school at Zamorano, near Tegucigalpa, endowed by the United Fruit Company and headed by Wilson Popenoe, a pioneer in the development of tropical fruits. This school, founded in 1946, has about 160 Latin American students, many from poor families, who take a three-year course. More than 95 per cent of the graduates are working in agriculture, some being employed in government services in Honduras, Guatemala, El Salvador, Costa Rica, Panama, Ecuador, Peru, and Venezuela. Also in 1946, Nelson A. Rockefeller established the American International Association, which has carried on active programs in Venezuela and Brazil, in co-operation with government agencies concerned with rural welfare and education.

Most recent of the private foundations to take up this kind of work as the movement gained momentum is the Ford Foundation, now the largest endowment in the world, with total assets of more than $500,000,000. I shall have occasion later to refer to the co-operative program this foundation is carrying out with the US Government in expanding agricultural extension and other community work in the villages of India. In Pakistan the Ford Foundation is helping in technical and industrial training and in establishing a women's college of home economics. More limited activities are under way or planned in other countries of the Far East and Near East.

Agencies of Governments

The exigencies of World War II resulted in a number of ventures in technical co-operation by governments in addition to those of voluntary organizations.

One of the first stemmed from the Office of the Coordinator of Inter-American Affairs established by the US Government in 1942 and headed by Nelson Rockefeller. This agency resulted from a resolution of the Hemisphere Solidarity Conference, held in Rio de Janeiro just after the attack on Pearl Harbor, calling for co-operation among countries in the Western Hemisphere on measures to improve health and sanitation. Because food and health go together, the co-ordinator's office set up a Division of Food Supply which worked with some of the Latin American governments on agricultural development programs. Later an Institute of Inter-American Affairs (IIAA) was created to take over the program. The Institute eventually became part of the TCA (President Truman's Technical Cooperation Administration) and then of FOA (President Eisenhower's Foreign Operations Administration). A characteristic feature of IIAA is the *servicio*, or service agency—essentially a government bureau—in each co-operating country. The director of the *servicio* is usually an American, and in the beginning most of the staff are Americans. As additional nationals of the co-operating country are trained, they gradually replace the Americans on the staff. Similarly the proportion of funds gradually shifts from being almost entirely contributed by the USA to being largely contributed by the co-operating country. In theory, the USA would eventually withdraw completely.

At about the time this work started in 1942, the US Department of Agriculture also initiated technical co-operation projects in Latin America, designed originally to stimulate production of such war-vital materials as rubber, quinine, fibers, insecticides. After the war, the work was extended to include coffee, tea, mahogany, vegetable oils, and other products.

The biggest US technical assistance undertaking in Latin America was the co-operative Mexico–USA foot-and-mouth-disease control program, which wiped out the disease in Mexico.

In 1944 the Organization of American States (of which the international staff is known as the Pan American Union) established an Inter-American Institute of Agricultural Sciences at Turrialba, Costa Rica, with 14 countries as members. The purpose of the Institute is to encourage and advance the development of agricultural sciences in the American republics through research, teaching, and extension work. By the end of 1952 it had given training courses for some 1200 students from 30 countries, distributed many new and improved varieties of plants, developed a defoliation control method for the most damaging coffee disease of the Americas, and had done much work on other important agricultural problems.

New Directions

UNRRA, largest of the war-born agencies, was set up in November 1943, through an agreement under which some 44 (later 47) governments were to assist liberated countries urgently in need of relief and rehabilitation (this included the technical assistance which in its final stages was taken over by FAO). Total contributions to UNRRA amounted to more than 3¾ billion dollars, of which 73 per cent was contributed by the USA and another 11 per cent by the United Kingdom and Canada. UNRRA carried on agricultural work on a large scale in 17 countries, providing such essentials as farm machinery, livestock, seeds, fertilizers, pesticides, veterinary supplies, fishing boats and gear, and services to go with these things.

After the creation of FAO, discussion of the technical co-operation approach to urgent economic problems became far more widespread. Then came the historic announcement of the Marshall Plan for US aid to Europe. "Our policy," said Secretary of State George C. Marshall in a speech at Harvard University on June 5, 1947, "is directed not against any country or doctrine, but against hunger, poverty, desperation and chaos. Its purpose should be the revival of a working economy in the world so as to permit the emergence of political and social conditions in which free institutions can exist." In April 1948 the US Congress passed the Foreign Assistance Act which set up the Economic Cooperation Administration (ECA) to administer the program for European recovery. Meanwhile, the governments of Western Europe established the Organization for European Economic Cooperation (OEEC) to work with ECA. So a vast drive for the development of agriculture, industry, and trade got under way. ECA made grants, provided loans, gave technical assistance. Eighteen countries, with a total population of some 250 million people, participated. The magnitude of the operation may be judged from the fact that during the first three years (through July 1950) US expenditures totaled about 10 billion dollars.

Thus by about the time FAO was established a good deal of the kind of activity that now goes by the name of technical assistance was in existence, and some of it had deep historical roots. (A little book by Edwin A. Bock, concerned with certain aspects of the work of the voluntary agencies and published in 1954, has the title *Fifty Years of Technical Assistance*.) What is new today is the sudden great expansion of the work, the rapidly growing awareness of its urgency to meet pressing world problems, and the fact that it is becoming a more or less united international effort with clear-cut aims, a definite philosophy, and increasing co-ordination of activities.

President Truman's 1949 Point Four proposals resulted not only in an expanded program of technical co-operation in the United Nations agencies but also in enlarging the bilateral programs of the US Government. In June 1950 Congress passed the Act for International Development "to encourage the flow of investment capital to countries which provide the conditions under which . . . capital can effectively and constructively contribute to raising standards of living, creating new sources of wealth, increasing productivity, and expanding purchasing power." Under this Act the Technical Cooperation Administration (TCA) was established for operations in the Near East, Africa, Asia (and in Latin America by absorbing IIAA). In October 1951 came the Mutual Security Act, setting up the Mutual Security Agency (ECA was ended shortly afterward). By January 1952 some 30 governments had signed agreements with the USA under this act, which incidentally resulted in rather extensive participation by voluntary agencies, including colleges and universities, in the government's technical co-operation program. The program has been continued under President Eisenhower with TCA and MSA consolidated in a new agency, the Foreign Operations Administration.

A significant movement started by the late Henry G. Bennett, first director of TCA, to involve US colleges and universities more extensively in the work of technical co-operation has been carried even further by FOA. That agency is making three-year contracts with universities under which the latter receive grants from FOA to carry out US bilateral projects, or in some cases entire programs, in other countries. Previously there had been many contracts of this kind between the government and universities, but all were for short periods only. It now seems that these US institutions of learning and research will play an increasingly active, intimate, and responsible part in the growth of world economic development.

The USA was not the only country to be caught up in the sweep of this technical co-operation movement. In January 1950 the Foreign Ministers of several of the British Commonwealth countries met in Colombo, Ceylon, and organized the Colombo Plan for Cooperative Economic Development in South and Southeast Asia (later extended to include most of the countries in the region). A consultative committee was established to survey needs and resources for assisting countries to raise standards of living through economic development, with special emphasis on food production. Each co-operating country in South and Southeast Asia drew up a development program covering a period of six years, beginning July 1, 1951. The total cost of these national programs for the six years was estimated at the equivalent of some 5 billion dollars. The funds for the work have been coming from private investments within the countries, the blocked sterling balances held by governments, and external financing (including considerable help from the USA). The work is co-ordinated with the programs of the USA and of the United Nations and the specialized agencies. A meeting of the Consultative Committee held in New Delhi in October 1953 heard reports on the first two years of operation, showing progress—nearly 200 experts sent out on field assignments; irrigation works, roads, factories, built or under way; a thousand Asians trained in non-Asiatic countries; some increases already made in food production.

In 1953 Norway started a program to provide assistance to India, King Haakon paying a tribute to the Hot Springs Conference in opening a campaign for a fund equivalent to about $1,400,000 to be raised by public subscription. Though Norway has a small population and limited resources, he said, it wants to do everything possible to help others because "this is the only way to a happier world [and] to better international understanding." Switzerland, as we shall see later, has had a technical mission in Nepal, the agricultural part of the work being subsequently taken over by FAO. Sweden has announced that its Central Committee for Technical Assistance will co-operate with the United Nations in projects in Pakistan and Ethiopia.

World Needs or World Fears

Future historians may come to regard this swift growth of an idea—the idea that is the foundation of FAO—as one of the most important and characteristic developments of this time.

Hundreds, perhaps thousands, of scientists and other experts from many different countries are now scattered all over the world, pushing the frontiers of knowledge and its practical application further outward and helping to effect the innumerable adjustments in age-old institutions and ways that are needed to make new advances possible. Other thousands of young people from lands that have been thought of as backward are attending universities, colleges, and technical schools abroad and returning to work as experts in their own countries. If this is a slow and sometimes disheartening process, it is no more so than were the voyages of Columbus, Magellan, Frobisher, and Drake, which must often have seemed hopeless yet brought immeasurable results; no more so than the slow creaking of oxcarts across America to open a continent of opportunity. These great outgoing movements stir the imaginations of men, stretch their souls, focus their energies on big creative achievements. This is happening now, as President Eisenhower showed so clearly in his address, "The Chance for Peace," made before the American Society of Newspaper Editors on April 16, 1953:

The fruit of success in all these tasks [limitation of arms and other safeguards of peace] would present the world with the greatest task, and the greatest opportunity, of all. It is this: the dedication of the energies, the resources, and the imaginations of all peaceful nations to a new kind of war. This would be a declared total war, not upon any human enemy but upon the brute forces of poverty and need.

The peace we seek, founded upon decent trust and co-operative effort among nations, can be fortified not by weapons of war but by wheat and by cotton, by milk and by wool, by meat and by timber and by rice. These are words that translate into every language on earth. These are needs that challenge this world in arms. . . .

We are prepared to reaffirm, with the most concrete evidence, our readiness to help build a world in which all peoples can be productive and prosperous.

This Government is ready to ask its people to join with all nations in devoting a substantial percentage of the savings achieved by disarmament to a fund for world aid and reconstruction. The purposes of this great work would be to help other peoples to develop the undeveloped areas of the world, to stimulate profitable and fair world trade, to assist all peoples to know the blessings of productive freedom.

The monuments to this new kind of war would be these: roads and schools, hospitals and homes, food and health.

We are ready, in short, to dedicate our strength to serving the *needs*, rather than the *fears*, of the world. . . .

I know of no course, other than that marked by these and similar actions, that can be called the highway of peace.

Today we face not only the possibility that civilization and even mankind will be rubbed out by a few violent thermonuclear reactions, but also more subtle dangers. According to a recent report by geneticist A. H. Sturtevant of the California Institute of Technology, "the entire human race, present and future," is risking damage by irradiation from atomic or thermonuclear bombs exploded in current experiments. "There is no possible escape from the conclusion that the bombs already exploded will ultimately result, in future generations, in the production of numerous defective individuals. And every new bomb exploded . . . will result in an increase in this ultimate harvest of defective individuals."

Though some of the biological effects of thermonuclear explosions are matters of dispute among experts, even these differences of opinion are evidence enough that we do not know what we are doing to ourselves by assuming the all-destroying powers without the all-embracing wisdom and compassion of divinity. But if we live in an age of anxiety, such words as those of the President make it clear that we live also in an age of faith.

PART
THREE

Technical Co-operation

CHAPTER EIGHT

Near East and Africa

REGIONAL PROJECTS

ONE OF THE prime uses governments make of FAO is to develop regional interests and foster co-operation among countries as neighbors. This kind of activity is peculiarly suitable for an international organization that works primarily in scientific fields. For years scientists have had their own international organizations for the exchange of information, a process that is essential to any scientific progress whatever. Because scientists are accustomed to thinking of their work as cutting completely across international boundaries, they can get together in a disinterested fraternity concerned with discovering and disseminating facts important for mankind as a whole. For agriculture, this is particularly useful in the case of neighboring countries in which conditions are similar.

In the Near East, the Mediterranean area, and parts of Africa, neighboring countries have been working together through FAO:

- To war against the age-old plague of locusts.
- To breed wheat and barley resistant to destructive diseases.
- To improve great stretches of range and pasture lands for the better nourishment of herds and flocks.
- To combat serious diseases of animals.
- To root out kwashiorkor, a widespread and often fatal nutritional disease of children.
- To train extension workers.
- To foster the development of sound co-operatives.
- To stimulate reforestation and better management of forests and woodlands.
- To develop nutrition services and improve the nutrition particularly of mothers and children.

Tyrant Locust

For numberless generations in the Near East, hunger has periodically driven herds of cattle and flocks of sheep and goats from exhausted or shriveled pasture to fresher grass. Other creatures in these vast sun-parched lands—notably the desert locusts—have been driven by the same need. When you are caught in a migrating swarm of these insects, they seem like millions of miniature yellow-green radar-guided missiles, hurtling toward some unseen target. Wherever they alight, they devour every green thing to the last grassblade, leaving the earth naked, the people starving.

This problem, too, has been going on for numberless generations. The locust was one of the seven plagues described in the Old Testament. A stoneworker of 2400 B.C. carved the hieroglyphic story of its devastations on the walls of an Egyptian tomb.

Perhaps worse than the ruin it brings is the hopelessness. What is the use of plowing and planting, the farmer asks, if these creatures are to get all my harvest? For when a plague once starts, it may continue for years, the swarms moving from country to country, continent to continent. The females spear their eggs into the ground at the rate of perhaps 2000 to a square foot. The larger migrating swarms may measure upwards of 50 miles square, fly 2000 miles at some 40 miles a day, and pile 700 tons of locusts on every acre where they settle.

The only good thing about locusts is that many Near East people use them, roasted, as food, along with dates and bread. John the Baptist, you remember, lived for a time on locusts and wild honey.

Individual communities, even countries, cannot by themselves effectively combat this menace. If outbreaks are to be controlled or prevented, it must be through mutual aid and co-ordinated strategy.

Research workers have been co-operating and pooling information for some 25 years through international conferences and the work of the Anti-Locust Research Center in London, headed by Dr. B. P. Uvarov. In field control work, co-operation began during the war, in 1942, when the British organized the Desert Locust Control, a hardy well-equipped corps ready to go anywhere on call, like a fire department. For three years British, Russian, Indian, Iranian, Sudanese, and Palestinian experts fought locust outbreaks together, and effectively, in a number of countries.

At present (1954) an outbreak that probably started in the Arabian peninsula as long ago as 1948-49 is plaguing the Near East and North Africa, attacking at various times in widely scattered countries from India on the east to Egypt on the west, Syria in the north to Kenya in the south. The grave threat of this current plague has stimulated widespread co-operation, with FAO as the chief co-ordinator of the work.

In 1951 FAO established a Technical Advisory Committee on Desert

Locust Control, with Uvarov as consultant. It brings together experts from Egypt, France, India, Iran, Jordan, Iraq, and Saudi Arabia, and material and personnel are contributed not only by these countries but by the USA (which has played an important part in the campaign), Pakistan, Egypt, Lebanon, Syria, Turkey, Kuwait, and the British Desert Locust Control. Among the FAO contributions was an airlift to bring supplies from India to Iran.

The next year, 1952-53, FAO agreed to provide a half-million dollars' worth of equipment and material, to be moved to danger areas as needed. Since this material must be transported in a hurry (usually by air), the organization established reserves of insecticides, spraying and dusting machines, and trucks at a number of strategic centers throughout the region, and purchased four spraying aircraft operated by the East African High Commission. In 1954 co-operation in the anti-locust work developed still further, thirteen countries contributing to a common fund about half of which was provided by FAO.

The modern locust control methods used in this vast campaign include the spreading of poisoned bran bait; dusting or spraying the insects on the ground with power or hand machines; and aircraft spraying of swarms in flight, settled swarms, and grasshoppers that have not yet become migrating locusts. The ultimate aim is to prevent plagues by destroying the creatures in their breeding or outbreak areas. In the case of some other locusts—the Moroccan locust in Algeria, for example—the breeding places are now known and preventive measures are highly effective. This is not yet true in the case of the desert locust; but the outlook for freeing millions of people from its antique tyranny is brighter today than at any time since the Pharaohs.

A God of Much Cunning

Except in Egypt where the fellaheen use corn, the bread of the Near East is made of wheat. It is ground between heavy stones, and the flour is mixed with water and salt. Sometimes yeast or other leavening is used, sometimes not. The dough is patted into big flat cakes, like the tortillas of Latin America but larger, which are cooked so they have a soft, pleasantly chewy consistency and can be readily torn apart with the fingers. People consume huge quantities of these flat loaves, maybe with vegetables or fruit, or a dab of meat or fish, or some thick clabber made from the milk of goats or sheep, water buffaloes or camels, or, occasionally, cows. Good bread it is, too, the best having an agreeable nutty flavor. All Westerners (Monsignor Ligutti noted) could learn something about breadmaking in the Near East. The nomads, he said, serve a thin wafer about 20 inches in diameter, folded like an old volume; you eat a page at a time.

Wheat is important for another reason: the straw is usually the only feed (a poor one) the farmer has for his animals when there is no grazing. An ox, cow, or ass that has subsisted for several months on straw and water is not the strongest of animals for plowing and hauling.

Where the soil is too poor or the climate too harsh for wheat, barley, adapted to greater hardships, often takes its place, though it is inferior for breadmaking.

Much of the Near East is climatically like the hot, semiarid parts of the West in the USA. Both grow mainly hard wheat. The area in wheat in nine countries (Egypt, Iran, Iraq, Jordan, Lebanon, Pakistan, Syria, Cyprus, plus Turkey in Europe) is more than 38 million acres, producing around 555 million bushels (1952). Diseases, insects, and drought do much harm. The worst enemy is black stem rust, which in this region, as in the USA and Canada, sweeps over large areas when winds carry the clouds of dustlike spores. The tiny rust fungus sends rootlike threads, mycelia, down into the individual cells of the wheat plant, sucking out water and food. Crop losses may run as high as 90 per cent in a severe epidemic. In 1935 almost a fourth of the wheat crop in the USA was lost, including 60 per cent of the crop in Minnesota.

Like locusts, stem rust is an ancient plague. It was called "mildew" in Biblical times. The Romans had a rust god, Rubicus. Their method of control was to placate Rubicus with a big festival every year.

Stem rust and other diseases have been conquered, more or less, in the USA, Canada, and some other countries by the breeding of resistant wheat varieties. But the work is never-ending. Rubicus is a god of much cunning. He can change his shape like the old magicians. The rust organism appears in various physiological forms or races (at least 59 have been identified in the USA and Canada), developed by mutation of genes and by crossbreeding among races. Thus the wheat breeder may produce a plant resistant to one form of rust only to find in a few years that it has been supplanted by another, which in turn is causing havoc. So he has to start all over again and develop a new variety resistant to the new form. Co-operative research among the states in the USA and between that country and Canada has been an indispensable tool in this work.

Stem rust is of course not the only enemy that can be overcome by breeding resistant varieties. Others are stripe rust, leaf rust, various smuts, some insect pests, cold, drought, weak stems that bend and break easily ("lodging"), and excessive soil alkalinity. Wheat can be bred also for good quality and yield—including a good yield of straw with which to feed animals.

Plant breeding, in fact, is one of the most economical ways to bring about some major agricultural improvements. In the USA and Canada during the past few decades one improved variety has often saved enough in a single year to pay for 50 years of research.

In 1952 six countries in the Near East sent representatives to a meeting at the Yesilköy Plant Breeding Station in Istanbul, Turkey, to explore the possibilities of a co-operative wheat-breeding project for this region, with emphasis particularly on producing strains resistant to stem rust. That meeting laid the groundwork for what should be a highly productive undertaking—the establishment of co-operative uniform rust nurseries at a number of points throughout the region, a co-operative program of breeding for rust resistance, a regional survey to determine what races of rust are present and how the spores travel from one area to another, the setting up of uniform bunt (stinking smut) nurseries, and co-operative uniform tests of barley.

The next year, at the second meeting (in Cairo), seven countries reported that they had started to grow stock in co-operative nurseries, and a few had organized national wheat- and barley-breeding committees.

The nine countries represented at this meeting are setting up 112 co-operative nurseries for wheat rust, wheat bunt, and barley testing. They have been expanding the rust survey and exchanging seed of hybrid material resulting from the program. Turkey and Egypt identify the races of rust involved in an outbreak (often a difficult job) in their laboratories, and Turkey makes milling, baking, physical, and chemical tests of wheat samples.

It will be several years before improved varieties from the program can be grown on a large scale, but this is a vigorous start and already some promising disease-resistant plants have appeared and are being distributed for testing.

Grass the Life-Giver

The world food problem is mainly a problem of grass. Human beings live primarily on the seeds of grasses—wheat, rice, corn, barley, millet. Sugar cane is grass. Meat, milk, eggs, hides, wool, and the work done by draft animals are grass transmuted in the bodies of domesticated animals.

Nowhere is the importance of grass more striking than in the Near East, where wandering herdsmen have for centuries grazed their flocks and herds on the vegetation of vast plains and pastures. These people are nomads because of their extreme dependence on grass. They can stay in one place only as long as there is enough grass and water for their animals. Then they are compelled to move on.

As a whole, the Near East and the Mediterranean area is dry country, with rain only in the winter months. In years when rain is plentiful, the cattle are fat; in years of drought, they are gaunt or die. The constant need for forage drives herdsmen to overgraze the sparse vegetation. Anyone who has seen much of the Near East realizes how punishing this practice has been to the land; and, as C. E. Kellogg has expressed it, when men punish the land, the land punishes men.

Throughout this region, then, water is the main limiting factor in agriculture. Grass and trees are the great conservers of water and soil. Land bared by overgrazing does not soak up and store rain when it comes; the water slithers off in sheets and rivulets, tearing much soil away as though with wet vindictive fingers. So the deeper stores of water for streams and wells are gradually depleted, and plant roots are as parched as the throats of men and beasts. Though irrigation is badly needed for agricultural development in much of this part of the world, often a more fundamental need is to build up the grasslands by systems of livestock husbandry which work with rather than against nature in making full use of all the water the heavens will provide. Wise man are perceiving this truth in the great agricultural awakening now taking place.

In 1951 the Organization for European Economic Cooperation (OEEC) and FAO sent out a team of grassland specialists to survey grazing and fodder resources in a number of Mediterranean countries. Afterward they held a Mediterranean Grassland Conference in Rome and ultimately set up an FAO Working Party on Mediterranean Pasture and Fodder Development, which met in May 1952 in Rome and a year later in Algiers. So far, the members of this group are Algeria, Cyprus (UK), Egypt, France, Israel, Italy, Libya, Morocco, Portugal, Spain, Tunisia, Turkey.

The undertaking is young; the problems are difficult and will require long persistent effort, which must include research to get basic facts on some important points. • What, for example, are the safe limits of grazing in different areas? • What feeding systems are practicable to supplement grazing with hay and ensilage? • What are the best plants to use in restoring damaged run-down grasslands? • What is the best way to bring about changes in grazing practices among nomadic people accustomed almost since time began to doing things in their own fashion?

Part of the experimental work needed to develop this kind of information will be carried on in uniform Mediterranean nurseries, of which there will probably be 20 or more, all told, in Algeria, Cyprus, Egypt, Greece, Israel, Italy, Morocco, Portugal, Spain, Yugoslavia. At this writing, seeds of some 60 grasses and 130 legumes have been contributed by countries in the Mediterranean and adjacent areas and obtained from other winter-rainfall environments in North America, South America, South Africa, Australia, to be distributed to the nurseries. In 1954 Turkey was host to an FAO-sponsored training center for grasslands workers.

Interest in the work is spreading. Arab governments not included in the Mediterranean group plan similar undertakings. On the loom of co-operation many countries are starting to weave a green garment to clothe the naked land.

As a further step extending beyond the region, representatives from a number of countries in the Near East, Far East, Latin America, North America, and Europe met in Rome early in 1954 to take up what are essentially world-wide problems of forest grazing.

Co-operation for Animal Health

In 1952 and 1953 a serious outbreak of foot-and-mouth disease struck livestock in parts of Syria. Fortunately two FAO veterinarians happened to be in that country on another assignment. They promptly obtained some 40,000 doses of vaccine (equivalent to 60,000 doses because of the number of small cattle), and a vaccination campaign was organized to stop further spread of the disease.

The situation was so bad that it aroused concern among neighboring countries and stimulated a move for regional co-operation in animal disease work; so in April 1953 representatives of a number of Near East countries met in Damascus under FAO auspices to consider the problem.

This was an exploratory meeting. Conditions that favor the spread of foot-and-mouth disease in the region, it was brought out, are the extensive seasonal migrations of flocks and herds in search of grass, both within and among countries; smuggling to avoid quarantine regulations; the shortage of trained veterinarians; and the lack of any systematic exchange of information about disease outbreaks.

The delegates agreed on the need for better control of cattle movements across frontiers, difficult though this will be, and for a region-wide disease-reporting service. There was much sentiment in favor of establishing a regional foot-and-mouth disease commission and maintaining supplies of vaccine at some central point so they would be quickly available to neighboring countries.

Meanwhile, before the Damascus meeting FAO had already arranged for a regional meeting on animal health to be held in Cyprus. This convened the latter part of June, with representatives of 12 countries attending and R. J. Roe (Cyprus) serving as chairman.

That meeting discussed and approved a draft constitution for a Near East Commission for Animal Health, which had been drawn up by FAO and has now been submitted to governments. The membership of this body, as proposed by the Cyprus meeting, would include Afghanistan, Egypt, Ethiopia, France, Iran, Iraq, Jordan, Libya, Pakistan, Saudi Arabia, Syria, Turkey, the United Kingdom, and Yemen. Headquarters would be at the FAO Near East Regional Office, Cairo. The budget would total $25,000 a year, contributed by the members in proportion to livestock numbers in each country.

Although the primary purpose of this commission is to combat foot-and-mouth disease, it would, as its name indicates, deal with other diseases as well. In fact much of the time at the session in Cyprus was devoted to a roundup of the whole livestock disease situation in all the countries represented, and to other aspects of livestock improvement as well.

As we shall see later, a regional foot-and-mouth disease commission has already been organized in Europe.

Deprived Children

Food, agriculture, and health are as inseparable as the sides of a triangle. People suffering from a disease such as malaria cannot work at full capacity. On the other hand, they cannot build up adequate resistance to a good many diseases unless they are properly fed.

So the efforts of FAO and other United Nations agencies must fit together in a sort of pattern, with particularly close co-operation at certain points. FAO and the World Health Organization, for instance, work together through a Joint Expert Committee on Nutrition. One of its major recent concerns has been to study and combat a serious nutritional disease of young children found in many parts of the world.

This work started in 1950 with an investigation of the disease known in Africa as "kwashiorkor." Dr. J. F. Brock (WHO) and Dr. Marcel Autret (FAO) surveyed the great middle belt of the continent south of the Sahara, from Zanzibar on the east coast to Dakar on the west. They found kwashiorkor prevalent in the whole area except among tribes that live on meat or use considerable quantities of milk. Among the people who live largely on starchy foods—cassava, plantains, yams, corn—the disease strikes young children shortly after they are weaned. Apparently the word *kwashiorkor* in the Ga language of the Gold Coast means "displaced child" or "deprived child," referring to the fact that a child nurses until it is deprived of the mother's breast by the next child to be born. The food the child gets when it is cut off from breast milk is almost totally lacking in protein. This severe protein shortage apparently affects almost every organ of the body, and children not treated are very likely to die.

A number of doctors have observed that dramatic cures are effected and the death rate can be cut from 50 per cent to practically zero by feeding dried skim milk. WHO and FAO promptly enlisted the help of the Children's Fund (UNICEF) in sending this product to Africa for use in hospitals and clinics. Prevention of the disease, however, must in the long run be based on a better-rounded local food supply.

The Joint FAO-WHO Nutrition Committee urged that a wider study of kwashiorkor be carried out in other regions. FAO has been conducting a survey in Latin America and finds that the disease is prevalent there, too. A search of medical and nutritional records shows, in fact, that it has been recognized at various times and in various parts of the world since as far back as 1910 and has been known by some 50 different names.

In November and December 1952 the nutrition committee joined forces with CCTA (the Commission for Technical Cooperation in Africa South of the Sahara, an organization formed by six governments in 1950 to foster co-operation in various technical fields) in convening a conference on protein-deficiency malnutrition in mothers, infants, and children, of which kwashiorkor is one manifestation. The meeting was held in Gambia, West

Africa, and brought together experts from Australia, Belgium, France, India, Italy, Jamaica, Portugal, Uganda, the Union of South Africa, the United Kingdom, and the United States of America under the chairmanship of Dr. F. W. Clements of the Institute of Child Health, University of Sydney.

The report of the group points out that today nutrition workers are concentrating more attention on protein than on any other dietary deficiency. This is partly owing to the fact that only recently have tools been developed for thoroughly exploring the complexities of protein nutrition. Investigations have now gone far enough to indicate that it might eventually be possible to add specific amino acids to foods to supplement low-quality proteins and achieve the kind of amino-acid balance that meets the needs of the body.

Following the Gambia meeting, conferences on protein malnutrition were held in Caracas and Jamaica for Latin America, and in Java for South and East Asia. It is too early to predict the outcome of the FAO-WHO investigations of protein malnutrition of children and mothers, including kwashiorkor; but from a practical standpoint they should provide more knowledge of the kinds and combinations of foods best adapted to meet protein needs economically in different areas.

A subsequent check-up of the results of the first kwashiorkor survey in Africa showed that the government of the Belgian Congo made prompt use of the findings in a widespread and vigorous campaign involving the distribution of powdered skim milk for use by children and pregnant and nursing women, with excellent results.

In the Near East, where the role of women has traditionally been circumscribed in community or public activities though their influence in the family and the home is often peculiarly strong, work in nutrition and home economics is beginning to assume greater importance. The staff of the Near East Regional Office of FAO in Cairo includes an expert in these fields. As a step in helping to train more workers and strengthen national services, the Egyptian Government, FAO, and WHO jointly sponsored a nutrition training institute in Cairo in the autumn of 1950 which set a pattern for other regions. The 36 trainees from eight countries were all either technicians or medical doctors, and the curriculum included appraisal and improvement of national dietaries, nutritional surveys, family budgets, production and marketing, food sanitation, and the public health aspects of nutrition. Later (April-July 1952) the two organizations sponsored another nutrition training institute in Marseilles, for French-speaking workers in North Africa.

Extension Wisdom

The awakening interest in extension work in practically every country in the Near East came to a head in the first extension institute in that region, held early in 1953 in Beirut, with Alfred Chamoun (Lebanon) as director. The 53 participants from 14 countries discussed the problems, methods, and philosophy of extension work, exchanged experiences and ideas, and prepared a series of recommendations designed to meet the needs of the Near East at this stage.

The record of these discussions is contained in a batch of mimeographed papers which look no more impressive than any other batch of mimeographed papers. But they contain passages of much wisdom drawn from the wide experience and thinking of men from several countries, including, for example, M. L. Wilson, who for many years headed the Extension Service of the USA and is known as a world leader in the movement.

For the most part it is not possible, the Beirut meeting emphasized, for Near East countries to apply directly the methods practiced in such countries as the USA, where conditions are so totally different. Extension work in the Near East must be rooted in and grow out of the ways and the thinking characteristic of each country, and at the start it must perforce get along with a minimum of expert guidance because there are so few trained workers. It must dig down into the village life and bring up native leaders who can be imbued with the aims and the philosophy of this great educational movement, now becoming world wide. It must, above all, seek the full understanding and co-operation of farmers and farm workers and their families. Any program not rooted in needs actually felt by these people will wither because it will not have the participation of those it is intended to benefit. It follows that the program can advance only as fast as the thinking of the majority of the people advances.

This meeting was a preliminary exploration of needs and possibilities in the Near East. It enriched the understanding of the participants and has accelerated the development of extension work in Egypt, Iraq, Iran, Jordan, and Lebanon; and it is to be followed up by a regional extension training center to be held in Egypt.

Training for Co-operation

There is also in the Near East a widening and deepening interest in rural co-operatives. Some co-operative ventures have been very successful, but serious mistakes have been made too, perhaps on some occasions from sticking too close to methods used in Western countries, which by no means always apply to conditions in Near East villages.

For three months in the autumn of 1952 FAO and the International Labour Organisation held a training institute on co-operatives in Nicosia, Cyprus, with 16 participants from five countries and two more sent by UNRWA (the United Nations Relief and Works Agency). These were people directly involved in planning, establishing, or conducting co-operative enterprises. Cyprus was chosen for the institute not only because conditions there are similar to those in other Near East countries but also because the co-operative movement on the island has a fairly long history, first of costly failure, later of remarkable successes.

W. J. W. Cheesman (UK), who served as director, organized the institute as a co-operative society. The participants studied (and applied in the society) the principles of co-operative organization, types of co-operatives, finance, management, audit and inspection, bookkeeping and accounts, thrift, credit, recovery of loans, arbitration, duties of the staff, education of officers and members, and the functions of government in relation to co-operatives. On the last day the society formally liquidated itself.

The members kept skeleton sets of account books, in English or Arabic, required for a credit and a consumer co-operative. On field trips they studied the work of organizations in the villages of Cyprus. They ended the course with strengthened belief in the co-operative approach to many economic problems and increased knowledge of the techniques needed for success.

Vanished Cedars

It is reported that when the late President Roosevelt was flying from Cairo eastward he looked down expecting to see the famous cedars of Lebanon and was amazed to find bare hills with only one or two patches of cedars left. The rest had been wiped out by centuries of deforestation. Such things could happen in any country, he was told, if it did not take care of its forests. Back in Washington, he made a note on a memorandum concerning the Food and Agriculture Organization (then in the Interim Commission stage): "Forestry most important. Request American delegation propose revision of FAO statute and include it in FAO charter."

I have discussed earlier in this book how dung cakes are commonly used in the Near East (and the Far East) as fuel for cooking. This waste of fertility that should go to enrich the soil results from stripping forest and woodland until there are no trees left. The millions of little charcoal fires that for generations cooked millions of meals (and tiny pots of thick sweet coffee) were picturesque but destructive of a great natural resource. Also destructive were the teeth of millions of sheep that have nibbled the grass too close, and goats hungrily munching the shrubs and saplings.

Of all regions, the Near East has the most serious and difficult forest problems, and it has also been the last to come around to a co-operative regional approach. Regional forestry commissions had been set up in Europe, Latin America, and Asia for some time when FAO held the first Near East forestry conference in Amman, Jordan, in December 1952, with Abdul Hannan Hiloue (Syria) as chairman.

Forest plantings are being made, however, and in many places there are vigorous efforts to improve management and increase production. Though rehabilitation of forest areas will be slow, farm planting of fast-growing species of trees can provide wood rather quickly, and the cash value of tree crops in this region compares favorably with that of the best agricultural crops.

It will not be easy to arouse the public interest required to recreate vanished forests. The Amman conference was a first step in bringing countries together to develop forest policies in concert. It recommended that a regional commission be established which would hasten progress and assure continued co-operation. On the part of FAO, the meeting resulted in stationing a forestry officer in the Near East to serve governments in every way possible.

Better Figures

Without good statistics—and plenty of them—modern agriculture, industry, and commerce could not function as they do in the more technically advanced countries. In many developing countries one of the most insistent needs is for better statistical services. Good statistical reporting and analysis, however, are difficult, highly technical procedures. FAO is doing a great deal to help individual governments strengthen and improve these services.

Early in the history of the organization regional training institutes were started as an economical and effective way of providing assistance. In fact, the first FAO training institutes in any field were those concerned with statistics, set up by Howard Tolley and Conrad Taeuber, formerly officers of FAO.

Since this work began in the Near East, it may be as well to set down a brief account of it here.

In the spring of 1948, 40 statisticians from Egypt, Iraq, Lebanon, and Syria met in Baghdad for a training course given by an FAO instructor. This venture was so well received that later in the same year a much more comprehensive one was organized in Mexico City. It lasted for three months and brought in 60 participants from 16 Latin American countries, of whom two thirds were government officers, including the director-general of statistics of one country and a number of other high officials. In this course the Bureau of Statistics of Mexico (*Dirección General de Estadística*), the United Nations Statistical Office, the Inter-American Statistical Institute, the US Bureau of the Census, and FAO all worked together. Mexico provided many of the teachers and lecturers, shared the expenses, and granted several fellowships.

The next year, 1949, statistical training institutes spread to New Delhi, Cairo, Paris; in 1951 to San José (Costa Rica) and Rio de Janeiro; in 1952 to Quito and Beirut (in co-operation with the International Statistical Institute). Also in 1952 a regional seminar was held in Beirut dealing with production and price statistics. In 1953 FAO conducted a statistical institute in Africa, with a large attendance from tropical areas where data are hard to get and badly needed. The training included field work under African bush conditions.

Because of the growing demand for this kind of assistance, FAO has also placed regional statistical officers in Cairo for the Near East and Bangkok for the Far East (and for a while had one in San José for Latin America) to help governments on specific problems and to follow up the work of the institutes.

Every improvement in the agricultural statistics of member countries is of course reflected in improvements in the coverage and accuracy of FAO's world-wide statistical reports, and the world statistical service is as useful to highly developed countries as to any of the others.

The early start on statistics was owing partly to the fact that one of the early projects of FAO was a world census of agriculture, the first to be taken in more than a decade. Collecting the data for an accurate census is a complicated business in any country even under the best of conditions. Where there is a shortage of trained people, little previous information on which to build, and inadequate means of communication and travel, the difficulties are greatly multiplied. Even in India, which has some of the world's best statisticians, there is a dearth of information on agriculture in certain areas.

In starting the census, therefore, many governments asked for help from FAO. The results of the 1950 world census of agriculture have now been provisionally published for 65 countries in FAO's *Monthly Bulletin of Agricultural Economics and Statistics,* and the first volume of the full report is in preparation.

Studies are under way for a 1960 world census.

Even in technically advanced countries census-taking is today undergoing some changes. The new methods of sampling, popularly associated with surveys of public opinion, have now been perfected to such a point that for some purposes, especially the analysis of relationships, they can be used where the slow process of recording every family and individual, every animal, every acre of land, is not necessary. If the right kinds of samples are taken, representing true cross-sections of a given group or population or area, these figures can be extended (*extrapolated* is the technical term) to give a fairly accurate picture of the whole.

The sampling technique has proved to be so useful (especially where funds for statistics are scarce) that in recent years there has been a rapid growth of interest in applying it all over the world. The services of FAO are in great demand to help government statisticians master the new techniques. The most ambitious project of this kind so far has been the regional sampling demonstration center for the Far East, held in Bangkok during seven months in 1952-53. A handbook on sampling techniques by P. V. Sukhatme has been prepared under the joint sponsorship of FAO, the Iowa State College Press, and the Indian Society of Agricultural Statistics, which has published the volume.

WORK WITH INDIVIDUAL COUNTRIES

Afghanistan

Bounded on the south and east by Pakistan, on the west by Iran, and on the north by the Turkmen, Uzbek, and Tadzhik Republics of the Soviet Union, Afghanistan is a country of unusual strategic importance. The Afghans know it; so do many other people, near and far. On its eastern frontier is the famous Khyber Pass, that narrow gorge winding between high cliffs of shale and limestone which for centuries was the gateway from the north and west to the plains of India, now of Pakistan.

This is how a former leader of the FAO team in Afghanistan, Tuure Pasto (USA), pictured that country:

Afghanistan is a semi-arid land covering about 250,000 square miles. It is dominated by a great central mountain mass running from east to west, splitting the country in half. The plains in the south approach desert conditions, with scant rainfall. The northern plains are characterized to a large extent by deep fertile soils, very productive when water is available.

Communications are extremely difficult, there being no railroads or surface highways. While most goods move in or out of the country by truck, substantial quantities are also moved by camel caravans and donkeys.

Agriculture supports 90 percent of the people. It also provides more than 80 percent of the total value of exports, largely in the form of karakul skins, fruit, cotton, wool, and hides. Nine-tenths of the dollar income comes from karakul skins.

Agricultural practices are primitive. Yields of many crops, notably cotton and sugarbeets, are only a fraction of what they could be per acre. Various diseases and parasites of animals take a heavy annual toll.

A large irrigation development is under way in the southern part of the country in the Helmand River Valley. Difficult and complicated problems are being and will be faced in the settlement of this area and in bringing it into profitable production.

The government is well aware of the urgent need for progress in agriculture, and FAO is playing a part in helping to develop the latent possibilities.

The Country of Karakul

An example is the work with karakul sheep. Afghanistan, South Africa, and the USSR are the world's biggest producers of Persian lamb (karakul) pelts. No country is so dependent as Afghanistan on these luxurious skins for its main support.

Recently there has been trouble. In times of poor grazing or heavy weather or deep snow, countless thousands of karakul sheep perish. In 1951 FAO sent Eugene Bertone, American sheep man from the Rocky Mountains to work with the Afghan sheep men of the Hindu Kush Mountains; and when Bertone's period of service was over, J. E. LeRiche (South Africa) went on with the assignment.

There are three main difficulties: too little feed, too little water, too many pests and diseases.

Bertone organized a karakul co-operative. Among other things it will cut and store fodder in good years for sale to flock owners in bad years. Cottonseed cake, a by-product of the expanding cotton industry, and beet pulp and molasses, by-products from the manufacture of sugar, will be used as sheep feed; they have not been fed before. In 1952-53 the co-operative distributed a million capsules of carbon tetrachloride for control of liver fluke.

The water situation is somewhat like that described by FAO's A. T. Semple in a letter from the USA:

I saw the excellent results of about 20 years of desert range rehabilitation experiments at the US Forest Service Station near Milford, Utah. Sheep men may practically double their income by conservative use of the range and other improved practices such as hauling water to the sheep. That really beats the old way of having them walk so far to water that they were too thirsty to eat when they returned to grazing, and therefore too weak to walk back to water again. So they died.

In a survey being made by the United Nations Technical Assistance Administration for underground water that can be tapped by wells, first priority is being given to the winter karakul range. FAO is helping to improve the grading, packing, and shipping of skins. Two FAO veterinarians are working to clean up sheep pox, liver fluke, lice, ticks, and other pests as part of a broader disease control program which includes rinderpest of cattle and Newcastle disease of poultry. Afghan crews do the vaccinating. LeRiche and FAO's R. V. Razmilic (Chile) and D. A. MacPherson (UK) have prepared a plan for the development of the whole livestock industry of Afghanistan. LeRiche has also outlined a program for better breeding as "the quickest and only sure means of rapid improvement of the average quality of Afghan pelts." He believes a breeding program should be comparatively easy to carry out in Afghanistan because sheep men there have behind them centuries of experience with karakuls. Some of the genetic problems are exceptionally interesting. For instance, Afghanistan is the only country that produces large quantities of gray skins; elsewhere, most of the skins are black. But the gene for gray pelts seems to be sublethal, causing the death of the lambs when inherited in pure (homozygous) form. Only sound scientific research in a breeding station established by the government or by commercial interests can discover the true facts regarding the genetics of this trait.

Farmers Learn New Ways

Producing more cotton, for home use and export, is another prime objective of the Afghanistan Government.

In the spring of 1951 FAO sent W. W. Dickinson (USA) to Kunduz to work on cotton production. Before he left at the end of 1952, he saw fundamental changes well on the way in some of the traditional production methods and tools. For instance, he promptly introduced the planting of irrigated cotton in rows on ridges, and also good timely hoeing with light hoes. These he had made by the local blacksmith to replace the heavy mattocks used in Afghanistan.

Farmers came great distances to see the demonstration plots, and before long a third or more of the cotton growers in the area were using methods Dickinson showed them. The Cotton Company bought tractors and trained operators, and Dickinson set up a cotton-grading and -classing school and started a program to grow a pure variety of cotton instead of the miscellaneous mixtures planted hitherto.

Later in 1951 three experts on small implements went to Afghanistan— Willi Sommerauer (Switzerland), and Wolfgang Faiss and Robert Hartmann (Austria). They traveled over the country by jeep, mostly demonstrating scythes for cutting grain and forage. They showed how a man could do three to five times as much work with a scythe as with the antique sickle. Sometimes every man in a village ordered a scythe after trying one.

The next year Sommerauer came back with about four tons of modern implements of many kinds from many countries, all selected for adaptability to Afghanistan conditions. The demonstrations roused great interest and proved once more that the farmers can take quickly to new tools. At a later date a farm machinery center may be established in Kabul to continue this work.

The government and some commercial concerns were interested also in extending and improving silk culture. In June 1952 FAO sent in a Chinese expert, Kintson Keh (assisted later by Tsong-Kiu Hsia). Climatically, he reported, Afghanistan is better suited to silk culture than Japan or China.

Keh got silkworm eggs by air from Japan. They went through many vicissitudes, some even hatching in the mail bags, but enough survived for a good start. He also set out tens of thousands of mulberry seedlings in nurseries for bud-grafting. The mother trees for supplying the bud-wood have been imported from Japan.

Keh has trained farmers and students in the production of mulberry trees and the rearing and handling of the worms. The latter is exacting work; "I am now training two young men," he noted at one point, "during my rearing of autumn silkworms. They are not so bad, but they are very afraid of getting up to feed the worms at midnight and 3 A.M. every night. I do not force them too much but try to lead them into habit gradually."

Other FAO work in Afghanistan has included improvement of sugarbeet production and use of the by-products, control of plant diseases and pests (with special attention to locusts), seed selection and distribution of improved seeds, improvement of fruit and vegetable production and marketing, dairy and poultry production, and agricultural education and research.

Pakistan

As in tearing apart a piece of cloth, the division of India and Pakistan left raveled ends (including great numbers of starving refugees) which have had to be knit up so that each part could become a whole.

The problems have been difficult, perhaps especially for Pakistan, which had to create a new government and build a corps of civil servants, of whom the larger proportion in the old days were Indians. But if the Pakistanis were short of trained people, they had the energy needed to start making a better-rounded economy.

One of the early steps was to draw on the services of FAO, which has provided experts on problems ranging from top-level planning and the organization of basic agricultural services to the control of diseases of chickens. Probably the most extensive country program FAO has had so far is the one in Pakistan. It has been concerned with farm machinery, including shops for repair and maintenance; refrigerated storage plants; a slaughterhouse in Karachi, where the population jumped from 700,000 to 1,500,000 in a short time; animal diseases and parasites; forests and forest industries; a census of agriculture; statistical services; co-operatives; the fishing industry; and, most important of all, irrigation.

Water for West Pakistan

Geographically, the partition split the old India into three parts. The western provinces became West Pakistan. Thence the new India stretched eastward for a thousand miles, including the western half of Bengal. Then came East Pakistan, which formerly was the eastern half of Bengal. West Pakistan and East Pakistan, separated by the thousand miles of India, are very different in climate, soil, topography, but in each irrigation is the dominant need.

Most of West Pakistan is dry—5 to 15 inches of rain a year. Its water supply comes from one of the world's great river systems, that of the Indus, which rises in the high Himalayas, flows northeastward into Kashmir, then, bending southeastward, twists and turns through Pakistan to the Arabian Sea near Karachi.

In this region during the past few decades some of the world's greatest water-diversion structures and canal systems were built, under British rule, to water an area equal to all the irrigated land in the United States. Part of this system is now in Pakistan, part in India. It was designed to supply enough water to grow one crop of wheat a year (this being formerly the breadbasket of the region), which is about a third of the quantity of water needed for year-round diversified farming.

In its northern reaches the Indus drops rapidly from 26,000 feet above sea level in the Tibet and Kashmir mountains to a few hundred feet in the Punjab plains. From then on, the fall averages only about a foot a mile. Thus the streamflow is very sluggish. The soil, moreover, is the kind that does not drain readily. So the water table gradually rises, the land becomes waterlogged, and alkaline salts accumulate to a point dangerous for crop plants.

The situation has become so bad that in the Punjab alone more than 300,000 acres are ruined for agriculture, and 20-30 thousand go out of production every year. This would be a serious problem anywhere; it is especially so in a region so dependent on irrigation for food.

Experts believe the condition can be corrected, the lost land reclaimed, and further losses prevented by pulling the water table down to a reasonable level and providing adequate drainage thereafter. FAO engineers and soils men, headed by Milo Williams (USA), concluded after a careful study that the best way to get quick results would be to sink tubewells. This would accomplish two objectives at once. The pumps would pull out enough underground water to lower the water table, and at the same time they would add a good deal of supplementary irrigation to the present canal system.

With government officials, Williams and his co-workers drew up plans for three big pilot projects as a starter to demonstrate what could be done and to make possible experimentation with farm management practices, cropping systems, machinery, and so on, adapted to the more intensive cultivation made possible by year-round water supplies—a type of farming new to this area.

One of the pilot projects was to be in the Punjab, one in upper Sind, and one in Khairpur State, each including 10 or 12 thousand acres; a fourth project, smaller, was to be undertaken in the lower Sind area.

The preliminary work in soil surveying and classification, groundwater geology, hydrology, engineering, and the determination of needed equipment was almost completed when the program broke down for lack of enough funds from internal or external sources to put it into effect. The projects in Baluchistan and the Sind had to be shelved, at least for the time being. The best that could be done was to go ahead with the project in the Punjab (the Chuharkana area), covering about 12,000 acres. Of the states in Pakistan, the Punjab has at present the largest economic resources and the most technically trained people. (It should be mentioned here that in both India and Pakistan states' rights are particularly strong.)

The Punjab therefore has decided to go ahead with some 500 wells for which equipment was on hand. Plans call for increasing the number to several thousand during the next few years. Water from the wells is being pumped into the present irrigation channels. The system is working excellently so far and is already increasing production.

This program includes extension work to demonstrate good modern farm practices. The area is adapted to many crops besides wheat, one of them being citrus fruits.

The new system in the Chuharkana district is not large. But water is the life-blood of this country, and the Chuharkana pumps, as one engineer remarked, are like a blood transfusion. Eventually they may lead to much greater development of irrigation from the rivers; vast quantities of river water now go to the sea unused by man.

Subsequently, work was resumed in Baluchistan, where a survey showed good groundwater supplies that can be tapped by wells.

Land of Many Rivers

In East Pakistan, a thousand miles away, the water supply is generous. Rainfall averages over 81 inches a year; in some places it is 255 inches, enough to cover the country with 20 feet of water. Most of this rain, however, falls during the monsoon season, June to September; from December to May there is practically a drought.

The country is cut by two great rivers—Mother Ganges, which flows eastward across India, and the Brahmaputra, which has its source in Tibet to the north. Innumerable smaller streams run into these two, making East Bengal a network of natural waterways, like the lines in the palm of a hand. The country is hot and moist part of the year, hot and dry the other part. It is admirably adapted to rice, but only one main crop can be grown, in the wet season; after that, there is too little moisture (although a small crop is produced in such places as the fringes of swamps).

East Pakistan is one of the world's most densely populated areas. Jute and cotton are the big cash crops. The people have long been subject to terrible famines; yet East Bengal has rich soil which in the lower third of the country is revitalized each year with deposits of silt brought down by the rivers and spread over the land during flood time. For four months this lower part is like a 7-million-acre lake. Here long-stemmed rice is grown. The seed is broadcast about the beginning of May. At the beginning of June the river begins to rise. The rice grows fast enough to keep above the water, which generally rises about 3 inches a day. At the height of the flood, in August, the rice is perhaps 20 feet high. Between August and November, when the rice is maturing, the flood waters gradually recede. At harvest time the people, whose houses are built on mounds raised above water level, come in boats and cut off the rice heads. From then on the water rapidly runs off.

The other two thirds of the cultivated area of East Pakistan comprises some 14 or 15 million acres of higher land. It receives plenty of moisture during the rainy season, little or none thereafter. The main crop is upland rice, which does not require flooding.

FAO engineer W. J. van Blommestein (the Netherlands) made a close study of East Bengal with other members of an FAO group. They concluded that by providing supplementary irrigation during the dry season on the two thirds of the cultivated land that is above flood level, it would be possible to grow two or even three crops a year instead of one. It may not even be necessary in many places to build canals because natural channels, now silted and dry, exist which could be used to carry irrigation water. What would be needed would be diversion works (barrages) and facilities for lifting the water to the natural channels. Such a development would be designed to distribute the flood waters carrying the "red gold," the alluvial silt, widely over the lower plain, supply water during the dry months, drain marshland, improve inland navigation, and control floods by removing surplus water at the end of the monsoon.

In 1953 the Provincial Government decided, in order to get started at once, to begin with a project covering about 200,000 acres in the Kushtia area. This work is now under way, and detailed farm management and soil surveys have been completed by Pakistan and FAO experts. The Canadian Government is providing an electric generating station under the Colombo Plan, and the U. S. Foreign Operations Administration is furnishing a considerable amount of equipment.

The rivers of East Bengal, as van Blommestein notes, are the principal sources of economic well-being of the people. Where they are still active and performing their original functions, the people are healthy and prosperous; but where they are deteriorating because of natural causes or human interference, the areas concerned are also deteriorating. The river problems of Bengal have to be solved if the country is to be saved from reverting to the swamps and jungles from which she was reclaimed.

Iran, Iraq, Syria

Since Iran, Iraq, and Syria are much alike climatically and physically, they have many similar problems in agriculture, forestry, and fisheries.

These countries have a rich cultural history. Iraq, once called Mesopotamia, the land between the rivers Euphrates and Tigris, includes the ancient kingdoms of Babylonia and Assyria, which dominated most of the civilized world. The Old Testament birthplace of man, the Garden of Eden, was in the western part of Iraq. South of Babylonia lay the kingdom of Chaldaea. Phoenicia, a land of restless and able merchant-seamen who established colonies all around the fringes of the Mediterranean, was a part of what is now Syria and Lebanon. Syria was a battleground for many peoples who settled there in successive waves. Aleppo became one of the great medieval trading centers, and the fame of Syrian artisans (Damascus steel, damask cloth) was world wide.

Iran, once called Persia, was a vital influence in Old World religion, philosophy, and art. Zoroastrianism, the Persian religion, had elements—one being the belief in a universal Father God—that later found their way into Judaism and Christianity. This religion had a deep rural undertone. Ahura Mazda, the creator of the universe,

... made the good earth and instructed man to till it. ... Ahura Mazda makes rigid demands of righteousness upon mankind. This righteousness consists of truthfulness, kindness, benevolence, justice, devotion to God, and good works, especially in the field of agriculture where weedless stands of grain are more efficacious in the matter of salvation than are prayers. Here is no place for a hypocrisy which may build a reputation for sanctity on pious words. ... A man's field may be seen! All matters connected with agriculture are given an accented religious importance.

Again and again each of these countries has been under the domination of foreign powers. Now all of them are independent, reaching out toward new ideas and new achievements, eager to apply modern science and technology to the development of their resources.

The dominant features of the three countries agriculturally are a semiarid climate, immense stretches of semidesert and desert land, nomadic herding of sheep and goats and cattle, extensive production of wheat and barley, and dependence on irrigation for intensive cultivation of crops. All three can support more people if water is brought to suitable areas. In all three of these countries, old systems of land tenure, rooted in part in a nomad society, inhibit increased production and better standards of living; hence there is a growing interest in improving land tenure. All three are carrying out plans for agricultural development which include land settlement ("homesteading"). The present evolution toward settled agriculture implies difficult changes in the ways of life of wandering pastoral people who have never cared to stay in one uninteresting place or punch the timeclock of farm chores.

In Iran and Iraq the USA has had bilateral technical co-operation programs involving far larger outlays than those of FAO; hence in these two countries FAO plays a relatively small though vital part in current agricultural development.

Syria does not at present have any USA technical assistance projects but draws fairly heavily on the co-operation of FAO. The Syrian Government also directly employs outside experts, mainly from other countries in the Near East. Early in 1954 the International Bank sent a mission to that country, including an agricultural expert provided by FAO, to prepare a five-year economic development program. In 1953 Carroll Deyoe (USA), head of the FAO mission in Syria, noted

... the rapidly increasing number of trained agriculturists returning to Syria and being absorbed by the Ministry of Agriculture. When I came to this country in January 1951 there were very few officials in the Ministry with degrees in agriculture. During the past two years at least 15 men have returned with Bachelor's or Master's degrees. Also a number of men trained under FAO fellowships are now back and working in fields related to their training. There are now in Syria nationals specialized in veterinary science, animal husbandry, agricultural statistics, geology, horticulture, agronomy, cotton culture, forage crops, locust control, forestry, soils, etc. This is resulting in a much improved atmosphere for technical and advisory assistance.

The same kind of thing is occurring throughout the region.

Animals in the Foreground

Livestock projects are an important part of the technical co-operation requested from FAO in these three countries.

In Iran there are some 29 million sheep and goats and 4 million cattle grazing on range which is so overstocked that losses from starvation, as well as disease, are heavy. Prime needs are controlled grazing, seeding with high-yielding grasses and other forage plants, development of irrigated pastures, and production of hay or ensilage to supplement range grass. FAO range management specialist J. A. B. MacArthur (Canada) worked for about two years in Iran on these problems.

In Syria the chief of the mission is a grazing land expert. Deyoe reports that in the past two years there had been a decided change in the attention given to livestock in the Syrian agricultural program as compared with the early days when the stress was entirely on cash and food crops. There is now a growing interest in crop rotations that include forage, and in irrigation of pasture land. Some of Deyoe's experimental plantings of grazing and forage plants have shown great promise. He demonstrated the first silo in Syria, a trench filled with greenstuff, packed down and covered with earth. Storage of feed reserves in the semidesert grazing area is an important part of these experiments.

In all three countries FAO is working with the governments on livestock diseases, helping to train veterinarians and get laboratories started for diagnosis and the making of vaccines and also to organize field services.

In Iran, FAO's R. L. Jorgensen (Denmark) helped to establish a modern milk plant and worked on other aspects of dairy improvement with assistance from the Children's Fund. This is a matter of some importance in reducing infant mortality. The government also obtained the services of FAO expert N. J. J. Houthuis (the Netherlands) to modernize slaughterhouses and meat inspection. (In the Near East and Far East conditions in slaughterhouses are often like those in the USA before the days of sanitary modern packing plants.)

Water Wizards

Iran, Iraq, and Syria have had centuries of experience with irrigation. It would be hard to surpass the engineering feats they have performed to get water, sometimes brought from distant mountains to the plains in long underground conduits or raised from the river by enormous waterwheels such as one sees at Hama in Syria, shrouded in wind-blown mist, eternally wailing a skreeky ear-piercing song.

In spite of this long empirical experience there is a dearth of scientific knowledge of geology and hydrology, the exact nature and needs of different soils, and the most economical and effective use of water in farming operations. Hence soil surveys, geological studies, and irrigation engineering have a high place in the work of technical co-operation.

Since irrigation has been rather fully discussed in connection with the FAO program in Pakistan, I shall not give details of the fruitful work in Iran, Iraq, and Syria. It should be noted, however, that irrigation is not the whole story of water in this parched area. Pure water for villages and watering places for animals in semidesert grazing lands are vitally important in helping people to make better use of the resources of a difficult land. During the summer grazing season, for example, a good well at the right spot can provide for perhaps 200 human beings, 200 camels, and 1000 sheep long enough to utilize the grass in a given area without being compelled by thirst to move on.

The author of this book has a vivid memory of Irish geologist David Burdon starting on an expedition into the desert in a battered jeep: a stringy enthusiastic man, dressed in sweated khaki shorts and shirt, wearing a battered hat and dusty desert boots, and draped with assorted objects hanging from his shoulders and stuck in his belt—water canteen, knapsack, altimeters, field glasses, geologist's hammer, camera—headed for the land where the Bedouins roam to live for weeks in the black goat's-hair tents, eat the Bedouins' food, share their life, and enable them, through the wizardry of science, to share the great blessing of water.

Better Crops

Much work is being done in these countries with crops.

In Syria cotton yields are high and production has been spreading rapidly in recent years. FAO entomologist A. E. M. Mistikawy (Egypt) has been working there on the control of insects, particularly the cotton bollworm and pink bollworm, which do much damage. Another entomologist, L. W. D. Caudri (the Netherlands), has been helping the government to develop a sound plant protection service for insects and diseases.

In Iran the government is getting help from FAO in the breeding of wheat and barley (partly in connection with the Near East regional co-operative program) and cotton, in the control of plant diseases, and in tea production and processing. Iraq also is increasingly interested in cotton production, which in fact is becoming more important throughout much of the Near East. FAO work in Iraq has been concerned with control of the spotted bollworm. J. L. Allison (USA) also worked on various plant disease problems, including those of wheat and dates.

Iraq is the world's greatest date exporter, and the hot country around Basra in the south is covered with palms rising like majestic columns in a vast green temple. The expert producers of this country wanted help in putting the processing of their dates on an equally high level. F. H. Winter (USA) has worked with them on modernizing and mechanizing the industry.

Growth of Research, Extension, Co-operatives

In some places in the dusty plains you go off the main highway and down a side road and suddenly come upon an agricultural experiment station—a neat new brick building, or two or three buildings, surrounded by flower-beds and shrubbery, and set in the midst of squared and numbered experimental plots. Here a group of eager young scientists will be growing cotton and other plants under controlled conditions. After seeing the field work, you sit down with them in a room perhaps cooled by the first air-conditioner (a good one—water dripping over camel thorn twigs packed between two layers of chicken wire set in a window), and you sip little cups of thick dark coffee while they talk eagerly about what they are doing and plan to do.

In Iraq, where large sums from oil production are used for economic development, expansion of agricultural research was started under the direction of Darwish Haidari Bey, Texas-educated, former Director-General of Agriculture. FAO has had W. V. Lambert, dean of agriculture in Nebraska and head of its experiment station, and Kenneth Kopf of Iowa State College in Iraq to help plan and organize the research setup. The government also established an extension service with help from FAO's H. C. Robinson (USA) and from experts of the US bilateral mission. Twenty-one main agricultural areas now have Iraqi extension leaders. Following the disastrous flood of 1954, Iraq obtained help from FAO in carrying out an integrated rehabilitation program for farms and communities.

Experiment stations and demonstration farms in Syria and extension work in Iran have also been included in the FAO programs.

Better agricultural credit arrangements which will enable small-scale farmers to get loans without becoming slaves to moneylenders are needed in all these countries. Iran and Syria are both putting more emphasis on the role of co-operative societies in the agricultural credit system. In Iraq FAO expert E. F. G. Haig (UK), who spent many years building up a co-operative system in Nigeria, has helped to reorganize some of the present societies and to establish new ones in connection with the government's extensive land settlement program. To break with tradition is by no means easy, even though the farmers know they are paying a cruel price for loans. Often, too, people with the right background to manage co-operative societies are hard to find. As Haig put it:

The work is unlike that of most other government servants. A co-operative superintendent in a rural area, if he does his work properly, must not only have a good knowledge of co-operative principles, the co-operative law, the working methods of different types of societies, and accounting; he must also live an arduous life. He has to travel frequently in all weathers, often on bad roads, sometimes by bicycle or on foot. He has to put up with poor accommodations. He must show an inexhaustible patience and courtesy in his dealings with simple and mainly illiterate people. He must have sound judgment and practical good sense to unravel human and economic problems. Lastly, as he is dealing constantly with matters of finance among uneducated people and is exposed to corresponding temptations, he must be a man of high personal integrity. To fulfill these duties successfully, men of an unusually good type are required.

Meanwhile co-operatives are now being established in various settlements where conditions are sometimes like those of the homesteading days in the western part of the USA. For instance, at one of the first meetings to organize a co-operative, the desert nomads arrived with loaded rifles and daggers, just as cattlemen might have come equipped with six-shooters in the old West. The belligerent appearance of the nomads, like that of the cattlemen, completely belied their genuine friendliness.

Machines, Figures, Forests, Fish

There is a rapidly growing use of farm machinery. A good deal of the extensive farming in the Jezireh or plains areas in each country is being done with tractors. In Iraq, three FAO specialists (H. R. Hare and R. L. Buck [Canada] and A. T. Petersen [USA]) have been helping with various aspects of mechanization and farm management.

Agricultural statistics are getting a good deal of attention; Iran, Iraq, and Syria have all been using FAO statisticians. The three countries are also getting help in forestry.

In Iran more forest is left standing than in any other Near East country; forests cover nearly 47 million acres, about an eighth of the total land area. The young seedling trees are often destroyed by grazing animals; hence adequate control of grazing is urgently needed. Such operations as sawmilling and the seasoning and impregnation of wood are also more important in Iran than elsewhere in the region. With its forestry problems the government has had help from FAO. Edmond Uhart (France) developed methods that greatly reduce the waste in charcoal-making, and later helped the government to formulate forest policy and law. Vittorio Carocci Buzi (Italy) was adviser on forest grazing, with a view to developing sound management methods. W. W. Varossieau (the Netherlands) set up a laboratory and training center for wood technology.

In Iraq FAO experts Ernesto Allegri (Italy) and L. D. Pryor (UK) have been working on the planting and management of poplar and eucalyptus trees, two of the best species for this region because of their many uses and rapid growth. In Syria FAO forester M. van Bottenburg (the Netherlands) is advising on forest policy, legislation, and the organization of the forest service. His efforts are concentrated particularly on the Latakia forest, one of the last remnants of the older forests of this region. In this northwest part of Syria the visitor sees a stubbly growth of evergreens sprouting like a new beard on hills that have long been as bare as a shaven chin.

There is much interest in expanding fisheries, and Iran and Iraq have both started work with FAO co-operation.

Nutrition and Home Economics

Syria and Iraq have had the services of FAO nutrition workers and home economists. Home economics has only recently begun to get the attention it deserves even in the better-developed countries. The time has not yet come when the governments of countries on the way to greater development are ready for full-scale work in this field. The fact that a demand for this kind of technical co-operation exists in the Near East and Far East may be significant of a new trend. A few decades or years ago this would probably have been regarded as an unthinkable invasion of the realm of women.

Ava B. Milam, dean emeritus of the School of Home Economics at Oregon State College, USA, was sent to Syria by FAO early in 1951 to help develop a program of education in home economics and to work with rural organizations on homemaking programs. She had previously had extensive experience in both the Near East and the Far East.

In Syria, as elsewhere, are wealthy homes, the homes of a growing group of middle-class people who live in city apartments and houses, and the far more numerous homes of the poor—mud villages, beehive huts of clay, Bedouin and gypsy tents, flimsy shelters of matting, crude stone huts of marshland dwellers—often practically without comforts or even furnishings and pre-Biblical in their primitive simplicity. The people in this last group of homes are the ones who will most need help in improving their living conditions as agriculture develops.

Dean Milam worked with teachers who had no formal training in home economics, no textbooks, no government pamphlets, but who were gallantly conducting classes to the best of their ability in elementary and secondary schools in the principal cities. One of her first steps was to get them together for a training course for which 98 students showed up instead of the expected 70.

Subsequently she made a study of home economics education in the Syrian schools and recommended improvements. She also recommended that a Department of Home Economics be established in the Syrian University where women could be trained for work in adult education, home demonstration, and hospital dietetics.

From Syria Dean Milam went to Iraq for five months to help the Queen Aliya College for Women in Baghdad organize a Department of Home Economics and to advise on home economics education in government schools. She emphasized the need to give more attention in elementary schools (since most girls marry soon after finishing their elementary education) to such subjects as planning meals, preparing food, making and caring for clothing, family relations, and child development.

Later FAO sent home economist Jessie Brodie (Canada) to Baghdad. She helped to equip the new laboratory in Queen Aliya College and get teaching started. Some time before this the efforts of FAO nutrition expert Hugues Gounelle (France) were successful in initiating the organization of a national nutrition committee and also in establishing a department of nutrition at the Faculty of Medicine in Baghdad.

Jordan

Jordan has so far called on FAO for only a little technical co-operation. • Early in 1951 economist L. D. Schweng (Hungary) went to that country and stayed for about a year making a survey which covered agriculture, forestry, and fisheries; basic government services relating to land use, agricultural co-operatives, and land tenure; and agricultural administration, including extension work and other services. • Agricultural economist C. H. Maliepaard (the Netherlands) went to Jordan in mid-December 1952 as consultant on economic policy. • FAO geologist David J. Burdon (Ireland) in 1952 made a preliminary investigation of the Yarmouk River Valley, where the government is planning a large-scale development project, including a dam which will impound water for irrigation and other uses. • A fisheries expert made a survey of fish-culture possibilities. • Experts on range management and on agricultural statistics went to Jordan for brief periods.

Saudi Arabia

Head in Fire, Feet in Water

Saudi Arabia, like Iraq, uses funds from petroleum concessions to some extent to finance economic development. Dates, next to petroleum, are the most important product. They take the place of bread as the staple food of many people and are also an important feed for livestock; every donkey in Saudi Arabia, it has been estimated, eats at least half a ton of dates a year. This remarkable tree, which according to the old Arab saying must have its head in fire and its feet in water, also provides sugar, alcohol, timber for building, leaf-thatch for houses, and fuel.

The date industry in Saudi Arabia has had trouble in recent years. Prices have fallen, sales have shrunk. Partly, this trouble is the result of a trend toward diversified agriculture, with grains replacing dates as the staple food, and toward greater use of machines which require petroleum rather than dates for fuel.

With this shift in internal markets, the possibility of exporting more dates is a matter of some importance.

But Saudi Arabians, unaccustomed to considering dates as an export product, do not handle and package the fruit in ways conducive to acceptance in foreign markets, where consumers demand high quality because dates are a luxury, not a necessity as in Saudi Arabia. Also, production as well as marketing can be improved in spite of the fact that dates have been grown in Saudi Arabia for thousands of years.

Two of the group FAO has sent to that country have been concerned with dates—Abdul-Jabbar El-Bekr (Iraq), production expert, and T. C. Carlson (USA), consultant on processing and marketing.

El-Bekr's work resulted in recommendations for improvements in irrigation, drainage, malaria control, use of fertilizers, methods of propagation, selection of varieties, and research in horticulture, insect and disease control, chemistry, and so on. He also came to the conclusion that Saudi Arabia could develop a date-export business, based on choice fruit, handled by modern methods.

Following these recommendations, the government asked for a processing and packaging expert, and FAO sent Carlson, who started processing and marketing experiments.

Carlson knew that the pilgrims who go in great numbers every year to Mecca, the birthplace of Mohammed, and Medina, where the Prophet is buried, like to buy a characteristic product (why not dates?) in these holy places which every Mohammedan aspires to visit at least once in his lifetime. To develop this special trade fully, it would be necessary to do things not done in 3000 years of date production in Saudi Arabia—sterilize the fruit, clean it with great care, control the moisture content, pack it by machinery in attractive souvenir packages.

A year or so after Carlson arrived he succeeded, in spite of frustrations and difficulties, in doing what he had in mind. He had rounded up electrical equipment in Europe and processing machinery in the USA, where he also had cardboard packages designed and printed. The first machinery, simple enough to be operated by inexperienced workers, washed, dried, and packaged 5 tons of dates a day. It was set up in an unfinished garage back of the Department of Agriculture in Jedda; Carlson did not want to go in for a big plant until there was some assurance of a profitable market. (Later, when this plant got into operation, it was moved to Medina, where Carlson, a non-Moslem, could not go.) In addition to the pilgrim trade, he also explored potential markets abroad in a preliminary way.

This project is doing well. In addition to the plant now at Medina, Carlson has helped to establish a date-processing and export business in the city of Hofuf.

Desert Dawn

Saudi Arabia is a land of extremes. As a visitor once remarked, on one side is a sea of water, on the other a sea of sand. East coast summer temperatures occasionally run as high as 130 degrees in the shade, which, with humidity at 90 per cent, makes the weather steamy. ("Drinking water kept in my tent is hotter than the skin can bear," an FAO engineer noted. "On a bad day the color of the sandstorm is that of cocoa cooked without milk, and visibility is under six feet.") The cool season is delightful, and someone once compared the climate of Jedda, on the west coast, with that of the French Riviera.

Half of Saudi Arabia is sand. Parts of the vast desert are unexplored, parts traversed only by camel trails.

Vegetation is poor over most of the semidesert pasture land—in some places unpalatable weeds and camel thorn, a rough, tough plant reputedly relished by that hardy beast but scarcely edible by any other. Three fourths of the people are Bedouin nomads whose camels, sheep, and goats are the backbone of the country's agriculture. Only a small part of the land is arable, and half of that is in fallow for lack of water. Half the arable land could be irrigated. The present irrigated areas are mostly along the Persian Gulf and the Red Sea. In the latter area they follow the wadis, streambeds which contain water only in times of flood. In the east irrigation is from wells. In the irrigated areas the people have been settled farmers—good farmers—for thousands of years. ("The desert is not an unfertile region," Lord Samuel once remarked. "It is only asleep.")

Oil now brings Saudi Arabia as much income as all other products put together. But much of the food for the cities and almost all the manufactured goods are imported.

The one large modern farm is the El-Kharj project near Kafa Daghara —1800 acres owned by the former Crown Prince (now the King) and operated at his request by the American Arabian Oil Company. The work done on this farm is stimulating much interest in agricultural development, and in research and extension. Six extension centers are now operating and five others are planned. A new dawn is breaking over the desert.

Following an FAO survey made in 1950, the government obtained a fairly large group of experts. The program that has since developed has several objectives.

The first is to extend irrigation and also make better use of present irrigation systems, for which the water comes down from the hills in flash floods in the rainy season. Such a flood can pile water 40 feet high, tearing away extensive earth banks used to divert the flow and sometimes wiping out whole villages. More often, there is not enough water, even in floods, to supply the entire system. A great deal of it percolates underground and escapes to the ocean.

FAO has begun with the most promising area, the Asir Tihama, in the south along the Red Sea. There, engineering surveys show excellent prospects for constructing dams to hold water, and also for storage under the plain itself, to be tapped by wells and pumps.

In the beginning the work will be concentrated on the Wadi Jizan. Here is a fairly dense population of industrious farmers who have built thousands of miles of earth banks for irrigation. More irrigation development and better use of the water will make it possible to increase production of present crops and add others—cotton and citrus fruits, for example.

For permanent results, such a development must eventually be managed and operated by Saudi Arabians. This means that they must have technical training, which in turn means a school system, a college, experiment stations. These are fundamental, and FAO is now helping to set up the first agricultural institute.

The government is also working on large irrigation projects on the east side of the country, to make use of water that goes underground from the Tuwaiq Mountains to the Persian Gulf. The projects involve hydroelectric plants for light and power, modern sewage systems, communications, warehouses, schools, hospitals. In connection with these tremendously significant developments Saudi Arabia is using FAO to help provide co-ordinated planning.

One of the interesting elements in this program is the extension training project near Jedda in charge of FAO's N. A. Lateef (USA). In addition to conducting a training course for extension workers, Lateef is single-handedly carrying out an extension program in 37 villages. He makes all-day visits to each community and talks to the individual farmers. Often all the men turn out at the headman's thatched hut or under the *nebaq* tree, Arabian equivalent of the New England village elm. Schoolteachers, leading farmers, elders tell about their local problems, difficulties, aspirations, and Lateef helps them make farm programs suited to their needs, including new crops adaptable to the area, sidelines such as bees and poultry, modern hand tools, and insect and disease control.

There is also considerable interest in doing more with fisheries, at present confined to waters close to shore, and conducted with small boats and hand nets. An exploration made in 1952-53 by FAO shows that there are untapped resources farther out to sea. As a result the government is starting a fishing company capitalized at more than £1,000,000 sterling, which will have powered vessels and ice plants.

A leader of the FAO group, W. Fred Johnson (USA), once remarked: "Our mission is truly international in composition. The 14 members represent 14 nationalities. We assist a fifteenth country, Saudi Arabia. Among

NEAR EAST AND AFRICA

us we speak, read, and write 10 languages, and most of them are used in the mission at some time. No better example of cooperation for peaceful and beneficial purposes could be offered." This is typical of more places than Saudi Arabia. So is the attitude of the Saudi Arabians, about which another FAO group leader, C. L. van der Plas, had this to say: "The kindness and courtesy we have received, and the keenness and capability of officials and farmers, were most heartening. At the same time they are healthily critical."

Israel

The recent settlement in Israel of immigrants from nearly 75 countries has brought many professional people to that land. Some fields are represented by world-famous scientists. In others there is a shortage of well-trained professional workers. FAO has tried to confine its aid to the kind of expertness of which the country does not yet have a large enough supply.

Priority for Soil Conservation

Israel's soil resources are so limited that the country has a special need to use them well, particularly since the population has doubled in four years, and new arrivals continue to pour in.

There is a shortage of trained people for work in soil and water conservation. Every two weeks the Jewish Agency has been locating three new settlements, each with 100 families. At this writing there was a backlog of applications from more than 200 of these settlements for help in classifying land and starting conservation measures. It would take the small Israeli staff 50 years to catch up with this work.

For some time FAO had world-famous conservationist Walter G. Lowdermilk (USA) in Israel, with three other USA experts (R. S. Murphy, W. H. Bender, D. W. Klauss) in fields connected with conservation.

Among other things, they have been introducing contour farming so that flood waters can sink into the ground or follow safe channels instead of tearing up the land. In 1951, for instance, a great storm did damage amounting to some £3,000,000 Israeli, washing away good topsoil and causing floods that drove many people from their homes. In a dry land like Israel such a rainstorm should be a blessing, not a calamity, and would be if there were adequate provisions for water holding. Lowdermilk thinks Israel has a unique opportunity, not generally open to older countries with set patterns of fragmented holdings, to change over from the traditional straight-line to contour farming. The land is held in trust and leased to farmers at a nominal rental. It should be possible to adjust the layout of large areas to contour farming and good storm-water disposal systems.

The FAO group working with Lowdermilk has been helping to set up a pilot project which is in charge of the Israel Soil Conservation Service. This project will serve as a demonstration center in the northern part of the

Negev. It includes about 25,000 acres, and here some 19 government people who have been taking an in-service training course at Midrisha (which proved to be so good that Cyprus sent 10 participants in 1954) have built diversion terraces, channels, grassed waterways, and dams to impound runoff, and have filled gullies, reseeded grasslands, and planted woodlots. (Bender, who set up the course, got amoebic dysentery and had to leave. Klauss came down with poliomyelitis.)

The Soil Conservation Service is training not only its own field staff but also one man in each settlement in the country, so that there will be a nationwide conservation corps.

Meanwhile an inventory of the land resources is under way as part of the broad program of soil classification, soil management, and land use. With the help of FAO's P. W. Manson (USA), the Haifa Institute of Technology has set up a Department of Agricultural Engineering which is also tied in with this program.

Long-term Livestock Program

FAO has given Israel a good deal of help in connection with livestock production.

Dairy cattle are the mainstay of the livestock industry in Israel. Some sheep are being imported. Irrigated pastures and fodder crops are being developed to supplement the range, especially in the dry season (May to December). FAO range expert Wayne Miles (USA) has been reseeding pastures and setting up a seed nursery. Samuel Lepkovsky (USA) has been studying Israel's needs for milk, meat, and eggs against her capacity to produce these foods. This study led to a survey of the agricultural research setup. Lepkovsky has recommended a long-term program, now getting under way, which includes a network of experiment stations to develop necessary information.

In assessing the possibilities for producing forage, he concluded that the carob tree, also called St. John's bread, is a valuable potential source of animal feed in Israel. This is an evergreen that produces a large quantity of pods filled with sweetish pulp of good nutritive value.

The Next Phase

FAO mission chief A. G. Black (USA) has helped the government with general agricultural planning and agricultural economics problems.

He notes that Israel is on the whole a land of small farms, about 7 acres apiece. They are not big enough for efficient production of grain, and large quantities of cereals (and other staple foods) must be imported. Agriculture has been thought of as a means of getting homes for people—each little farm having a cow, chickens, a vegetable garden, perhaps some fruit—rather than as the source of the nation's food.

Farmers are making unusually good incomes from these small plots, but it is likely that they will soon be producing more vegetables than the country can use. These products cannot well be exported fresh, nor can they be processed under present conditions.

There is already a considerable loss of food between the farm and the table. FAO dairy expert Aage Jepsen (Denmark), for example, estimated that at least 30 per cent of the milk produced on farms was unfit for food before it reached the consumer; he has been working with the government to improve sanitation and quality control of animal products. E. L. Crossley (UK) drew up plans for a dairy training institute for technicians which is being financed by the USA and for which FAO is providing part of the equipment.

Black came to the conclusion that in the next phase of its development Israel will need to pay much more attention to the handling and marketing of foods; to production to meet the country's food needs, including price policies, production incentives, farm credit; to practical arrangements for growing grain on considerably larger areas of land; to commodities for export, particularly fruits and possibly also processed foods; and to the whole business of marketing.

FAO fisheries experts George Napier (USA) and A. E. Hofstede (the Netherlands) have worked in Israel on the improvement of boats, craft, and gear, and on inland fisheries; forestry expert D. Roy Cameron (Canada), on forest policy; home economist Elda Robb (USA), on the setting up and equipping of a School of Home Economics at the Institute for Education in Jerusalem.

Egypt

The Cairo office of the Food and Agriculture Organization handles FAO affairs for the Near East, with M. T. Hefnawy as Regional Representative. Egypt is participating fully in the regional work, but so far FAO has had little opportunity to provide technical co-operation within that country. Recently, however, the government has requested a number of projects on which work is beginning. As this is written, six FAO technical experts are in Egypt: C. L. Pan (China), rice production; Oliver S. Mabee (Canada), general agriculture; S. T. Farouky (Jordan), extension work; Mona Khoury-Schmitz (Lebanon) and Grace K. Nadig and Mary Ross (USA), home economics.

Rice, the Bright Pearl

Pan finds promising possibilities for improving rice production. The chief handicap in Egypt is lack of enough water to increase the rice acreage or to use water generously in shortage years. Pan has approached this problem mainly from the standpoint of using water more economically.

When rice is grown under flood conditions, as it is in Egypt, the seed is planted in nursery plots and later the seedlings are transplanted to the field.

Pan found that Egyptian farmers may be inclined to use too much water in the nursery beds. He took four experimental nursery plots and tried handling them in four different ways: plot 1, kept flooded continuously, the usual Egyptian practice; plot 2, flooded for 15 days, thereafter merely kept moist; plot 3, kept continuously moist without any flooding; plot 4, kept moist for 15 days, then kept flooded.

Plot 3, with no flooding, produced twice as many seedlings as plot 1, which was flooded continuously and required 10 times as much water; and the seedlings in plot 3 were bigger than those in any other plot. Too much water may actually inhibit germination and early growth. In Egypt an acre of nursery provides enough plants to set out 5 to 8 acres in the field. In Japan and China 1 nursery acre supplies plants for 15 to 20 field acres. The difference may be owing in part to the use of excessive amounts of water in the nurseries in Egypt.

Another way to cut water use would be to select or breed rice tolerant to dry conditions. Pan is working on this also, getting breeding material from many countries. These experiments include breeding for other characteristics, such as large seed.

The excellent breeding work that has been carried on by the Egyptian Government in recent years shows among other things that a given rice variety may produce three times as much in one location as in another. Examination of these results seems to indicate that rice is more productive in the south than in the north. It would save water to use the limited supply in areas where productivity is highest.

In another approach to the problem, Pan is experimenting with upland rice grown before floodtime. As no upland rice is produced in Egypt, this is a new venture. At the opposite extreme, he plans to experiment with floating rice in the extensive irrigation and drainage ditches.

Pan came to the conclusion that "if cotton is the white gold of Egypt, rice is the bright pearl." Analyzing comparative yields, he found that it compares very favorably with either corn or wheat in food production and that the net profit per acre at domestic prices is much greater than that from cotton.

A third of the cultivated land in Egypt cannot be used in summer for lack of water. About a thousand artesian wells are now operating. Some experts estimate that a large supply of underground water exists throughout most of the Delta in the north—much more, perhaps, than the amount held by the Aswan Dam—which could be used by sinking wells to augment the supply from the Nile. Pan figured that if 500 wells were drilled as an experimental beginning, they would provide enough water to irrigate about 100,000 acres and that if this area were planted in rice, the cost of the project could be rather quickly recovered. He also proposed stocking the rice fields with fish during floodtime, as in the Far East, to increase their yield of food.

An Arab States Program

In an earlier chapter I mentioned the government's village improvement program, which takes in agriculture, nutrition, health, living conditions, with a number of villages serving as demonstration centers. That this work can have a good deal of significance for other countries is recognized in the establishment of an Arab States Fundamental Education Center at Sirs-al-Layyan in which UNESCO, FAO, WHO, ILO, the United Nations, and the Egyptian Government are co-operating.

Here Farouky's extension training program for rural leaders in agriculture in the Arab states includes students from Egypt, Iraq, Jordan, Lebanon, Saudi Arabia, and Syria. The center is attempting to work out techniques for extension work especially suited to this region. At the start, the aim is the practical one of increasing farm incomes in the immediate neighborhood; hence much attention is given to such sidelines for the fellaheen as the better production of eggs, milk, and honey. All the improved equipment is made from local materials. If the million hens in this area would each lay only four more eggs a year, Farouky remarks, that would be 4 million more eggs to sell. But he adds, regarding this kind of work in general, in other countries besides Egypt:

I have noticed that most distribution stations interest themselves in the number of seedlings they distribute and the number of baby chicks they give to farmers. But no one follows with any interest what happens to this material. It is more important to distribute 500 citrus seedlings and keep in constant touch with the farmers to teach them how the trees should be irrigated, fertilized, and so on than to distribute 20,000 seedlings and stop at that.

At this center, also, Grace Nadig has been working on home economics. Mona Khoury-Schmitz, Mary Ross, and Oliver S. Mabee are now stationed at the Sindibis center.

Surplus Milk

In the summer of 1954 FAO sent an unusual mission to Egypt, at the government's request, to study the possible use of considerable quantities of dried skim milk in that country. The study grew out of a proposal for importing the milk powder (and possibly other dairy products) from the USA, as a result of the surplus commodity disposal program in that country. Earlier, the FAO Committee on Commodity Problems had expressed some concern over the possible harmful effects of large-scale disposal of imported dried skim milk on the development of the dairy industry of the importing country; it might provide a kind of competition which would be highly discouraging to greater milk production at home.

The mission, headed by M. J. Dols (the Netherlands), made a careful survey of the situation, with the help of a committee made up of representatives of all the appropriate Egyptian ministries. Its conclusions showed that with the proper precautions very sizable amounts of skim milk powder can be usefully distributed in Egypt through specific outlets without discouraging expanded local production; on the contrary, the plan could be used to the advantage of producers by stimulating consumer demand for milk. The report also analyzed the difficulties of the current dairy production and market situation in Egypt and the steps needed for sound and successful expansion.

This was a small and inconspicuous project, but it deserves special attention as an example, useful to both exporting and importing countries, of an intelligent approach to the problem, often an acute one, of disposing of a surplus product with benefit to the producers as well as the consumers of the receiving country.

Ethiopia

Of legendary King Prester John it was said that there were "no poor in his dominion, no thief or robber, no flatterer or miser, no dissensions, no lies, and no vices." He had a mirror which showed him everything that went on in his dominions; he was waited on by 7 kings, 60 dukes, 365 counts; he ruled over a fabulous country called Ethiopia, which was supposed to extend from Africa through India.

Such legends are understandable when you realize how difficult it was, until the age of airplanes, for outsiders to get into this isolated mountainous country and bring back accurate reports. The proud sovereign land of Ethiopia was unconquered until Mussolini's invasion—a conquest not long-lived.

This is one of the most beautiful of countries and one with exceptionally rich agricultural possibilities. Thinly populated, it is suitable for growing almost anything from coffee and pineapples to temperate-zone crops. There are deserts where camels provide transport, grassy plains grazed by great herds of cattle, humid river valleys where hippopotamuses yawn and lions rumble, plateaus where the Blue Nile and other streams are born, in surroundings of breathtaking loveliness. The plateau country inevitably reminds visitors from the USA of the mountains of the West; but in place of ranch houses are little round *tukuls,* thatched huts made of mud, clustered in small groups under graceful eucalyptus trees. The individualism of the people and their eagerness to learn also remind visitors from the United States of the United States.

Emperor Haile Selassie is keenly aware of the great production potentials of his country and wants to see them used for the benefit of Ethiopia and of other less generously endowed lands in this region. There is a vast amount to be done, but beginnings are everywhere being made. Ethiopia obtained the help of FAO in formulating its agricultural program, and it has been getting FAO help also in carrying out various parts of the program.

Virus Bondage

Here, cattle are a traditional form of wealth, regarded as an investment, like savings deposits, rather than as commodities for sale. Yet Ethiopia could supply considerable amounts of meat and livestock to near-by countries if rinderpest could be wiped out so that quarantines might be lifted. Livestock constitute one of Ethiopia's most important economic assets, but the rinderpest virus has blocked full use of this wealth.

One of the first things FAO undertook after inheriting the UNRRA work in Ethiopia was to develop a program for rinderpest control. This program began in 1947. The work was slow at first because laboratory and other services had to be set up. Now it is in full swing, and teams of trained Ethiopian vaccinators are working under the direction of a few FAO veterinarians, who travel by jeep to remote areas over primitive roads and cattle trails, sometimes under conditions involving a good deal of hardship. FAO veterinarian Nels Konnerup (USA), for instance, was sleeping on the ground under his jeep as the only way to keep dry in torrential rains (the canvas top being in rags) when he woke up one night gazing into the eyes of an unpleasantly close unlaughing hyena. This beast has been known (so it is said) to devour a sleeping man so thoroughly that not even bones were left, only indigestible clothing. Konnerup's startled yell startled the hyena, which ran away, and from then on he (Konnerup) slept inside the car. Better wet, he thought, than et.

In this rinderpest campaign the government is co-operating fully, and the veterinarians seem to have gained the confidence of livestock owners, who in the beginning, naturally, were suspicious and even hostile, like cattlemen in the USA in the early days when government veterinarians first came snooping around during disease epidemics. In the four years through 1953, about 3 million head of cattle were vaccinated, and rinderpest is on its way to being cleaned out of Ethiopia. Work has now started on other serious diseases, in particular pleuropneumonia, anthrax, and blackleg.

Hides and skins are a big export, but methods of handling and preparing them are primitive; often they are so badly damaged or so inferior that they bring low prices. FAO has been carrying on an active program to help the Ethiopians produce hides of better quality. This would bring immediate cash returns. So simple a change as using a blunt instead of a pointed flaying knife brought a marked reduction in the number of cuts in hides. Said FAO's C. M. Anderson (UK): "The skins of Ethiopia's Bati goats and Salale sheep rank among the highest-priced in the world. There is no reason why Ethiopian hides, properly prepared, should not have a similar proud place on the world market."

Wild and Tame Coffee

Coffee grows wild in very few places in the world. Ethiopia is one of them. Some botanists believe coffee first originated in that country; if so, this area should be a good source of breeding material for use elsewhere, including trees resistant to coffee diseases.

Coffee makes up about half of Ethiopia's exports. Here again is a product that could bring greatly increased returns if production and processing were improved.

Early in 1952 FAO sent coffee expert Pierre Sylvain (Haiti) to Ethiopia. Large areas, he found, are suitable for production. A considerable part of the crop comes from coffee forests, which may possibly not be true forests but old neglected plantations. Present plantations, sometimes extensive, are, in general, not too well cared for.

Sylvain found a number of types of coffee with different taste characteristics that might be the result of differences in genetic constitution or environment or method of preparation. Diseases and pests are not very troublesome. For the most part yields are low, and the quality of the product is poor because of the methods of processing. Government regulations for cleaning and grading have not yet overcome these difficulties. Sylvain personally processed samples of Ethiopian coffee and sent them to the Kenya Coffee Board for tests. They proved to be as good as the average Kenya types, which are among the world's best.

Sylvain has proposed the setting up of a coffee organization, including representatives from the industry and from government agencies, to coordinate all aspects of production, processing, and marketing. He recommends that settlements of coffee producers be established, the settlers to be carefully instructed by a good extension service in the best methods of production and preparation. A central plant would do the processing for each area, and the Imperial Ethiopian College of Agricultural and Mechanical Arts would undertake research and training so that Ethiopians could replace technicians from abroad. Students with a degree in agriculture might be sent to South America for specialized study.

Subsequently, a coffee experiment station was established at Jimma Agricultural College, and the FAO instructor there has been carrying on extension work in all the main coffee districts.

Tools, Textiles, Trees

The farmers use primitive tools; one usual spading implement, for instance, is a long forked stick. FAO expert Kaspar Gabathuler (Switzerland) has been demonstrating better tools in Ethiopia since 1952 and getting an extraordinarily enthusiastic response. More efficient tools are especially important in this country where there is not an overplus of labor. Some entries from his diary for the first several months might read like this:

Near East and Africa

August—Arrived in Addis Ababa. Moved into the Ras Hotel, where several other FAO technicians live.

September—Found that few improved small tools or machines are used.

October—It will be possible to manufacture all wooden parts for tools in Ethiopia. Metal parts need to be imported. Native plows must be used four times to make a good seedbed. First demonstration of tools to 200 teachers and others was a complete success, especially the scythe. I plan to run a training course, then sell tools to people who have learned how to use them.

November—On a trip to Moggio I demonstrated scythe to farmers working in their fields. I can see increasing confidence in new tools. An Austrian firm has obtained an order from the Ethiopian Government.

January—I have been asked to demonstrate a small Japanese pedal thresher for grain.

February—More and more farmers come to my experiment station set up at Akaki to ask about tools and machines. The government is now giving UNRRA plows and other equipment, left over from the period just after the war, to farmers who learn how to use them.

March—Ethiopian farmers do not cultivate crops in rows. I began demonstration of that kind of cultivation with vegetables, maize, and alfalfa. My Ethiopian assistant also started a demonstration in his own village. [The Swiss girl to whom Gabathuler was engaged arrived in Addis late in January. After they were married they moved from the hotel to a house where they put in a demonstration garden for their Ethiopian neighbors.]

April—Out of ten kinds of hoes we have tried, only two or three are really good for Ethiopia.

May—Found that bush knives brought in by UNRRA were not used because they seemed to be no good. They had never been sharpened. After sharpening they worked well. Forestry workers are now using them. Also found that people did not know how to sharpen saws. Farmers like to learn about new tools and talk about new ways. I am making plans to start repair shops.

Cotton grows wild in Ethiopia, yet cotton goods make up about 40 per cent of imports. (The characteristic garment of men and women is the *shamma*, homespun and homewoven, a loose cotton wrap about 10 feet long and 4 feet wide, draped over the shoulders like a Mexican serape.) The government is taking steps, with some help from FAO, to increase production of cotton, and also to expand manufacturing.

Flax too could be produced to make linen, which would help to meet the need for textiles and might also be a valuable export product. FAO is encouraging experiments in that direction. In fact, seeds of a considerable variety of plants are being brought into Ethiopia from several countries for experiments. The generosity of the donors of such material from all over the world, said E. S. Archibald (Canada), former head of the FAO mission, is phenomenal and heartening.

In connection with forest development, which is especially important, E. H. Swain (Australia) spent two years in Ethiopia for FAO helping to work out the government's forest policy and program, and arranging for FAO fellowships to train young Ethiopians who will form the nucleus of the forest service. FAO also had a team in Ethiopia planning fairly extensive irrigation works in the Awash River valley.

Ethiopia has great need for home economics work and FAO home economist Thyra Andrén (Norway) started work there in July 1953, training teachers and advising on the introduction of home economics courses in the schools.

Libya

Libya, once called Rome's granary, now almost all desert, presents difficult problems of development.

In the south the Fezzan is an extension of the Sahara, almost rainless, dotted with occasional oases—infrequent emeralds strung on old trade routes. Farther north lie half-desert areas where 2 inches of rain (or, in some places, 10 inches) may fall in a year; but even this is fickle. The coastal belt gets a bit more, and in the low mountain areas back from the coast of Tripolitania the rain may amount to 20 inches a year.

A harsh and erratic climate, little water, hot days, cold nights; and though the desert soils respond to irrigation, they are not so rich as in some other dry countries; nor in most places is water easy to come by.

The people are mostly Arab and Berber nomads and seminomads, keeping flocks of sheep and goats, cultivating wheat and barley in little patches when there is enough rain, producing dates and vegetables, and driven by circumstance, fate, the will of Allah, to be going almost always from one place to some other place that seems a little less unpromising. In the north, where the larger towns are located, the population is more settled and Italians are the principal minority group.

Most production is for home subsistence. The income of the average person equals about $35 a year. Production methods are crude, but they were born of long experience in coping with formidable handicaps and on the whole are well adapted to the harsh mandates of this climate, these soils, this poverty.

Not until recently has Libya been free of foreign rule. The Phoenicians conquered the country in 1100 B.C. In successive waves came Greeks, Egyptians, Romans, Vandals, Arabs, Turks, Italians. After World War II, Britain and France held the country under a United Nations mandate until the beginning of 1952, when Libyans could at last create a government of their own.

Near East and Africa

In preparation for independence, Libya for two years or more had a group of experts from the United Nations and the specialized agencies making detailed surveys, drawing up plans and programs, getting new work started.

The results of much of the FAO survey were summed up in a report submitted to the government in November 1952. It covered all important aspects of agriculture and made recommendations concerned with:

- Sand dune fixation, windbreaks.
- Tools and equipment (yields of grain have been markedly increased in FAO-fostered experiments with better soil preparation and seeding).
- Cereal production.
- Trees and tree crops.
- Water resources and irrigation.
- Grading, processing, marketing.
- Grazing conditions, animal health, livestock breeding (two livestock experiment stations and a forage nursery have now been established), wool, hides, skins (export prices for skins soon went up 10 per cent because of the use of methods proposed by FAO).

Sheep are the most important animals among the nomads for meat, milk, and wool. An FAO range-management specialist succeeded in having three areas set aside for sheep grazing experiments; two breeding stations have now been established, FAO supplying the nucleus of breeding stocks.

Two other FAO reports deal with forest needs and possibilities and with fisheries—the rather extensive sponge-fishing industry and tuna and sardine fishing.

As the surveys make clear, this is not the kind of desert land that is likely to blossom like a rose or flow with milk and honey. But real achievements are possible in increasing livestock production, mainstay of the country's agriculture, and the production of cereals and vegetables, dates and olives (two of the principal products), and such fruits as citrus, figs, apricots, grapes, and pomegranates.

As this is written, 12 FAO experts are working intensively in Libya and several more are to be recruited.

Everything must be planned with a realistic appreciation of the limits imposed by nature and man. Agricultural development that might come easily in countries long accustomed to settled farming will be more difficult where most of the people have always been nomads, and also where there is no source of development funds except external loans or grants. But for generations the people of Libya have shown that they can wrest a livelihood from adversity. This is their great asset, for which they deserve the admiration of all men. Nor is this country without certain natural advantages. The challenge is to make the most of them, with the friendly co-operation of many countries.

Somalia

On the northern coast of Somalia are several fish canneries which pack yellowfin tuna, the species caught off California, Hawaii, and Japan. In recent years these plants have not been able to get enough tuna to operate at more than half capacity. The government asked for assistance.

FAO bought a California baby tuna-clipper, the *New Hope,* fitted it with up-to-date gear and instruments, and sent it to Somalia with engineer H. W. Ogilvie (USA), biologist A. F. Fraser-Brunner (UK), and skipper Donald Byrd (USA). The three men with two Somali counterparts operated it as an exploratory fishing vessel during the 1953 season.

The Arab and Somali fishermen use two types of boats, both clumsy, slow, unsafe—the *huri,* a dugout canoe, and the *bedan,* a larger craft made of planks tied together with fiber. The fishermen can never go far enough from shore to reach the main tuna population at the edge of the continental shelf. Even such simple vessels as outrigger canoes and catamarans would be more efficient.

As a demonstration of an improvement that could be made with the native craft, the FAO team harnessed two *huris* together with a platform between them, like a catamaran. This type of boat carries more sail and can use a motor. The fishermen were highly enthusiastic; they could catch much more bait and use trolling and longlining, neither of which is possible with native boats.

Most of the catch with the simple hand lines used is small-size tuna; the bigger ones are at deeper levels than these lines reach. At Bender Cassim the FAO crew showed that with multiple Japanese-type longlines their boat could catch ten times as much tuna in a day as the whole local fleet with its usual equipment.

The best bait for tuna are certain sardines which cannot usually be caught on this coast with Mediterranean-type nets. Using light California-type nets, and also tanks in which to keep both live and dead bait, the *New Hope* got more bait in one haul than the cannery boats could catch by fishing all night. The use of live bait kept in tanks also enabled company boats to triple their catch of tuna. Throwing the bait into the water quadrupled the catch of the fleet of 150 craft.

The original opposition or skepticism of the Somali fishermen has changed to enthusiasm for these new methods.

In addition to fisheries experts, FAO sent an agronomist and a range and livestock expert to Somalia as members of a UN-FAO mission in 1951. The organization also has had a nutrition expert in that country.

Liberia

Next door to the equator is Liberia, land of tropical forests. From May to October, 200 inches of rain make it a warm wet place. The big industry

Near East and Africa

is rubber, produced on the plantations of the Firestone Rubber Company. Otherwise the people depend almost entirely on subsistence farming. This is shifting cultivation: a man hacks down trees and brush with a machete, burns the wood so the ashes serve as fertilizer, puts in a crop for a year or two, then moves elsewhere. A piece of land is cropped once in 8 to 15 years.

More than a third of the country is forest; less than 20 per cent is cultivated. There are almost no roads, no carts or other vehicles, no animals for work, no animals for hauling (all of which is done on people's heads). Upland rice and cassava are the principal foods, with some sugar cane, taro, yams, and bananas. Wild palms furnish oil and palm kernels, source of most of the cash income. A few cattle, pigs, goats, chickens, and some fish provide a little protein food.

The government is eager to advance the development of the country and in co-operation with two USA technical missions has formulated a long-term program which includes roadbuilding and other engineering works, agricultural and health projects, basic education (schools are unknown in some areas), and public administration. Prime emphasis in the early stages is on increasing food production.

FAO has been helping to some extent in connection with fisheries, rice processing, cocoa production, agricultural extension, and statistics.

The brothers Hubertus and Jan Van Pel (the Netherlands) have been working on fish production and processing. The fishing fleet consists of some 850 canoes. Engineer Hubertus Van Pel brought a motor which he rigged on one of the canoes and also got a small motorized fishing boat from Denmark. He taught Liberians how to operate and maintain this equipment and how to make and use better fishing gear. Jan Van Pel worked to improve salting and smoking, which for the present are the best ways to preserve fish in Liberia; refrigeration and canning are not yet practicable. With larger supplies of smoked and salted fish, people back from the coast can enjoy these foods, which they have not had hitherto.

This kind of work is on a relatively small scale. It is simple. It may seem trivial. It takes much patience and much walking and perspiring. But the fishermen are eager to learn, and for them the results are far from trivial. Two fishing companies have now been organized. It has been possible to reduce the retail price of fish from $1 to 15 cents a pound.

Since rice is the main food, processing and storage are matters of great importance; the rubber plantations, for instance, use a pound of rice a day for each worker, a total of a million pounds a month. The rice is threshed by treading or beating and milled by pounding in a hollowed-out log. Storage conditions are conducive to much damage by fungi and insects in this hot humid climate. T. T. Hogan (USA) worked out plans for better storage; for a rice mill which is now in operation and for which FAO contributed $6,000 worth of machinery; and for the production of unpolished rice of high nutritive value. He also arranged for two FAO fellowships for Liberians to study rice processing and storage abroad.

FAO agronomist Gustaaf E. Doornberg (the Netherlands) found that soils in Liberia are well suited not only for cocoa but for coffee, citrus, mango, pineapple, and other fruits. Very little cocoa is grown, however, and the methods used result in many failures. Following Doornberg's recommendations, the government plans to establish three demonstration gardens, and religious missions and farmers are planting cocoa according to his instructions. Doornberg died in Liberia in the course of his work for FAO.

D. E. Kimmel (USA) was in Liberia for six months as an FAO agricultural extension specialist in the fundamental education project conducted by UNESCO, and Efraim Murcia Camacho (Colombia) went there for several months to help establish a permanent central statistical office for agriculture. He carried out a pilot survey of farms in one area and started the training of a small staff. More detailed and accurate data will help a great deal as underpinning for sound agricultural development.

CHAPTER NINE

Far East

REGIONAL PROJECTS

Rice

THE IDEA of a regional attack on the perennial and then acute Far East rice problem was broached by India in the meetings of the FAO Preparatory Commission on World Food Proposals in the winter of 1946-47. The Commission approved, and in May 1947 FAO called an international rice conference in Trivandrum, Travancore, with 10 governments sending delegates. This meeting planted the seed that was to grow into the International Rice Commission, an organization that has had a steadily increasing significance, particularly in the Far East.

Before the war, 95 per cent of the world's rice was produced (and eaten) in that region. A few countries, especially Burma, Indochina, Indonesia, Thailand, grew more than they consumed and exported the surplus to other countries that did not grow enough. The importers included Ceylon, China, India, Japan, and Malaya.

The war hit the rice industry hard. It has now recovered in most areas, but production has not fully caught up with population growth.

Rice is grown in the Far East mostly on small patches of land by many millions of subsistence farmers. There is little large-scale production. In the main areas of Burma, Thailand, Cambodia, and parts of Vietnam, farmers produce for sale on farms ranging from 10 to 30 acres. Under these circumstances, little rice is stored from year to year, and since transportation is also inadequate, any crop failure is likely to mean local famine.

Though all countries represented at Trivandrum agreed on the need for co-operative action, there were two views about its nature. One group thought a small statistical and technical FAO office in Southeast Asia would be enough. Another, urging more vigorous action, favored a rice board under the general auspices of FAO to handle all rice production problems.

In a broad sense the second view prevailed at the next meeting, held in

Baguio in March 1948. There, 19 governments and six organizations were represented, with Joaquin Elizalde of the Philippine Republic serving as chairman.

The Baguio meeting had a draft constitution for an international rice commission ready for discussion. FAO was to provide the secretariat; the member governments were to pay all other expenses that could not be met by FAO. The delegates reviewed the current rice situation and the programs and plans of governments, suggested tentative production goals, and made proposals for work which included co-operative breeding of better rice varieties, fertilizer experiments, and better control of diseases that kill and cripple the animals used to cultivate the paddy fields. Plant breeding alone, it was estimated, could raise production at least 10 per cent; it had doubled yields in Japan in three or four decades. In discussions on nutrition, emphasis was given to the need for increasing the nutritive value of milled rice by better milling practices, a campaign to cut down huge losses of harvested rice (perhaps 12 million tons a year), and school feeding programs. These questions were considered in detail by the Regional Nutrition Committee in South and East Asia, which met in Baguio at the same time as the rice meeting.

That autumn (1948) the FAO Conference approved the proposal for an international rice commission, and in March 1949 it was ready to hold its first meeting, in Bangkok. The 17 charter members were Burma, Ceylon, Cuba, the Dominican Republic, Ecuador, Egypt, France, India, Italy, Mexico, the Netherlands, Pakistan, Paraguay, the Philippine Republic, Thailand, the United Kingdom, and the United States of America. Since then Australia, Cambodia, Indonesia, Japan, Korea, Laos, and Vietnam have joined.

At this writing the International Rice Commission has held four regular meetings—Bangkok, March 1949; Rangoon, February 1950; Bandung, May 1952; Tokyo, October 1954. Special meetings on economic aspects of the rice industry, not under the aegis of the Rice Commission, were held in Bangkok in January 1953 and in Rangoon in November 1954. Economic problems of the industry were also the subject of discussion at the Far East regional meeting at Bangalore in July–August 1953, which I shall discuss later. Most of the detailed work of the commission has been in the hands of two working parties, on rice breeding and fertilizers. The FAO-sponsored Nutrition Committee for South and East Asia co-operates with the commission. Prince Sithiporn Kridakara of Thailand has from the beginning contributed much wisdom and experience as commission chairman. His term of office ended at the Tokyo meeting, where he was succeeded by Seiichi Tobata of Japan.

The program is not startling, but step by step it has been coming to grips with basic problems. At the second meeting, for example, Prince

Sithiporn was able to report that "For the first time in the history of rice improvement, a co-operative program for breeding, selection, and seed exchange has been worked out on an international basis." The following year, 1951, the Director-General of FAO noted in his annual report that a recent meeting of the working party on rice breeding, which then included 30 technicians from 15 countries,

. . . gave evidence of a refreshing upsurge of interest in rice breeding in those countries. The discussions were on a high technical level, and six governments contributed the equivalent of $1,000 each to help along the work, in addition to the sums made available by FAO. As a result, many new projects have been undertaken, and information and breeding materials are now being extensively exchanged among member countries.

To appreciate what this means, it is necessary only to recall that two years ago there was practically no exchange of seed or information. The workers in each country were isolated from one another and unable by themselves to attack major problems of varietal improvement.

Altogether, there are probably about 5000 varieties of rice; some 2000 are grown in India alone. Each locality has its own kind, good or bad. Except in Japan and parts of India and Indonesia, the area planted to improved varieties is almost negligible. This is one reason why production is so low; but on the other hand the great mass of heterogeneous material offers unusual opportunities for scientific selection and breeding.

The commission decided that at the start the program should emphasize the development of hybrids between the two types of rice grown commercially. One, the Indian (*indica*), is a lowland rice, widely produced under irrigation in Southeast Asia. It has a long grain, is adapted to hot climates and poor soils, but does not respond well to fertilizers. The other, the Japanese (*japonica*), is an upland rice, grown without flooding. It has a short round grain, is adapted to cooler climates, needs good soils, has stiff straw, and produces very high yields in response to fertilizers. The aim of hybridizing is to create a type combining the good qualities of both, and in particular having good fertilizer response.

India gave the plan a practical sendoff by generously offering the facilities of its Central Rice Research Institute for the hybridization work. With almost 75 million acres planted to rice in 1952 (the largest area of any country in the world), India has 48 rice research institutions, of which the biggest is the one at Cuttack, where 3000 genetic stocks are maintained. The head of this institute was K. Ramiah, who at the outset directed the international hybridization project.

This work started in August 1950. Under present plans it will continue until April 1956. At this writing, second-generation seed of some 200 crosses are being grown at experiment stations in the participating countries for selection of the most promising material. Expenses during the first three years have been about $26,000, of which individual governments contributed about $11,000 and FAO the remainder.

As in almost all technical fields, the shortage of trained workers is a great handicap. Again India came forward with an offer for the use of the Cuttack station, this time for an FAO training institute, and a course was given there in the latter part of 1952. Twenty-three professional workers from 11 countries took this training, living in a hostel built with funds provided by the Commonwealth Colombo Plan. There is a demand for another course.

The fertilizer work got a somewhat later start. As a first step, an FAO soils expert surveyed most of the rice area in Southeast Asia, collecting and analyzing a mass of useful data on soils, rainfall, water supply, cultural and fertilizer practices, and current experimental work in 12 countries. Since then, an active exchange of information among the member countries has been going on through the Working Party on Fertilizers. Eleven cooperative research projects have been started, one of them involving as many as 10 countries. Just before the course on rice breeding, an FAO soil-fertility training institute was held at Coimbatore, Madras, with 19 trainees from seven countries attending, and with P. D. Karunakar, principal of the Agricultural College and Research Institute at Coimbatore, serving as director.

In 1952 Ramiah was appointed to the staff of FAO to serve as liaison officer with governments. He visited eight countries during the year to help in the breeding work and other aspects of the rice program. Among many recommendations for national and regional action made after this survey, he emphasized three principal needs: more breeding stations, more technicians, more double cropping—raising two crops of rice on land where only one is raised now.

Equipment and machinery (for irrigation, cultivation, harvesting, threshing) has come in for considerable attention by the Rice Commission, as have economic problems, which I shall discuss in a later part of this chapter. (It may be noted, however, that international trade has not so far been included in the commission's work.)

So many people live almost exclusively on rice that its nutritive values are especially important. The FAO Nutrition Committee for South and East Asia has brought out some striking facts. In ordinary milling, for example, three fourths of the thiamine (vitamin B_1) and 15 per cent of the protein in rice is lost. Some 80 per cent of the remaining thiamine and 10 per cent of the remaining protein ordinarily disappear in the washing and cooking of the grain. In other words, an already poor diet is made much poorer by the ways in which the food is commonly processed and prepared.

If the consumer could get cleaner rice it would not have to be washed so much. If he used undermilled rice, which has some of the outer layers

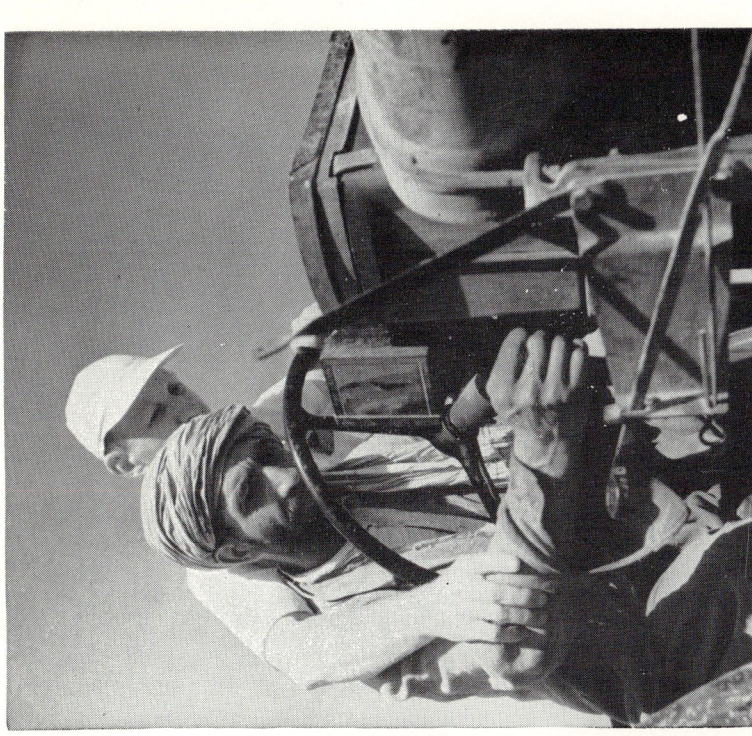

The plow most commonly used is a heavy pointed stick fastened to a beam to which one or more animals are hitched. The first and simplest improvement is a metal point at the tip of the stick. This implement does not turn the soil over but scratches the surface, and in many cases it must be dragged across the same piece of ground many times to prepare a good seedbed. This farmer in Afghanistan is using a team of bullocks for plowing.

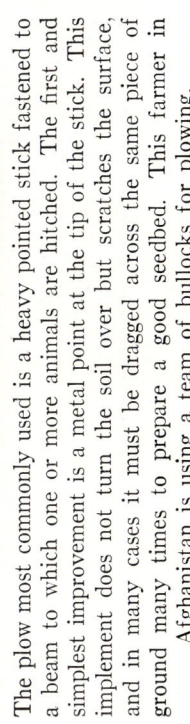

Nevertheless, tractors are being used more and more, especially on large farms and in clearing and leveling tracts of land, and in many countries FAO has been helping to set up properly equipped and manned tractor stations and repair shops. The Afghan farmer here is a beginner but an apt and interested pupil.

Water for human beings and animals and for irrigating crops on arid land is a must. Ancient devices for lifting and spreading water, invented thousands of years ago, are still in use. Simplest of all is an ordinary bucket. Here a number of buckets are tied to the rim of a wheel, the so-called Persian wheel, which is turned by a man or an animal—water buffalo, donkey, camel, bullock. Irrigating an acre of land by such methods is slow backbreaking work.

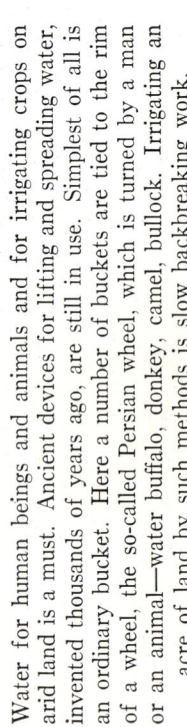

Extensive irrigation works are being built by modern machinery in many places. Here, tractors dragging heavy chains knock down trees in an area in northern Ceylon, long overrun by jungle, where ancient irrigation tanks are being restored and new water facilities created.

One result of Ceylon's irrigation and land settlement program. These farmers are cultivating their new rice fields in the Gal Oya area. The development program as a whole aims to double the amount of land in agricultural production.

Often it is desirable to use human labor rather than machines for much of the work on large-scale construction projects. Underemployed rural people welcome the chance to supplement their scant earnings. These workers hauling dirt from a big excavation on an irrigation project in Java are literally using their heads to make increased food production possible.

There can be no more arduous or slower way to rip down a big log. This one is being split at a plywood factory in India. The modernization of forest work and forest industries is only beginning in many of the world's main wooded areas.

Here is a case in point. The homemade overhead traveling pulley for handling logs, and the truck trailer itself, readily do the work of many grunting elephants and puffing men. This is in Thailand, where a long-term program is under way for improving forest management and operations.

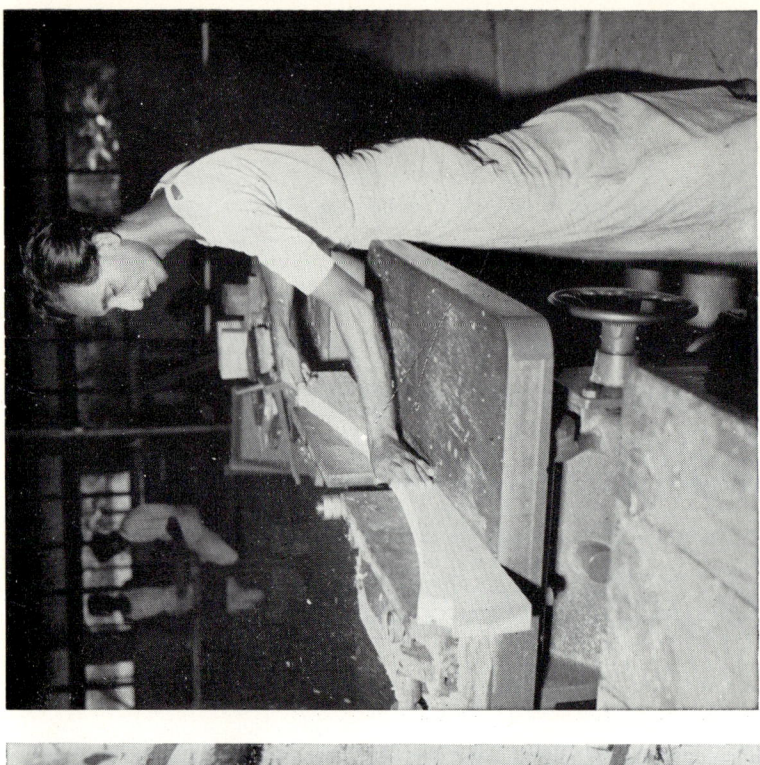

The use of primitive tools means slow work but not necessarily less expertness. The boatbuilder on a beach in Pakistan is drilling a hole with a bow drill, an ancient device consisting of a cord wrapped around a spindle, which twirls as the bow is pulled back and forth. These craftsmen build some of the best boats to be found anywhere.

A man who is expert with hand tools, and whose ancestors have been expert for generations, often takes quite readily to machinery. This worker in a shop in Ceylon is running a wood-molding machine. New machine shops installed in Ceylon are reported to be already operating at a high level of efficiency. There is no inherent reason why Eastern people cannot make as effective use of machinery as Western.

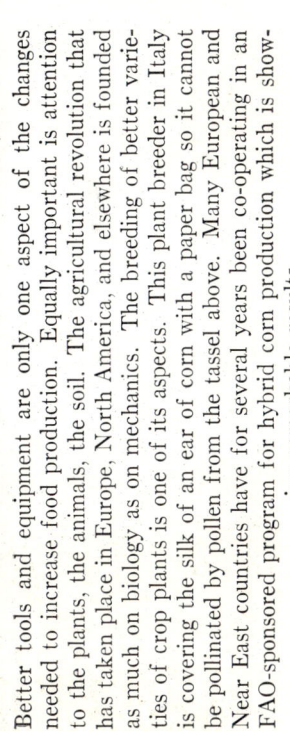

Better tools and equipment are only one aspect of the changes needed to increase food production. Equally important is attention to the plants, the animals, the soil. The agricultural revolution that has taken place in Europe, North America, and elsewhere is founded as much on biology as on mechanics. The breeding of better varieties of crop plants is one of its aspects. This plant breeder in Italy is covering the silk of an ear of corn with a paper bag so it cannot be pollinated by pollen from the tassel above. Many European and Near East countries have for several years been co-operating in an FAO-sponsored program for hybrid corn production which is showing remarkable results.

In the Far East there is the International Rice Commission, an FAO agency through which member countries are doing a great deal of co-operative work to increase the production of this grain, the staple food of more than half of mankind. Here an Indian scientist has brought his microscope to the rice field in the course of his work on the big hybridization project now centering at the Central Rice Research Institute at Cuttack and carried out for the benefit of all contributing countries.

Yes, it's certainly good and strong! An Ethiopian farmer admires the quality of flax fiber, a new crop being experimentally introduced with FAO help in connection with Ethiopia's agricultural development program.

left on the grain, he would have a nutritionally better product. But undermilled rice must be stored under the best of conditions because it does not keep as well as rice from which all the outer layers have been removed.

To retain nutritive values and at the same time prevent spoilage, rice may be parboiled. This process is traditional in some countries. The unmilled paddy rice is soaked in water, steamed, and dried before milling. Steaming diffuses the thiamine and other nutrients from the germ and outer layers through the entire grain so that even after milling a large proportion is left. About one fifth of the world's rice is parboiled, but the product has a flavor that some people do not like. The Government of India is studying possible improvements in parboiling methods. There are processes that yield a product of excellent quality. Rice can also be "fortified" with thiamine and other nutrients, and this is being done rather extensively in the Philippines. There is evidence that rice enrichment can reduce the incidence of beriberi and help in educating people in better dietary habits. But one of the prime needs throughout the Far East, as governments are well aware, is to produce more vegetables (including soybeans and other pulses), fish, meat, and milk, to balance the limited rice diet.

Rinderpest

Most of the tractors in the Far East have four feet. Because cattle do the farm work, they are especially important in any program for increased food production. In improving these animals, disease control probably comes first if only because serious diseases can cancel out all efforts at better feeding and breeding.

Among cattle diseases, rinderpest is by all odds the worst in this region, which makes it the worst in the world, since most of the world's cattle are in the Far East. FAO is spearheading an international program—a natural counterpart of the Far East rice work—to control and, in fact, wipe out this disease. Recent developments in vaccines, which the organization helped to foster, have made the latter a not-far-fetched possibility.

Vaccinating against rinderpest is not new, and most countries had some sort of control program before FAO existed, using either immune serum or inactivated virus. Immune serum is blood serum containing antibodies that combat rinderpest virus. The antibodies develop in the blood of an animal infected with the disease. When its immune serum is injected into the blood of another animal that has not had the disease, the ready-made antibodies provide that animal with some measure of borrowed immunity, which, however, lasts only a short time. Inactivated virus is made from infected tissue taken from an animal with rinderpest and then disinfected (inactivated) with formalin or chloroform. When this vaccine is injected into a susceptible animal, the animal produces its own antibodies just as it would if it had an attack of rinderpest. This immunity is more certain and lasts longer than borrowed immunity. Developed in the latter part of the 1920's, the inactivated-virus method was used on millions of head of cattle, but it was cumbersome and costly because many animals had to be destroyed to make the vaccine.

The new methods make use of laboratory animals, usually goats or rabbits. One of these animals is infected with the disease; virus from its blood is used to infect a second one, virus from the second to infect a third, and so on, until the virus has been "passaged" through scores or even hundreds of laboratory animals. The last in the series provides the vaccine for immunizing livestock. By that time the virus is so modified and attenuated that it produces only a mild reaction, but enough to stimulate the processes that create positive immunity.

According to experience in Nigeria and Kenya, two or even three doses of attenuated goat virus vaccine can be produced for the equivalent of two cents in US currency—much less than by any previous method.

The efficacy of attenuated virus vaccine has been proved by rigid tests in which a vaccinated animal is "challenged" by injecting into it a heavy dose of deadly rinderpest virus—perhaps enough to give a thousand animals the disease. Such tests have shown that immunity lasts for at least four years; some authorities believe it may prove to last a lifetime.

The first work with goat-attenuated virus was done in India as far back as 1932 and the first significant work with rabbits in Japan in 1938. A particularly successful program using goat vaccine was carried out in Africa between 1942 and 1949, when 15 million head of cattle were immunized, with very small losses.

In an earlier chapter I mentioned the method of rinderpest control developed by the United States and Canada during World War II; this method uses hens' eggs as the attenuating medium. With a large supply of fertile eggs and adequate sanitation, an inexpensive vaccine may be produced which also has the advantage of being nonvirulent to animals so susceptible to rinderpest that neither goat nor rabbit virus can be used with complete safety.

The freeze-drying of vaccines is another recent contribution to effective disease control.

Consider the making of goat virus as an example. Spleens of infected goats are removed, quick-frozen, chopped fine by machine, converted to pulp, dried in a vacuum chamber at a very low temperature for 22 hours, ground to powder, and then transferred to small glass containers (ampoules). The ampoules are submitted to drying by vacuum for another 24 hours, after which they are sealed by melting the glass tips with a hydrogen flame and stored in a deep-freeze cabinet ready for use in the veterinarian's hypodermic needle.

FAO's function is to spread information about these and other effective techniques, train people to use them, train field crews of vaccinators, help organize veterinary services, help to bring laboratories up to date, and so on. Most of this work is necessarily done in individual countries, but an essential part of it is international.

The work started in China, where potent lots of avianized (egg) vaccine first arrived from Grosse Isle, Canada, in July 1946, for use in the UNRRA rinderpest control campaign. The following year FAO took over this program and carried it on with remarkably good results until the teams had to leave the mainland. The FAO work was then transferred to Thailand, where veterinarians had been waging an uphill fight against rinderpest. Starting with lapinized (rabbit) vaccine brought by FAO from Nanking and also using their own caprinized (goat) vaccine, they pushed the program with new vigor and soon immunized all the cattle in areas where the disease existed. Since then there has been only one small outbreak, which was quickly controlled. A number of other countries have had or are now receiving help from FAO.

The first steps toward international action on the part of FAO date back to a meeting on animal health held in London in August 1946. In October and November 1948 came a meeting in Nairobi, Kenya, sponsored jointly by FAO and the British Colonial Office, in which 22 countries and territories participated. The Kenya conference started the campaign now under way with the support and endorsement of veterinarians throughout the world.

A few months later, in June 1949, FAO convened a Rinderpest Conference for Asia and the Far East in Bangkok. There a number of governments agreed to take all possible steps to control outbreaks, co-ordinate their programs with those of neighboring countries, and work toward ultimate eradication. Early in 1953 FAO held a training institute in Izatnagar, India, on the manufacture of rinderpest and other virus vaccines (Newcastle disease, fowl plague, fowl pox, sheep pox), with Dr. S. Datta, Substantive Director of the Indian Veterinary Research Institute at Izatnagar, serving as director.

It would be fair to say now that another major plague of rinderpest is unlikely. The countries have the means and the knowledge to produce vast quantities of vaccine—enough to control any outbreak, and ultimately to achieve complete eradication.

Fisheries

Fishing, sometimes called the oldest occupation of man, may well have begun in the Far East. Some of the gear and the boats used there today are probably much the same as those men used before history began—spear, hook and line, simple nets, rafts, dugout canoes. As in ancient days, the fishermen are still confined mainly to inshore waters since they do not have boats or equipment that would enable them to go far out to sea—except, of course, the Japanese, who are well in advance in adopting up-to-date methods. So the deep-sea fish are in general uncaught.

Ninety per cent of all fish caught in the world are caught in northern waters. Until recently it was thought that only the northern waters were very productive. This idea has been upset by recent research, showing that in a broad belt near the Equator are movements of the ocean current which bring phosphates, nitrates, and other minerals from great depths to the upper zone of the sea, where there is enough light for green plants, which depend on photosynthesis, to exist. The light from above and the chemicals from below combine to nourish a generous growth of minute one-celled plants, which are consumed by minute animals. These plant and animal plankton are food for shrimps, squids, and small fish, which in turn are food for tuna, bonito, albacore, and other large fish, which are food for man.

Thus some of the world's best fishing grounds apparently lie in the Equatorial belt—a fact that may have considerable significance in the food developments of the future.

Meanwhile, along the interminable crinkled shores of Asia live many thousands of humble folk who have always been fishermen (and in many cases very skillful fishermen), as were their fathers, grandfathers, and great-grandfathers, but who are handicapped by primitive tools and methods. A boat with one or two men may, and frequently does, go out for a whole day and return with only a tiny basket of fish.

Inland, tens of millions of human beings need more protein food. Fish could help supply it. But the inland people do not get fish not only because the fishermen do not catch enough but also because facilities are meager for processing it so it will keep and transporting it for any distance. Much time, effort, and money will be needed to change this situation materially. (In a later chapter I shall have occasion to describe some of the interesting processing methods in use in Asia.)

As one practical step, FAO fostered the organization of the Indo-Pacific Fisheries Council, which now has 16 members. Since it was set up in 1949, the council has held five annual meetings and has been responsible for starting a number of far-reaching projects and for many investigations of technical problems.

In the main, these are the things the countries in the Far East need to do, and are doing, to expand and develop fisheries:

- Build up a much larger corps of trained people with a good background of technical knowledge—scientists, engineers, marketing experts, economists, statisticians, fisheries extension workers, administrators—to stimulate and carry out the work of development.
- Gradually improve boats and gear, starting with the equipment the fishermen now have and to which they are accustomed.
- Wherever possible, develop better basic facilities—harbors, wharfage, storage plants, curing and processing plants, markets, transportation.

- Expand fish resources in ponds, lakes, streams, brackish shore waters, flooded rice fields.
- Encourage the organization of co-operatives among fishermen as a means of economic betterment.
- Educate consumers to like fish and want more of it.

Between a modern tuna clipper, which costs half a million dollars to build and is fitted with the most up-to-date gear (sometimes including even a motion picture theater for the recreation of the crew) and a dugout canoe or homemade catamaran lies a world of difference. To try to jump from the dugout to the tuna clipper would be much more difficult than substituting a tractor-drawn gang plow for a bent stick pulled by a water buffalo, because the knowledge required to run the clipper is far more complex than that required to run the tractor, and the costs are far greater.

Often the first step in improving fishing boats is to put a motor into an existing craft. This in itself is a long step forward. It has been proved many times that a fisherman can double his catch, or sometimes multiply it tenfold, with a motorized vessel. Suppose it takes him four hours to row to the fishing grounds and four hours to row back. With a motor he might cut this time in half and have the extra time for fishing. Also, he would be confined to shore less often by bad weather, and he could go farther from shore where the big fish are more likely to be.

This first step in mechanization is now well started in the Far East. (In fact, as one expert remarked, it is spreading like a virus infection.) The fourth meeting of the Indo-Pacific Fisheries Council brought out that it is taking place in every country—started, moreover, by the fishermen themselves. Malaya, Singapore, Hong Kong, and Bombay State are outstanding examples. The council is fostering this development, and FAO naval engineers and architects are assisting governments in their programs.

There is much more to the process of mechanization than putting a motor in a boat. People who have never known anything about machines must be taught to handle them. If they are to go out for longer trips, which mean staying away from shore more than a day at a time, they frequently must learn different attitudes. Many people who have always made their livelihood from the sea have a deep fear of it; some of the best of northern fishermen, for instance, refuse to go on a long voyage unless at least two ships accompany one another. Much more is this fear present in people who have never gone farther from shore than the distance they can paddle out and back between dawn and dark.

Similarly, when boats are able to go to deep water the fishermen need different gear from that for shallow water, and the skill to use it. Finally, they must know more about navigation, including the use of the compass, than most of them do at present.

All this means training. Without it, new equipment can even be disastrous. For example, the following incident is said to have occurred not long ago in a large fishing harbor in the Far East (and if it did not, it easily might have).

In this place, as in so many others, the fisherman lives on the boat, with his family if he has one. He goes out with his family and fishes during the day, returning in the evening to the harbor, where scores or hundreds of boats just like his are tied up side by side for the night. One bright young fisherman managed to save enough to get an outboard motor. He learned how to start and stop it; he went out for his first day's fishing; he came back elated with the catch. Dreaming of a bright future, he got ready to cook his evening meal, making a charcoal fire in a small brazier, which he placed in the stern as he had always done. The gasoline tank offered a convenient spot, so he set the brazier on it. Came the explosion, which burned up quite a few boats in the crowded harbor before they could get away. Had the young fisherman had a little more training before using his wonderful new motor, the tragedy would not have occurred.

Lack of funds has unfortunately so far prevented FAO from holding the training courses it had planned for marine fishermen in the Far East. For inland fish culture, the organization has sponsored two regional courses, one in 1951 and another, somewhat more ambitious, in 1952, both in Djakarta. To the second course came 18 participants from India, Indonesia, Pakistan, the Philippines, Taiwan, Thailand, and Vietnam, all of whom held responsible positions in fisheries departments. Java was chosen for this demonstration and training because fish culture is a very ancient practice there. In particular, the culture of milkfish, or *chanos*, in specially built brackish-water ponds (*tambaks*) is a remarkable achievement which historically goes back as far as 1200 B.C., or even 1400 B.C. East Java may in fact be the place where pond fish culture originated.

Less interesting to most people but not less useful were the six-week regional training institute on fisheries statistics which FAO held in Bangkok in the summer of 1952 and the institute on fish marketing held in Hong Kong in July–August 1954.

Special reports on practical and scientific aspects of fisheries in the Far East are one of the useful products of the meetings of the Indo-Pacific Fisheries Council. One meeting, for instance, included a symposium on fish culture, with contributions on such subjects as the fish-spawn industry in India, where certain people make a business of collecting fish eggs in the spawning season and selling them in the market for stocking ponds; methods of transplanting fish fry; and the physiological requirements that have to be met in transporting eggs, larvae, and fry. Another report described fishing gear and fishing methods used in the region. The seaweed industry and the use of plankton as food (in Asia large quantities are converted into pastes and other products) were among the items on the agenda of the 1954 meeting. The most ambitious project is perhaps the series of handbooks and studies now in preparation covering the main technical and economic aspects of fisheries. One of the first was a detailed account of fish culture in Java by W. H. Schuster, who had many years of experience there and later served for a while on the FAO staff.

Better Use of Tropical Land

For a long time many northern Caucasian people looked on the tropics as a region of romance—and profits—but also of sinister mystery, of dark adventure, of dreadful diseases, where "civilized" people could not live normally and, in particular, had to have all physical labor done for them by natives. A whole literature was built up around such concepts. Now they are being swept away by a new look at the reality. The sinister effects of the climate have been shown to be somewhat exaggerated; northerners can live and work in the tropics as well as anywhere else, provided they take sensible precautions. Modern medicine shows that tropical diseases are no more mysterious than other diseases; they are caused by the same kinds of organisms; they yield to sanitation, vaccination, and other preventive measures; they are as likely to be cured by modern drugs.

There is now a new surge of interest in the development of the tropics and subtropics, partly because half the world's people live there, partly because recent political changes have freed many of them from foreign domination and brought new demands for better living, partly because this is a region where food production can be expanded.

In September 1951, FAO convened a conference in Nuwara Eliya, Ceylon, on the utilization of land in the tropical areas of Asia and the Far East, with K. Kanagasundram of the host country as chairman. This meeting dealt with such fundamental questions as the methods or techniques needed to assess the basic land and water resources of tropical countries, to determine what they can actually produce, and to draw up sound agricultural programs for their further development.

In a lively debate several delegates emphasized that it is not possible to apply a neat development plan where people are already too densely crowded on the land; where they cannot shift from one occupation to another; where farmers have almost no money to invest in improvements; where most of them are tenants who must hand over perhaps half their year's proceeds to landlords; where for all these reasons the return to the family working the soil is a pittance. The discussion brought out, however, that in seeking possible remedies for these extreme conditions, accurate knowledge of basic resources is, if anything, even more important than it is in countries where the problems are less stark and difficult.

The Ceylon conference gave special attention to shifting cultivation. In Southeast Asia this is essentially the same practice I have discussed in connection with Liberia: burning off the trees and brush (the fires often spreading unchecked over immense areas); planting a crop for a year or two, or until the heavy tropical rains have washed the plant nutrients out of the upper layers of the exposed soil, greatly reducing its fertility, and sprouting brush has made cultivation difficult; then moving on to another location, leaving the clearing abandoned for 10 or 15 years.

In addition to resulting in a great loss of timber, this practice results in floods, silting of streams, serious erosion in the hills; and it damages settled farmers who carry on a permanent agriculture in the valleys by eventually cutting down their water supply.

Shifting cultivation has been widely condemned, yet there is a growing recognition that it has a legitimate place in certain tropical rain-forest areas where almost no other kind of crop production is possible. The problem, for which some countries are working out interesting solutions, is to develop methods that eliminate or greatly reduce the damage involved.

In Cambodia there have been experiments with a system which, as described by Huberman, involves settling groups of farm families in temporary villages built in forest clearings.

[They] cut the low-value indigenous forest, haul the best logs to a sawmill for house-construction lumber, and deliver the rest of the wood to kilns where it is burned into charcoal. The debris is burned under controlled conditions.

The areas thus cleared are assigned by lot to the villagers, who then plant teak seeds or cuttings in rows about six feet apart, and sow their crops between the rows. . . . Cultivation continues until the trees shade the crops. Then the villagers move on to another area. This process is repeated until that portion of the forest reserve within reach of the village location is completely converted to teak or other valuable species. The village is then moved to another area in need of such conversion.

This is practically the same as the *taungya* system of Burma, or a similar system in Java. It seems to be working satisfactorily where the people are willing to settle down instead of roaming freely over the hills.

Partly as a result of the Nuwara Eliya meeting, consultants and working parties are collecting detailed information about shifting cultivation from countries in the Far East and Africa with a view to recommending possible changes and remedies.

Among other interesting points emphasized at the meeting were these:

- Research specifically related to tropical soils is often badly needed as a foundation for sound programs of mechanization and irrigation; there has been too great a tendency to apply in the tropics the results of experience and research in temperate zones, and this has been responsible for some of the failures of agricultural development programs.
- In large areas certain grasses and sedges have run wild and made cultivation practically impossible; co-operative investigations are needed to find the best ways of eradicating them.
- Much more attention should be given to the needs of peasant farmers. Great advances have been made in management techniques on large planta-

tions, but these are not applicable to small-scale producers. Land reforms may be required to achieve the kind of efficiency on small farms that is possible in plantation agriculture.
* A permanent land and water commission should be set up in each country. (A number of governments have since established such agencies.)

Animals—Fewer, Better

There are many excellent cattle in the Far East and Near East. That humble sturdy citizen of Egypt, the *gamoosa,* is, as we have seen, not only a good plower and hauler but also a producer of exceptionally rich milk. It can stand heat; it is not bothered much by the hosts of tropical insects; it is resistant to some of the tropical diseases. The humped cattle of India and Africa are similarly adapted to tropical conditions. (On one of these breeds FAO has published a handbook, *The Zebu Cattle of India and Pakistan.*) Practically every country has its native domestic animals, what the Latin Americans call *criollos* (creoles), well fitted to local conditions through generations of survival.

But in many cases these animals are not so productive as breeds developed in countries in the north temperate zone—for example, Holstein-Friesians, Brown Swiss, Ayrshires, and Jerseys for milk; Shorthorns and Aberdeen Angus for meat. The farmer in the tropics is often tempted, if he can afford it, to import northern animals of high productivity. But then he runs into other difficulties. These animals are not, in general, adapted to tropical conditions—heat, insects, diseases, poor rations. Thus the producer who switches enthusiastically to some foreign breed may be in for costly disappointments.

There are three possible solutions to this problem. He can select the best native stock and by careful breeding gradually build up a herd or flock with high productive capacity. He can import a northern type or breed that seems reasonably adapted to tropical conditions and try to provide a special environment (some have even used air-conditioned barns) that will help to maintain production. He can cross native and imported stock to produce new types combining high productivity with adaptation to the environment.

The first method is slow. The second is likely to be expensive and troublesome. The third is being used successfully in a number of countries, including the USA, where, in Texas and Louisiana particularly, European breeds have been crossed with humped cattle from Africa and India.

Recently there has been a somewhat new approach based on attempts to determine more exactly what it is that enables certain animals to tolerate heat so much better than others. Dr. D. H. K. Lee of Johns Hopkins University, an authority on animal physiology in relation to climate, has been carrying on certain investigations in this field for FAO. In his FAO document, *Manual of Field Studies on the Heat Tolerance of Domestic Animals,* he writes:

If permanent improvement is to be effected, steps must be taken to concentrate desirable characters in each new generation. To do this successfully we need to know, not only what the desirable characters are, but how they are inherited. . . . Genetic improvement based solely on the criterion of productivity must necessarily be slow and costly. It would be very much better if one could recognize what character or small number of characters are responsible for high heat tolerance, and direct breeding programs to the concentration of such characters.

At the present juncture there are more beliefs than certainties. . . . Increased surface area, greater density of sweat glands, greater activity of sweat glands, increased respiratory activity, shorter coat, presence or absence of pigmentation, and many other characters have been postulated as responsible for heat tolerance. . . . None, however, has really been proved to be *the* factor. . . . The possibility that tolerance may be due to efficiency in metabolism with a consequently lower heat production, rather than efficiency in heat loss, has not received adequate attention.

In the present state of our knowledge it would be premature to indicate the characters a concentration of which should be attempted in breeding. The chief reason for advocating field studies, and the motive behind the preparation of this manual, is to promote the gathering of the evidence which will make such instructions possible.

The livestock producer in the tropics must, of course, also try eternally to improve feed supplies, especially grass and forage, and to combat diseases and pests.

The lively interest in these questions found expression in a regional meeting in Lucknow, India, in 1950, under the chairmanship of Sardar Datar Singh, where people directly concerned with livestock problems in the tropics and subtropics agreed on the fundamentals of programs needed to solve them. These discussions included a frank exchange of experiences in introducing European breeds and Indian and Pakistani types in various countries, and in crossing tropical and European animals. The Indian delegate told about the "key village plan" under which a great many villages or groups of villages are assigned good bulls for breeding while all others are castrated or removed. Artificial insemination is also being used to speed up progress. This key village plan is a practical means of reducing the great numbers of poor animals, which are a heavy burden on feed resources. Somewhat similar programs are under way in a number of countries.

In fact in this region, where so many animals are needed for farm work, the pressure of livestock (as well as people) on land resources makes it imperative to seek every means not only of improving animals by breeding but also of increasing supplies of fodder and other feedstuff that cannot be consumed directly by human beings. This, in turn, requires a better integration of crop and animal husbandry than can be found in most places in the Far East at present.

FAR EAST

Mainly Economics

A little over two years after FAO was established, the governments in the Near East held a regional meeting in February 1948 to review what FAO had done and what they wanted it to do. This was the first of a series of regional meetings on Food and Agriculture Programs and Outlook that have continued ever since—for the Near East, in Beirut (1949), Bloudane (1951), Cairo (1953); for the Far East, in Singapore (1949) and Bangalore (1953); for Latin America, in Quito (1949), Montevideo (1950), Buenos Aires (1954); for Europe, in Rome (1950).

At first tentative and diffuse, these meetings have steadily gained in substance and definition until they are now extremely useful forums for exploring regional needs, agreeing on concerted policies, and fitting the work of FAO into national development programs. The Bangalore meeting is an example.

In advance, the FAO staff visited most countries of the region to discuss with national policy-makers, administrators, and experts in various fields specific problems and programs for food and agricultural development. On the basis of these discussions the staff officers prepared a rather detailed account, country by country, covering production trends and goals for principal commodities, international trade, and related government policies and programs.

Most countries in Asia and the Far East have prepared agricultural programs for increased production of food and, insofar as possible, of nonfood products as well. Very few countries, however, are in a position to carry out agricultural development on a comprehensive scale. Many of the FAO member nations that have gained independence since the war are still faced with the problem of restoring peace and security and otherwise establishing an economic climate conducive to expanding production and consumption.

In most parts of the region agricultural production per person and per acre is too low. But the food situation is already showing signs of a radical change. India is fast approaching its goal of national self-sufficiency in basic food and some of the fibers. The Indonesian food situation has also changed for the better. The Philippines has more than regained its prewar status of national self-sufficiency in rice. Burma, which has yet to recover all the rice area abandoned to jungle growth, is confronted with the problem of disposing of a current surplus at reduced prices. Were it not for production setbacks in Pakistan and Japan, the problem of distribution would have become more pressing than the problem of expanding production. The conclusion emerges that in their approach to economic development governments should take into account the need and possibilities for raising effective demand for food and agricultural products more than they have so far.

Some of the main points brought out in the meeting follow.

Although the cultivated area almost everywhere can be expanded and production per acre can be increased, the obstacles to rapid development are formidable. Any increase in purchasing power, unless backed by adequate supplies of food and consumer goods, brings on inflation. Earning capacity for foreign exchange in most countries is low. A large part of the limited funds must be used to import food rather than capital goods. Income from exports is very unstable because prices of such products as natural rubber and fibers fluctuate widely; the Bangalore meeting stressed the need for international action to stabilize export prices. In sum, speedier economic development depends on ability to import more capital equipment, which in turn depends on expanding agricultural exports and reducing imports of food.

Low incomes mean little savings for investment. But in many countries substantial sums that might be used for economic development are invested in real estate or spent for consumer goods (often imported), which contribute little to improving the general standard of living. Most governments, however, are now investing a larger share of the national budget in economic development. They are also encouraging co-operative credit societies. But in spite of all efforts, the sums needed are far greater than can be supplied under present conditions, from governmental and private sources combined. To increase agricultural production by 2 per cent a year, according to evidence presented at Bangalore, would require some 2 billion dollars of investment capital annually, exclusive of Japan. Only about 900 million dollars is available from all sources. The gap seems impossible to bridge unless domestic savings for agricultural development are greatly increased and foreign capital is attracted on a larger scale.

One of the ideas discussed at Bangalore was for governments to set up national agricultural finance corporations to mobilize domestic investment. "Buffer funds" were also suggested, on the analogy of the buffer stocks of commodities discussed in an earlier chapter. In years of high national income, money paid into such a fund would be earmarked for development projects, which could thus be kept going in years of low income. The meeting also favored the establishment of an international finance corporation and a special United Nations fund for projects that might not be self-liquidating.

On the industrial side, development should not be thought of only in terms of city factories. There is often a place for more rural and cottage industries, which can absorb much manpower with relatively little capital; and where rural manpower is not fully employed, use of manual labor in place of heavy machinery under certain conditions, as in road-building, is not necessarily as wasteful as it seems to Westerners. Forest industries producing timber, plywood, pulp and paper, fiberboard can also be useful in countries that have an abundance of both raw materials and labor.

Many farmers need more incentive than they now have to increase their production—for instance, remunerative prices, secure tenure, and enough available consumer goods to make better living possible with increased earnings.

Besides the more strictly economic questions, the Bangalore meeting dealt with nutrition, crop and livestock production, farm mechanization, forestry, and fisheries.

How to Develop

When the expanded technical co-operation program first began to get into its stride, the countries eligible to participate began preparing plans for suitable projects. Some of the proposals that came to FAO and other agencies proved on critical examination not to be as sound, urgent, or well thought out as they should be to justify the expenditure of funds and effort they would require. Although some countries had long had development plans of one kind or another, this program was something new in size and scope.

It would be worth while, FAO decided, to provide some special training for government officials and others directly concerned in formulating economic development projects and preparing material for presentation to the agencies expected to provide co-operation. The first training institute of this kind was held in Lahore, Pakistan, late in 1950, under the joint sponsorship of the Pakistan Government, the United Nations, the International Bank for Reconstruction and Development, and FAO.

It aroused a good deal of interest, and 54 people from eight countries took part. Each national group worked up reports on a specific project for its country and presented the case to the whole meeting for critical review. Two series of lectures were also given, one on the fundamentals of project planning, the other on specific kinds of projects—roads, agricultural extension, public health, grain storage, forest development, reclamation, irrigation, flood control, fisheries, fertilizer manufacture, agricultural credit, and so on. Later, the Lahore lectures were published by the United Nations in two thick volumes, for which there has been a considerable demand.

The institute was so successful that in 1951 FAO conducted two more of the same kind, one in Ankara, Turkey, with 60 participants from 11 countries, and one in Santiago, Chile, with 62 from 19 countries. An Arab training institute was held in Cairo in the autumn of 1954.

Far East Co-operatives

Work on co-operatives began for FAO with a technical conference for Asia and the Far East, held in Lucknow in October and November 1949, with V. L. Mehta of India as chairman. This meeting dealt with such practical problems as administrative control, legislation, auditing, training of personnel, research, government departments concerned with co-operatives, and the special problems of various types of societies.

There is a remarkable range of co-operative activity in Asia and the Far East, the meeting showed, though in many cases the organizations are relatively new and some may not survive. Among the kinds of co-operatives represented or discussed were organizations concerned with rice processing and marketing, consumer goods at wholesale and retail, credit (many people believe that co-operative credit is the best answer to the need of the small-scale farmer for operating funds), commodity marketing, fisheries, building, cottage industries, joint farming and land colonization, livestock improvement, land improvement, supplying of farm machinery, malaria control and other medical problems, village improvement and rural life, schools, and mutual insurance. As evidence of the high degree of interest, it was reported, for example, that the co-operative movement in Bombay hoped to enroll more than half the population in multi-purpose co-operatives within the next 15 years, and that the Government of the United Provinces (now Uttar Pradesh) planned to have at least one society in each village.

Since then the movement has been steadily on the march. FAO has held another conference for Asia and the Far East, in Ceylon in February 1954, with the International Labour Organisation as joint sponsor. Eleven countries were represented as compared with seven at the meeting more than four years earlier in Lucknow.

Lumber Economy

At the opening session of the FAO Timber Grading School at Kepong, Malaya, on February 8, 1952, His Highness Tengku Ya'acob ibni Al-Marhum Sultan Abdul Hamid Halim Shah said:

If a merchant in one country wants to buy rubber, pepper or rice (or any of a host of other natural products) from another country, or if he wants to buy manufactured products like textiles, jam, or beer and so on, he will call for a representative sample of the product that the seller can supply. If the sample meets with his approval, and the price is right, he will place an order. That in short is the method of buying and selling in the world today. But a few sheets of rubber, a packet of pepper corns, a yard or two of cloth, or a bottle or two of beer take up little space and can easily be sent as samples.

He went on to point out that it is not possible to supply small representative samples of timber so that a buyer can determine its suitability for particular uses. It would be necessary (but too expensive) to send several logs or a score of boards cut from different logs. The alternative to samples is the use of accurate written descriptions of the qualities and characteristics of timber. A good system of grading provides such descriptions. The buyer who purchases on the basis of honest grades can be sure he will get what he asks for. Adequate grading, in turn, depends on inspection and classification of timber by qualified experts. The purpose of the Kepong school was to train grading officers for the timber trade in the Far East.

To the school came 19 students from seven countries. They studied 25 different timbers which go by names strange to the Westerner—Bintangor, Geronggang, Jelutong, Kedondong, Kempas, Keruing, Medang, and so on. All day every day except on week ends they went to lectures on the theory of lumber grading and saw its practical application in sawmills, in factories, and on the Singapore docks.

This was one of the regional projects developed by the Forestry Commission for Asia and the Pacific, an organization set up under the auspices of FAO at a meeting in Bangkok in October 1950, with Mom Chao Suebsukswasti Sukswasti (Thailand) as chairman.

A second meeting was held in Kuala Lumpur and Singapore in 1952, with J. P. Edwards (UK) as chairman. The groundwork for the commission was laid at a regional forestry conference in Mysore, India, in 1949, which stirred widespread interest in the development of forests and forest industries in the Far East.

After the timber-grading institute at Kepong, the commission sponsored another training course in the Philippines, beginning in October 1952 and lasting for six months. This was concerned with modern logging and milling practices, particularly the use of mechanical equipment, with H. G. Keith (Canada) and Florencio Tamesis (the Philippines) as co-directors. Much of the work of felling and moving timber in the Far East forests is done by primitive methods involving the most arduous hand labor. Government and the industry alike are increasingly interested in modernizing these operations. The Philippines was chosen for this training course because it is the only country in the region where mechanical logging is the rule rather than the exception.

Forty people from 11 countries took the course. They not only received theoretical instruction, putting in about two months at the College of Forestry of the University of the Philippines; they also spent four months visiting the logging camps of four big lumber companies where they saw many kinds of equipment used under many kinds of conditions. The program was a stiff one. Sometimes the group had to start out at 4:30 in the morning; frequently they made field trips all day and listened to lectures at night.

"It may be said with confidence," as Keith put it at the close of the institute, "that none will return to his country without a reasonably intelligent appreciation of the possibilities as well as the limitations inherent in mechanized extraction."

WORK WITH INDIVIDUAL COUNTRIES

India

Census Commissioner R. A. Gopalaswami reported that the population of India in 1951 was 360 million, equal to about one out of every six of the people on earth, as much as the population of the United States and the Soviet Union combined, crowded on about a tenth of the land area of those two large countries. If the Indian population should continue to expand at its present rate, it would number 520 million in three more decades. This fact helps to explain why the government is so deeply concerned about increasing food production and why it is interested in studying the question of population control.

China is the other land with a population numbering hundreds of millions. Each of these countries is going through profound economic and social changes. In China they are following the pattern of communist Russia, in India the pattern of the Western democracies. The world is deeply concerned with the outcome in both cases.

India hopes to double the average income of her people in about 25 years. As Prime Minister Nehru has expressed it, this means advancing suddenly and by democratic means from the age of the bullock cart to the atomic age.

According to a recent report by the Government of India Planning Commission, the program covers these principal fields of activity: agricultural production including land reclamation, crops, fertilizers, finance, animal husbandry, fisheries; rural extension services and community projects, including village roads and housing; irrigation and power; industrial development; transport and communications; social services—health, education, labor, housing; land reform, including abolition of rent collectors, reform of tenancy, ceilings on holdings, subdivision and consolidation of holdings, and reorganization of agriculture.

The irrigation and land reclamation work is one of the biggest operations of its kind in the world, and the village and community development program is actually the biggest ever attempted. In the latter, the Indian Government is co-operating with the United States Government and the Ford Foundation in a comprehensive program covering 120,000 villages, about a fourth of the rural population, in the first five years. In 70,000 of these villages, extension services are being established for 49 million people as part of an intensive program. Thirty-four centers have been organized to train extension workers, who are being chosen from the village people. Each of the trainees must, as Ferdinand Kuhn said, "be willing, first of all, to work with his hands. No matter what his caste . . . nobody is exempt; everyone has to wash dishes, clean latrines, dig compost pits, cultivate a seed-bed by hand and do all the other things which, in time, the village worker will have to teach the farmer to do. . . . In the setting of India, with its rigid social stratification of hundreds of years, what is going on in the training centers is in truth a revolution."

In a sense, then, India is now making itself a vast laboratory for working out ways of hastening changes in agriculture and rural living that have become imperative in many lands. If the undertaking succeeds, that country

Far East

will be proof that the transition from the old world to the new by peaceful means is possible even under difficult conditions. It seems to be succeeding, and a new dynamic spirit is now evident among millions of Indian villagers.

Not extensively but in significant ways India is using the services of FAO in this great enterprise. The government has taken a leading part in the regional work of the Rice Commission, the Forestry Commission, the Fisheries Council, and the training institutes and conferences described earlier in this chapter. On a country-wide basis, the most important FAO projects have been connected with farm machinery and livestock.

The Tractor and Machine Stations

India's large irrigation and reclamation projects require mechanical equipment of all kinds for land clearing, leveling, and other operations. There is also some large-scale colonization, particularly in the State of Uttar Pradesh, which involves tractor plowing and tillage. A dozen large farms are used as demonstration and training centers for mechanized farming.

Tractor and machine stations are located at various points to service the equipment in the field, obtain and distribute machines and parts, provide training for operators and mechanics, and in some cases manufacture certain kinds of equipment. Some of this work is done by the Government of India through its Central Tractor Organization, some by the state governments.

Modern farm machinery is not new to India, but its use is being expanded faster than at any time in the past. This involves many difficult problems, since facilities for repair and maintenance are scarce, and so are experienced workers.

FAO has been able to provide some technical co-operation which helps to fill the gaps. The former head of the FAO mission, J. C. Hansen (Denmark), is a machine expert, and eight other machinery experts have been assigned to India at various times, mainly in Uttar Pradesh. They have worked in the machine centers and workshops at Lucknow, Bareilly, Talkalore, and Jhansi. At one place less than 15 per cent of the tractors and implements on farms were in working order. Starting in temporary sheet-iron shacks with tools salvaged from an old mobile army shop or made from scrap, the Indian workers, with FAO help, built up a center that now does all kinds of repairs and major overhauling. This is an area, moreover, where tractors frequently have to operate in clouds of gritty dust, and where dust storms sometimes make keeping the fuel and oil clean almost impossible. All this has meant giving much in-service training for machine workers.

Some of the government workshops are now as good as can be found anywhere, and India may well be proud of them. They take care of privately owned as well as government-owned tractors. But mechanical equipment is still only a small part of the farm picture. Practically all the work on small farms is done with hand tools and animal-drawn equipment, much of it crude. The new machine centers are playing a part in introducing better small tools, in some cases manufacturing the new types by line-production methods.

Multitudes of Cattle

There are 198 million cattle and buffaloes in India, more than twice the number of cattle in the USA (and of course millions of other animals). How to feed and manage them for more efficient work and better production is one of the big problems of agricultural improvement. Its importance is by no means universally recognized. Where cows often wander freely in the streets, cattle are so taken for granted that few people give thought to the penalties of bad management. Overgrazing is almost universal. Many animals may be half-starved during much of the year, and in a drought huge numbers perish.

As a step in attacking this problem literally at the grass roots, India obtained the services of FAO grasslands expert R. O. Whyte (UK). He made the first survey of grazing conditions throughout the country; prepared a handbook that should be fundamentally useful for a long time to come on grazing resources, especially those that do not compete with foods that can be used directly by human beings; and laid out a program of research and demonstration for improving grass and forage production.

The livestock disease-control program is also being stepped up. Because of the enormous number of animals involved, it will take several years for immunization against serious diseases such as rinderpest to blanket the country effectively. The central government and some of the states are making good progress in the manufacture of vaccines by modern methods and are expanding both their research and their field campaigns. Some of the veterinary colleges are reorganizing and improving their training courses. The key village plan, as I have previously noted, is extending the use of artificial insemination. In all of this FAO has been able to provide considerable help through a team of eight animal production experts, of which the senior member was R. L. Daubney (UK).

One of the most striking livestock developments in India, or indeed the Far East, is the milk distribution program of the city of Bombay. In this, FAO experts S. B. Sorensen (Denmark) and Ian D. MacRae (UK) have helped on technical problems. The Bombay Milk Scheme was started in 1944 and has become more or less a model for other cities in the region. Previously the milk was as bad as that in many other cities around the world. The bacterial count was high, and the unclean milk was diluted with equally unclean water. In a few years the city authorities have revolutionized production and handling. This has involved removing most of the buffaloes that supply the milk from the city and establishing them in dairy units several miles away, providing free veterinary services, purchasing feed in bulk, and carefully collecting manure and using it as fertilizer for growing green fodder rather than letting people burn it for fuel. The standards of cleanliness in milk handling are said to be as high as those found almost anywhere in the West. Subsidies are used to stimulate production and at the same time keep prices reasonably low for consumers. An interesting experiment has been the production of a blend of buffalo milk with reconstituted dry skim milk, which results in a product containing less butterfat but more protein. The FAO Mission to Egypt concerned with dairy problems recommended a similar procedure for that country.

Because of the large numbers of animals in India, hides and skins are important products, but every year large quantities are ruined or seriously damaged by bad handling and processing. With help from FAO expert F. H. Hoek (the Netherlands) and US co-operation, several community centers have now been established where people are trained in leather production, and co-operative societies are being formed to market leather and leather products. This kind of work gives quick returns, provides employment for many young people, and raises the prestige of an occupation that has hitherto been at a low level in the hierarchy of trades.

In the State of Uttar Pradesh, FAO experts G. R. Upward and H. W. Newton (Australia) have given technical assistance in sheep and wool production. They helped set up an experimental farm which may eventually become a stud farm for the production and distribution of breeding flocks for the village shepherds. The nucleus of the flock was provided by FAO from Australia. A wool analysis laboratory has been established also. Government officers are regularly trained in improved methods at these centers.

Fish, Forests, and Food

As elsewhere in the Far East, India has a growing interest in fish production and marketing. FAO expert W. F. L. van der Heyden (the Netherlands), assigned to West Bengal, has recommended a program that is fairly typical. It includes steps to protect fishermen from exploitation by middlemen, who under present conditions get most of the profits; to improve transportation so the fish will reach the market in better condition; to improve craft and gear, which might practically double the number of days the fishermen can go to sea; to stop the depredations of sea-gangsters who prey on fishermen; to raise the status of fishing as an occupation.

FAO naval architect P. B. Ziener (Norway) has been in India studying the adaptability of native craft for the use of motors, and M. O. Kristensen (Norway) has given some help to the federal government in the work of the fisheries research stations in Bombay, West Bengal, and Madras. F. O. Botke (the Netherlands) carried on experiments with hormone weed killers to destroy water hyacinths and other aquatic plants that often choke inland bodies of water and are the greatest single obstacle to fish culture.

India has a highly developed forest service and an excellent training school at Dehra Dun. FAO has provided some co-operation in working out ways to carry on logging operations in the Himalayan Mountains, in the northwest, on a year-round basis rather than only in the summer as hitherto, as well as in timber research and the development of wood industries. In the Himalayas Alfred Huber (Switzerland), traveling on foot over winter snows, found that the production of railroad ties (the chief product) could be made much more efficient by such steps as making use of the half of the tree that now goes to waste; shaping the ties with a portable sawmill, accomplishing in an hour as much as two men can do in a day with axes and hand saws; skidding the logs out on snow chutes in winter instead of carrying them laboriously out by hand in summer.

In Uttar Pradesh the government is taking steps to make use of fruits and vegetables now wasted during seasonal periods of peak production. With FAO technical co-operation, several canneries have been started and others are under construction. A grading system for fruits and vegetables has been established, a Directorate of Fruit Utilization has been set up, and classes in home food preservation have been held for the women of Lucknow. FAO has also given some assistance in the program of the All India Women's Council in setting up cafeterias in large cities to serve good meals at low cost. The cafeteria or "Annapoorna" movement is proving so popular that the Council is having difficulty in responding fully to the demand. The work of the FAO expert has also contributed to the establishment of a College of Catering and Nutrition, to help in raising catering standards throughout the country.

Ceylon

Ceylon, lying like a pearl off the eartip of India, is divided climatically into two parts. The northern and eastern area, the so-called Dry Zone, has a rainfall of 50 to 60 inches a year, concentrated in the monsoon season. In the southwest third, the Wet Zone, rainfall averages around 135 inches a year.

Some five centuries B.C., Dravidian peoples from lower India swept down over northern Ceylon, founding a culture which in the succeeding centuries developed to a high level. These people built up an elaborate irrigation system of ditches and ponds to catch and spread rainwater for rice growing. Eventually their civilization was smashed by invaders from other parts of India and by internal strife. During a long period of decay, the northern part of the island, including all the great irrigation works, reverted once more to jungle.

Later, Ceylon was dominated by European peoples—Portuguese in the sixteenth century, Dutch in the seventeenth, British toward the end of the eighteenth. Thus for generations the island has been ruled by foreign powers. Then in 1948 it became an independent country with membership in the British Commonwealth.

The Europeans were concerned mainly with export crops grown on large plantations—on the high land, coffee, eventually wiped out by a fungus disease and replaced by the famous Ceylon tea; at middle elevations, rubber; on the lowlands, coconut palms. For subsistence, the peasants grow rice and other food plants on millions of handkerchief-size farms. Agriculture has been confined mainly to the Wet Zone, where the population is compressed into a comparatively small area.

The overwhelming emphasis given by the colonial powers to crops for export left Ceylon short of enough food for its people. Each year the country imports about twice as much rice as it produces, as well as considerable amounts of other foods. This extreme dependence on exports creates a precarious situation in view of the uncertainties in the overseas markets. Meanwhile, since DDT practically freed the country of malaria, the population is expanding faster than almost anywhere else in the world.

How to produce more food is the crucial problem. Ceylon has been tackling it vigorously and before independence had started on a course of economic development. Since then the country has been getting help from the Colombo Plan (born in Ceylon's capital city), the International Bank, and FAO and other United Nations agencies. The program includes agriculture, industry, transport, communications, power, education, and health. Unfortunately the work has been slowed by financial difficulties following an adverse turn in export trade.

The biggest and most dramatic undertaking has been to clear vast jungles in the north and east, restore ancient irrigation systems, build new ones, and colonize the area with farm families from other parts of Ceylon.

According to a recent report by the International Bank, the total area of Ceylon is $16\frac{1}{4}$ million acres, of which $6\frac{3}{4}$ million is suitable for agriculture. Of this, $2\frac{1}{4}$ million acres is in tea, rubber, and coconuts, and $1\frac{1}{4}$ million in rice and miscellaneous crops. About $3\frac{1}{4}$ million acres, almost as much as the area now cultivated, is not yet developed. Much of this is in the Dry Zone, now receiving major attention.

FAO has helped by providing 35 technicians from a dozen different countries who have been concerned with soil chemistry, production of synthetic nitrogen fertilizer, control of crop insects and diseases, dairy and poultry production, agricultural statistics, forest management and forest industries, fisheries, and the organization of a food research institute.

For instance, dry-farming expert Evan Hardy (Canada) carried out groundwater surveys, classified land, and helped to establish cropping and tillage systems in the north. One of the main problems there, as in other hot climates, is to slow the swift breakdown of organic matter in the soil, especially when it is exposed by clearing. Hardy grew cover crops of velvet beans and *dhal* (pigeon peas) and seeded the main crop with special machines underneath this plant cover, which keeps the soil relatively cool, supplies and conserves organic matter, and saves plowing and disking for weed control. *Dhal* is also a useful plant in many other ways.

At the big Gal Oya River Valley development in the east a great dam has been built for the government by an engineering firm. Here the plan is to settle some 25,000 families on about 250,000 acres over a period of 10 years or so. The area is divided into village units, each housing 150 families and provided with a school, co-operative store, village hall, marketplace, and heavy machinery for community use. Each family also receives farm implements, and as many families as possible are given a minimum number of animals. In this area FAO agronomist S. T. Farouky (Jordan) has been doing somewhat the same kind of work that Hardy has done farther north.

Squads of tractors dragging heavy chains knock down the thick jungle growth, haul off the stumps, and pile up tree trunks, brush, and earth to make the banks (bunds) that are the walls of the reservoirs. Farouky has been putting these bunds to use for growing crops; they equal about 20 per cent of the total land area and include much of the topsoil, which is scraped off the fields in the clearing operation.

There is a good deal of interest in producing sugar in Ceylon for domestic use; some 100,000 tons are now imported annually. FAO's C. van Dillewijn (the Netherlands, with long experience in Indonesia) was assigned to explore possibilities for sugar production. He noted that the island is in the center of the great tropical sugar belt, yet sugar has never been grown there. His experiments indicated that yields in Ceylon could be as high as anywhere in the Far East. A rice-sugar cane rotation, moreover, would benefit the rice by returning much organic matter to the paddy fields. Van Dillewijn started a sugar-development program which is continuing with the help of another Netherlands expert, H. V. Reerink, though it, too, has now been slowed down by shortage of funds.

In the extensive land clearing and other operations, adequate maintenance and servicing of tractors and machinery is of vital importance. Australia and New Zealand have supplied a good deal of machinery under the Colombo Plan. FAO sent six machine experts to the Gal Oya Valley and the northern dry zone to help set up service organizations and train mechanics.

The Ceylonese have reason to be proud of what they have accomplished in the machine program. For example, the FAO experts report that "the workshops of the Gal Oya Development Board at Amparai are second to none in the East and equal in many ways to those in the United Kingdom and United States." This unit has been gaining a reputation abroad and has received applications for training from Thailand, Indonesia, Malaya, and India. Ceylonese mechanics, many of them without any experience until recently, are able and ingenious in working out mechanical devices and improvements; one, for example, designed and made a device for straightening nails (as many as 2000 can be recovered from a single big packing crate) and a device that makes buckle clips for electric wiring from bits of scrap aluminum. The supervising officers, according to FAO reports, can compete with those in any country. In other words, the people of Ceylon have no lack of innate mechanical and inventive ability; what is needed is a chance to develop it.

Ceylon is short of livestock, and FAO animal husbandry specialist Henry Hirst (UK) has been working on the livestock part of the government's six-year plan. Six government stock farms carry some 400 head of cattle, and there are several other experiment stations with considerable numbers. Careful records are now being kept to provide basic information for programs of improved breeding and feeding.

FAO dairy specialist E. A. Danbom (USA) has been helping in a project to improve the processing and distribution of milk, especially for the city of Colombo.

Eggs are imported and in great demand. FAO poultry expert J. W. Brant (USA) has done a great deal of work to help make more production possible, especially in small farm flocks.

Two FAO veterinarians have been helping on problems connected with animal diseases, which are under better control in Ceylon than in some other countries in the Far East. FAO has also had two forest experts in Ceylon working on equipment and machinery for opening up rough or inaccessible areas, and on the use of machines for forest planting. At the UNESCO fundamental education center FAO expert George Reisner (USA) helped to develop extension activities, mainly with young people, organizing boys and girls in "paddy clubs" to improve rice production, poultry clubs to do the same thing with chickens, and snail-eradication groups to wipe out the snails that harbor liver flukes. All these young people are eager to learn, and what they are learning and doing should in the long run profoundly affect farm practices. FAO is co-operating in home economics work too at the UNESCO center.

Earlier in this chapter I discussed the regional interest in motorizing fishing boats. Ceylon is a good example of this trend. At the end of 1951 the only motor-powered fishing boat in Ceylon was one steam-trawler. At that time FAO sent a master fisherman, and later a marine engineer, to advise on mechanization. In April 1953 FAO supplied three small diesel marine engines, which were installed in three fishermen's boats. The men were given some instruction on how to maintain and use the motors and then left to their own devices. At the end of six months they were asked if they wanted to buy the motors; if not, FAO would take them out and restore the boats to their original condition. The fishermen all jumped at the chance, and others clamored for motors, too. So another 40 small diesel marine engines are being provided under the Colombo Plan, to be sold on easy terms, and more will be provided later.

Thailand

Thai means free; Thailand is the free land, the Thai people are the free people. Thailand had never been conquered by a foreign power until the Japanese invasion in World War II. In this country of innumerable winding waterways traversed by slender boats, great stretches of rice fields, majestic teak forests, lovely temples, and a warm-hearted, intelligent, singularly courteous people, FAO has its Far East Regional Office headed by W. H. Cummings (born and raised in Burma, of US missionary parents).

Besides its participation in FAO regional activities, Thailand has had help mainly in surveying production potentials and needs, in improving the economic position of small-scale producers of rice and rubber, and in fish culture, poultry production, and veterinary services.

In another chapter I described the earlier FAO surveys of agriculture, forests, and fisheries in Thailand. Many of the recommendations made, particularly those concerned with irrigation, have been gradually put into effect, with help from the US Government and the International Bank.

Burma was once the most important rice exporter in the Far East, before the long wartime and postwar setback. Then for a time Thailand became the largest exporter. Rice yields per acre in Thailand, however, are somewhat less than in Burma. In Thailand the producer receives about a fourth of the sale price of his rice; about three fourths goes to the government and middlemen. (This problem was discussed briefly in Chapter Six.) The producer usually has to sell as soon as the crop is harvested, when prices are lowest; he has no storage facilities, and he could not afford to wait for his money in any case. If he could, he might get a materially better price.

FAO's J. W. Coddington (USA) recently made a study of the rice economy in Thailand to advise officials on a plan to provide granaries holding about 500,000 tons of rice. On that part of the crop put in storage, the farmer would receive a loan of 80 per cent of the current market price. The other 20 per cent he would get later on, including any addition resulting from higher prices at that time. Thus he would realize a larger gain on whatever part of his crop he could afford to store on the basis of an 80 per cent cash loan. This operation would cost the equivalent of about 5 million dollars (US) a year for the first five years, but it should be self-liquidating.

The storage program would be combined with a program for improvements in rice milling. Much of the milling equipment is so old that it damages the grain, which then brings a lower price. This loss could be avoided if millers would install new and better equipment. Under the proposed program the government would set up a modern mill as part of a demonstration to stimulate these changes.

Installation of equipment to extract the oil from rice bran would be the third aspect of the program. Including the oil it contains, bran sells for the equivalent of about 1½ cents (US) a pound. If the oil were sold separately, it would bring 10 times that much, about 15 cents a pound; and the bran, useful for livestock feed, could be stored longer without spoiling. The oil project also would pay for itself.

As part of this proposed program the government and FAO held a training institute on rice grading, inspection, and storage, with FAO providing much of the equipment, which was later bought by the government for its new grading laboratory.

Next to rice, rubber is Thailand's most important export product. Although Thailand is the world's third largest producer of natural rubber, rubber is not a big plantation crop there but, like rice, is produced mainly by small-scale farmers. The processing of the latex is crude—so much so that only a very small part of it fetches a good price. This is a matter of some importance since most of the rubber goes to the USA and is one of Thailand's main sources of dollar earnings. FAO's William Lloyd (UK) has been helping the Thai producer co-operatives to turn out a much better product. Six co-operative processing plants and a testing station have been built, and several others are on the way. The government has also worked out a plan for running a fairly large plantation to demonstrate better production methods and distribute improved trees to farmers.

The Thai people are co-operative-minded and have a number of other types of co-operative organizations besides those concerned with rubber. FAO co-operatives expert Gordon Ward (USA) has been in Thailand for about two years helping to work out scores of specific improvements in practices and procedures—selling, buying, investment, bookkeeping, and so on.

The third major Thailand export is teakwood. Since its forest survey several years ago, FAO has provided a number of experts who have helped with a forest inventory, a program for reforestation and improved forest management, and the modernization of sawmilling. It will take time for this work to show large-scale results.

In inland fisheries FAO expert S. W. Ling (China) has helped effectively to expand production. To get beyond the limitations of artificial ponds, he turned to producing fish in large areas of water—flooded rice fields, canals, swampland. The Thai people have performed wonders in making use of these resources. They converted swamps into lakes, stocked every possible stretch of water with fry and fingerlings, made widespread use of that almost unbelievably prolific and adaptable fish, tilapia (10,000 copies of a leaflet on tilapia by Ling were published and distributed), built up and strengthened the government fisheries department, and created a fisheries extension service.

Somewhat similar work has been under way in connection with poultry. A Thai university professor, Luang Suwan Kasikit, has for years been a tireless prophet and exponent of expanded poultry production. He and a few other enthusiasts enlisted the interest of the King and high officials in poultry production, started one or two poultry journals, put on a unique radio program, and did other remarkable things. FAO has been able to help by providing the services of three experts, F. N. Fronda (Philippines), J. E. Lancaster (UK), J. G. Campbell (UK). A systematic program of breeding, feeding, management, and disease control is now well under way; the last is especially important since Newcastle disease has been the main limiting factor in expanding production. Poultry is essentially a backyard industry in Thailand and therefore particularly significant for the small-scale farmer.

Work in animal disease control has been mentioned earlier in connection with the rinderpest program. Progress in improving veterinary services has been outstanding, but much still needs to be done to build up a veterinary organization adequate to take care of the large number of animals in Thailand. An interesting development is the research of FAO's R. V. S. Bain (Australia), first in Burma, later in Thailand, on an improved vaccine for hemorrhagic septicemia, a troublesome disease that causes considerable loss of livestock all over the world and is now especially important in Thailand.

FAO has also had an agricultural economist helping to set up the economics unit in the Ministry of Agriculture and an extension man working with the UNESCO Fundamental Education Center in Bangkok. FAO nutrition workers have co-operated with the government in organizing surveys, planning a National Nutrition Council, and setting up a Nutrition Research Institute.

Burma

The Government of Burma, an independent country since 1948, is young, forward-looking, eager to carry out new plans and ideas. The country is not overcrowded; there is room to increase production considerably without straining natural resources; education is widespread; the literacy rate is high; the future seems promising. But simmering guerrilla warfare made any steady peaceful development impossible for some time. In many places the technical experts from both FAO and the USA were unable to carry on their work, and technical co-operation had to be reduced to the minimum.

The help given by FAO has been concerned mainly with forests and timber industries, livestock diseases, poultry, and silk production. Work in dairy development, nutrition, and agricultural statistics is getting under way, and the government has started a program for bringing new land under cultivation, with FAO assistance in organizing tractor and machine shops.

Burma has very large forest resources which can be further developed. Since forestry was tied in with the work of the institute at Dehra Dun, India, there is a good background of knowledge and training in the Burma service. The forests and wood industries now provide a livelihood for about

600,000 people, 3 per cent of the population; this number could be greatly increased.

Aside from teak for export, wood is used mainly as fuel for cooking. Bamboo is the common material for building houses, since it is cheap and easy to handle. There are many possibilities for using wood, especially chipboard and wallboard, in house construction. FAO forest experts J. A. von Monroy and K. A. Miedler (Austria) sent 60 tons of wood of nondurable types from Burma to Germany, where it was processed, returned to Rangoon, and used to build two sample houses, one made of conventional kiln-dried lumber, the other of chipboard. These buildings—even the chipboard roof—have stood up well under monsoon rains.

The comprehensive FAO survey brought out many possibilities for the development of integrated forest industries. The government is now endeavoring to carry out these proposals step by step and is setting up equipment, provided by FAO, for kiln-drying wood and for treating it chemically for decay resistance.

There were a million less cattle in Burma in 1951 than 10 years before. During the Japanese invasion many animals were slaughtered for food and rinderpest has been serious. Lack of draft animals was one reason for the falling off of rice production in Burma, which before the war exported 3 million tons a year—as much as Thailand and Indochina together.

Twice within the last 10 years the laboratory and clinic of the veterinary center at Insein, a few miles north of Rangoon, were destroyed, and the training institute there was stripped of equipment. They have now been restored and are functioning well. The Burmese veterinary force, however, is far too small to handle the disease problem for 5 million cattle.

FAO veterinarians I. W. Kelton, R. V. S. Bain, and G. Edgar (all from Australia) studied the disease situation, helped to refit the laboratory and clinic with equipment provided largely by the USA, and introduced modern methods of producing vaccines and other biologics. FAO poultry expert P. J. Schyns (Belgium) also concentrated mainly on disease control.

Burma started silk production early in the 1920's and by 1941 had a number of experiment stations and a fairly large acreage of mulberry trees. Everything came to a standstill with the war. Now some 20,000 families are eager to take up silk culture. FAO expert S. I. Kano (Japan) has been helping to re-establish the central experiment station and to get improved types of mulberries, better species of silkworms, and better hand-reeling equipment. This program is well on its way, and a new silk-culture school was opened in 1953.

Indonesia

Indonesia consists of some 2000 tropical islands like flowers strewn by the Creator across 3000 miles of sea. Until recently they were the Dutch East Indies; earlier, as the Spice Isles, many of them were famous in history and romance as well as commerce; and they still produce a good deal of the world's pepper, nutmeg, mace, cloves, cinnamon—and natural rubber. About 74 million people, equal to nearly half the population of the USA, live on these islands; perhaps 4½ million of them are able to read.

Two thirds of the people are concentrated on one ninth of the land area, the islands of Java and Madura. In some places in northern Java there are 1500 people to the square mile; few spots in the world are as crowded. On another of the islands, Borneo, there are 13 people to the square mile; few spots are less crowded.

The Dutch had a highly developed agriculture, with 20 experiment stations on Java alone. Most of the research was carried on by Dutch scientists, who trained very few Indonesians for this kind of work; hence one of the most urgent concerns of the new government is to get many more Indonesians trained and, meanwhile, to borrow experts from abroad.

Some indigenous institutions hold much promise for further progress. The rural banks, for instance, each owned by a village community and operated by the village headman, were perhaps the first credit agencies of the kind in the Far East. Unfortunately they were victims of years of war and civil disturbance, but they might be revived. Extension services, too, are better developed in Indonesia than in most places in the region.

The government is now engaged in a difficult struggle to modernize agriculture and help the people attain better living standards. There are programs for improving and expanding irrigation, increasing the use of fertilizers, establishing seed farms, and colonizing parts of the outer islands with people from overcrowded Java. In developing its general program, the government during the past two years has used the services of FAO agricultural expert J. van der Ploeg (the Netherlands).

Hundreds of millions of acres of forests, capable of extensive development, cover these islands (over three fourths of Borneo is forest). FAO has helped to get mechanical logging under way in three typical areas.

The infant mortality rate is very high, and many of the deaths of young children are the result of undernourishment. The government is working hard to establish a sound nutrition program. An FAO staff officer who had long experience in the famous Eyckman Institute in Java helped to plan the program and set up a nutrition organization, and another staff nutrition expert, following up experiments made several years ago in the Institute, worked on a project to use so-called soya milk (*saridele*) for feeding in health centers, schools, and hospitals. This could be produced in large quantities to compensate to some extent for the shortage of cow's milk. The *saridele* will be distributed mainly in dehydrated form, which simplifies packaging and lowers costs. To improve taste and flavor, some peanut milk and malt extract are added before dehydration. FAO's J. W. B. Visser (the Netherlands) has organized and conducted courses to train local dietitians.

Indonesia is also using FAO services in soils work, extension, horticulture, and agricultural economics.

Nepal

Nepal, a slice of the Himalaya Mountains sandwiched between India and Tibet, has been bypassed by the scientific and mechanical developments of modern civilization more than have most countries. Beautiful and difficult of access, it is inhabited by people who have Mt. Everest and Mt. Annapurna in their back yard. Though much of the upper part of the country is cold and vertical, the southern edge is nearly at sea level and is warm enough to grow rice and subtropical fruits. North of this area the land rises abruptly to spectacular snowclad peaks. At present the country has less than 200 miles of road that can be traveled by automobile and only a few miles of railroad; those who have to make extensive journeys, including FAO workers, are likely to travel half the way on horseback, half on foot. A 14-mile ropeway hauls freight up the mountainside to the capital city, Katmandu.

Nepal grows rice, wheat, cotton, jute, and a considerable variety of other products. Cattle, buffaloes, yaks, oxen, sheep, goats, and poultry are kept on small farms. Animals are not used for farm work in the mountains. The land is turned with heavy mattocks, not plowed or even spaded. The lumps are broken up with wooden mallets. Grain is cut with sickles. Very little milk can be sold fresh; it is made into fermented products or ghee.

Life smacks less of the twentieth century than of the Middle Ages. But the Nepalese are a vigorous, intelligent, skillful people who have mastered a hard environment that would crush the average "civilized" Westerner; and they are as capable of doing new things as any other people, once they have the chance and the desire.

The government is anxious to initiate changes. In 1950 another mountain country, Switzerland, sent a group of experts to Nepal at the latter country's request, to work out possibilities for agricultural improvement. Later FAO continued the program with some of the same group.

Outstanding among the projects is the work in dairying. Dairy expert W. G. Schulthess (Switzerland) traveled by foot and horseback over much of the country, lived and worked with the cattlemen on their little farms, saw what was being done in each village, compared the practices in different villages and areas, found out what improvements the people could effect by their own efforts, and helped them—by giving practical demonstrations in the hut of every herd owner—to use their own skills to make changes in the production, handling, and marketing of milk.

In northeast Nepal, Schulthess found that the Sherpas, rugged folk living high in the mountains, cross yaks with local dairy cows. (You will remember that Tenzing Norkey, who accompanied Sir Edmund Hilary to the top of

Mt. Everest in May 1953, is a Sherpa guide.) Above the snowline, the heavy, hairy, long-horned yak is often used for transport. Yak cows produce little milk, nor do the local dairy cattle do much better. But when yaks and dairy animals are crossed, the result is a spurt of hybrid vigor expressed in higher production than that of either foundation stock.

Schulthess gained the confidence of these cattlemen, and the government asked him to stay on after finishing his first assignment. An FAO fellowship was granted to a Nepalese to study in New Zealand and Switzerland.

FAO has also had a farm management expert in Nepal, an agronomist, an expert in soils and irrigation, and a forester. All of them have made proposals for development programs. There is no doubt that great improvements can be made, but the beginnings are likely in most cases to be small and local, gradually widening as they prove their value. These people live on a margin of safety as precarious as a footpath along the edge of one of their own dizzy ravines. They must climb carefully.

FAO WORK IN OTHER FAR EAST COUNTRIES

FAO has so far been able to do little work in other countries of the Far East except Korea. There a sizable FAO unit has been concerned with crops, fertilizers, irrigation, marketing, agricultural economics, rural community problems, nutrition, forestry, and fisheries. This group is part of a mission sent by the United Nations Korean Relief Administration, which is responsible for reporting on the work.

In Cambodia an FAO economist has served as consultant on the government's agricultural development plans and the organization of agricultural services. In Malaya an expert has surveyed the farm economy in general— the status of farmers, prices, financial aid to producers, economic incentives for increased production, grading, marketing, and storage facilities. In the Philippines, where some 60 per cent of the land is in forests, FAO has had a number of forestry experts on short-term assignments concerned with specific problems of timber extraction and logging and with reforestation and forest legislation. I have previously discussed the regional training course on mechanical logging held in the Philippines.

CHAPTER
TEN

Latin America

REGIONAL PROJECTS

Trees

TREES are one of the great resources of Latin America; a fourth of the world's forests are in that region, and just as a magnificent green mantle once covered most of the United States, so it still covers large parts of the southern continent. Not quite half (40 per cent) of the area is woodland, much of it unused but in many places scourged by fire or destroyed by shifting cultivation.

The region is rich in tropical and subtropical tree species, about many of which very little is known. Certain kinds of trees that grow in these forests—mahogany, greenheart, cedar, for example—have great value; men seek them only a little less eagerly than they seek gold. But these trees are rare and widely scattered, and are expensive, therefore, to obtain. For the sake of the forests (and in most cases for the sake of the national income) it would be better not to concentrate on the rarities but to take timber of all kinds, at the proper size for cutting and in accordance with the requirements of sustained yield.

But if there are vast quantities of unutilized timber in Latin America, there are also areas, especially near large cities, where land that should have the protection of trees has been stripped bare and opened to serious damage.

The great extent and value of the forest resources make all the more imperative their use to good advantage. Perhaps the most significant development in that direction was the move to set up a regional Forestry and Forest Products Commission, made at a meeting in Rio de Janeiro in May 1949, following a session in Teresopolis the year before (April 1948) which laid the groundwork for such an organization. At the Teresopolis meeting 20 countries and four organizations were represented, with Virgilio Gualberto (Brazil) as chairman. Subsequent sessions of the commission met at Lima in November 1949, Santiago (Chile) in December 1950, and Buenos Aires in June 1952.

One of the foremost needs in all Latin American countries is for a great deal of research and investigation to get more facts (very few are available) about the real extent of the forest resources of Latin America, the species of trees, the uses to which the timber can best be put. This kind of investigation lends itself to a regional approach. So does the training and education of forestry people and the building up of the knowledge and skill essential to good modern forestry practice.

To accomplish these ends, the commission decided to establish a Latin American Forest Research and Training Institute and six subregional research centers, for Mexico and Central America, for the Caribbean, for the tropical Andes, for the southern Andes, for the Paraná-Plata-Paraguay area, and for the Amazon area. Final proposals for establishing and financing the institute are to be presented at the next meeting of the regional commission in Venezuela in March 1955.

At its 1954 session the commission asked FAO to foster an association of Latin American foresters. At this session many countries reported that a good deal of progress has been made in forestry work and the development of national forest policies. For instance, Venezuela has a school of forestry; Chile is starting one with FAO help; forestry training courses are being given in schools of agriculture in Argentina, Brazil, Cuba, Costa Rica, and Peru; research is under way in Argentina, Chile, Puerto Rico, Surinam, and Trinidad; in several countries development corporations (*corporaciones de fomento,* semiprivate, semigovernmental institutions peculiar to Latin America) are keenly interested in expanding forest industries or starting new ones.

This ferment of activity is significant not only for Latin America but for other parts of the world. For in relation to population and rising standards of living, the world's forest resources—and especially those of the north temperate zone—have been dwindling. As they grow smaller, the great under-used resources of the tropical regions assume an increasing importance for all who live outside the tropics.

Paper Work

Increasing literacy and education create a demand for more printed matter; expanding commerce and industry means more paper work, more wrapping paper, boxes, cartons; rising standards of living are accompanied by greater household use of paper; and even without all these factors, population growth itself steps up the total demand for paper. The great suppliers are Europe and North America. They make 90 per cent of the world's paper and paperboard, but they use 87 per cent of it themselves and have only a small margin for export. Although these areas could increase their output materially, their own requirements are also rising; and in addition, the deficit countries are restricted in what they can buy by the limitations of their available foreign exchange. In the deficit areas, the gap between local production and requirements is widening rather than narrowing.

Thus on a long-term basis there is need for sensible and realistically planned increases in production in these areas.

This need is notably true of Latin America, where the demand is rising faster than in any other deficit region. It is estimated that almost 80 per cent more paper and paperboard will be needed in that region in 1960-62 than was used in 1950-52.

Ample resources are available for greater production of pulp. Latin America has some coniferous forests, traditional source of pulping material; but, more important, it has immense areas of tropical and subtropical hardwoods which, with the new techniques recently developed, can be used for pulpmaking. There are large resources of other fibrous material, such as sugar cane bagasse and bamboo. With new techniques, these also can be utilized for papermaking.

Raw materials are, of course, not the sole requisite. Adequate supplies of water, power, fuel, and chemicals are needed, together with capital, technical knowledge, transport facilities, economically accessible markets, and so on.

FAO has now completed the first phase of a long-term program looking toward adequate pulp and paper production and distribution to meet the world's growing needs. This first phase consists in assessing present and prospective demands, surveying resources, and studying production possibilities. Surveys made by FAO experts during the past two years or so have covered 25 countries, of which half were in Latin America and the other half mainly in the Far East and the Near East. The work was started on the initiation of the Economic and Social Council and UNESCO and has been carried out with the co-operation of the regional United Nations economic commissions. A report of the findings (*The World's Pulp and Paper Resources and Prospects*) has recently been published by the United Nations.

Animals

FAO and the Inter-American Institute of Agricultural Sciences held a Latin American regional livestock meeting at Turrialba, Costa Rica, in October 1950. A larger FAO conference (150 delegates from 19 countries, João Soares Veiga [Brazil] presiding) met at Baurú in December 1952. The Baurú meeting concluded by asking the FAO Director-General to prepare proposals for setting up a Latin American Livestock Commission, to be presented to a third meeting scheduled to be held in Argentina in 1955.

This would be the first regional organization in the Americas devoted to the broad interests of livestock production. Essentially, it would be like the FAO regional organizations for rice, forests, and fisheries.

The size of the Baurú meeting is evidence of the prominence of livestock in the economy of Latin America. If the early Spanish explorers sought gold, in many cases they found more lasting wealth later in their great herds of cattle and flocks of sheep, mainly kept on the vast land grants called latifundia. Today, production of cattle and sheep is important everywhere in Latin America, but particularly in Argentina, Brazil, Uruguay, Chile, and Mexico.

Regional co-operation may develop first in connection with the control and prevention of livestock diseases; of these, the most important in Latin America is foot-and-mouth disease.

The Baurú meeting recommended that FAO, the International Office of Epizootics, and the Center for Foot-and-Mouth Disease near Rio de Janeiro explore the possibilities of co-operative work for the control and ultimate eradication of this disease in the region. Whether this work would be undertaken by the proposed livestock commission remains to be seen. There is already some measure of co-operation—witness the work of the Rio center, established in 1951 by the Organization of American States and the Pan-American Sanitary Bureau, which is concentrated primarily on classifying samples of virus from disease outbreaks to determine which of the several types of the foot-and-mouth organism is involved in each case. This information is essential in any prevention or control program based on vaccination.

Earlier, in 1951, eight Central American countries that are free of the disease—Costa Rica, Cuba, Dominican Republic, El Salvador, Guatemala, Haiti, Honduras, and Nicaragua—held a meeting in Panama City, under the auspices of FAO and the Organization of American States, to initiate co-operation in keeping the disease out of their countries and in controlling outbreaks quickly if they should occur. Since then, FAO has had two animal disease experts in Panama helping the government of that country on its own disease-control program and working with the other Central American countries concerned (and to some extent with countries in the Caribbean area also). Such regional movements as this are almost always slow to materialize, but the outlook is promising. Panama promptly contributed $5200 to the proposed common Central American fund, and that country and Costa Rica are preparing legislation which might serve more or less as a model for other governments. El Salvador is also strengthening its livestock disease work.

At the Baurú meeting almost every aspect of livestock production—veterinary medicine, breeding, nutrition, climatology, and so on—was the subject of detailed reports and discussions. Though much needs to be done to improve livestock services, the meeting showed what an impressive amount of work is now under way. To mention a few random examples:

• In Brazil, selection of high-producing native Caraçu cattle has produced cows averaging 3500 pounds of milk a year, with at least one individual making a record of more than double that amount. Forage studies in Brazil have emphasized the value of guinea grass for tropical and subtropical areas. Under drought conditions, this grass sends its roots down more than 18 feet to reach water. • Brazil and El Salvador are working on the feeding of by-product coffee pulp to livestock, both dried and as ensilage. • Jamaica has been crossing Zebus and Jerseys to produce its Jamaica-Hope breed of dairy cattle, which is giving milk yields as high as 13,000 pounds. • Costa Rica, Uruguay, Argentina, and Chile all reported programs of testing dairy cows for milk production, to provide records for selecting sires with proved ability to beget higher-yielding offspring. • Argentina and Chile have unique projects for graphic presentation of the adaptability of different types and strains of cattle to various climatic conditions. • Nicaragua is making a study of pasture management in the humid, hot Atlantic coastal plains, which are not adaptable to crops but could sustain large numbers of animals. • Chile has been working on the use of seaweed, treated with lime and then washed with water to reduce the salt content, as a feed for horses. • Brazil is working on a trivalent vaccine which might protect against three strains of foot-and-mouth disease with a single injection.

There have been at least two other regional projects in Latin America connected with livestock production. One was a pasture management training center in Argentina in October and November 1953, sponsored by the Turrialba Institute (IAIAS) with FAO co-operation, to demonstrate and teach techniques for better production of animal feeds. The 34 trainees were all experienced people holding positions of responsibility in their governments. A good many ranchers also took part, unofficially but enthusiastically.

In Costa Rica a training center on the production, handling, and processing of milk was held in August–September 1953, under the auspices of FAO and the Costa Rican Government. This was for the benefit of Latin American countries in which UNICEF has established milk plants. Co-operatives and herd testing were the subjects that aroused the liveliest interest among the trainees.

Land

All human beings live off the land, even though they may not live on it. Since the days, ages ago, when nomadic hunters first took to settled farming, land has been associated with some of man's deepest emotions and highest ideals. Land is home, land is livelihood, land is security, land is life. Perhaps more blood has been spilled fighting about land than about any other factor in human affairs.

In certain places at certain times land tenure problems occupy the thoughts of great numbers of people. This is doubtless when the suffering and hardship arising from bad conditions of ownership create so sharp a sense of injustice as to explode in violent revolt. In any period of social and economic stress, it is safe to say, land problems are likely to be deeply involved, somewhere.

We are now living in such a period, and in many countries land problems are in the foreground of pressing social and economic difficulties.

As we have seen, land reform was prominent in the Interim Commission's groundpattern for the work of FAO—and even before that, in the thinking at Hot Springs and even before Hot Springs. In 1950 the United Nations began to take an active interest in these essential underpinnings of agricultural development and asked FAO to prepare a report showing the effects of unsatisfactory conditions of land tenure on economic progress. FAO did so. Then the 1951 Conference asked the Director-General to take the lead among international agencies in meeting the needs of member governments for guidance in land tenure reform. It said forthrightly,

That in many countries the agrarian structure has most serious defects, in particular the uneconomic size of farms, the fragmentation of holdings, the maldistribution of landed property, excessive rents, inequitable systems of taxation, insecurity of tenure, perpetual indebtedness, or lack of clear titles to land and water; that these defects prevent a rise in the standard of living of small farmers and agricultural laborers and impede agricultural development; that reform of agrarian structures in such countries is essential to human dignity and freedom and the achievement of the aims of FAO.

Subsequently representatives of UN, ILO, UNESCO, and FAO met in Rome to agree on lines of work. FAO then started the preparation of a series of studies dealing with questions fundamental to agrarian reform in any country, with the idea that they might help governments in shaping sound national programs. (Three studies completed so far deal with *Communal Land Tenure, Cadastral Surveys and Records of Rights in Land, Inter-relationship between Agrarian Reform and Agricultural Development*.)

The first international conference on land problems was held in Madison, Wisconsin, in 1952, sponsored by the United States Government and the University of Wisconsin, with the participation of FAO. It drew a considerable number of delegates from countries widely scattered over the world, and they in turn stimulated some governments to devote increasing attention to land reform.

FAO next began a series of regional seminars on land tenure problems, with Latin America taking the lead. (A Far East meeting was held late in 1954 and a Near East meeting will be held in 1955.) It stood ready to meet requests by member governments for technical co-operation in connection with land reform programs. The Latin American seminar was held in 1953 in Campinas, near São Paulo, and Brazil's João Gonçalves de Sousa served as director.

Well prepared and publicized in advance, the Campinas meeting attracted an able representation from 15 countries. Mexico, for example, where land reform began with the constitution of 1917, sent an outstanding group of participants who brought a report—the product of six months' hard work—appraising the country's entire land program, failures as well as successes. Brazil presented a mass of information on the conservation aspects of land problems. Cuba dealt comprehensively with the agricultural credit aspects. Bolivia sent a five-man delegation which was keenly interested in the bearing of the conference on Bolivia's own difficult land problems, and at the request of this delegation the seminar appointed a subcommittee to discuss the Bolivian situation. (Subsequently FAO sent a land expert, Edmundo Flores [Mexico], to Bolivia.) Chile announced after the Campinas meeting that it was setting up an agricultural commission to study the possibility of changes in the land tenure system.

Perhaps the most important outcome of Campinas was the clear demonstration that a reasoned and scientific approach is possible even in the case of situations so explosive that the common tendency is to avoid talking about them—in which case they drift to the stage where talk will no longer help because violence has become inescapable.

In general, there are three main types of land holding in Latin America, with many gradations and variations between: the latifundia, vast estates on which the work is usually done by landless peasants; the minifundia at the opposite extreme, tiny farms, usually too small to be effective economic units; and lands owned not by individuals but by the community, a pattern handed down through generations of Indians, who are a large element in the population of many countries.

There was a frank and realistic discussion at Campinas of all types of ownership and operation. The delegates were mainly concerned with such questions as these:

What should be the main long-term objectives of a sound land policy?

What modifications of the existing land system are desirable under a given set of conditions to achieve increased production from the soil to meet the needs of the community, and increased production per person to make better living possible?

In cases where changes in the land system are under consideration, how can land distribution be financed?

What is the role of credit in bringing about a better land tenure system?

What are the right sizes of farms under given sets of conditions?

How should settlers be selected?

What kinds of title and tenure are best adapted to new settlements?

The effects of the seminar are probably already being felt in various parts of Latin America. New legislation in several countries appears to have been influenced by the discussions, and several governments have set up institutes or commissions to explore ways of resolving land tenure and settlement problems. At the end of the seminar the delegates proposed that a permanent center be established, possibly in Mexico, for research and training, at the request of any Latin American country, in land problems and related fields.

Money

Some self-sufficing communities—including quite a number among the Indians of Latin America—get along practically without money, but they are capable of only a very limited kind of development. In general, land and money for material and equipment to use on the land or in connection with the land must go together in modern economies. Hence the overwhelming importance of credit in agriculture. If this is an old truth or truism in technologically advanced countries, it is only now becoming recognized as a new truth in some others.

In 1948 FAO, in co-operation with the United Nations Economic Commission for Latin America, began collecting data on the agricultural credit situation in the region, with a view to arranging a conference on credit in the next couple of years. That work continued through 1951, and it did a good deal to help focus attention on the credit needs of agriculture, especially of small-scale farmers, who hitherto have had practically no way to borrow money. Positive action resulted in a number of countries.

In 1952, after the Wisconsin land problems seminar, a similar international meeting devoted to agricultural credit convened in Berkeley, California, sponsored by the University of California and the US Government, with FAO participating.

For Latin America regionally, all this work came to a focus in two meetings on credit sponsored by FAO in 1952 and 1953. In both, the delegates were not official representatives of participating countries as is usual in such conferences; they were chosen as experts on money and credit. Both meetings brought results that should have continent-wide— even world-wide—usefulness.

The first conference, held in Guatemala City in September and October 1952, brought together experts from 13 countries and seven organizations, with Cuba's Alfonso Rochac directing the discussions and Guatemala's J. Roberto Fanjul G. and Nicolás Brol serving as joint chairmen. This meeting was concerned, in the main, with the ordinary types of credit, including sound collateral and repayment at usual interest rates, for farmers and for organizations concerned with economic development. The group canvassed every aspect of that subject in relation to existing conditions, practices, and needs in Latin America. The discussions were in effect a form of professional collaboration among people from many countries, and they resulted in a jointly prepared handbook on agricultural credit in Latin

America (*Seminario de Crédito Agrícola*) which is the only volume of its kind in the Spanish language, and as authoritative as it can be made.

Intentionally, this meeting devoted little attention to supervised credit, which, however, is especially important in Latin America. This type of lending was developed especially to meet the needs of small-scale farmers who do not have the resources necessary for ordinary borrowing. Supervised credit was the subject of the second meeting, held in Asunción, Paraguay, in December 1953, and sponsored jointly by FAO, the Institute of Inter-American Affairs, and the American International Association. Twenty-eight experts came to Asunción, and their work is an outstanding example of international collaboration. Out of this too came a manual (the title, somewhat abbreviated, is *Crédito Agrícola Supervisado para la América Latina*) which is unique not only in Latin America but anywhere. It fills the gap left in the previous handbook and should be widely useful.

Supervised credit is the cornerstone of improvement for the great majority of farm families, including those involved in land distribution and colonization projects. Being noncommercial, supervised credit is a function of government. Some people consider it costly. It should not be thought of, however, as exclusively lending to foster the creation of wealth through increased production; it is equally an investment in education, rural improvement, and human welfare, and as worthy of public financing as are schools or roads.

In supervised credit the borrower usually does not put up ordinary collateral. Funds are advanced on the basis of a financially sound farm plan. The money must be used to improve the farm and home in ways that will as nearly as possible guarantee better production, better use of land resources, and better living. To make these results possible, the loans are accompanied in each case by expert guidance for the family, both in drawing up the plans and in carrying them out. Hence it is essential that there be a corps of people—extension workers in agriculture and home economics—adequately prepared to give this guidance sympathetically and capably. Supervised credit and extension work go hand in hand. The results have been good; and incidentally, the record of repayments, where the programs have been well handled, is high.

Counsel

The corps of extension workers needed to provide advice and counsel for this and other aspects of agricultural development is gradually expanding in Latin America, although the number is still very small in comparison with the need. The Institute of Inter-American Affairs has for some years fostered the growth of extension services in a few countries, notably Peru and Costa Rica; the Turrialba Institute has been actively engaged in the work; Wilson Popenoe's school in Honduras has done yeoman service in training young men from many countries for extension work; some national institutions such as the National Agricultural School at Chapingo, Mexico, do extension training.

FAO has been able to get countries and organizations to pull together in co-operative regional efforts that are both effective and economical.

The work started in Central America with an extension meeting at Turrialba, Costa Rica, in 1949, before the beginning of the technical assistance program, followed by another at Turrialba in 1951, and a third in nearby San José in 1952. In each case, collaboration among FAO, the Inter-American Institute of Agricultural Sciences, and the Costa Rican Government made success possible. In fact, interest quickly spread beyond Central America to other parts of the continent.

The next step was an Andean center in Lima, Peru, which ran for three months in 1953. Peru has a well-organized extension service, developed originally by John R. Neale, of the *Servicio Cooperativo Inter-Americano de Produccion de Alimentos* (SCIPA), the organization through which the Peruvian Government and the Institute of Inter-American Affairs co-operate. SCIPA is now staffed almost entirely by Peruvians. The extension work is headed by Ingeneiro Enrique Labarthe, who directed the Andean training center, in which FAO and SCIPA joined forces.

This was a hard-driving, effective training course. During the first two weeks the 18 trainees from five countries spent their time in lectures and discussions. Then they scattered over the country, each to an area where conditions were somewhat like those in his own land. For more than two months they worked as extension agents beside the Peruvians—visiting farmers, giving advice on the problems they met, helping to conduct demonstrations, and taking part in meetings of farmers and of farm youth. In fact, they learned by example and practice what a good extension agent needs to do and how he does it. They then gathered again in Lima to review all they had been doing and get it into proper focus for maximum usefulness in their own countries.

The first Andean training center was so successful that another one was held in Peru in 1954, and probably others will follow in the future.

Plans are also under way for an extension training center in the Caribbean area, which has characteristic problems of its own. As a first step, FAO sponsored a preliminary discussion meeting in Jamaica in August 1954 with the co-operation of a number of regional and bilateral organizations.

Locusts

As with fire, so with locusts—prevention is better than attempting to stop them after they start. Preventing locust outbreaks requires accurate knowledge of the kind of locust concerned and the details of its life history. Locusts normally live as solitary grasshoppers in relatively limited areas, minding their own business and causing little serious damage. Under certain abnormal conditions, however—apparently those conditions, such as drought or certain changes in cultivation practices, that threaten shortage of food for the grasshoppers—they gradually change to a gregarious phase, multiply with great rapidity, and gather in swarms that in effect go berserk, travel great distances, and do tremendous damage. The swarming phase may last for several years; it then gradually gives way to the solitary phase again. Thus to prevent swarming it is necessary to know exactly when and where solitary locusts are becoming gregarious so they can be destroyed before the swarming fever really takes hold. To illustrate how this knowledge pays: Algeria spent some 7 million francs a year between 1925 and 1932 fighting swarms of Moroccan locusts. In 1934 the government began work to prevent swarming. Since then, annual costs have been less than 1½ million francs a year, and not one locust outbreak has occurred.

FAO locust expert Morales Agacino (Spain) has paid much attention to research in the locust laboratory in Managua, Nicaragua, in order to lay the foundation for effective regional work to prevent outbreaks in Central America. He also gave technical training to experts in the area who serve as a task force in Central American locust control operations. As a result of this work, the majority of the outbreak centers have now been discovered.

FAO serves as adviser to the International Committee of Coordination for Locust Control (CICLA), set up in 1949 by the Conference of Ministers of Agriculture of Central America and Mexico, meeting in Tapachula, Mexico. The co-operating governments (Nicaragua, Costa Rica, El Salvador, Guatemala, Honduras, Mexico) picked Managua as headquarters for the regional work, for which they contribute about $15,000 apiece every year, and chose Ingeneiro Francisco Seravalli Céspedes (Costa Rica) as executive director. The Tapachula agreement was renewed and broadened in San Salvador in 1951 and again in 1953.

This work is as good an example of effective regional co-operation as can be found anywhere. CICLA is becoming widely known. Each member country has its own locust committee and technicians. Five of the countries are now practically free of locusts as a result of co-operative control work; the sixth, Honduras, recently had a bad outbreak, and efforts are under way to discover hitherto unknown outbreak centers in that country. The whole undertaking has now been turned over to the countries concerned. In France, authorities had the CICLA convention translated and distributed to French overseas territories as an example of what can be done by united action.

Meanwhile there is also an important locust program in countries farther south, including Argentina, Bolivia, Brazil, Paraguay, and Uruguay. In this region the locust is considered to be the worst of all insect pests; it is said that the area is never entirely free from swarms, and in fact that the insect has never been found there in the nonswarming solitary phase. A permanent Inter-American Anti-Locust Committee with headquarters in Buenos Aires has been in existence since 1947, mainly to exchange information on swarm movements.

Fish

The most eager and able fishermen in South America are the cormorants off the west coast—keen-eyed divers, ceaselessly traversing sky and sea in great dark flocks. They live on anchovies, which must crowd these waters in vast quantities, nourished by hosts of minute sea plants in the upwelling cool currents off the coast. In a year, each of the several million hungry cormorants, it has been estimated, nabs and guzzles 172 pounds of these tasty fish (so commonly served as *hors d'oeuvres* at diplomatic receptions). On the rocky islands off the coast of Peru where the cormorants nest, their droppings are deposited to form guano; and before the days when this natural nitrogen fertilizer was exploited by man, the deposits (which incidentally insulate the nesting birds from the terrific heat of the sun-baked rocks which otherwise might cook their eggs) were in some places a hundred feet deep.

Peruvian guano bears witness to the richness of life in the sea in this part of the world, and therefore of its potential fisheries resources. Fisheries production in the region could be very considerably expanded. It did expand as a result of wartime and postwar demand, when exports jumped from the equivalent of 5 million dollars in 1938 to 55 million dollars in 1950. Since then the export market has fallen off so much that in some places available facilities and equipment are idle or are not fully used. For the time being, the main opportunity for growth seems to be in enlarging the domestic market.

This will not be easy to do. Consumer purchasing power is low. The kind of transport needed for fresh fish is often completely lacking. Processing facilities except in a few places are not well developed. Boats are for the most part small or primitive—dugout canoes, dories, and other rowing and sailing craft which have to keep close to shore. Production per man is low and prices high. It has been estimated that the 13,500 fishermen of Latin America, where the industry is more or less incidental, catch less fish than the 6300 fishermen of Iceland, where it is paramount.

This is not to say that Latin America does no fishing or fish processing with modern equipment and has no fisheries research. It does, in a few places; in fact, in certain centers in Brazil, Chile, Mexico, Peru, and Venezuela, mainly near growing industrial communities, there has been an almost spectacular expansion because there were remunerative markets.

These and other facts are contained in a report on the "present status and prospects of the fisheries industry in Latin America" prepared by FAO for the Economic Commission for Latin America. The regional surveys on which the report was based, and a regional fisheries training center held in

1952 in Valparaiso, Chile (near the Marine Biological Laboratory at Viña del Mar), have been the outstanding fisheries activities of FAO in Latin America so far.

The training institute, directed by Chile's Commander Ezequiel Rodriguez, brought together representatives from Brazil, Chile, Ecuador, El Salvador, Paraguay, Peru, and Uruguay. To use an American slang phrase apt for fisheries, the course "covered the waterfront," dealing with practically every aspect of fisheries, scientific and practical. Some of the material resulting from the lectures and discussions cannot be found elsewhere in technical literature in the Spanish language. If anything, the course was too comprehensive, but it was a good pioneering start and the participants apparently got a great deal from it which they used to encourage advances in fisheries in a number of countries after they got back home.

A second regional training institute was held in Mexico in the autumn of 1954.

A movement to start a Latin American fisheries council like those in the Indo-Pacific and the Mediterranean areas got under way in the autumn of 1951 but has not yet reached the point where establishment of a permanent organization has been possible.

Food and Home

People think a good deal about food but very little about the alimentary processes that go on quietly and unobtrusively (except in times of trouble, such as a stomachache). Perhaps the hidden unspectacular nature of the body's chemistry is one of the reasons why nutrition is often so difficult to dramatize.

Nevertheless, the unfolding of the science, mentioned earlier in this book, has been responsible for great advances in human well-being which have affected the countries of Latin America as well as those of all other regions. Thus, today, all Latin American countries have nutrition organizations and services, some highly developed and including school lunches, workers' canteens, food control laboratories, and so on; others, still small or rudimentary.

One of the duties assigned to FAO was to help countries to expand and improve this work.

In July 1948 the first FAO-sponsored regional nutrition conference met in Montevideo. There, technical and administrative people got together from 19 countries and 10 international organizations, partly to exchange views and experiences, good, bad, encouraging, discouraging. They decided, among other things—

- That, malnutrition in Latin America being widespread, much more work is needed to find out just how well- or ill-nourished large population groups really are.
- That there is a need for education in nutrition which would teach people

to make better use of the foods available to them, and also for expanding services that provide additional good food for certain groups such as school children and industrial workers.
- That too little is known about the true nutritive value of local foods and diets, which may be better or poorer than the scientists think, and which in any case should have more scientific study.

As a follow-up of the Montevideo meeting, during the next year an FAO nutrition expert visited almost every country in South America, going over programs and plans in detail with officials and technical workers.

Two years later came the second nutrition conference, in Rio de Janeiro in June 1950. There delegations from 18 countries reported on progress since the first meeting, especially in school feeding programs, the study of local foods, and the training of nutrition workers.

The third conference, this time sponsored jointly by FAO and WHO, met in Caracas in October 1953, with 13 countries and nine organizations represented. After hearing reports on work in various countries during the previous two years, this meeting felt that a good deal of progress had been made. Special attention was given to protein malnutrition, following the work on kwashiorkor in Africa, the recommendations of the 1952 Gambia meeting, and the recent FAO–WHO surveys in Central America and Brazil showing that the disease is widespread in Latin America. Endemic goiter was also considered; the conference was convinced that this disease could be eradicated within a few years if governments would use the necessary preventive measures. Subsequently, in November 1953, another conference on protein malnutrition, sponsored by WHO and FAO, was held in Jamaica, with the Josiah Macy, Jr., Foundation contributing substantially to the cost. This was a technical meeting dealing particularly with unsolved problems, and hence of special interest to research workers.

Meanwhile, in September 1949 the Institute of Nutrition for Central America and Panama (INCAP) had been established, with headquarters in Guatemala City and with a membership that eventually included Costa Rica, El Salvador, Guatemala, Honduras, and Panama. In 1950 FAO assigned a staff nutrition officer to INCAP to help in carrying out a nutrition survey in near-by Guatemala villages, where an experimental school feeding program was being started. She lived with Indian families in their homes in order to learn as much as possible at first hand about their foods and ways of preparing food. The co-operation between FAO and the Institute has continued ever since. The same worker has organized surveys in Honduras and Costa Rica, and all the surveys together give a picture of food habits in Central America which will help to guide practical nutrition work in this region. The continuing co-operation between FAO and INCAP has led to other useful undertakings. For example, FAO provided fellowships for a number of workers from different countries in the region to attend INCAP nutrition training courses in 1952 and 1953.

In the Caribbean area FAO started some work in nutrition and home economics early in 1950 by making a survey of organizations concerned with the interests of women and children. Following this, the United Nations provided fellowships that made it possible for 16 workers in home economics and related fields to attend a summer workshop and seminar at the University of Puerto Rico, in which FAO participated. FAO work in the Caribbean region has also included informal counseling and advising on home economics curricula in educational institutions and on some of the programs of welfare agencies.

The Puerto Rican Workshop was followed in 1952 by a joint Caribbean Commission-FAO conference in Port-of-Spain, Trinidad, which showed clearly that interest in nutrition and home economics is growing rapidly throughout the area. This conference in turn resulted in a second home economics training course given in Puerto Rico in 1953 with the co-operation of the University, and financed by FAO. Twenty-five students from the Caribbean area took this course. To follow up these promising developments, FAO provided a home economist to work for a year or more with the Commission, helping various countries to organize teaching programs. There are great obstacles to co-operation and greater unification of this work because the islands are so widely scattered and diverse.

More

In previous chapters I discussed the Latin American statistical training institutes, the institute on economic development, the grain storage work.

A number of Latin American countries have come together through FAO to deal with the question of fertilizer requirements, supplies, and production. This is a matter of persistent concern. Some years ago an appraisal made by FAO and the Economic Commission for Latin America showed that an acute shortage of some fertilizers, particularly phosphates, exists, with prices increasing faster than the value of the crops for which they are intended. This cuts down the use of fertilizers and is a drag on increased crop production. A number of countries are now either carrying out or planning fertilizer enterprises which may be very important for the future.

This was one of various aspects of agriculture discussed at the second Latin American Regional Meeting on Agricultural Programs and Outlook, held in Montevideo in 1950, with FAO and the Organization of American States collaborating. The first conference, an exploratory one, met in Quito, Ecuador, early in 1949. A third regional meeting planned for 1953 was held in September 1954, in Buenos Aires.

The Montevideo meeting spotlighted the fact that with some minor exceptions, per acre yields of basic crops in Latin America had not increased in 15 years. There are many modern farms and progressive farmers, but not enough. There is a fair amount of experimental work, but not enough. The possibilities for increased production per acre and per man are very great. Also, there are large resources that are not yet used; at most, 5 per cent of the land area is under cultivation, and only two thirds of that portion is cropped in any one year.

The discussions at Montevideo were a milestone on the road of frank appraisal of a regional situation by the countries concerned. The progress being made in some parts of Latin America is as striking as that anywhere in the world, including the most highly developed countries. By contrast, in many places the conditions of production and living cry out for change.

One of the interesting and potentially important movements in the region is the effort now being made to bring a number of Central American countries together for unified action in certain aspects of administrative, industrial, and agricultural development. Although this project is still in an early stage, there have been meetings of top-level officials sponsored by the Economic Commission for Latin America with representatives of international agencies, in particular the United Nations Technical Assistance Administration, the Technical Assistance Board, and FAO. A number of projects have been proposed involving co-ordinated technical co-operation among several countries. Co-operation has already started with plant protection, livestock sanitation, and quarantine regulations, which are particularly suitable for international agreement, and projects are likely to be under way soon in various aspects of livestock and forest production.

In the Caribbean area FAO undertook a survey of co-operatives, the results of which were published in a report used as the main document for a joint FAO–Caribbean Commission meeting held in Trinidad early in 1951. The recommendations that came out of this meeting have been useful in stimulating further development of co-operatives in the area. As this is written, a three-month Caribbean training institute is under way in Puerto Rico, with Señora Aida Péres de Rivera as director.

WORK WITH INDIVIDUAL COUNTRIES: CONTINENTAL SOUTH AMERICA

Brazil

Brazil is big, bigger than the USA but much more thinly populated—56 million as compared with more than 160 million. There are more people in Brazil than in the United Kingdom or France or Italy, and almost as many as in all the rest of continental South America; the people all speak one language, Portuguese, with only slight local differences in accent. Resources too are remarkable: Brazil is the world's biggest coffee producer (48 per cent of the world supply in 1952), the second biggest citrus producer (California's navel oranges came originally from Bahia), and the biggest rice producer outside the Orient. It is second in the extent of its forests (the USSR being first), third in corn production, fourth in cotton, perhaps

LATIN AMERICA

fourth in number of domestic animals. And it is perhaps the world's most civilized country from the standpoint of racial understanding.

In Rio de Janeiro, FAO has an office, in charge of W. G. Casseres (Costa Rica) which services the countries on the east coast of South America.

Brazil's Fabulous Forests

Half the trees in South America grow in this country. The most extensive forests are in the hot, humid Amazon Valley, which covers nearly half (42 per cent) of Brazil's area. This is a land of many trees and few people. Its immense forests have been tapped only to skim off the cream—the more expensive hardwoods, mainly mahogany.

Now Brazil is taking an interest in more systematic development of this fabulous, almost uninhabited tropical region. Under a new law, 3 per cent of the national revenue and of the revenue of the states and municipalities in the area is to be devoted to Amazon Valley development. Since this area at present provides only 1 per cent of the national income, it must more than treble production to meet expenses. An Amazon commission (*Commissão de Valorisacão da Amazonia*) has been set up to plan development and land use. Meanwhile the Brazilian Institute of Geography and Statistics has a special staff of geographers, geologists, soil scientists, and other experts who are sifting and evaluating the great mass of material already in existence about this region.

The most important work in Brazil so far undertaken by FAO has been to provide help in these early stages of assessing and shaping the potentially vast Amazon program. Three experts—René Gachot (France), wood industries; M. N. Gallant (UK), timber marketing; K. P. McGrath (Australia), logging—spent a year making a thorough study of the valley and of possible markets in Brazil, and in other countries that might use Amazon timber. To put a complex subject as briefly as possible, they concluded

- That the development of the Amazon forests presents no insuperable technical difficulties. The problem is mainly one of organization, plus capital, equipment, and skills. At present it is not possible to insure a sufficient supply of timber even for the small capacity of existing sawmills.
- That as a short-term objective Brazil could treble its timber production from these forests within 10 years through simple improvements and modernization without radical change in the structure of the timber industry.
- That though this achievement would not require much extension of operations, it does involve establishing a forest policy, legislation, and administration for well-rounded and rational development of the Amazon forests.

The Indian forest workers are expert woodsmen, quite capable of using modern tools and methods. The only tool they now use, however, is the most primitive one, the ax. With an ax as the sole tool, great quantities of wood are wasted in felling—sometimes a ton from one tree. Losses are even greater in the process of getting the logs out of the forest. They have to be rolled to the waterside (mainly temporary streams filled only at floodtime), down which they are floated to the bigger waterways. The whole operation is so uncertain and precarious that a third to a half of the felled logs, sometimes even more, must be left to rot.

Since very little food is grown locally, most of the food for the forest workers has to be brought in, some from 4000 miles away. Naturally, this food is extremely expensive. The standard of living is a miserable one; the workers are paid only enough for the most elementary necessities.

To modernize and increase timber production in this immense, difficult area requires a change in the fundamental attitude from one of speculative exploitation to one of permanent and settled use—including near-by production of food for the forest workers. The FAO team believes that the Amazon Valley is well suited for colonization, but for forest development rather than crops. First steps would be to get a more accurate picture of the nature and extent of the forest resources (surveys have now begun) and to demonstrate extracting and milling equipment. Two centers have been started, one for logging, one for sawmilling, and FAO is contributing $44,000 toward the purchase of equipment to be used for demonstration and training. The FAO mission is now attached to Brazil's Amazon Valley commission and work has begun on the development program.

In the southern part of Brazil are extensive areas of Paraná pine, a fast-growing species especially good for pulpwood. Brazilians are worried about the permanence of the present stands. FAO forest expert L. J. Rogers (UK) surveyed the Paraná pine area and estimated that at the present rate of exploitation the trees will all be gone in about 40 years. Working with the *Instituto do Pinho,* he suggested methods of cutting, regenerating forest stands, and planting new forests that would maintain the timber supply while continuing to meet the needs of industry. He also outlined additional research needed to find answers for some of the Paraná pine problems.

Land Use and Rural Development

The fact that Brazil was host for the FAO Regional Land Problems Seminar shows that that country is keenly interested in better land use.

Brazil is so large that hitherto there has been little pressure for land-use planning and conservation. As in the early days of the USA, settlers could exhaust one area, then move on to another. Now the attitude is changing, and a number of organizations—religious, civic, governmental—are devoting a good deal of attention to the interrelated problems of land use, farm incomes, and rural welfare.

After the Campinas seminar, FAO's Manlio Rossi-Doria (Italy) stayed on in Brazil to help the government on land policy questions. He has been analyzing the land tenure systems, suggesting useful lines of research, and making a critical examination of proposed land laws.

New colonization is an important aspect of the problem in Brazil with its vast areas where there is little or no agriculture. Land settlement projects in the past have been more or less haphazard and subject to abuse. Now the government is proceeding more carefully and has had the help of three FAO experts: the late Jacques de Coulon (Switzerland) who died during this assignment "in the service of humanity," J. M. J. Brantjes (the Netherlands), and L. A. Foulon (Argentina), as well as of an irrigation man, J. B. Hammon (USA). These men helped to lay a foundation of careful planning for new settlements. The recently established Brazilian Institute for Colonization will carry on the work. In soil surveying, FAO's Luis Bramão (Portugal) has been working on irrigation, drainage, and colonization programs and training graduate students in soil science. The government is also actively developing its extension service, and FAO's W. J. Timmer (the Netherlands) has worked on that program.

There is a keen interest in other aspects of rural welfare. Two FAO experts, Raymond E. Wakeley and J. H. Kolb (USA), have been concerned mainly with helping to lay the groundwork for research projects and training schools, improvements in census and other reporting, strengthening community organizations, training rural leaders, and making surveys to find out why farmers do or do not do certain things—for example, why some take readily to the use of hybrid corn whereas others do not—as a step in developing more effective and persuasive ways to improve agriculture and rural living. FAO agricultural economist Henrique de Barros (Portugal) has been surveying possibilities for extending wheat production in the south (Brazil now imports much of its wheat).

Cattle—and Fish

A very small part of Brazil is cultivated; 3 per cent of the land, in fact, grows all the 21 principal crops. Three fourths of the people live within a hundred miles of the coast. Back of this is a vast hinterland, a good deal of which, outside the Amazon Valley, is devoted to the grazing of cattle. The life of these cattle producers is rugged and picturesque and the business is important, for the value of livestock products in Brazil exceeds that of the biggest export crop, coffee. Contributing to this value are intensive livestock operations around large cities, for instance, dairying near São Paulo and Rio de Janeiro.

That control of animal disease is a matter of vital concern is evidenced by the amount of research under way in Brazil and the part played by that country as host to the recent inter-American livestock meeting. In the way of direct co-operation, FAO has provided the services of an expert on brucellosis, A. F. Valiente (El Salvador). Conditions are not ripe for an extensive vaccination campaign, but it has been possible to take steps to reduce the incidence of brucellosis among cattle and sheep. In parasite control, FAO's H. T. Carroll (Australia) has worked mainly on sheep parasites. He has also done much to make both technicians and laymen realize the tremendous importance of this aspect of animal (and of human) health.

Fish production in Brazil is greater than in any other Latin American country. There is need for still more production, however, since about half the fish consumed are imported. An FAO expert, C. J. Bottemanne (the Netherlands), helped the government in drawing up plans for modernization of fishing equipment and for further development of preservation and processing, storage, and distribution. Three other experts—in fishing operations, in marine biology, and in fish preservation—are also being provided.

Chile

Chile has long been the world's greatest exporter of copper and nitrate of soda. Competition from other sources has now drastically shrunk these once-booming Chilean industries. As they have dwindled in importance, some others have been expanding. Chile has coal and iron deposits; it is now making steel and fabricating steel products. There are rich forest resources which are being used to provide raw material for the manufacture of wood products. Manufacturing centers have grown rapidly. Unlike most other South American countries, Chile is not today primarily agricultural; it is predominantly an industrial nation. Only four out of every 10 people are engaged in farming (including livestock production) compared with at least seven out of 10 in the other countries.

This development has been uneven, and in the process Chile has suffered from economic growing pains and from a steadily rising inflation. Industrial wages and profits brought increased consumption of food and other things that go with a better standard of living. Meanwhile agriculture has been falling behind in providing enough for the enlarged market. Chile has had to import considerable amounts of wheat and other agricultural products. But its very narrow range of exports with which to pay for the imports is characterized by uncertainty and extreme price fluctuations.

Inside and outside Chile, many competent observers believe that one of that country's great needs today is modernization and expansion of agricultural production, including forestry and fisheries, to bring it more nearly in balance with industrial development and market demands. For this, Chile has excellent natural resources of water, climate, and land. It also has excellent human resources. The European settlers were a vigorous breed; so, apparently, was the Indian population that preceded them. The descendants of these peoples have sometimes been called the Yankees of the South because of their psychological drive and talent for business and industry.

Farming still largely follows the pattern of the great Spanish estates. Some of the landowners are very progressive, but in general the system is one in which the owner does not feel a compelling need, and the landless laborer has no opportunity, to make improvements.

These and many other conclusions, in considerable detail, were included

LATIN AMERICA

in a report made by a joint agricultural mission which the International Bank and FAO sent to Chile in 1951 at the request of the government.

Agricultural development and settlement in Chile are concentrated mainly in a great central valley lying between the dry north (at the upper end of which are the nitrate deposits, which are never washed away because this is one of the world's few completely rainless deserts, white and sharp as a wolf's tooth) and the cool forested land in the south, ending in the fury of Antarctic seas.

In the central valley are many cattle. Everywhere the visitor sees the picturesque Chilean cowboy, wearing a broad-brimmed, flat-topped hat and a bright-colored small poncho and riding on a mignificent saddle almost as big as an armchair. The cattle for the most part roam over the range without shelter, and little effort is made to supplement the range grass with fodder crops or with improved pastures. The same is true in the case of sheep, which graze farther to the south, especially in Magallanes province, one of the largest sheep-producing areas in South America. Livestock production could in fact be considerably improved by paying more systematic attention to feeding, breeding, and shelter. Widespread use of better farm practices would likewise step up wheat production.

This ribbony land, narrower in relation to its length than any other country in the world, is squeezed between majestic wrinkled mountains on one side (where the moonlight can be so beautiful that some Chileans claim they have a special moon of their own) and the crinkling sea on the other. Water comes down from the mountains in natural streams which can be tapped for irrigation so easily that the landowners have developed their own irrigation systems. But these sources are by no means adequate for large-scale expansion of irrigated agriculture. Much could be done to increase agricultural production through an irrigation program financed from public funds.

To carry out such developments as these would require adjustments in government administration and in the fundamental attitude toward agriculture, which has been more or less forgotten while attention was concentrated on industrial growth. City people, who are the workers in industry and commerce, have been well protected by laws that hold down the prices of foods, but farmers have been offered no corresponding incentives to increase production. Here is one of the changes most urgently needed for better balance in Chile's economy.

The Bank–FAO mission, working with government representatives and others, proposed a program of agricultural development which, if inflation is controlled, should bring increases in production averaging about 3 per cent a year for several years. After studying the proposals, the government set up a special economic commission to work out an eight-year plan, which is now being put into effect.

Some time before the joint mission went to Chile, FAO sent a sizable technical assistance group, headed by E. I. Kotok, US forest expert, to that country. In Santiago, FAO also has an office, in charge of B. F. Osorio-Tafall (Mexico), which services the countries on the west coast of South America.

One of the chief undertakings in technical co-operation has been to help the government shape an administrative setup adequate to cope with the complicated problems of agricultural expansion. R. A. Lovald (USA), who has had this assignment, has also been concerned with planning future irrigation developments in Chile. R. M. Carslaw (UK), agricultural economist, has been setting up a demonstration center for modern management practices. E. D. Sandvig and Wayne Miles (USA), range experts, have worked mainly on improving the sheep ranges in the Magallanes area, but their assignment will cover other aspects of livestock production. The marketing expert, R. F. Burdette (USA), started working on a long-range market improvement program, which is badly needed, but has had to concentrate on developing meat refrigeration plants near points of production to cut the heavy losses now sustained in shipping animals alive (or driving them on the hoof as in the days of the great cattle trails in the US Western states) to the big consuming centers. He has also conducted a course on marketing methods at the University of Santiago. W. F. Ewert (Canada), the statistician, has principally helped to prepare for the taking of an agricultural census.

In forestry, one of the important developments carried out with FAO aid has been the establishment of a forestry school at the University of Chile, in Santiago, with a curriculum based on the experience of the best schools in Europe and the United States. This school should be of great value regionally as well as nationally. To assist Chile's Professor Valenzuela in making plans for the school, FAO obtained the services of Dean Paul M. Dunn (USA), who taught there with two other American professors and a Chilean staff. A forestry center has been set aside on public land at Llancacura, some 500 miles south of Santiago, where modern methods of forest management and timber extraction will be demonstrated, and where university students and others can receive part of the training needed for careers in forestry and in wood-using industries. This center plays a vital part in showing the possibilities of a sound forest policy.

The FAO forestry group of eight experts has also worked on drafting forest legislation, making a forest inventory, drawing up plans (with the *Corporacion de Fomento*) for an integrated forest industry in the Valdivia area, making soil conservation surveys, and so on. In fact, no important aspect of the development of the forest resources of Chile has been neglected.

The coast of Chile is rich in fish resources. Hake is the most common fish; caught in large quantities, it is comparatively inexpensive. The government is greatly interested in expanding the market for fish within the country, for both nutritional and economic reasons. A primary need is to popularize fish as a food, and a fairly extensive sales campaign is now under way, started with a big demonstration by FAO expert John Fridthjof (Denmark), the setting up of five pilot projects for processing and distribution, and the enlistment of schools, press, radio, and government services in the campaign. The benefits of all this work are already substantial. Chile is also co-operating with FAO in investigating the use of fish flour as a food —mixed, for example, with wheat flour to make bread. This might be an inexpensive way of adding significantly to the protein value of some common foods. Taste tests so far indicate that the product is well accepted.

Chile has a program of biological research in fisheries in which FAO has provided some help. The regional fisheries training center held in Valparaiso has been described earlier in this chapter.

Wheat is Chile's staple food and baking is an industry of major importance, particularly in the cities. The government has been keenly interested in trying to bring down the price of bread and to improve its quality. FAO assigned bakery expert J. A. Silva, Jr. (USA)—the man who made a practical commercial product out of the nutritionally famous formula for bread developed at Cornell University—to demonstrate modern methods in the industry and work out a program of improvement.

Ecuador

The first help given by FAO to Ecuador was in 1949. The country had just been rocked by an earthquake which shook up some 2000 square miles of farm and pasture land, wrecked irrigation works, killed 7000 people, injured 20,000, and left 100,000 homeless. This occurred in August.

The government gallantly insisted that FAO go ahead with its first Latin American regional meeting, scheduled for Quito in the high Andes in September. During the meeting the Director-General surveyed the earthquake's harvest of ruin. Shortly afterward an FAO engineer, Donald W. Gilfillan (USA), was sent in to help plan rehabilitation and, in particular, to mobilize all available resources to build a new canal to restore water to the land.

This was done. Since that time the government has been carrying on an extensive program for increasing the area of irrigated land, mainly for cereals, alfalfa, sugar cane, and cotton.

Up-country, in the high Andes, livestock (particularly sheep) are the mainstay of agriculture on the part of the descendants of the early Spanish settlers, who own the big estates, and also of the Indians, who follow the ancient pattern of communal ownership of both grazing and grain lands. In charge of an FAO livestock program in Ecuador is John C. Tauber (USA), who also is head of the FAO Ecuadorian mission.

In recent years production from sheep has been falling off for one reason or another. The fleece weight, for instance, now averages around 2 to $2\frac{1}{2}$ pounds; in Australia the average is 10 pounds. There is also much room for improvement in the quality of the wool. The government and the sheepmen alike are eager for technical help.

FAO sent in J. M. Jones and Eugene Bertone (both of the USA) to help improve breeding, feeding, and management. One of their first steps was to organize a national sheep and wool growers' association, which has taken an active part in an improvement campaign.

Two prime needs are improvement of mountain ranges by bringing in better grasses and legumes to replace poor herbage and development of better animals by selection and by crossbreeding with imported stock. Bertone is also helping to introduce improved equipment such as shearing machines better than the crude tools now commonly used, to develop better veterinary services, to spread the practice of dipping sheep for control of external parasites, to provide shelter for ewes during lambing time, and to obtain tax-free salt so that sheepmen can afford to use it for their animals. High-grade breeding stock has now been imported from Mexico under FAO supervision.

The benefits of the program are not confined to the big producers. "The first lamb born in an experiment station in Ecuador—a half-breed Corriedale ram lamb—was dropped on June 20," one of the experts reported in July 1953. "This, and about 150 others like it, we hope to sell or give to small farmers for flock improvement in 1953."

Among the highland Indians the sale of wool and wool products is an important source of income. The weaving is done on ancient hand looms, and the possible earnings with such primitive equipment are pitifully small. Two craftsmen, W. A. Ames and Florence M. LaGrande, with long experience in a handicraft school for Indians in the southwestern USA, were sent in at the request of the government to develop better methods of grading, testing, dyeing, spinning, and weaving wool. They found the Ecuadorian craftsmen eager and quick to learn new ways. The weavers soon organized a co-operative, built a shop-laboratory as a craft center in Otavalo, brought an improved loom from the USA, found that they could multiply their earnings several times by using better practices, and did so. Subsequently, steps were taken to have a large number of the new-type looms built locally.

The Ecuador coast is low-lying hot country, well adapted to rice, cacao, bananas, and other tropical and semitropical crops under irrigation. On this coast Guayaquil, the chief commercial city, is located.

There is good fishing along the mainland and around the Galapagos Islands. FAO expert E. C. A. Schweigger (Peru) made a study of the situation, suggested some practical steps to strengthen the fisheries, proposed a program for better development and conservation of lobster and shrimp, and outlined some needed research.

The native fishermen are exceptionally skillful with primitive equipment. They use a canoe called a *bongo,* 18 to 40 feet long, with decked-over bow and stern and a triangular sail. One of their remarkable feats on catching a marlin—weighing perhaps 200 to 350 pounds—is to haul it alongside the little boat, keep it tied there until it is dead or weakened, dive into the water, turn the boat over to cover the marlin, then turn it right side up with the big fish inside. Sometimes two or three marlin are caught in a day and brought to shore in this fashion. Other fish commonly caught are yellowfin tuna, skipjacks, bonito, swordfish, mackerel, pompano, corvina, and grouper. The income of the fishermen is fairly good compared with that of people in other occupations. Demand is brisk along the coast but does not spread inland; better transportation and processing are needed to provide fish for the people up-country. In 1952 FAO expert Carlos Gonzalez (Argentina) carried out a project to distribute dried and salted fish in the Andean region of Ecuador.

Other FAO work has been concerned with nutrition, food technology, milk production and handling (in connection with a UNICEF program), modernization of a slaughterhouse in Guayaquil, the feeding of cattle and pigs, agricultural extension, agricultural machinery, and forestry.

Uruguay

The government of this beautiful and progressive country, which has such natural advantages as a temperate climate, evenly distributed rainfall, and excellent grasslands, has from the beginning played an active part in the development of FAO. Montevideo was the scene of the second FAO Latin American Regional Meeting and of the first regional nutrition conference. But Uruguay has so far asked for little direct technical co-operation from FAO. The main work there so far has been participation in a survey mission with the International Bank in 1950 which included nine specialists in fields related to agriculture and forestry.

Since Uruguay is one of the world's leading exporters of meat products and wool, the survey and the proposals for agricultural development made by the Bank-FAO mission paid a good deal of attention to the livestock industry, although they also covered all other important aspects of agricultural production, including marketing, transportation, storage, research, and extension services. One important outcome was a carefully prepared program for pasture improvement, now under way. Carroll, the Australian parasitologist who worked in Brazil, has been sent to Uruguay by FAO to help on sheep problems.

Paraguay

This "little country that somehow missed being a paradise," as Preston James puts it, has had direct technical assistance from FAO only in connection with forestry developments. Partly as a result of two exhausting wars, against Brazil, Argentina, and Uruguay in 1865-70 and against Bolivia in 1932-35, Paraguay is poverty-stricken and thinly peopled. Yet it is blessed with much good soil and good grass, with immense untapped forests which cover over half the land, and with a climate that is mild but not too mild. Tannin and rough logs are the main exports, going to other countries in South America. In 1955 an FAO expert will begin consultations with the government on its agricultural development programs.

The FAO forestry mission of two experts—Eino A. Saari (Finland) and J. J. French (USA)—believe there are immense possibilities for development of forest industries. Their work so far has been mainly confined to the preliminary steps: helping to draft forest laws that would insure rational exploitation in the best interest of the country as a whole and to prepare plans for a capable forest administration which could explore the possibilities for development of industries and attract the necessary capital.

The USA has for some years had a bilateral assistance program in Paraguay, until recently under the direction of Albion Patterson. This group and the Paraguay Government co-operated with FAO in the highly significant regional project concerned with supervised agricultural credit, about which I have written earlier in this chapter.

Peru

The co-operation between FAO, the Peruvian Government, and other agencies in the Andean extension training institute has proved to be fruitful, and it should have even greater possibilities in the future. I have discussed this work briefly in earlier pages. Otherwise, Peru has so far requested very little technical co-operation from FAO.

The government is much interested in nutrition and has had the help of a number of organizations in nutrition programs. An FAO staff nutrition officer made surveys in three typical areas (a coastal cotton plantation, a fishing village, and a farming village in the highlands near Cuzco) which included training some 30 Peruvians in survey techniques and laying out a program for further work during the next few years.

Peru is sharply divided into three types of areas: the coastal strip, mainly bleak desert interspersed with 40 or more productive, oasislike farming communities, each with a distinctive character and supplied with water from mountain streams and irrigation ditches; the high Andes, once the site of a remarkable Inca civilization and today dotted with Indian communities raising sheep, llamas, and alpacas, and producing potatoes and grain in the same way their ancestors did; and the jungle area in the east, beyond the Andes, where at Tingo Maria in the upper reaches of the Amazon interesting experiments in tropical farming on cleared land are being conducted.

A United Nations mission has been working in the Cuzco area, in the Andes, where a destructive earthquake occurred in 1950, and FAO has been co-operating in agricultural aspects of the project.

Bolivia

Bolivia, too, is a country of sharp contrasts, from the high mountains in the west (La Paz, at 12,000 feet, is the world's highest city), including the more or less level Altiplano, to the tropical lowlands and river basins in the east. Roads and other means of transport and communication are meager, and the eastern lowlands are difficult of access from the Altiplano, where most of the Bolivians live.

The country imports a good deal of its staple food—wheat, flour, meat, sugar. In 1949, before the expanded technical assistance program began, the government asked for advice on how to increase food production in the Altiplano area and FAO sent H. G. Dion (Canada) to make a thorough study. He concluded that production can be stepped up enough to eliminate or greatly reduce the need for imports: wheat, rye, and barley by careful selection and breeding, a good system of fallowing, and the use of phosphate fertilizers; potatoes by similar means, plus control of certain pests and diseases; meat by pasture improvement, control of grazing, the use of mineral supplements in cattle feeding, the production of silage and hay, and the introduction of good breeding stock.

Quinoa, a species of *Chenopodium* (which includes the common and edible weed, lamb's-quarters), is extensively grown because it can be produced where corn will not grow. It has long been the staple food of the Indians. The grain is richer in protein, fat, minerals, and the B vitamins than is wheat, but it has two main drawbacks: low yield and a high content of soapy-tasting saponin, which the Indians wash out in the process of preparing the grain for food. It cannot by itself be used to make bread, but it can be blended with wheat for breadmaking. Dion reported that the plant has good possibilities for improvement by selection and breeding. In Peru, some experiments are now being made with quinoa as a prepared breakfast cereal.

Some time after the Altiplano survey the United Nations signed a contract with the government to undertake many administrative functions in Bolivia. FAO has been involved to some extent in an advisory capacity in connection with agriculture. Several projects are scheduled to begin in 1955. I have already mentioned the Bolivian land reform program in connection with regional work in Latin America.

Colombia

In Colombia one of the outstanding FAO projects has been technical cooperation in establishing a laboratory at Bogotá for the rapid diagnosis of virus diseases of cattle, particularly foot-and-mouth disease. This work—carried out by E. Traub (Germany), W. J. Capps (USA), and Nels Konnerup (USA)—followed a serious outbreak of foot-and-mouth disease in Venezuela which spread to Colombia. Besides its regular analytical work, the laboratory has trained Colombian students, sent others to Europe for study on FAO fellowships, and done significant research, which I shall have occasion to mention again in the next chapter, on the possibility of producing foot-and-mouth disease vaccines by passaging the virus through chicken eggs.

In forestry, FAO's von Bottenburg (the Netherlands) did a good deal of work which resulted in recommendations for enlarging and improving the forest service, carrying out a sizable reforestation project near Bogotá, conducting an intensive campaign against the burning of forests, and establishing a forestry school at the agricultural college at Medellin. Some of these proposals are now being put into effect as part of the government's forest program.

FAO expert Carl Fritzle (Switzerland), after making extensive surveys prepared proposals for agricultural development with emphasis particularly on extending the production of oil-bearing and fiber plants. FAO livestock expert A. I. Staffe (Austria) is now in Colombia working on broad aspects of the government's animal production program, including further development of the excellent breeds created during $4\frac{1}{2}$ centuries by Colombian cattlemen. FAO has also furnished considerable help in connection with agricultural statistics, particularly the use of modern sampling methods. Other work is either under way or will soon start in connection with water development, dairying, agricultural economics, fisheries, and nutrition.

Venezuela

Venezuela has taken an active interest in the work of FAO. An early FAO project was the survey, discussed in a previous chapter, concerned with expanding the production of oil-bearing plants. Venezuela is now undertaking expansion of its dairy industry, with technical co-operation from FAO, and projects are planned for animal nutrition, extension development, and economics and statistics.

WORK WITH INDIVIDUAL COUNTRIES: MEXICO AND CENTRAL AMERICA

Mexico

Mexico covers as much territory as ten countries of Western Europe together: Austria, Belgium, France, Germany, Italy, Luxembourg, the Netherlands, Portugal, Spain, and Switzerland. Physically, the country ranges from rugged mountains to arid plains to lush tropical lowlands; culturally, it is characterized at one extreme by the highly developed commercial and industrial capital, Mexico City, and at the other by the isolated primitive Indian communities in the forests of Yucatan. In the background is a rich history, from the complex ancient culture of the Aztecs conquered by Cortes, through long periods of foreign exploitation (around 1900, only 5 per cent of the Mexican people had any land of their own) and of internal strife and revolution, up to the vigorous drive of modern Mexico for economic development and betterment.

In Mexico City, FAO has an office which services Mexico, Central America, and the Caribbean area. The government has taken an active part in FAO's regional work, including locust control, forestry, livestock disease control, and the recent land problems discussions in Brazil, in which, as I have noted, Mexico was especially interested because of its own long-standing land tenure program.

The UNESCO fundamental education project at Patzcuaro, in the State of Michoacan, in which FAO, ILO, and WHO collaborate, is largely a regional undertaking to train teachers and community leaders, which places a good deal of emphasis on agriculture. FAO has participated by providing experts in extension, home economics, and co-operatives.

Nine FAO experts, headed by D. T. Griffiths (UK), have worked in Mexico on the government's vigorous forest development program. The 1948 forest law is unique; in line with provisions of the 1917 constitution on land ownership, it provides for a mixture of communal, private, and state-owned forests, and it authorizes state control and regulation in the public interest, even in private forests. This works favorably for private industries using forest products because the state must guarantee that they will have a sustained supply of timber to meet their needs; but the industries, in turn, may be required to provide certain technical forest services to insure proper management of timber lands. The undertaking is new and the government is understandably anxious to make an outstanding success of forest management. The help obtained from FAO has included silviculture, entomology, forest inventories, and pine lumber and other forest products industries. Co-operation between the government and FAO has been excellent, and a promising long-term program is now well under way. The FAO forestry group in Mexico has been drawn from seven different countries.

Since Mexico is a large producer of livestock, it is seeking to improve range and pasture lands. During much of the year, extensive areas of the overgrazed range are yellow and parched, and the thin vegetation has little or no nourishment left. Experience with similar conditions elsewhere (in the Western plains of the USA, for example) has shown that much can be accomplished by selecting or introducing well-adapted grasses, making the best use of limited areas of irrigated pasture, and preserving forage either dried as hay or fermented as ensilage. (Similar work, as I have noted, is under way in the Near East.) Many Mexican livestock owners are much interested in this kind of improvement, and FAO has been helping with a team of three experts—the late D. A. Savage (USA), R. L. Robb (Union of South Africa), and A. L. Brown (USA). UNICEF and FAO are assisting in the development of a milk-conservation plan.

Other FAO work in Mexico is concerned with agricultural machinery and with fisheries economics (the regional fisheries training center in Mexico has been mentioned earlier). A minor but interesting project was a survey made by an FAO plant pathologist of pineapple growing around Vera Cruz, primarily in connection with the marbled-fruit disease.

Honduras

Honduras is mountain country with much forest, comparatively few people, and a sky full of magnificent clouds. Rough land, likable folk. Scattered among the hills are peaceful villages where oxen amble meditatively along the roads, dragging carts with creaky solid wooden wheels, and horsemen ride small native ponies, ax and machete slung from the saddle. Tegucigalpa, the capital, has a good airport but no railroad connection with any other place, and in the streets there are sometimes long trains of burros, each carrying a pair of big saddlebags stuffed with goods. Characteristic of Honduras are large estates, often owned by landlords who stay elsewhere. Farmers and farm laborers tend to live in scattered isolated houses rather than in village communities, the usual pattern in Latin America; they practice shifting cultivation, stripping and burning the hillsides, planting corn or other crops, and then abandoning the land to weeds for a time.

Along the northern coast lies a rather narrow strip of low level land devoted to the growing of bananas by methods that have now become so intensive and scientific as almost to constitute factory production on the soil. About a fourth of all the bananas exported from Latin America come from this area. There is only one other small area of intensive cultivation, devoted to coffee.

Many people in and out of Honduras are confident that the country can support a considerably larger population and achieve considerably higher standards of living. A vigorous development program got under way in 1950 when the Congress organized a National Development Bank and a Central Bank, started a development fund, and asked for technical co-operation of an unusually fundamental kind from FAO.

Agricultural economist H. J. L. Joosten (the Netherlands) then made a detailed survey of the country's agricultural situation and possibilities, which provided a basis for the government's subsequent plans and programs. An early decision was to undertake fairly extensive colonizing of selected areas, beginning with a colony near Catacamas which could be used as a model. Supervised credit accompanied by guidance from farm and home extension workers were basic in this plan.

In preparing and carrying out the development program, particularly the aspects concerned with colonization, which included setting up credit facilities and training extension workers, one of the guiding spirits has been

FAO's G. Insfran Guerreros (Paraguay). The whole program is a truly pioneering effort in which a number of the government agencies have been working together in a way that is highly promising for the future. The project was started on a modest scale, and its further development will be watched with intense interest both in Honduras and in other countries.

FAO has helped in setting up a bureau of animal industry which includes a bacteriological laboratory and will eventually develop a veterinary field service. This is the first undertaking of the kind in the country; it soon resulted in quick control of an outbreak of anthrax and in the drafting, in Tegucigalpa, of a Sanitary Livestock Convention which involves co-operation among six Central American countries. Here, too, UNICEF and FAO are now working with the government in preparing a milk-conservation plan.

Forest development has considerable possibilities. Honduran forests contain such valuable species as mahogany, rosewood, and cedar—all rather overexploited for many years. Probably the most important timber resources, especially for domestic needs, are the pine and oak forests, which are greatly in need of protection from burning, clean-cutting, and, in the case of pines, unnecessarily destructive methods of tapping the trees for resin. With some co-operation from FAO, the government has been preparing comprehensive forest legislation and organizing a forest service in a new approach to the use and conservation of woodland resources.

Guatemala

Guatemala, home of an ancient Mayan civilization, still has among its people a high percentage of pure-blooded Mayans who follow the ancestral pattern of group ownership and use of the land. Two regional projects involving FAO, both discussed earlier in this book, have centered in Guatemala: the FAO agricultural credit seminar in 1952, and the work of the Institute of Nutrition for Central America and Panama. Guatemala has also participated in other FAO regional programs.

Direct FAO technical co-operation has been confined almost entirely to advice on the reorganization of the sugar industry, and to forestry. Gunther Becker (Germany), F. Schwerdtfeger (Germany), and Marc Rocher (France) helped the government to work out a broad program of forest development and forestry training. Entomology bulked large because considerable areas of valuable pine forests in Guatemala have been heavily infested with insects, particularly a local species of bark beetle. The results of the entomology work are useful to all Central American countries.

An FAO expert recently went to Guatemala as a consultant on the economics of grain production and marketing.

El Salvador

In crowded El Salvador 80 per cent of the land, including the mountainsides, is cultivated, in sharp contrast with 5 per cent in Honduras. The population per square mile is among the highest in Latin America; income per person is among the lowest. The people are hard-working, however, and the government is making a determined effort to do something about their difficult problems. The high price of coffee—almost the only export—has brought a certain prosperity to El Salvador, but with increased purchasing power has come increased pressure for more food and other products not sufficiently available. An active economic development program is now under way with help from a mixed UN mission, FAO, UNICEF, WHO, and US bilateral agencies.

FAO has given special attention to improving farm management, which is perhaps the key to better rural living in El Salvador. This means not only better techniques of crop and livestock production but improvement of the land tenure system. Other work has included help in developing the dairy industry and the milk distribution system (dairy men have been attending training courses after morning chores and before evening chores) and in the production and processing of sugar, which at present is largely imported.

Nicaragua

Managua is the headquarters of the Central American locust control program, serviced by FAO and described in earlier pages. A good deal of other work is under way in that country, which has resources far greater than its present stage of development might indicate.

In 1949, before the days of the expanded technical co-operation program, FAO sent a mission to Nicaragua to survey agriculture and forestry. In the same year the International Bank also made a preliminary survey, which was followed by a loan for building roads, purchasing farm machinery, and other purposes.

In 1951 came a joint Bank–FAO mission, which prepared a comprehensive program of agricultural development. According to this mission, crop yields can be stepped up at least 25 per cent by applying some of the methods normally practiced in more highly developed countries. Coffee production should be expanded; since Nicaragua's high-aroma coffee can be used for blending, it has a favorable long-run outlook. Dairy producers can raise milk production by 50 per cent as a first step even before starting a cattle breeding program.

FAO dairy expert H. M. Morrison (Australia) spent a year and a half in Nicaragua working on dairy improvement, and veterinary expert Paul Emsbo (Denmark), who died in the course of his work there, advised the government on livestock disease control in general and on slaughterhouse problems.

Other proposals given high priority in the Nicaragua program were production of African oil palms, soil conservation, irrigation, a machinery repair shop, homesteading (land colonization) for small-scale farmers (Insfran Guerreros was transferred from Honduras to help with colonization and farm credit), grain storage, better forest management, and further development of extension and other agricultural services. An FAO nutrition expert has helped to develop a national campaign and train school teachers and nurses in nutrition work, and has also co-operated with the United Nations Children's Fund on a school feeding program.

Costa Rica

This small hilly country, where gentle mists and rains make the land as green as Ireland, is agriculturally advanced. In the densely settled central part, at least, most farmers own their farms, and farm practices are likely to be good. The people are democratic, literacy is high, and there is no dominant group of large-scale absentee landlords.

So far FAO has been called on to do comparatively little work in Costa Rica except in connection with the regional projects already described in which various international, regional, and national organizations have collaborated.

The government has a nutrition program in which FAO expert Lirica Barreto (Argentina) has worked with the ministries of health and education for two years helping to organize a school feeding project using local foods, train people to carry it out, and plan village demonstration centers. UNICEF and FAO have also co-operated in a national milk project.

Panama

Earlier in this chapter I discussed regional work, centering in Panama, on the prevention and control of foot-and-mouth disease in Central America.

Direct technical assistance on a national scale has been provided only in the case of two short-term projects. P. C. Tang (China) helped in improving the system of collecting agricultural statistics, which included making two sample surveys. The other project was an intensive study of the economically important shrimp fisheries, carried out by Leslie W. Scattergood (USA), succeeded by M. D. Burkenroad (USA). The main object so far has been to trace the migrations of shrimp in the waters of Panama and adjacent Costa Rica so that fishermen will be able more readily to locate areas of abundant supplies at different times and seasons.

WORK WITH INDIVIDUAL COUNTRIES: CARIBBEAN COUNTRIES

Haiti

In 1948 the United Nations and some of the specialized agencies, including FAO, sent a technical mission to Haiti. Out of this visit came an economic development program, started in 1950. Haiti was chosen for the mission partly because its problems—those of a large, rapidly growing population crowded on a small mountainous land—are more than usually difficult.

Among the people in the 1948 mission was FAO fisheries expert E. F. Thompson (USA). He reached the conclusion that the development of inland fish culture could be remarkably useful in Haiti to provide an economical source of much-needed protein food, especially since marine fish in Haitian waters are far from plentiful.

Thompson's idea proved to be a sound one. In 1950 FAO fish culture expert S. Y. Lin (China) went to Haiti to start a five-year program for fisheries development. It has been steadily progressing ever since. Lin has recently been succeeded by Shimon Tal, fish nursery expert from Israel.

The work started with the construction of a number of small propagating ponds and the importation from Alabama of a few carp—each more than 100 years old, incidentally—as breeders. Some months later Lin brought in several hundred tilapia (African in origin) from the British West Indies. Progress was slow in the early stages. By now, however, lakes, rivers, and canals in Haiti, stocked from the original ponds, are swarming with tilapia and carp, and for the first time fresh fish are becoming plentiful and cheap in food markets. This is a boon to very poor people. Tilapia in particular have multiplied with almost magical speed. In 1951, for instance, a few were released in the Artibonite River. By 1953 large quantities were being caught—more fish than Haitians had ever seen before. Flooded rice fields, too, now yield fish as well as rice. When the fields are drained, the fish collect in hollow places and are dipped out. Later, as the river overflows and again floods the fields for a new crop, it automatically restocks them with fish. Thus the fish supply in the rice fields is self-perpetuating. In addition, fish ponds have now been built on farms in a number of communities, and more will follow, to be stocked with carp of especially high quality brought from Israel.

There are two main river valleys in Haiti. In one, the Artibonite, the level alluvial land is suitable for rice growing. Here agriculture is being developed mainly with help from the USA. The other, the Marbial Valley, is a cut between hills, and more difficult to utilize well. There the problem is mainly to teach farmers better ways of managing the slopes by terracing, contouring, using well-adapted plants, and so on. This is largely an undertaking for extension workers, and FAO for a time provided the services of extension expert Tuure Pasto (USA), who worked with a UNESCO fundamental education team that was engaged on a sizable program in the valley.

One of the urgent needs in Haiti is a vigorous program of reforestation and soil conservation to halt some of the heavy soil losses that have by now taken a good deal of land practically out of production. FAO forestry expert L. Vinton Burns (Jamaica) has worked on this project since the

One of the biggest jobs is to cut the heavy loss caused by animal diseases, which in many places are very inadequately controlled. Some of these diseases run rampant in sporadic outbreaks that may kill most of the animals in a large area. In the Far East and Near East, rinderpest is the deadliest. Research has in recent years developed vaccination methods that for the first time open up the possibility of wiping out this scourge. FAO is spearheading an international drive with that objective and is helping many countries to strengthen their veterinary services. Here Ethiopian technicians are inoculating an animal against rinderpest. Great herds of cattle are one of Ethiopia's most important agricultural assets.

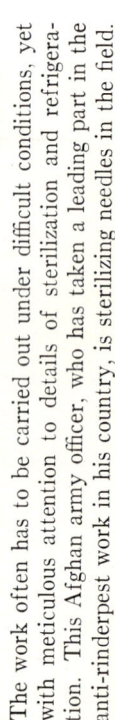

The work often has to be carried out under difficult conditions, yet with meticulous attention to details of sterilization and refrigeration. This Afghan army officer, who has taken a leading part in the anti-rinderpest work in his country, is sterilizing needles in the field.

Getting men and equipment to the places where they are needed is not always easy when jobs like vaccinating have to be done in remote areas. These Afghan villagers have turned out in force to make a passable road so the jeep carrying an FAO veterinary team can proceed on its way.

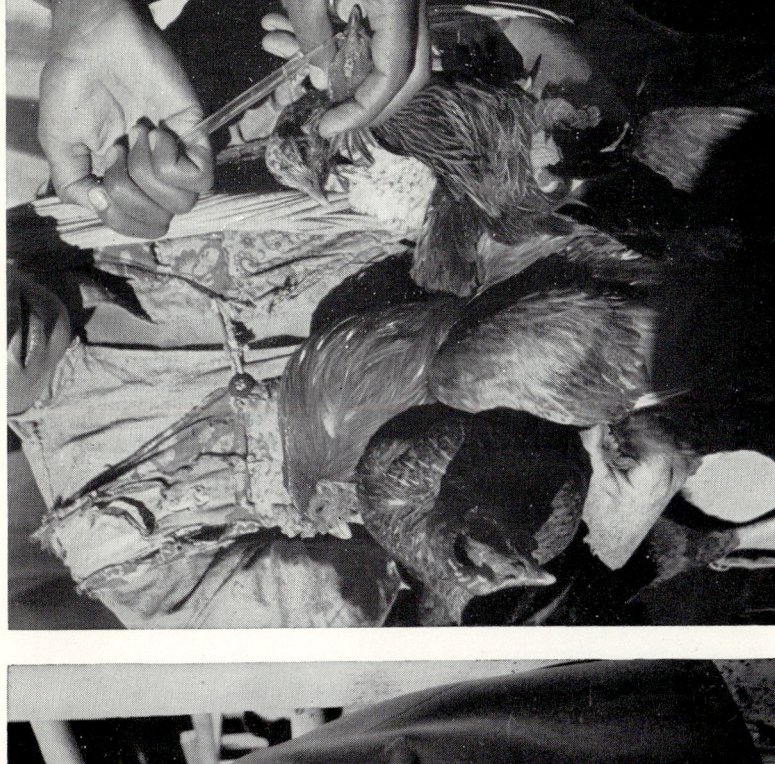

Poultry comes in for a good deal of attention because in many places small home flocks make a real contribution to the food supply. In the Far East and Near East, Newcastle disease is often the greatest handicap to increased production. Here, too, new and inexpensive vaccines are making it possible to control the disease. This Afghan boy is getting his birds inoculated.

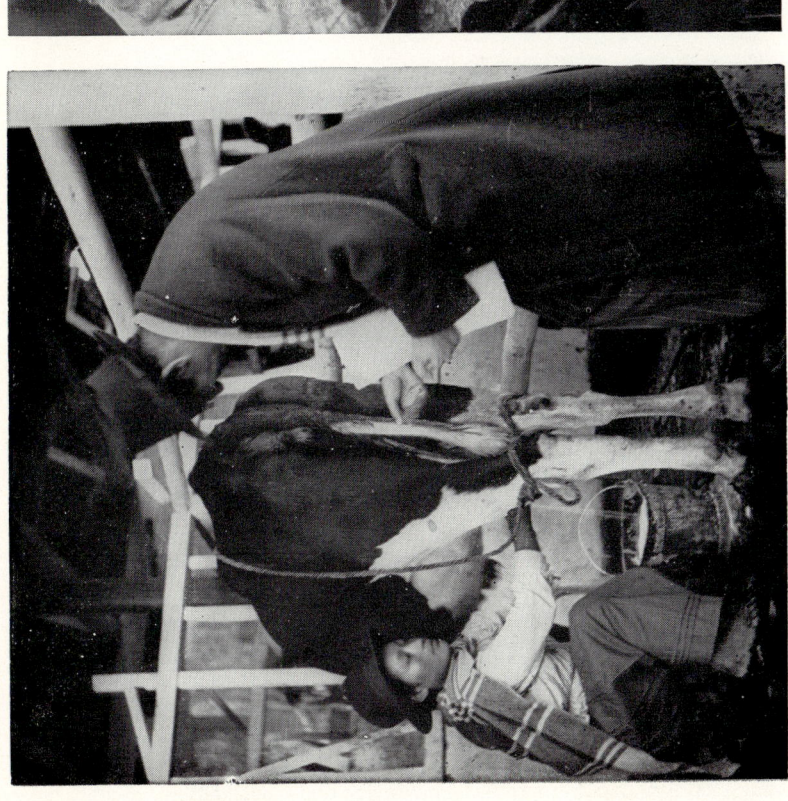

Better production of animals and livestock products does not depend only on disease control. Animal breeding and better animal feeding are also important, and so is better handling of livestock products used for human food. Often clean milk is one of the prime needs. Here a sanitary inspector in Ecuador explains elements of hygiene to a girl working with dairy cows.

Insects annually consume vast quantities of food needed by human beings. The locust is perhaps the worst of all man's insect enemies. Since the days of the Pharaohs, swarms of desert locusts like this one have traveled in airborne armies over countries of the Near East and Far East, destroying every green thing in their path. Now, with FAO as the main co-ordinating agency, these countries are working together more than at any time in history, using modern methods to combat these pests.

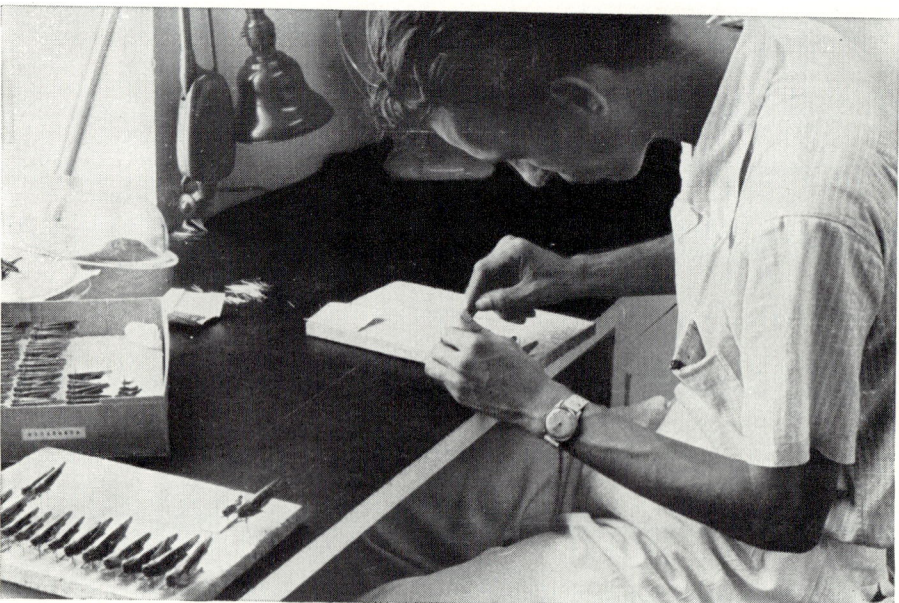

The Central American countries and Mexico also have a continuing fight on their hands to control swarming locusts, and they too are working effectively together, with technical help from FAO, in an International Committee for Coordination of Locust Control. Here a laboratory worker at the organization's headquarters in Managua, Nicaragua, prepares locust specimens.

Better production is only part of the battle to enlarge supplies of food for the world's people. Food processing, marketing, storage, transportation can all be vastly improved, to make more and better food available. This lively, colorful marketplace in Guatemala is typical of those in untold thousands of communities in various parts of the world where all the local food is bought and sold, in little heaps, mostly placed on the ground beside the squatting seller. Market day is a big event in the social life of the community, but also it often involves much preventable waste.

Other agricultural products besides food need attention from the marketing standpoint. Afghanistan, for instance, is introducing cotton grading as a step in the production of cotton of standardized staple lengths instead of the heterogeneous mixture now common. Standardization should help both to bring better returns for producers and to reduce the cost of manufacturing cloth.

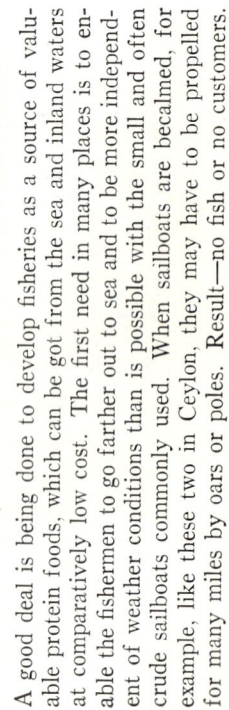

A good deal is being done to develop fisheries as a source of valuable protein foods, which can be got from the sea and inland waters at comparatively low cost. The first need in many places is to enable the fishermen to go farther out to sea and to be more independent of weather conditions than is possible with the small and often crude sailboats commonly used. When sailboats are becalmed, for example, like these two in Ceylon, they may have to be propelled for many miles by oars or poles. Result—no fish or no customers.

Interest in using motors to increase the speed and range of their vessels is spreading rapidly among fisherfolk. Both of these boats in Ceylon have been equipped with motors as part of a development program in which the country is getting help from FAO and the Colombo Plan. Note the good catch in the boat just back from the fishing grounds; yet the average catch of a Ceylonese fisherman in a whole week, using sail, is only about 20 pounds. No wonder the fishermen are clamoring for motors.

Inland fish culture in ponds, streams, lakes, and flooded rice fields is another source of valuable foods which is being extended in many places with FAO help. Pioneers in this art and science are the Javanese, who began raising fish in ponds some twelve or fourteen hundred years ago and have had time to become extremely adept. (Obviously in Java as elsewhere fishing is likely to go with a leisurely, contemplative attitude toward life.) Because of the skill and experience of the Javanese, FAO has held two of its regional training schools on that island.

Also intensely interested in inland fish culture are the people of Thailand, and they have been making rapid strides in increasing production in recent years. The Thai women here are using plunge baskets, which are open at the bottom and serve as traps. The captured fish are removed by hand from the top.

spring of 1951. He has been carrying on a crusade, aimed principally at general protection of the Artibonite Valley, in which he enlisted the support of churches, schools, and any other organizations or individuals able to reach the peasant farmers, of whom he says:

They do not read nor can they communicate by writing, but they can see good examples and they can talk about them. On our side, we can befriend them, win their confidence, and show them in as simple a fashion as possible how the existing ill practices may be remedied. Generally they are very conservative and have a tendency to resist change and new ideas, but we can approach them through a few key individuals in whom they already have confidence. In this way truly great progress can be made, arising from desire on the part of the peasants themselves and not imposed on them from an external source.

FAO has also worked in Haiti on livestock improvement, on the production of sugar and of cotton, on school feeding and other nutrition programs, and on coffee production.

Dominican Republic

In 1953 the Dominican Republic asked for S. Y. Lin's services to start inland fish culture in that country. The Dominican Government undertook the business of constructing ponds with vigor and efficiency, and a number are now stocked with carp and tilapia which were brought from Haiti in special tanks carried by trucks that drove without stopping for 14 hours. (The first truck overturned with a loss of all the 6700 small carp in the tank. This is one of the minor tragedies that occur in such work.) A few months later, by the end of 1953, the ponds had produced 3300 pounds of carp ready for marketing, plus several thousand tilapia descended from the original 150. Lin also imported a few carp from Indonesia of a type characterized by especially quick growth and superior flavor, which are being used for breeding.

Jamaica, Barbados

From Jamaica FAO received an emergency call for help after the great hurricane of August 1951 which destroyed the island's banana plantations (one of the main sources of exports) and most of the food crops needed to feed 1½ million people. The organization at once sent Ralph W. Cummings (USA) to help on a general program of rehabilitation and development. Early the following year the International Bank sent a mission to the island, with FAO co-operating.

The farm organizations and the government have gone ahead vigorously with the comprehensive programs that have grown out of the work done by Cummings and the Bank–FAO mission. As part of the drive for agricultural improvement well beyond conditions existing before the hurricane, Jamaica has brought in several other FAO experts on agricultural credit, rice production, soil conservation, and the surveying and classification of soils. The Jamaicans are especially anxious to make a success of their development program. In the near future they will be taking steps to become a self-governing member of the British Commonwealth.

As I have noted earlier in this chapter, Jamaica is to be host for an agricultural extension conference for the Caribbean which it is hoped will greatly stimulate the development of extension work throughout that area.

FAO technical co-operation in Barbados has been confined to counseling on the government's program of home economics education. The people are poor; the chief work is labor on the sugar plantations; much of the island's food has to be imported; many mothers have to work, in addition to keeping house and taking care of children, in order to make ends meet; and education does not normally extend beyond the sixth grade. Under these circumstances, home economics work is especially important in schools and among adults. An FAO home economist has proposed certain changes in the present program designed to strengthen the valiant efforts of the small staff doing this kind of work in Barbados.

The Guianas

In British Guiana and Surinam (Dutch Guiana), FAO and the International Bank have worked together on economic surveys designed to strengthen the development programs of the two countries.

Most of the people in British Guiana live in a narrow coastal strip two to eight miles wide in the eastern part of the country, reclaimed from the sea by dikes and walls. Inland are dense tropical hardwood forests, much open savannah, a few scattered agricultural settlements on the rivers, and some limited mining and timber operations. The principal crops on the coast are sugar and rice. Beef cattle are raised in one of the savannah areas in the inland forests, and there is some dairying along the coast. Although the country is in a sense very underdeveloped, much of it in fact being unexplored, educational and health standards are, in general, good. Most of the people are East Indians, who grow rice, and Africans, who originally worked on the sugar plantations.

The Bank–FAO mission made recommendations designed to achieve a 20 per cent increase in national income within an initial five-year period, and to expand the cultivated area by about the same percentage. The agricultural work includes a land settlement program, expanded research, a start on forest industries (particularly for export), and a considerable expansion of credit for agriculture, forestry, fisheries, and rural housing.

Later, FAO range and pasture expert Peter Hogg (USA) worked on further developments of the cattle industry in the savannahs, where possibilities are good, with a view particularly to expanding meat exports to Great Britain. Much would need to be done, however, to provide better pastures, better livestock management, and the price incentives that make it profitable for producers to spend money on fertilizers, machinery, fencing, breeding stock, and so on.

In Surinam, too, the population is concentrated on a narrow strip along the coast. The country is five times the size of the Netherlands, but has only one fiftieth as many people. Here too health and education standards are fairly high. The Bank–FAO recommendations on agriculture fit in with the government program and include the opening up of a large area of new land, rehabilitation of some of the deserted plantations, more cattle production, development of pond fish culture, and expansion of logging operations and wood-products manufacture to treble the value of timber products from the Surinam forests within 10 years.

CHAPTER
ELEVEN

Europe

THE PRECEDING CHAPTERS on the Near East, the Far East, and Latin America have been concerned in the main with the technical assistance work of FAO in these regions. The situation in Europe, or Western Europe at any rate, is quite different. Many countries in the other regions are now going through the kind of evolution that Western Europe (the birthplace of Western civilization) went through long ago; indeed, the agriculture, industry, commerce, science, art, literature, philosophy of Europe generated and shaped developments in these fields in modern North America and Oceania. At each stage in the inception and growth of FAO, Europeans have played a dynamic part, and in the case of technical co-operation they have been on the giving more than the receiving end, providing a considerable number of the field experts and headquarters staff who do the work of FAO.

It is a temptation at this point to discuss the achievements of European agriculture, which among other things raised grain yields to astonishingly high levels in a comparatively short period, developed many of the most valuable horticultural crops grown today, perfected breeds of livestock used all over the world, and led in the wise management of grasslands, which must be regarded in many places as the most fundamental resource of agriculture. At the beginning of this book, however, I devoted a good deal of space to telling about some of the farm conditions in Egypt and in the USA as a means of helping the reader to see the nature of the problems involved in the work of FAO. Instead of Jim Barton, I might have chosen a farmer in some country in Western Europe; but I did choose Jim Barton and in writing about him described certain characteristics of modern agriculture anywhere in the world, regardless of nationality. So I do not feel justified in repeating much the same kind of material here, even though the background of Europe differs in various ways from that of the USA.

In discussing FAO work in Europe in the present chapter, I shall follow the same pattern as in the others, dealing first with regional projects and programs, then with individual countries. The reader should keep in mind, however, that much of the work of FAO in Europe is somewhat different from that elsewhere. In many activities, particularly those of a regional character—connected, for example, with fish marketing, forest policy, control of foot-and-mouth disease, and extension services—FAO has acted as a convenient international agency through which member governments could carry out technical investigations, focus diverse viewpoints and interests on common objectives, and develop useful co-operation among countries that already have well-trained technicians and highly developed services of their own. (The US reader should remember that, though international co-ordination of this kind would not be useful in the USA, where the states are cohesive parts of a single government, it does have an important function in an area composed of many states with entirely independent governments.) In other cases—for example, artificial insemination in the dairy herds of Luxembourg, and rehabilitation of forest industries in Austria—the need has been primarily to help repair wartime damage as quickly as possible. But there have also been technical co-operation projects like those we have described in other regions, arising from the need and desire for economic development. This work has been mostly in Eastern Europe, where agriculture has not in general been modernized to the same extent as in countries to the west.

REGIONAL PROJECTS

The European Fisheries

Commercial fishing in Europe is highly developed, especially in England, Holland, Portugal, and the Scandinavian countries. The standby of North European fisheries is the humble, nutritious, versatile herring, which every year slithers in sleek shiny millions up from the sea and down into the welcoming holds of innumerable fishing boats. Both Holland's Amsterdam and Norway's Haugesund, according to legend, were built on heaps of herring bones.

In recent years the industry has been going through a troubled period, largely because of reduced popular demand for this fish, especially in its common traditional form, salt herring, once universally relished but today increasingly supplanted by more tempting or sophisticated foods. In connection with their marketing problems, the fishery folk in Western Europe have made use of the services of FAO for a number of meetings and studies: a fisheries meeting in Rome in 1947; an FAO commodity study of herring and related species in 1949; a meeting at The Hague in the same year; two meetings in Bergen in 1950; an intensive survey of marketing made in 1951 by the Organization for European Economic Cooperation and FAO; the setting up of a committee to co-ordinate technology research in northwest Europe.

This is the Interim Committee on Fish Handling and Processing, which has functions similar to those of the FAO regional fisheries councils, although its work is limited to practical technology since another organization, the International Council for the Exploration of the Sea, co-ordinates research in biology and hydrology in the European region. The FAO committee has four working groups, all designed to expand markets—one concerned with possibilities for making inexpensive processed foods from surplus fish, another with herring products especially suited for Africa, a third with edible fish flour for possible overseas markets, and the fourth with certain liquids and pastes made from fish in the Far East which have aroused considerable interest and perhaps deserve special mention here.

Salting and drying, being economical, are the most common methods of preserving fish in the Far East, as in many other areas; but fish condiments or pastes are also traditional products in much of Southeast Asia, including South China and the Philippines (though not India). They go by various names—*pra-hoc* and *mam* in Cambodia, *padec* in Laos, *kapi* in Thailand, *bagoong* in the Philippines, *trassi* in Indonesia—and there are many variations in the products and processes, according to whether fish, fish entrails, fish eggs, or shrimp are used as the base and whether or not a carbohydrate such as sugar, rice, or rice husks is added.

The method of preparing these pastes varies from place to place, but commonly involves placing the headed and gutted fish in a wicker basket or earthenware jar, pounding, salting, and pressing them (sometimes they are trampled in much the same way as grapes in a wine press), then decanting the liquid that rises to the top and finally fermenting it in the sun for a period varying from 10 days to three months. This becomes a paste that will keep for several years in hermetically sealed jars. It is used to flavor soups and rice but may also be eaten as a main dish with rice or vegetables.

Fermented fish sauces or pickles, known as *nuoc-mam* in Viet-Nam and Cambodia, *nam-pla* in Thailand, and *patis* in the Philippines, are perhaps even more common than pastes. In the preparation of these products, the fish are usually placed in a vat or earthenware jar with salt, and the liquid products are decanted off, with or without pressure, after an aging period of a few months to a year or more, during which the receptacle may be buried in the ground to insure an even temperature. A feature of the manufacture of fermented fish sauce is that the fish are used ungutted since the visceral enzymes are essential to the hydrolization process.

Nuoc-mam is a clear, brown, salty liquid, and the better qualities are rich in soluble nitrogenous compounds, although it is impossible to eat enough for a significant intake of protein because of the high salt content. The product is mainly a condiment, but in some places the small amount of fish sauce used to flavor rice may be the only source of animal protein.

Although early European and American workers were inclined to label these products as repulsive and unhygienic, further investigation and rigorous chemical analysis has proved otherwise. There is now a voluminous literature on the chemistry of these processes. As is the case with all food processing, unsanitary conditions may result in a spoiled product; but fermented fish is basically no less acceptable than fermented milk (cheese and yogurt), fermented grape juice (wine), or various fermented meat and vegetable sauces manufactured in the West. Nor is fish sauce any more odoriferous than some fermented cheeses, and the best qualities are similarly sought for their bouquet; in fact, it is said that fermented fish sauce was greatly relished at their banquets by the ancient Romans, who called it *garum*.

The governments of the countries of Southeast Asia, particularly Cambodia, are taking steps to introduce quality standards, involving the kinds of controls used in modern food industries, in order to establish a uniformly hygienic product with a high protein content.

Whether it may prove to be possible or desirable to utilize surplus herring in Europe for the manufacture of cheaper fish pastes and sauces like those made in Asia, and to what extent, remains to be seen; processing and marketing methods, and especially consumer taste, are not changed overnight, nor as a rule are extensive new markets quickly developed. The present interest in these processes is evidence, however, of the intense concern to improve and expand distribution.

The Bergen meeting also considered many other aspects of fish processing, including new developments in the techniques of canning and freezing.

The Mediterranean region of Europe has its own fish problems, quite different from those that plague the northern countries. Here the question is rather markets-looking-for-fish than fish-looking-for-markets. Like so many countries in the Far East, the Near East, and Latin America, those in the Mediterranean area are for the present interested mainly in modernizing the industry. In July 1952 they established a regional organization, the General Fisheries Council for the Mediterranean (modeled on the lines of the Indo-Pacific Council), which so far has 11 members—Cyprus (UK), Egypt, France, Greece, Israel, Italy, Monaco, Spain, Tunisia, Turkey, and Yugoslavia. The third meeting was held in October 1954.

The Mediterranean Council agreed in the beginning to stick closely to practical problems rather than scientific research. Its three technical committees (exploration, production, utilization) are concerned mainly with exploration for new fishing grounds, research on new gear and new methods for tuna and sardine fishing, maintenance of boats and gear, problems of pollution of waters, the effect of fishing methods on overfishing and natural restocking, health hazards of fishermen, fisheries training, and, finally, the collection of statistics and technical information.

Two other FAO fisheries meetings in Europe were international rather than strictly regional in character. One was the first international meeting ever held on fisheries statistics, in Copenhagen in May 1952. Accurate figures on manufacturing, processing, and trade are especially lacking in the fish industry. For several years FAO has been regularly publishing volumes of fisheries statistics, but large gaps still remain in the information collected. More accurate and complete reporting is badly needed, and the Copenhagen meeting was a step in that direction.

The other meeting in Europe of world significance was the International Fishing Boat Congress held in Paris in October 1953, and followed by a meeting on the same subject in Miami, Florida, in November.

The Paris and Miami meetings were the first international discussions of what is without doubt the most important factor in the fishing industry, namely, the boats that do the fishing. More capital is invested in fishing boats than in any other single element in fisheries. It has been estimated, for example, that in the USA of the total capital value of fisheries in 1946 nearly half was invested in boats and gear.

Obviously, the boats which require such heavy investments should be designed to perform as efficiently and economically as possible. Yet comparatively little research, study, and governmental support has been given to the design of fishing boats in any part of the world. There is a dearth of technical literature on the subject, although it is known that improvements in boat design can result in better performance and great savings in costs of operation. Such factors as length in relation to girth, hull shape, round or V-shaped bottom, shape of stern, location of the center of buoyancy, fuel consumption at different speeds—all have a marked influence on the seaworthiness of vessels, their stability or seakindliness (as one expert puts it, "a vessel can be seaworthy and still pitch and buck so that only a cowboy can stay aboard her"), and efficiency and economy of operation.

Research and testing in this field is too expensive for most owners or builders, and even for some governments. Under such circumstances, regional co-operation among countries can be particularly fruitful. The experience of FAO in advising and assisting governments in connection with fishing-boat design shows that there is marked interest. The Paris and Miami meetings were attended by some of the world's best boat designers and builders. They dealt not only with design and construction but with engines, propellers, deck equipment, safety at sea, the handling of fish aboard ship, factory ships on which fish is processed at sea, and other technical problems. The meetings should have a marked effect in drawing attention to the prime importance of improvement in this most fundamental aspect of fisheries.

Forestry in Europe

In 1947 Europe faced a postwar shortage of wood—almost as serious as the shortage of food—for rebuilding homes, factories, railroads, bridges, and other structures. To help European governments cope with this situation, FAO called a conference at Marianske-Lazne (Czechoslovakia was then a member of the organization) where in spite of conflicts of interests a program was hammered out which successfully stepped up timber production and increased the flow of timber from east to west sufficiently to meet the need. By 1949 Europe had achieved an equilibrium, though a somewhat precarious one, between supply and demand.

The European Forestry Commission was a product of the Marianske-Lazne meeting. Its membership is confined to the countries that are members of FAO, which provides the commission's secretariat. Another major European forestry organization is the Timber Committee of the United Nations Economic Commission for Europe. This committee has in its membership countries that are not members of FAO, including the USSR and Eastern European governments closely allied with it. The timber supplies from this eastern area are very important for Europe as a whole. FAO co-operates with the ECE Timber Committee, and, in fact, the director of the forestry division of ECE is an FAO officer.

Besides playing an active part in achieving the needed postwar increase in timber supplies, the FAO European Forestry Commission has done much other work. Perhaps the most important to date is the recently completed study of European timber trends and prospects which was made by the joint secretariat of the commission and the ECE Timber Committee. This report was three years in the making, beginning in 1950, and it constitutes the most exhaustive analysis of European timber consumption, production, and trade ever produced. The conclusions are likely to influence forest policies on that continent for a long time to come. They might be summed up briefly this way:

The demand for wood for industrial use has not kept pace with the rate of industrial expansion and population growth. In other words, forest products are falling behind and other materials are taking their place.

Probably this recession in relative demand has been owing to sharp price increases, which were caused by the shortage of supplies in recent years.

In spite of the downward trend, it has been estimated that the need for wood for industrial purposes in Europe by 1960, assuming normal economic growth and prices unchanged from current levels, will be about a third more than the supplies that will be available at that time if production schedules continue as they are at present.

Thus, by 1960 other materials will inevitably have taken the place of wood to an even greater extent than they have so far, unless in the meantime a great deal more wood is available for normal needs. The loss of markets for the timber trade in the former case would probably be permanent.

The only way to avoid this further loss is to increase timber supplies through enlarged production and increased imports to Western Europe from the USSR, Canada, the USA, and other sources.

Major elements in the program in Europe would include opening up less accessible forests not now exploited, stepping up the rate of reforestation, somewhat more intensive cutting in present woodlands, further reduction in the use of wood for fuel, economies in industrial use (for example, greater utilization of wood waste), and maintaining careful forest inventories.

Such a dynamic program of forest management and use means planning for a long time ahead as well as for the immediate future. Long-term planning is not unusual in forestry; trees take a long time to grow, and it is not visionary but essential to think in terms of a hundred years.

The findings of the working party that made the timber-trends study are embodied in a detailed report which was carefully considered and approved in the autumn of 1953 by a joint meeting of the European Forestry Commission and the ECE Timber Committee.

Next, the findings were considered by the 1953 session of the FAO conference, which reaffirmed the conclusions and strongly urged European governments to put the measures outlined in the report into practice. The conference also asked the Director-General to undertake similar studies of timber trends in Latin America, the Far East, and the Near East. As the Director-General noted in discussing the question at the conference, the European report shows that sound investments in forestry and forest industries by European governments, bankers, and businessmen should be directed toward the twofold purpose of increasing supplies and reducing costs of production, conversion, and distribution.

Mainly under the aegis of the FAO Forestry Commission, European governments have established a number of smaller or subsidiary organizations for special needs—for instance, a Mediterranean subcommission to deal specifically with problems in that area, including the cork oak, which is especially important in Spain and Portugal; a committee to foster advances in logging techniques and the training of forest workers; a Chestnut Commission and an International Poplar Commission, both international rather than strictly European in character; and a working party on the control of torrents and avalanches, which is studying the difficult problem of reducing the hazards of these destructive forces in mountain areas.

The Regional Hybrid Corn Program

One of the most successful undertakings by a group of countries anywhere is the hybrid corn program in Europe, mentioned in an earlier chapter. This program has made steady progress and now has a record of achievement which includes increasing production by the equivalent of 24 million dollars' worth of corn in 1952 and 40 million dollars' worth in 1953 above what it would have been without the use of hybrids introduced through the program. The 64 million dollar value added to the European corn crop in two years is more than the total amount spent by FAO for all its work since the organization came into existence, including both the regular and the expanded technical assistance programs. Yet the hybrid corn development has so far hardly started, and during the first five years

Europe

FAO has spent only $40,000 on the work. Although the use of hybrids practically doubled in 1953, as compared with 1952, it still covered only 6 per cent of the total corn area of the region. As it really gets into its stride, hybrid corn should add far more to food and feed supplies.

Since 1947 there have been annual meetings of European corn breeders each winter to go over what they had done the previous year and to lay plans for the co-operative work of the next season. In the beginning the program was confined to importing and testing US and Canadian hybrids—since hybrid corn originated in North America—to find out which were best adapted to local conditions in Europe, this specific adaptation being in general the key to the big yields of hybrid corn. Complete records of the performance of the hybrids were kept, analyzed, and exchanged among the co-operating countries. All of this preliminary work was a foundation for the next step, the development of national programs designed to breed hybrids especially suited to local environments. Throughout the program FAO provided the services of Merle T. Jenkins, an outstanding US hybrid corn expert, as consultant.

The 1954 meeting was held in Belgrade, Yugoslavia, in February. To that session 38 delegates came from 18 countries and territories. In addition to the European countries, Algeria, the Belgian Congo, Egypt, Israel, Lebanon, and Morocco sent representatives. According to the director of the hybrid corn work in FAO,

Successful though previous meetings in this series have been, each succeeding one appears to be even more so. The improvement in the general level of technical discussion at Belgrade was particularly striking. European workers are now commencing to bring in their own fresh ideas in relation to hybrid maize breeding, and in certain directions—for example, in breeding for cold tolerance—may soon progress at least as rapidly as their colleagues in the United States. A considerable part of this advance may be attributed to the opportunity provided through these annual meetings for the exchange of information between breeders in the various countries and the planning of co-operative investigations.

Control of Foot-and-Mouth Disease

The control of foot-and-mouth disease provides another field where co-operation among European experts could be immensely useful to all countries. Europe has long been subject to periodic severe outbreaks of foot-and-mouth disease, and efforts have been made since 1949 to bring about international action for more effective control through FAO. In 1950 and 1951 a very bad outbreak swept over most of the continent, causing losses that have been estimated conservatively at 400 million dollars. This catastrophe brought a wave of new interest in a regional control program.

New methods of vaccination have now been developed which make a large-scale regional program to stamp out foot-and-mouth disease more practicable than it has been in the past. With the older method, the virus was cultivated on the tongues of living cattle, which subsequently had to be destroyed. This practice made the production of the vaccine extremely expensive, since only a comparatively small amount of virus can be obtained from each animal. A vaccination campaign covering the 2½ million head of cattle in the Netherlands, for instance, would require the sacrificing of 500 animals every week.

It was a Netherlands research worker, H. S. Frenkel, who developed the new technique, which involves growing the virus on the covering membrane removed from the tongues of healthy cattle immediately after they have been killed in the slaughterhouse. By this method the vaccine can be produced for about 10 cents a dose, whereas the cost with the older method is about $1 a dose. The cost of vaccinating 5 million head of cattle in West Germany, which was hard hit by the recent outbreak, was the equivalent of 5 million dollars.

Still more recent work in Bogotá, Colombia, mentioned in an earlier chapter, might eventually result in producing foot-and-mouth disease vaccines even more cheaply by culturing the virus in the incubating eggs of chickens, much as in the case of avianized rinderpest vaccine.

Whether or not this research should result in new techniques, the Frenkel method is already usable. European governments and the FAO staff have worked out a pattern for effective regional co-operation which was approved by the 1953 conference. This envisaged a European Commission for the Control of Foot-and-Mouth Disease, following the general lines of other FAO regional organizations. Commission headquarters would be in Rome; the staff would be appointed by the Director-General of FAO and paid by the commission; expenses would be met by assessment of the member countries (the budget is estimated at the equivalent of $50,000 a year for the first five years); the International Office of Epizootics would co-operate in the work. As this is written, six governments have ratified the constitution so that the commission came into existence on June 12, 1954. The commission held its first meeting during the last week of July, when J. C. Nagle of Ireland was elected chairman.

Each member country of the commission agrees to undertake a rigorous control program using one or more of four methods: Slaughter of infected animals and animals exposed to infection (as in the USA, Great Britain, Ireland, Finland); slaughter of infected and vaccination of exposed animals (as in Switzerland and Sweden); maintenance of a totally immune cattle population by vaccination of all animals (as in a number of European countries); vaccination in zones surrounding outbreaks to create barriers of immunity.

The commission will serve as an agency through which European governments will exchange information on outbreaks, determine the type or types of virus responsible in each case, register stocks of virus and vaccines available in various countries, and (possibly) establish international laboratories for the production of vaccines. It will also have broad powers to take "suitable action" for producing and storing virus and vaccines for distribution to any member country in case of need.

Other Regional Work in Europe

Two Bad Insects. The fall webworm came to Eastern Europe from the USA. It weaves a nest much like that of the tent caterpillar and produces two generations a year, one in the spring, one late in the summer. In large areas in Austria and Yugoslavia it sometimes strips all the leaves off the trees. The especially bad outbreak of 1952 was kept under partial control only by energetic measures which included recruiting thousands of people to cut out nests and using airplanes to spray forests, orchards, and parks. Countries in Western Europe have a well-founded fear that these insects may invade them also.

FAO has been providing some financial help and starting a co-operative program of research on controlling this pest. Special attention is given to biological methods, which would involve bringing in natural parasites of the worm; there are 40 or more such parasites in the USA and Canada, where they effectively prevent the webworm from being a serious pest.

In the Mediterranean region the great enemy of the olive tree, a major source of food for local consumption and export, is the olive-fly larva, which makes the olives unfit to eat and reduces the quantity and quality of the oil. This pest is responsible for losses estimated at many millions of dollars a year. An FAO meeting on the olive-fly problem, held in Florence early in 1952, laid the foundation for new research and a regional control program. Through a working party much like those concerned with grasslands and with wheat-breeding in the Mediterranean area, the work has begun with experiments designed to compare the value of older control methods with those using some of the new insecticides.

For Better Extension Services. European governments are much interested in enlarging and strengthening extension services in agriculture and home economics. In 1949 a conference on extension work met at Brussels and at The Hague under the sponsorship of FAO. One outcome was a rather extensive study made by FAO early in 1950 of the extension services in 14 countries (and later a fifteenth, Finland). The experts who made this survey were themselves drawn from 12 different countries. The visits brought candid evaluations of work and exchange of views, and reports made later by most of the countries showed the results in various improvements.

In the summer of 1953 the Netherlands Government co-operated with FAO and the US Mutual Security Agency in running a training institute on extension in agriculture and home economics at Wageningen. Nearly 100 extension workers, women as well as men, took this course. They came from 30 countries, more than half of which were outside Europe, mainly in the Near East. In fact trainees came to Wageningen from as far away as Argentina and Burma. A second training course was held in the summer of 1954, and it has been proposed that the Wageningen institute be made an annual event.

This work on extension activities has been summarized in a recent FAO report *Improvement of Agricultural Extension Services in European Countries*.

Special European Committees. The European Committee on Agriculture, set up by the FAO Conference, has been mainly concerned with research needs and improvement programs. One outcome of its work was an FAO study of methods of milk-butterfat recording which resulted in the signing of an agreement by national organizations responsible for this work in 12 countries. This is a matter of considerable importance to breeders of dairy and dual-purpose cattle since superior breeding animals are chosen partly on the basis of milk-butterfat records; but there were so many divergent ways of keeping the records in different countries that it had become extremely difficult to make comparisons.

The European Committee on Agriculture has also taken a keen interest in work co-ordinated by FAO on livestock feeds. The production of animal feedstuffs has long been one of the major problems of European agriculture. In much of Europe livestock products bring in the larger part of agricultural income—60 to 80 per cent in the northern, western, and central areas, and 30 to 40 per cent in the south. Hence in most European countries a very large share of plant production is used to feed animals—as much as 88 per cent in Denmark, for example, and 70 per cent in Germany. Before the war a large part of the necessary concentrates were imported from outside Europe to supplement home-produced feeds. Today, with changed economic conditions, European countries are trying to reduce their imports, particularly those requiring hard currency, and are thus forced to rely more and more on home production—a change that involves important technical problems in agriculture. So far, FAO has sponsored two meetings dealing with these problems, one in Zurich in December 1949 and the other, convened jointly with the European Association for Animal Production, in Paris in 1953. The material prepared for the latter meeting is in effect a detailed study of the whole situation, including advice to governments for the shaping of production policies.

The European Association for Animal Production is an FAO-sponsored organization, and a highly successful and useful one. Its beginnings go back to the autumn of 1947 when the idea of a continent-wide agency was first broached and FAO was asked to provide the secretariat for a preparatory committee. This committee later held two meetings, in Milan in 1948 and Paris in 1949, to prepare a constitution for the agency, which was formally established at another meeting in Paris in November 1949. The association is now one of the most active professional organizations in Europe.

FAO is also investigating the possibility of developing uniform methods of recording agricultural research in European countries. As a step in avoiding duplication of effort wherever possible and fostering co-operation, a number of governments some years ago set up a working party on land and water use and conservation under FAO auspices. European meetings on the problems of mountain peasants have also been organized with FAO sponsorship. Austria, France, Germany, Italy, Switzerland, and Yugoslavia all have mountainous farming areas with many difficult agricultural problems. The first work has been concerned with establishing sound methods of surveying economic and other conditions in such areas, and a seminar on that subject met in Switzerland in August 1953, with 36 participants. Plans have been made for detailed surveys in the six countries involved, and further work may be carried out by the European Confederation of Agriculture, which co-operated with FAO in conducting the seminar.

Economic Studies. FAO co-operates with the United Nations Economic Commission for Europe on comprehensive economic studies of European agriculture. The most recent report (*European Agriculture: A Statement of Problems*), published early in 1954, points out that "developments in agriculture in southern and most eastern European countries contrast sharply with developments in the northwest." In the former group, half the population is still engaged in producing food, and it is still only enough for a meager diet. This corresponds to the situation in most of Western Europe some 70 years ago. The principal goal of agricultural policies in the eastern area must still therefore be the twin one of improving yields from the land and productivity of labor on the land. In northwest Europe, on the other hand, the industrialized countries face the problem of determining how much of their food they will produce themselves and how much they will import in exchange for manufactured goods. In the depression period between the two world wars the countries in this area deliberately reduced their dependence on the outside world for foodstuffs and built up their own production. The food shortages immediately after World War II again necessitated tremendous emphasis on home production. Since then, the remarkable recovery of agriculture in most Western European countries and the large increases in such high-producing countries as the USA, Canada, and Australia have materially changed the situation.

The discussion in an earlier chapter of the emphasis given by the 1953 FAO conference to "selective" rather than general expansion of agricultural production, and the continued efforts of FAO to bring about effective international action on agricultural commodities, clearly indicate that member governments have recognized these changes in formulating the policies of FAO.

In the highly developed agriculture of Western Europe, economic questions such as these are of paramount importance, and the countries in this area have called on FAO for a good deal of help in providing information on which both national and regional economic programs can be based. The FAO statistical yearbooks, commodity bulletins, and similar publications are only one of the ways in which this demand is met. For example, FAO has furnished much of the data used for the current efforts to establish a so-called "Green Pool" in Europe—a union which would try to accomplish for agriculture what the Coal and Steel Community aims to do for heavy industries. Much work has been done also in bringing officials together for agreement on standards and grades for fruits and vegetables in international trade. In the period of intense struggle to solve postwar agricultural reconstruction problems, the services of FAO, ECE, OEEC, and the US bilateral agencies were all needed and useful, and there was constant co-operation among these groups.

WORK WITH INDIVIDUAL COUNTRIES

Austria

Hard-hit by the war and struggling for rehabilitation, Austria must depend on its extensive forests for a large share of its exports, which had fallen to alarmingly low levels by the last half of the 1940's. A considerable part of the US bilateral aid to this country has therefore been devoted to building up forest resources.

FAO was called in as expert adviser to help the government work out a balanced program for investment in forest industries, with an underpinning of sound long-term policy. In 1949 two FAO staff officers began detailed surveys, followed later by periodic visits which included other FAO forestry experts, to consult with Austrian officials as the program progressed.

Since 1949, capital equivalent to about 90 million dollars has been invested in forestry and forest industries in Austria, most of it in accordance with FAO proposals. Much has been accomplished with this investment; it made possible, for instance,

- The building of a thousand miles of forest roads to open up new areas which have added more than 20 per cent to the timber output.
- Extensive reforesting.
- Greater production of pulp and paper.
- Building and modernizing sawmills—now among the most modern in Europe —and factories to make plywood, fiberboard, chipboard.
- An increase in the output of roundwood.
- Substantial growth in the export of forest products and improvement of their quality.
- A new forest products laboratory and forest research institute.
- Expansion of the sawmilling school.
- Building and equipping a new sawmill which cuts manufacturing costs in half compared with most of the country's mills.

EUROPE

- Completion of a forest inventory.
- A promising start in revising the government's forestry and forest products administration for greater efficiency.

These are first-rate achievements in any country, and they will lead to greater results in the future. The work as a whole is in fact an outstanding example of fruitful co-operation among three groups—a national government, a bilateral technical assistance agency, an international agency. Anyone visiting Austria today who was familiar with the forestry situation before the present program began must be struck with the vitality and vigor that have replaced discouragement and decay.

Two other FAO projects in Austria are associated with European regional programs discussed earlier in this chapter—the campaign against the fall webworm, in which Austria is participating, and the control of foot-and-mouth disease, which may become part of the proposed region-wide operation. FAO provided some of the equipment for a new vaccine laboratory and helped to start vaccine production, and shipped from Rome 2500 liters (equivalent to about 2600 quarts) of vaccine to meet an emergency call for help.

Finland

This second most northerly country in the world—Iceland being the farthest north—is progressive, vigorous, and thrifty in managing its natural resources. But Finland lost more than a tenth of its land as a result of the war. It has also suffered from some of the ills that beset so many other countries: failure of agricultural production to keep pace with the increase in the number of people; inflationary pressures resulting partly from improvements in living standards without enough goods to meet the enlarged demand; a growing need to import foodstuffs.

In 1952 the government asked FAO for advice on strengthening its program to improve and expand farm production. The man chosen to undertake this assignment was G. S. H. Barton (Canada), who went to Helsinki in the latter part of 1952 and the early part of 1953. An outstanding veteran of agricultural science, Barton was until recently Canadian Deputy Minister of Agriculture, and he has been closely associated from the beginning with the development of FAO.

In Finland, Barton found many conditions favorable to further advances in agriculture. Co-operatives are developed to a high degree and have dynamic functions much like those of co-operatives in the neighboring Scandinavian countries. Farms are for the most part family-owned and family-operated. Almost every farm includes an area of woodland, and these farm woodlands produce most of the forest products that are so important in Finland's economy. Research in agriculture is rather well developed through a number of experiment stations. In general, crop and livestock production are fairly well advanced.

After a careful study of Finland's agriculture, Barton came to the following conclusions, which are the basis for detailed recommendations made to the government:

Finland is capable of producing enough grain (wheat and rye) and livestock products to meet its own needs and provide some surplus for export. In future agricultural programs strong emphasis should be placed on increasing the production of bread grains and livestock products.

The country is admirably adapted to certain kinds of specialized farming, for example, production of seed (grains, grasses, forage plants, potatoes) and of certain livestock products.

More attention might well be given to producing improved equipment for small farms, training boys in rural schools in the handling of machinery, and training agricultural engineers. At the same time, mechanization should not be overdone or pushed at too fast a rate.

Good drainage is especially necessary for the soils of Finland. There might well be considerably greater use of underground drainage systems, with less reliance on open ditches.

Grasslands are not so productive as they should be. They are capable of becoming one of the country's most profitable resources. Along with the improvement and extension of grasslands it would be worth while to increase the number of silos for preserving green fodder.

Extension work might be reorganized to some extent to prevent overlapping and improve co-ordination. (Proposals along this line have been made by the Finnish Agricultural Organization Committee, largely as a result of the survey made by FAO in 1950, mentioned earlier in this chapter.)

Research work should be strengthened by progressively increasing appropriations for that purpose during the next five years, providing traveling fellowships for technical staff and scholarships for postgraduate study abroad, and arranging for more participation by Finnish technicians in meetings and conferences in other countries.

There is room for considerable expansion of agriculture in the northern half of the country, where perhaps as much as 5 million acres of swampland might be made productive. (The present arable area in Finland totals about 6 million acres.) The area actually under cultivation could be further enlarged by reducing the size of the woodlots on many small farms, where the amount of land devoted to trees is often disproportionally large.

Finland is bent also on improving and increasing fish production from the sea and inland waters. FAO expert A. C. Taft (USA) made a survey in 1952 and proposed a number of improvements in the government's fisheries services. These suggestions are being carried out, and FAO has awarded six fellowships for fisheries technicians in Finland to study abroad.

Since Finland has no school equipped to give a full course in veterinary science, Finnish veterinarians have had to get their final training in other countries. Plans for a school that will give a full course have now been drawn up with the advice of FAO expert G. Schmid (Switzerland). FAO fellowships have been granted for prospective teachers in this school, and X-ray equipment is also being provided.

In 1951 FAO and the United Nations co-operated in holding a training seminar on agricultural statistics in Helsinki. A large number of employees in the government and in nongovernmental organizations took advantage of this course, which brought experts from Sweden, Denmark, Switzerland, Italy, and the USA to serve as instructors.

Greece

About the mission to Greece and the later work of Tsongas, who for more than two years acted as nutrition counselor to the government, I have told in an earlier chapter.

One result of this program was the building of two plants for pasteurizing milk and making dairy products, at Volos and at Salonika. (This doubles the number of milk-pasteurizing plants in Greece.) FAO dairy expert E. A. Jensen (Denmark) has spent about three years planning and supervising the construction and equipment of the two new buildings. By the end of 1953 the Volos plant was in operation and taking in about 6000 pounds of milk a day from neighboring farmers, with an increase anticipated soon. Ultimately this plant expects to handle about 20,000 pounds a day. The Salonika plant is completed and the equipment is being installed as this is written. To take care of periods of peak production, both plants expect to make ice cream, butter, and yogurt as well as pasteurizing milk.

This project is a good example of co-operation among a number of agencies. The money for the building and equipment came from several sources: funds raised by Greek farmers through their dairy co-operatives, which will operate the plants; contributions from the US Government's comprehensive bilateral assistance program in Greece, the agricultural part of which has been directed by Brice Mace; counterpart funds from the Greek Government; contributions from the United Nations Children's Fund. Finally, FAO provided technical supervision for the whole undertaking. Irritations and delays are unavoidable in such operations, but on the whole all of these groups have worked together effectively and in a friendly spirit.

FAO has also given some assistance to Greece in connection with foot-and-mouth disease control, which may eventually be part of the regional program discussed earlier.

Iceland

The cold surrounding sea is pasture for numberless finny creatures which are Iceland's principal business. The land provides pasture for cattle and sheep, although during the long twilight months of winter, when the sun is in the south, feeding these animals is a problem.

Once upon a time there were rather extensive forests in Iceland, but during a thousand years of grazing and erosion the birches that clothed the lower slopes of the mountains have almost disappeared. The government is much interested in reforestation, and FAO sent R. F. Taylor, of the US Forest Service in Alaska, to Iceland to serve briefly as expert adviser.

At great cost Iceland imports all its timber, including a great deal for making boxes for export fish. Taylor reports that the government's reforestation program, planned for the next hundred years, will eliminate the need for imports; Iceland will grow its own wood. As a start, a million trees have been planted during the past four years. Although as yet there are only the beginnings of forests, a forest service has been active for many years, areas have been set aside for trees, laws have been passed to protect future woodlands, and an effort is being made to arouse public awareness of forest values.

The present program calls for planting conifers on some 70,000 acres of brush (there are nearly 250,000 acres of such land), to produce eventually at least as much timber as is now imported. The forest service has found after a period of testing that certain Alaskan trees grow exceptionally well in Iceland. But as Taylor points out, the success of the program will depend to a considerable extent on importing the right seed from the right sources. He advises more research and controlled experiments, using several Alaskan species not yet fully tested in Iceland. Also, he notes, "Iceland has a much bigger land use problem than that of growing timber. Sheep and cattle grazing have eroded the land to an incredible degree." Better range management therefore should rank high in agricultural planning.

Sheep production has been going through a discouraging 20 years. In the middle 1930's three serious lung diseases with high mortality rates were apparently brought into Iceland with imported karakul lambs. By 1950 the number of sheep in the country had dropped more than 40 per cent in spite of strenuous efforts and large expenditures to check the diseases. Since 1941 eradication campaigns have been undertaken which involve slaughtering all the sheep in any area where the diseases appear. This plan may prove to be successful, but there is always the danger of reinfection.

FAO veterinarian W. Lyle Stewart (UK) went to Iceland at the end of 1952 as adviser on these and other troublesome sheep diseases. His recommendations dealt mainly with the further research and experiment needed to find adequate control methods, particularly in the case of paratuberculosis. Stewart also initiated an investigation of bone diseases of cattle suspected to be caused by mineral deficiencies. He outlined additional research on important nutritional, parasitic, and other diseases of sheep as well as a disease of cows (*bradadaudi,* "sudden death") which kills without apparent warning symptoms.

A long-term program for expanding the sheep industry in Iceland, worked

EUROPE

out by Stewart with the government officials, would bring sheep numbers by 1958 approximately back to the level of 1930, before the lung diseases appeared.

Luxembourg

Luxembourg received help from FAO primarily in connection with an artificial insemination program for dairy cattle which was an important part of the effort to rebuild dairy herds following the heavy wartime losses. FAO veterinarian Erik Blom (Denmark) went to Luxembourg in the autumn of 1952 to get this program under way. Some 40,000 Holstein-Friesian cattle make up the dairy herds in the southern part of the country, where the land is level. In the northern part, which is mountainous, there are about 10,000 red-and-white Dutch cattle. Most of the artificial-insemination work has concentrated in the south, since farmers in the north were not yet ready for intensive use of this technique. Blom set up an artificial insemination center, using bulls imported from Holland, helped to select the director and other officials, trained technicians, worked out a system which makes it possible for all the farmers in the country to share in using the services, and was able, incidentally, to help control an outbreak of foot-and-mouth disease. The work is now proceeding with the Luxembourg staff in charge.

Portugal

Contagious bovine pleuropneumonia is a serious cattle disease which fortunately occurs in few countries—principally Australia, Portugal, and parts of Africa. An outbreak in Europe or Africa is of course a potential menace to neighboring countries as well as to the one directly concerned.

Portugal is anxious to undertake control of this disease, and FAO sent T. S. Gregory (Australia) to that country early in 1953 to help the veterinarians formulate a policy and program for eradication based on Australian experience.

Quick decisive action, Gregory points out, is essential. The method of control recommended involves quarantining and testing, elimination of animals with a positive reaction, followed by vaccination of all animals that have been in contact with the disease and retesting after three to five months.

In the spring of 1951 FAO nutrition expert N. M. Bottomley (UK) went to Portugal to help in shaping the food and nutrition program being carried out in that country by public and private organizations. She advised primarily on the training of nutrition workers and on the further development of supplementary feeding programs for school children.

Turkey

In 1950 the International Bank sent a mission to Turkey in which FAO participated. The report of this mission emphasized that at present the prime need in Turkey is for agricultural development. Further industrialization, which Turkey greatly desires, depends fundamentally on making it possible for industry to draw a supply of workers from the rural population and also to develop profitable markets in rural areas. These two developments, in turn, depend on a stepping up of the productivity of agriculture and raising farm incomes.

Turkey has now undertaken a comprehensive program of agricultural development in which the primary factor is the sturdy, intelligent Turkish peasant. He is beginning to use farm machinery on a wide scale, and today repair shops and extension workers are to be found in thousands of villages. In this program the government is receiving a great deal of assistance from US bilateral agencies. FAO has been called on to give some assistance, mainly in connection with sheep production, fisheries, and nutrition. FAO's A. G. Black (USA) also helped the government in co-ordinating the various aspects of its agricultural economics work and agricultural planning.

In 1950 and thereafter Andromache Tsongas, the FAO nutrition worker formerly in Greece, spent a good deal of time in Turkey consulting with government officials on the setting up of national nutrition services.

FAO sheep expert Eugene Bertone (USA) went to Turkey after his assignment in Afghanistan, to explore the possibilities of expanding karakul production. Turkey has only a small number of pure-bred karakuls (a thousand or so) and about twice as many karakul crossbreds. Bertone examined each of these sheep and recommended a rigidly controlled breeding program to improve and expand pelt production, based on the present stock plus small importations of high-quality rams.

More important, perhaps, was his review of wool production in Turkey from breeds of sheep other than karakul. Turkish carpets have long been world-famous. The wool comes from some 18 million sheep, which the visitor sees in many parts of the country. (In the north the flocks are guarded by powerful dogs wearing massive collars studded with iron spikes to help in fighting wolves.) As a result of his survey Bertone pointed out that a good deal of improvement could be made in the production of carpet wool by a program of selection and crossbreeding to produce larger sheep with heavier fleeces, which would also have longer staple and better luster. This program, too, was to be based in part on imported breeding stock from abroad, particularly Border Leicesters from the United Kingdom. A third type of sheep in Turkey, the Merino, can also be improved to produce more and better wool as well as more meat and milk. (Since a fifth of the milk supply of Turkey comes from sheep, high milk production is important in any breeding program.) Bertone made suggestions for crossing the Turkish Merinos with Rambouillets from the USA.

A foot-and-mouth vaccine production center is being built in Turkey with US aid. FAO is providing experts to demonstrate techniques and is training fellows in laboratories in Amsterdam.

As part of its assistance program in Turkey the US Government is helping to finance plants for refrigerating and processing fish. FAO has provided the services of four fisheries experts—a biologist concerned with research in oceanography and biology, an engineer carrying out practical fishing operations and training local fishermen, an economist advising on general development and administration and also on a project to produce fish meal and oil at Trabzon, and an engineer concerned with freezing and cold storage plants.

I have mentioned earlier that Turkey has been host to a regional training institute on agricultural development projects and has participated actively in the Near East wheat- and barley-breeding program. This country also acted as host for a regional training institute in 1954, concerned with Mediterranean grasslands.

Yugoslavia

Yugoslavia is engaged in an intense struggle to speed industrialization and improve agriculture. The government has received help from FAO in various aspects of this work, mainly in the form of brief visits by experts to survey situations and problems and provide on-the-spot advice. Often this was accompanied by field demonstrations and training and followed by the granting of fellowships for Yugoslav technicians to study abroad. Sometimes the FAO expert brought groups of Yugoslav agricultural, forestry, or fisheries technicians together for professional seminars. FAO has probably provided a greater variety of technical assistance to Yugoslavia than to any other country, although the help asked for has usually been for much briefer periods than in other countries. The results should gradually become evident in many different ways during the next few years.

Cotton is grown on a small scale. Production could be expanded to help supply the country's textile needs. An FAO expert has reported on the possibilities and outlined necessary experimental work, for which the organization has supplied equipment, machinery, and seed to be used at one of the new cotton experiment stations.

Fruit is extensively grown; Yugoslavia is especially proud of its plums, produced in large quantities. In the winter of 1952-53 an FAO horticulturist held 10 seminars in different parts of the country concerned with insect control, pruning, nursery management, and the selection of varieties. He also supervised experiments on pest control, for which FAO supplied raw materials.

Control of weeds, insects, plant diseases, which are responsible for tremendous losses in Yugoslav agriculture, is in general receiving much more attention than in the past. A new plant-protection laboratory has been set up with the help of an FAO expert; and, as noted earlier, Yugoslavia is cooperating in the European regional program for control of the fall webworm.

Irrigation and drainage could be extended to large areas to make possible a considerable increase in production. Three FAO experts have been advising on developments of this type. One is a multipurpose canal for irrigation, drainage, and navigation in Vojvodina province, the country's big grain-growing region. This waterway, called the Danube-Tisa-Danube canal, would run from a point on the Danube River across country to the Tisa River and then on to the Danube again at a point farther south. The canal would eventually irrigate a huge area and would be comparable in size and importance to the Zuider Zee in the Netherlands. The FAO experts consider that the project could be completed fairly rapidly. In Macedonia, in the south, large areas in several river valleys are suitable for irrigation. Other projects are also being considered. The FAO advisers believe that in particular thorough study should be made of the possibilities of well irrigation in several places.

Range management and soil conservation need more emphasis. In the mountainous Karst area two FAO men found that thousands of acres of overgrazed, eroded land could be reforested and used in part for growing forage plants. The government has started demonstration plantings of grass, the seed being supplied by FAO. Four FAO seminars held during the winter of 1952-53 were attended by 200 agricultural officers directly connected with range and livestock management, and these get-togethers have led to further promising experimentation. FAO has also provided advice on the control of mountain torrents.

Livestock diseases are coming in for increased attention. FAO has given help particularly in connection with the control of foot-and-mouth disease and tuberculosis.

Farm machinery work is in charge of an Institute of Agricultural Mechanization. An FAO expert was called in to survey machinery manufacturing and field operations. He found the Yugoslavs eager to adopt suggestions for improvements in the training of operators and mechanics and in setting up better-equipped maintenance and other services.

Dairy production is receiving special attention around the city of Belgrade, where in the short period of three years the government set up a remarkably good milk processing and distribution system. Here an FAO expert has been asked to iron out certain difficulties and help make needed improvements.

Canning is an important industry which should be considerably expanded and improved to take care of large quantities of perishable fruits, vegetables, meats, and fish that now go to waste during the peak seasons. Here, too, an FAO expert has made a series of practical recommendations from the manufacture of the cans through all aspects of food processing, not omitting the production of foods for canning and the establishment of community canneries.

Agricultural marketing has been reorganized, partly on the basis of FAO advice, including changes in the system of price incentives to put it on a more realistic basis. An FAO marketing specialist has been especially concerned with the export trade, which is only half what it was before the war. He organized a traveling training institute for Yugoslav marketing officers during which they visited market centers in Germany, Switzerland, and the United Kingdom to study up-to-date methods of handling products in urban markets and the quality standards required for export commodities. Among other things, this work resulted in arrangements for shipping frozen pork from Yugoslavia to the United Kingdom, opened up possibilities for shipment of poultry products, and brought in high-quality pigs for breeding in exchange for hay and other feedingstuffs.

Forests cover about a third of the land; Yugoslavia is one of the countries on which Western Europe must depend for timber. For some time after the war Yugoslav forest experts were out of touch with recent technical developments elsewhere. Now forestry is feeling the stimulus of the new drive for development and modernization. FAO has sent 11 forestry experts to Yugoslavia, mainly on short-term assignments. The national program includes a 20-year plan for rehabilitating 3¾ million acres of present forests and reforesting another 1½ million acres. Equipment for research has been provided by FAO to the extent of $27,000. A good deal of attention is being given to the use of wood waste for the manufacture of fiberboard and other products and to modernizing the veneer and plywood industries.

Fisheries too have been expanding. Along the Adriatic coast, marine fisheries are getting more modern equipment and developing better facilities for preserving and processing fish. Here FAO has provided two experts. An FAO biologist is also investigating inland fish culture; there are many fish ponds but in recent years fish culture has been set back by the spread of diseases, which have also affected the fish in rivers and lakes.

Home economics, the government recognizes, deserves more attention for the dynamic part it can play in raising levels of nutrition and of living in general. Pellagra, for instance, is an unnecessary disease in the light of modern knowledge of nutrition; but it is still prevalent in parts of Yugoslavia where the diet consists too largely of corn, not balanced by enough of the available vegetables and fruits. FAO has surveyed home economics teaching in Yugoslavia, suggested certain improvements, and provided the services of a Canadian home economist to help the government develop its program further.

Appendix

CHAPTER 1. ABU LIBDA

Page 17

Summary of the main points of the Egyptian Land Reform Decree, September 9, 1952: No one may own more than 200 feddans of agricultural land (exceptions are made in the case of land for industrial use and for reclamation and lands dedicated to religious use). (Articles 1 and 2)

Within the next five years the government shall expropriate land exceeding the limit allowed. One fifth of the total area subject to expropriation is to be seized each year, and expropriation is to start with the largest estates. (Article 3)

Large landowners can transfer 50 feddans each to their children, but the total land property so transferred shall not exceed 100 feddans. (Article 4)

Transfers of 5 feddans each can also be made to small holders who do not own more than 10 feddans provided they are not related to the landowner beyond the fourth degree of kinship. (Article 4)

Expropriated landowners have the right to compensation at 10 times the annual rental value plus the price of buildings, trees, and machinery. (Article 5)

The rent is to be estimated at seven times the annual tax imposed on the land. (Article 5)

Compensation is to be paid in the form of bonds on the public treasury bearing 3 per cent interest, redeemable in 30 years. The bonds cannot be transferred except to Egyptians. (Article 6)

The expropriated land is to be redistributed in each village to small peasants in such a way that each of them shall have no less than 2 feddans and no more than 5, according to the quality of the land. (Article 9)

Those benefitting from the redistribution must be adult Egyptians not previously convicted of crime, cultivators by trade, and owners of less than 5 feddans. (Article 9)

Land distribution is to be based on the following priorities: (1) persons who are actually working the land as tenants or farmers; (2) inhabitants of the village who support big families; (3) the most needy of the inhabitants; (4) inhabitants of other villages. (Article 9)

In the case of orchards, however, the land is to be distributed in parcels of no more than 20 feddans to graduates of agricultural and technical institutions who do not already own more than 10 feddans. (Article 10)

The new owners are to pay for the land what the State paid to the expropriated landowners, plus 3 per cent annual interest, plus an additional 15 per cent to pay the costs of requisition, distribution, and other expenses. The total sum is to be paid back to the State in 30 annual installments. (Article 11)

A committee of 12, headed by the Minister of Agriculture, is to supervise the expropriation and distribution of lands and may consult experts and technicians in the process. (Article 12)

The peasant who benefits from the redistribution of the land must farm it himself with all due care and attention. (Article 14)

Redistribution is to be completed within five years. (Article 15)

The owner of the land and his heirs shall not have the right to dispose of the land until its price is fully paid to the State and it cannot be expropriated to pay any debt except one due to the government, the agricultural and co-operative bank, or a co-operative society. (Article 16)

Any person obstructing the enforcement of certain articles of the Decree is liable to imprisonment. (Article 17)

An agricultural co-operative made up of peasants who acquire the requisitioned land and who own not more than 5 feddans is to be set up in each village (or in some cases in a group of villages). (Article 18)

The co-operatives are to issue agricultural loans to members; provide seeds, fertilizers, cattle, agricultural machinery, and means of storage and transport; organize the tilling and exploitation of the land in the most efficient manner, including seed selection, pest control, and the digging of canals and drainage ditches; sell the main crops on behalf of the members and deduct land payment installments, taxes, and loans; undertake all other agricultural and social services required by members. (Article 19)

Limitations are placed on the inheritance, sale, exchange, and giving of land with a view to preventing its fragmentation into plots of uneconomic size. (Articles 23 and 24)

Agricultural land can be rented only to those who cultivate it themselves (Article 32); the rent is not to exceed seven times the basic tax, or in the case of sharecropping the owner cannot take more than half the crop after deduction of all expenses (Articles 33 and 34); all leases are to run for at least three years (Article 35); written contracts should be used whenever possible (Article 36).

Wages of agricultural workers in the various agricultural districts are to be fixed every year by a committee of six members with a high agricultural official as chairman—three members representing landowners and tenants and three representing agricultural workers. (Article 38) Agricultural workers may form trade unions to defend their common interests. (Article 39)

APPENDIX

CHAPTER 3. NARROW THE GAP

Page 31

TABLE 1

DIFFERENCES AMONG COUNTRIES IN FOOD
CONSUMPTION AND CHANGES SINCE THE WAR
(CALORIES PER PERSON PER DAY)*

	Prewar†	*Recent*
Australia	3300	3290
Brazil	2150	2300
Canada	3070	3020
Ceylon	2140	2010
Colombia	1860	2400
Cuba	2630	2740
Denmark	3390	3220
Egypt	2410	2350
Greece	2600	2490
India	1970	1620
Indonesia	2040	1880
Iraq	2210	1930
Italy	2510	2480
Japan	2180	2100
Mexico	1800	2210
United Kingdom	3100	2990
United States of America	3150	3160

* Sources: *Second World Food Survey* (FAO 1952); *The State of Food and Agriculture; Review and Outlook—1953* (FAO).
† Recent figures may be more realistic than prewar since national statistics have been improving.

TABLE 2

WHAT THE AVERAGE PERSON EATS YEARLY
(1949-50, IN POUNDS)*

	In the United States of America	In India
Cereals and starchy roots	279	277
Beans, peas, lentils, etc.	15	44
Fruits and vegetables	447	90
Meat, eggs, fish, milk	856	110 or less
Fats	42	7
Sugar	103	29

* Source: *Second World Food Survey* (FAO, 1952).

Page 32

TABLE 3

AMOUNTS OF CERTAIN TEXTILES USED IN DIFFERENT COUNTRIES (POUNDS PER PERSON PER YEAR, 1952)*

Australia	27.9	Indonesia	2.4
Brazil	8.1	Iraq	6.8
Canada	25.1	Japan	12.3
Ceylon	4.6	Pakistan	3.7
Cuba	10.6	Thailand	3.1
Denmark	17.2	United Kingdom	21.6
Egypt	7.9	United States of America	37.2
India	4.4	Yugoslavia	5.5

* Source: *Per Caput Fiber Consumption Levels* (FAO, March 1954).

TABLE 4

LAND RESOURCES*

	Acres per person—all kinds of land	Per cent of arable land
Afghanistan	13.4	4.2
Australia	247.0	2.3
Brazil	41.2	2.2
Canada	247.0	3.9
Ceylon	2.0	22.9
Colombia	24.7	2.1
Cuba	5.2	17.2
Denmark	2.4	64.4
Egypt	11.8	2.5
Ethiopia	17.5	10.4
Greece	4.2	26.4
India	2.2	40.0
Indonesia	4.8	5.8
Iraq	21.1	5.3
Italy	1.6	51.5
Japan	1.1	13.8
Mexico	17.6	7.6
Thailand	6.7	9.3
United Kingdom	1.2	30.0
United States of America	12.4	24.7
Yugoslavia	3.8	30.3

* Sources: *Yearbook of Food and Agricultural Statistics: Production, 1953* (FAO); *United Nations Demographic Yearbook, 1953.*

Appendix

Page 33

TABLE 5
Percentage of Working People Who Are Farmers*

Australia	14	Indonesia	66
Brazil	58	Italy	39
Canada	16	Japan	47
Colombia	72	Mexico	58
Cuba	41	Thailand	85
Denmark	23	United Kingdom	5
Egypt	65	United States of America	11
Greece	58	Yugoslavia	75
India	66		

* Source: *Yearbook of Food and Agricultural Statistics: Production, 1953* (FAO).

TABLE 6
Energy Used for Each Person
(in Terms of Metric Tons of Coal per Year, 1951)*

Australia	3.21	Indonesia	.06
Brazil	.24	Iraq	.18
Canada	6.96	Italy	.81
Ceylon	.08	Japan	.87
Colombia	.29	Mexico	.66
Cuba	.52	Pakistan	.05
Denmark	2.08	Thailand	.02
Egypt	.23	United Kingdom	4.65
Greece	.27	United States of America	8.02
India	.10	Yugoslavia	.40

* Source: *United Nations Statistical Yearbook 1952.*

Page 34

TABLE 7

ANNUAL PER CAPUT INCOME, INCLUDING INCOME IN KIND (IN TERMS OF US DOLLARS, 1949)*

Afghanistan	50	India	57
Australia	679	Indonesia	25
Brazil	112	Iraq	85
Canada	870	Italy	235
Ceylon	67	Japan	100
Colombia	132	Mexico	121
Cuba	296	Pakistan	51
Denmark	689	Thailand	36
Egypt	100	United Kingdom	773
Ethiopia	38	United States of America	1453
Greece	128	Yugoslavia	146

* Source: *National and Per Capita Incomes, Seventy Countries, 1949* (Statistical Office of the United Nations).

TABLE 8

INFANT MORTALITY (DEATHS OF INFANTS UNDER ONE YEAR OF AGE FOR EVERY 1000 LIVE BIRTHS)*

	1930-34	Recent
Australia	43	24
Canada	79	38
Ceylon	165	78
Colombia	120	111
Denmark	73	29
Egypt	163	130
Iceland	47	26
India	176	116
Italy	106	64
Japan	124	58
Mexico	135	100
Netherlands	47	23
Thailand	93	62
United Kingdom	63	29
United States of America	60	29
Yugoslavia	155	105

* Source: *United Nations Demographic Yearbook 1953.*

APPENDIX

CHAPTER 5. BIRTH

Page 50

Hot Springs Conference on Food and Agriculture, Hot Springs, Virginia, USA (18 May–3 June 1943): Australia, Belgium, Bolivia, Brazil, Canada, Chile, China, Colombia, Costa Rica, Cuba, Czechoslovakia, the Minister of Denmark, Dominican Republic, Ecuador, Egypt, El Salvador, Ethiopia, French Delegation, Greece, Guatemala, Haiti, Honduras, Iceland, India, Iran, Iraq, Liberia, Luxembourg, Mexico, Netherlands, New Zealand, Nicaragua, Norway, Panama, Paraguay, Peru, Philippine Republic, Poland, Union of South Africa, USSR, UK, USA, Uruguay, Venezuela, Yugoslavia.

Page 52

Members of the Interim Commission on Food and Agriculture (June 1944): L. B. Pearson (Canada), Chairman; P. I. Tchegoula (USSR) and P. W. Tsou (China), Vice-Chairmen; F. L. McDougall (Australia); Viscount Alain du Parc, Charles Léonard (Belgium); René Ballivián (Bolivia); C. M. de Figueiredo (Brazil); Carlos Campbell del Campo (Chile); Guillermo Eliseo Suárez (Colombia); Francisco de P. Gutiérrez, Jorge Hazera (Costa Rica); Felipe de Pazos, Mariano Brull (Cuba); Václav Myslivec (Czechoslovakia); Mario E. de Moya (Dominican Republic); S. E. Durán-Ballén, Emilio A. Maulme (Ecuador); Anis Azer, Monir Bahgat (Egypt); Carlos Adalberto Alfaro (El Salvador); Yilma Deressa (Ethiopia); André Mayer, Christian Valensi (French Representatives); Kyriakos Varvaressos, Athanasios Sbarounis (Greece); Francisco Linares-Aranda (Guatemala); Elie Garcia (Haiti); Julián R. Cáceres (Honduras); Thor Thors (Iceland); Sir Girja Shankar Bajpai (India); Ali Akbar Daftary, H. Hadjeb-Davallou (Iran); Darwish Haidari (Iraq); Gabriel L. Dennis (Liberia); Hugues Le Gallais (Luxembourg); Rafael de la Colina, Vincente Sánchez Gavito (Mexico); M. P. L. Steenberghe, L. A. H. Peters (Netherlands); Walter Nash, A. G. B. Fisher (New Zealand); Alberto Sevilla Sacasa (Nicaragua); Anders Fjelstad (Norway); Ricardo A. Morales (Panama); París E. Menéndez (Paraguay); Juan Chávez (Peru); Joaquin M. Elizalde, Urbano A. Zafra, Amando M. Dalisay (Philippine Republic); Wieslaw Domaniewski (Poland); A. T. Brennan, W. C. Naudé, J. A. Siegruhn (Union of South Africa); Edward Twentyman (UK); Paul H. Appleby (USA); Juan Felipe Yriart (Uruguay); M. A. Falcón-Briceño (Venezuela); Branko Cubrilovich, George Radin (Yugoslavia); Henrik de Kauffmann, Count Benedict Ahlefeldt-Laurvig, J. V. Rechendorff (the Danish Minister). Howard S. Piquet (USA), succeeded by Gove Hambidge (USA), Executive Secretary.

Panels of the Interim Commission: *Science Panel:* J. A. Scott Watson (UK), Chairman, E. C. Auchter (USA), G. S. H. Barton (Canada), Frank G. Boudreau (USA), R. E. Buchanan (USA), André Mayer (France), L. A. Maynard (USA), París E. Menéndez (Paraguay), T. H. Shen (China), R. D. Sinclair (Canada), M. L. Wilson (USA).

Economics Panel: Howard R. Tolley (USA), Chairman, H. F. Angus (Canada), Antonin Basch (Czechoslovakia), J. D. Black (USA), R. R. Enfield (UK), A. G. B. Fisher (New Zealand), Alexander Loveday (USA), Ansgar Rosenborg (USA), T. W. Schultz (USA).

Reviewing Panel: F. L. McDougall (Australia), Chairman, Monir Bahgat (Egypt), Joseph A. Becker (USA), Frank G. Boudreau (USA), D. B. Finn (Canada), Henry S. Graves (USA), Roger Makins (UK), André Mayer (France), L. A. H. Peters (Netherlands), Robert Rae (UK), J. A. Scott Watson (UK), Howard R. Tolley (USA), Edward Twentyman (UK), Leslie A. Wheeler (USA). Gove Hambidge (USA), P. Lamartine Yates (UK), Rapporteurs, Sherleigh G. Fowler (USA), Assistant Rapporteur.

Page 53

Constitution of FAO

ARTICLE I

(Functions of the Organization)

1. The Organization shall collect, analyze, interpret, and disseminate information relating to nutrition, food and agriculture.
2. The Organization shall promote and, where appropriate, shall recommend national and international action with respect to
   (a) scientific, technological, social, and economic research relating to nutrition, food and agriculture;
   (b) the improvement of education and administration relating to nutrition, food and agriculture, and the spread of public knowledge of nutritional and agricultural science and practice;
   (c) the conservation of natural resources and the adoption of improved methods of agricultural production;
   (d) the improvement of the processing, marketing, and distribution of food and agricultural products;
   (e) the adoption of policies for the provision of adequate agricultural credit, national and international;
   (f) the adoption of international policies with respect to agricultural commodity arrangements.
3. It shall also be the function of the Organization
   (a) to furnish such technical assistance as governments may request;
   (b) to organize, in co-operation with the governments concerned, such missions as may be needed to assist them to fulfill the obligations arising from their acceptance of the recommendations of the United Nations Conference on Food and Agriculture; and
   (c) generally to take all necessary and appropriate action to implement the purposes of the Organization as set forth in the Preamble.

APPENDIX

Scale of Contributions to FAO, 1955 (expressed in percentages): Afghanistan 0.12, Argentina 1.60, Australia 2.06, Austria 0.55, Belgium 1.76, Bolivia 0.08, Brazil 1.71, Burma 0.15, Cambodia 0.05, Canada 5.69, Ceylon 0.20, Chile 0.41, Colombia 0.65, Costa Rica 0.05, Cuba 0.50, Denmark 0.91, Dominican Republic 0.07, Ecuador 0.06, Egypt 0.60, El Salvador 0.08, Ethiopia 0.13, Finland 0.56, France 7.49, Germany 5.66, Greece 0.38, Guatemala 0.10, Haiti 0.05, Honduras 0.05, Iceland 0.05, India 4.55, Indonesia 0.83, Iran 0.34, Iraq 0.12, Ireland 0.27, Israel 0.19, Italy 2.99, Japan 2.79, Jordan 0.05, Korea 0.16, Laos 0.05, Lebanon 0.05, Liberia 0.05, Libya 0.05, Luxembourg 0.07, Mexico 1.14, Nepal 0.08, Netherlands 1.26, New Zealand 0.58, Nicaragua 0.05, Norway 0.65, Pakistan 1.15, Panama 0.06, Paraguay 0.05, Peru 0.21, Philippine Republic 0.74, Portugal 0.37, Saudi Arabia 0.09, Spain 1.62, Sweden 1.97, Switzerland 1.54, Syria 0.10, Thailand 0.30, Turkey 0.79, Union of South Africa 0.77, UK 10.49, USA 30.00, Uruguay 0.23, Venezuela 0.57, Viet Nam 0.21, Yemen 0.05, Yugoslavia 0.60.

Page 60

First Session of the FAO Conference, Quebec, Canada (16 October–1 November 1945): Australia, Belgium, Brazil, Canada, China, Colombia, Cuba, Czechoslovakia, Denmark, Dominican Republic, Egypt, France, Greece, Guatemala, Haiti, Honduras, Iceland, India, Iraq, Lebanon, Liberia, Luxembourg, Mexico, Netherlands, New Zealand, Nicaragua, Norway, Panama, Peru, Philippine Republic, Poland, Syria, Union of South Africa, UK, USA, Venezuela, Yugoslavia. Observers: Argentina, Byelorussian Soviet Socialist Republic, Ukrainian Soviet Socialist Republic, USSR.

FAO Executive Committee (elected at the First Session of the FAO Conference): André Mayer (France), Chairman; Howard R. Tolley (USA), Vice-Chairman; Sir Girja Bajpai (India), Edouard Baker (Haiti), G. S. H. Barton (Canada), Newton de Castro Belleza (Brazil), R. R. Enfield (UK), E. J. Fawcett (New Zealand), Anders Fjelstad (Norway), Alfonso González Gallardo (Mexico), Darwish Haidari (Iraq), Stanislaw Mikolajczyk (Poland), P. W. Tsou (China), P. R. Viljoen (Union of South Africa), Arthur Wauters (Belgium).

CHAPTER 6. GROWTH

Page 62

World Food Survey Working Groups: *Nutrition Targets:* Frank G. Boudreau, John M. Cassels, L. A. Maynard, Francisco de P. Miranda (Mexico), Esther F. Phipard, Lydia J. Roberts, Hazel K. Stiebeling.

Prewar Food Consumption: Joseph A. Becker, Charles A. Gibbons, Werner Klatt (UK), H. V. Knight (UK), Wilfred Malenbaum, Hollis W. Peter, O. V. Wells.

Page 63

Special Meeting on Urgent Food Problems, Washington, D.C., USA (20–27 May 1946): Argentina, Australia, Belgium, Brazil, Canada, Chile, China, Cuba, Czechoslovakia, Denmark, France, Greece, India, Netherlands, New Zealand, Norway, Peru, Poland, Thailand (Siam), Union of South Africa, UK, USA; Combined Food Board, United Nations (UN), Emergency Economic Committee for Europe, International Bank for Reconstruction and Development, International Labour Organisation (ILO), United Nations Relief and Rehabilitation Administration (UNRRA).

International Emergency Food Council (July 1947): Australia, Austria, Belgium, Brazil, Canada, Chile, China, Cuba, Czechoslovakia, Denmark, Ecuador, Egypt, Finland, France, Greece, Hungary, India, Ireland, Italy, Mexico, Netherlands, New Zealand, Norway, Peru, Poland, Portugal, Philippine Republic, Sweden, Switzerland, Thailand (Siam), Turkey, Union of South Africa, UK, USA.

Page 64

FAO Mission to Greece: Franklin S. Harris (USA), Chairman; Panos D. Caldis (USA), Vice-Chairman; Mordecai Ezekiel (USA), Rapporteur; G. Belloc (France), Louise A. Bryant (USA), R. E. Buchanan (USA), G. H. K. Hewison (UNRRA), William L. Newmeyer (USA), A. G. Plakidas (USA), Henri Roy (France), Afif I. Tannous (USA), Norman C. Wright (Scotland).

Page 68

FAO Preparatory Commission on World Food Proposals, Washington, D.C. (28 October 1946–24 January 1947): Australia, Belgium, Brazil, Canada, China, Cuba, Czechoslovakia, Denmark, Egypt, France, India, Netherlands, Philippine Republic, Poland, Thailand, UK, USA. Observer: Argentina.

Page 70

Council of FAO:

1947: Australia, Brazil, Canada, Chile, China, Cuba, Czechoslovakia, Denmark, Egypt, France, India, Italy, Mexico, Netherlands, Philippine Republic, Union of South Africa, UK, USA.

1954: Argentina, Australia, Canada, Chile, Colombia, Cuba, Egypt, Finland, France, India, Iraq, Italy, Japan, Lebanon, Liberia, Netherlands, Pakistan, Philippine Republic, Spain, Switzerland, Thailand, UK, USA, Uruguay.

Page 71

Committee to Study World Commodity Problems, Washington, D.C. (August–September 1949): John B. Condliffe (USA), Colin Clark (Australia), J. K. Galbraith (USA), D. Ghosh (India), Gustavo Polit (Economic Commission for Latin America), A. Radomysler (UK).

APPENDIX

Page 72

Committee on Commodity Problems (1954): Argentina, Belgium, Brazil, Burma, Canada, Ceylon, Cuba, Denmark, Egypt, France, Germany, India, Japan, Netherlands, New Zealand, Pakistan, Spain, UK, USA, Yugoslavia.

Working Party on Surplus Disposal, Washington, D.C. (23 February–18 March 1954): Argentina, Egypt, France, India, Netherlands, New Zealand, UK, USA.

Consultative Sub-Committee on Surplus Disposal (August 1954): Argentina, Australia, Canada, Ceylon, Cuba, Denmark, Egypt, France, Greece, India, Iraq, Israel, Italy, Jordan, Netherlands, New Zealand, Pakistan, Sweden, Turkey, UK, USA. In addition 35 countries and 7 organizations are observers.

Page 76

FAO Mission for Siam (Thailand): R. H. Walker (USA), Chairman; G. N. Danhof (Indonesia), Karl O. Kohler, Jr. (USA), H. S. Purchase (UK), R. L. Pendleton (USA), K. Ramiah (India); W. W. Cochrane, H. Greene, Franklin C. H. Lee (FAO staff).

Page 77

FAO Mission for Poland: Noble Clark (USA), Chairman; M. J. L. Dols (Netherlands), Vice-Chairman; C. H. Edelman (Netherlands), Paul J. Findlen (USA), T. J. Harrison (Canada), Aksel Milthers (Denmark), James Morrison (Northern Ireland), Edward N. Munns (USA); Mordecai Ezekiel, A. B. Lewis (FAO staff).

Page 78

FAO Oilseed Mission for Venezuela: K. S. Markley (USA), Chairman; Carl E. Claassen (USA), Dale W. Jenkins (USA), Jorge Succar Rahme (FAO staff). Consultants: Miriam L. Bomhard (USA), N. G. Nhavi (India).

CHAPTER 7. NEW DIRECTIONS

Page 84

Contributions to the United Nations technical assistance program (in national currencies or dollar equivalents) pledged at the Technical Assistance Conference, June 1950, for the first financial period (18 months):

Afghanistan	119,084 Afghanis
Argentina	1,000,000 Argentine pesos
Australia	$400,000
Austria	500,000 Austrian shillings
Belgium	13,500,000 Belgian francs

Bolivia	750,000	Bolivianos
Brazil	8,500,000	Cruzeiros
Burma	$7,500	
Canada	850,000	Canadian dollars
Ceylon	$15,000	
Chile	5,400,000	Chilean pesos
China	$10,000	
Colombia	100,000	Colombian pesos
Costa Rica	$5,000	
Cuba	50,000	Cuban pesos
Denmark	660,000	Danish kroner
Ecuador	94,500	Sucres
Egypt	28,500	Egyptian pounds
El Salvador	$5,000	
Ethiopia	$20,000	
France	422,625,000	French francs
Greece	$5,900	
Haiti	30,000	Gourdes
Honduras	16,000	Lempiras
India	$250,000	
Indonesia	463,000	Rupiah
Iran	$40,000	
Israel	10,000	Israeli pounds
Italy	$93,000	
Korea	$5,000	
Lebanon	$6,500	
Liberia	$8,000	
Luxembourg	$2,500	
Mexico	300,000	Mexican pesos
Monaco	1,000,000	French francs
Netherlands	1,520,000	Florins
New Zealand	45,000	New Zealand pounds
Norway	250,000	Norwegian crowns
Pakistan	467,000	Rupees
Philippines	100,000	Philippine pesos
Sweden	500,000	Swedish crowns
Switzerland	1,000,000	Swiss francs
Syria	25,000	Syrian pounds
Turkey	$182,000	
United Kingdom	760,000	Pounds sterling
United States of America	$12,007,500	
Uruguay	151,000	Uruguayan pesos
Venezuela	$44,000	
Yemen	20,000	Indian rupees
Yugoslavia	2,500,000	Dinars

APPENDIX

Page 94

Members of the Inter-American Institute of Agricultural Sciences, Turrialba, Costa Rica: Colombia, Costa Rica, Cuba, Dominican Republic, Ecuador, El Salvador, Guatemala, Haiti, Honduras, Mexico, Nicaragua, Panama, USA, Venezuela.

Page 95

Countries which participated in the Economic Cooperation Administration: Austria, Belgium, Denmark, France, German Federal Republic, Greece, Iceland, Ireland, Italy, Luxembourg, Netherlands, Norway, Portugal, Sweden, Switzerland, Free Territory of Trieste, Turkey, UK.

Page 96

The Consultative Committee of the Colombo Plan for Cooperative Economic Development in South and Southeast Asia (1953): Australia, Burma, Cambodia, Canada, Ceylon, India, Indonesia, Laos, Nepal, New Zealand, Pakistan, UK (and its territories in Malaya and North Borneo), USA, Viet Nam.

CHAPTER 8. NEAR EAST AND AFRICA

Page 104

Near East Wheat Breeding Conference, Istanbul, Turkey (16–20 June 1952): Iran, Iraq, Pakistan, Turkey, UK, USA. Observer: United Nations Educational, Scientific, and Cultural Organization (UNESCO).

Page 105

Second FAO Meeting on Wheat and Barley Breeding in the Near East, Cairo, Egypt (13–18 April 1953): Egypt, Iran, Iraq, Jordan, Lebanon, Pakistan, Syria, Turkey, UK. Observers: French Agricultural Mission in Lebanon, Technical Cooperation Administration (USA), UNESCO.

Third FAO Meeting on Wheat and Barley Breeding in the Near East, Damascus, Syria (26 April–2 May 1954): Egypt, Iran, Jordan, Lebanon, Pakistan, Syria, Turkey, UK. Observer: UNESCO.

Page 107

Special Meeting on the Control of Foot-and-Mouth Disease in the Near East, Damascus, Syria (27–29 April 1953): Egypt, Iran, Iraq, Jordan, Lebanon, Syria, Turkey, UK (for Cyprus). Observers: British Middle East Office, International Office of Epizootics, Mutual Security Agency of the USA (MSA), Near East Foundation, Royal College of Veterinary Surgeons (England).

Near East Meeting on Animal Health, Prodhromos, Cyprus (15–20 June 1953): Afghanistan, Egypt, Ethiopia, French territories, Iran, Iraq, Jordan,

Lebanon, Libya, Syria, Turkey, UK territories. Observers: Sudan, American University of Beirut, International Office of Epizootics, MSA, World Health Organization (WHO).

Page 108

Joint FAO–WHO Expert Committee on Nutrition: *FAO:* E. J. Bigwood (Belgium), P. Gyorgy (USA), R. Jacquot (France), G. J. Janz (Portugal), L. A. Maynard (USA), V. N. Patwardhan (India), A. J. Wakefield (UK). *WHO:* J. F. Brock (Union of South Africa), F. W. Clements (Australia), G. Frontali (Italy), B. S. Platt (UK), M. V. Radhakrishna Rao (India), H. C. Trowell (Uganda), J. C. Waterlow (UK).

Page 109

Nutrition Training Center, Cairo, Egypt (October–December 1950): Cyprus, Cyrenaica, Egypt, Iraq, Lebanon, Syria, Thailand, Turkey.

Nutrition Training Course for French-Speaking Nutritionists, Marseilles, France (May–June 1952): Belgium, Eritrea, France, Haiti, Italy, Portugal.

Page 110

Near East Regional Extension Development Center, Beirut, Lebanon (6–16 January 1953): Cyprus, Egypt, Ethiopia, France, Iran, Iraq, Jordan, Lebanon, Liberia, Pakistan, Somaliland, Syria, Turkey, UK. Observers: French Legation in Syria, ILO, Near East Foundation, Technical Assistance Board, Technical Cooperation Administration of the USA, United Nations Relief and Works Agency (UNRWA).

FAO–ILO Near East Cooperative Training Center, Nicosia, Cyprus (8 September–5 December 1952): Iraq, Jordan, Lebanon, Sudan, Syria, UNRWA.

Page 111

Near East Forestry Conference, Amman, Jordan (13–20 December 1952): France, Iraq, Italy, Jordan, Lebanon, Syria, UK, USA. Observers: International Poplar Commission, UNRWA.

Page 112

Statistical Training Centers, Mexico City, Mexico (2 September–10 December 1948): Bolivia, Brazil, Colombia, Costa Rica, Cuba, Dominican Republic, Ecuador, El Salvador, Guatemala, Honduras, Mexico, Nicaragua, Panama, Paraguay, Peru, Venezuela.

New Delhi, India (1949): Burma, Ceylon, India, Indochina, Indonesia, Korea, Nepal, Pakistan, Thailand.

Cairo, Egypt (10 October–22 December 1949): Cyprus, Egypt, Ethiopia, Jordan, Syria.

Paris, France (September–December 1949): Belgium, France, Germany, Greece, Italy, Luxembourg, Netherlands, Switzerland, Turkey, Yugoslavia.

APPENDIX 255

Statistical Meeting on Census Schedules and Plans, Bogotá, Colombia (July 1949): Bolivia, Brazil, Colombia, France, Guatemala, Nicaragua, Panama, USA, Venezuela.

Latin American Training Center for Agricultural Statistics, San José, Costa Rica (8 January–28 March 1951): Brazil, Colombia, Costa Rica, Ecuador, El Salvador, Guatemala, Honduras, Nicaragua, Panama, Paraguay, Puerto Rico, Uruguay, Venezuela.

Regional Laboratory in Census Statistics, Rio de Janeiro, Brazil (August 1951): Bolivia, Brazil, Costa Rica, Dominican Republic, Ecuador, El Salvador, Panama, Paraguay, Uruguay, Venezuela.

Latin American Center for Training and Demonstration in Agricultural Statistics, Quito, Ecuador (7 July–29 October 1952): Bolivia, Brazil, Chile, Colombia, Costa Rica, Dominican Republic, Ecuador, Guatemala, Nicaragua, Panama, Venezuela.

Seminar on Production and Price Statistics, Beirut, Lebanon (1–14 July 1952): Cyprus, Egypt, Iraq, Jordan, Lebanon, Sudan, Syria, Turkey. Observers: American University of Beirut, British Middle East Office, Centre d'Etudes Mathématiques et Physiques de Beyrouth, French Technical Mission in Lebanon, US Technical Cooperation Administration, UNRWA.

African Training Center in Agricultural Statistics, Ibadan, Nigeria (July–September 1953): Angola, Belgian Congo, Bechuanaland, Cameroons, Dahomey, France (Overseas Statistical Service), French Equatorial Africa, French West Africa, Gold Coast, Ivory Coast, Liberia, Madagascar, Moyen Congo (French), Mozambique, Nigeria, Sierra Leone, Southern Rhodesia, Spanish Guinea, Sudan, Tanganyika, Togo, Ubanqui-Chari, Uganda.

Page 113

Regional Demonstration Center for Agricultural Statistical Sampling, Bangkok, Thailand (September 1952–March 1953): Cambodia, Ceylon, India, Indonesia, Japan, Korea, Laos, Nepal, Pakistan, Thailand, Viet Nam.

CHAPTER 9. FAR EAST

Page 145

Rice Study Group, Trivandrum, Travancore, India (16 May–6 June 1947): Australia, Burma, China, France, India, Netherlands, Philippine Republic, Thailand, UK, USA. Observer: United Nations.

Page 146

Rice Meeting, Baguio, Philippines (1–13 March 1948): Australia, Burma, China, Ecuador, Egypt, France, India, Italy, Liberia, Mexico, Netherlands, Pakistan, Paraguay, Philippine Republic, Thailand, UK, USA, Venezuela. Observers: Portugal, Economic Commission for Asia and the Far East (ECAFE),

League of Red Cross Societies, Supreme Command–Allied Powers, US Army Military Government in Korea, UNESCO, WHO.

Page 148

International Training Center on Rice Breeding, Cuttack, India (15 September–15 December 1952): Ceylon, Egypt, French Sudan, India, Indonesia, Iran, Laos, Madagascar, Pakistan, Philippine Republic, Thailand.

International Training Center on Soil Fertility, Coimbatore, Madras, India (15 July–15 October 1952): Ceylon, India, Indonesia, Pakistan, Philippine Republic, Thailand, Viet Nam.

Page 151

Nairobi Rinderpest Meeting, Nairobi, Kenya (October–November 1948): Anglo-Egyptian Sudan, Belgian Congo, China, East Africa High Commission, Egypt, France, Gambia and Sierra Leone, Great Britain, India, Kenya, Nigeria, Northern Rhodesia, Nyasaland, Portuguese East Africa (Mozambique), Portuguese West Africa (Angola), Somalia (British Military Administration), Southern Rhodesia, Tanganyika, Uganda, Union of South Africa, Zanzibar; International Office of Epizootics, USA Research and Development Board.

Rinderpest Conference for Asia and the Far East, Bangkok, Thailand (June 1949): Australia, Burma, France, Korea, Netherlands, Philippine Republic, Thailand, UK; International Office of Epizootics.

International Training Center on Living Virus Vaccines, Izatnagar, India (16 February–7 March 1953): Afghanistan, Burma, Ceylon, India, Japan, Malaya, Pakistan, Thailand.

Page 152

Indo-Pacific Fisheries Council, Australia, Burma, Cambodia, Ceylon, France, India, Indonesia, Japan, Korea, Netherlands, Pakistan, Philippine Republic, Thailand, UK, USA, Viet Nam.

Page 154

Indo-Pacific Fisheries Statistics Training Center, Bangkok, Thailand (June–July 1952): Burma, Cambodia, Ceylon, Hong Kong, India, Indonesia, Japan, Korea, Malaya, North Borneo, Pakistan, Philippine Republic, Singapore, Taiwan, Thailand, Viet Nam.

International Training Center in Fish Marketing, Hong Kong (12 July–21 August 1954): Burma, Ceylon, Hong Kong, India, Indonesia, Japan, Malaya, Pakistan, Philippine Republic, Thailand, Viet Nam.

Page 155

Regional Meeting on Land Utilization in the Tropical Areas of Asia and the Far East, Nuwara Eliya, Ceylon (17–29 September 1951): Australia, Bel-

APPENDIX

gium, Burma, Cambodia, Ceylon, France, India, Indonesia, Netherlands, Pakistan, Portugal, UK, USA, Viet Nam. Observers: ECAFE, the Holy See.

Page 158

Meeting on Livestock Breeding under Tropical and Sub-tropical Conditions, Lucknow, India (13–22 February 1950): Australia, Belgium, Burma, Ceylon, Egypt, France, India, Indonesia, Iran, Italy, Pakistan, Thailand, UK.

Page 159

Regional Meetings on Food and Agricultural Programs and Outlook

Near East: Beirut, Lebanon (12–17 September 1949): Egypt, Ethiopia, France, Iraq, Jordan, Lebanon, Saudi Arabia, Syria, Turkey. Observers: the Holy See, ILO, UNESCO, UNRWA, WHO, Yemen.

Bloudane, Syria (28 August–6 September 1951): Egypt, Ethiopia, France, Iraq, Jordan, Lebanon, Pakistan, Saudi Arabia, Syria, Turkey, UK. Observers: ILO, Near East Foundation, UNESCO, United Nations Children's Fund (UNICEF), UNRWA.

Cairo, Egypt (1–9 September 1953): Egypt, Ethiopia, France, Iraq, Jordan, Lebanon, Pakistan, Saudi Arabia, Syria, UK. Observers: Anglo-Egyptian Sudan, ILO, League of Arab States, Near East Foundation, UN, UNESCO, UNRWA, WHO.

Far East: Singapore (26 September–1 October 1949): Australia, France, India, Netherlands, Pakistan, Thailand, UK. Observers: Korea, USA, ECAFE, the Holy See, ILO, Supreme Command Allied Powers, UNESCO, WHO.

Bangalore, India (27 July–5 August 1953): Australia, Burma, Ceylon, France, India, Indonesia, Japan, Laos, Netherlands, Thailand, UK, USA, Viet Nam. Observers: ECAFE, ILO, World Federation of UN Associations.

Latin America: Quito, Ecuador (18–25 September 1949): Bolivia, Brazil, Chile, Colombia, Costa Rica, Cuba, Dominican Republic, Ecuador, France, Guatemala, Haiti, Italy, Mexico, Netherlands, Nicaragua, Panama, Paraguay, Peru, UK, USA, Uruguay, Venezuela. Observers: Economic Commission for Latin America (ECLA), the Holy See, ILO, International Refugee Organization (IRO), WHO, representatives of 15 Ecuadorian organizations.

Montevideo, Uruguay (December 1950): Bolivia, Brazil, Colombia, Costa Rica, Chile, Cuba, Dominican Republic, Ecuador, El Salvador, France, Guatemala, Haiti, Mexico, Netherlands, Nicaragua, Panama, Paraguay, UK, USA, Uruguay. Observers: Argentina, Canada, ECLA, the Holy See, Inter-American Council for Trade and Production, Inter-American Indian Institute, Inter-American Institute of Agricultural Sciences, Inter-American Statistical Institute, International American Institute for the Protection of Childhood, International Federation of Agricultural Producers (IFAP), ILO, IRO, Pan American Sanitary Bureau (PASB), UN, UNESCO, WHO.

Europe: Rome, Italy (10–15 October 1950): Austria, Belgium, Finland, France, Greece, Italy, Netherlands, Norway, Switzerland, UK, Yugoslavia. Observers: the Holy See, IFAP, ILO, Organization for European Economic Cooperation (OEEC), WHO.

Page 161

Asian Center on Agricultural and Allied Projects, Lahore, Pakistan (2 October–15 December 1950): Australia, Burma, India, Indonesia, Japan, Nepal, Pakistan, Thailand.

Mediterranean Training Center on Appraisal of Development Projects, Ankara, Turkey (1 October–22 December 1951): Cyprus, France, Greece, Israel, Malta, Morocco, Portugal, Sudan, Tunisia, Turkey, Yugoslavia.

Latin American Training Center on Agricultural Plans and Projects, Santiago, Chile (26 September–20 December 1951): Bolivia, Brazil, Chile, Colombia, Costa Rica, Cuba, Dominican Republic, Ecuador, El Salvador, Guatemala, Haiti, Honduras, Mexico, Nicaragua, Panama, Paraguay, Puerto Rico, Uruguay, Venezuela.

Arab Training Center on Economic and Financial Appraisal of Agricultural Plans and Projects, Cairo, Egypt (4 September–18 November 1954): Egypt, Jordan, Iraq, Iran, Libya, Syria.

Technical Meeting on Cooperatives in Asia and the Far East, Lucknow, India (24 October–2 November 1949): Australia, Ceylon, France, India, Pakistan, Thailand, UK. Observers: IFAP, ILO, Supreme Command for the Allied Forces in Japan.

Page 162

FAO–ILO Technical Meeting on Co-operatives in Asia and the Far East, Kandy, Ceylon (February–March 1954): Burma, Ceylon, France, India, Indonesia, Japan, Laos, Pakistan, Thailand, UK, Viet Nam. Observers: American International Association, Cooperative League of the USA, UN, the Holy See.

Page 163

Timber Grading School, Kepong, Malaya, and Singapore (January–February 1952): Burma, Cambodia, Ceylon, Formosa, Indonesia, South Korea, Thailand.

Forestry Commission for Asia and the Pacific: Afghanistan, Australia, Burma, Cambodia, Ceylon, France, India, Indonesia, Japan, Korea, Laos, Nepal, Netherlands, New Zealand, Pakistan, Philippine Republic, Portugal, Thailand, UK, USA, Viet Nam.

Forestry and Timber Utilization Conference for Asia and the Pacific, Mysore, India (28 March–8 April 1949): Burma, Ceylon, France, India, Netherlands, New Zealand, Pakistan, Philippine Republic, Thailand, UK. Observers: Indonesia, Korea, Nepal, Portugal, International Meteorological Organization, UNESCO, Supreme Command–Allied Powers (Japan).

APPENDIX 259

Far Eastern Mechanical Logging Training Center, Philippine Republic (3 October 1952–24 March 1953): Burma, China, India, Indonesia, Laos, Malaya, North Borneo, Pakistan, Philippine Republic, Thailand, Viet Nam.

CHAPTER 10. LATIN AMERICA

Page 179

Latin American Conference on Forestry and Forest Products, Teresopolis, Brazil (19–30 April 1948): Brazil, Chile, Cuba, Dominican Republic, France, Guatemala, Honduras, Mexico, Netherlands, Nicaragua, Paraguay, Peru, UK, USA, Uruguay, Venezuela. Observers: Argentina, Canada, Italy, Portugal, Inter-American Institute of Agricultural Sciences (IAIAS), ILO, UN, UNESCO.

Page 181

Countries in which pulp and paper surveys were made (1953–1954): Brazil, Cambodia, Colombia, Costa Rica, Cuba, Dominican Republic, Ecuador, Greece, Haiti, India, Indonesia, Iraq, Laos, Mexico, Northern Rhodesia, Pakistan, Paraguay, Peru, Philippine Republic, Portugal, Thailand, Turkey, Venezuela, Viet Nam, Yugoslavia.

Inter-American Meeting on Livestock Production, Turrialba, Costa Rica (9–20 October 1950): Costa Rica, El Salvador, Guatemala, Honduras, Netherlands, Nicaragua, Panama, Peru, UK, USA, Venezuela. Observers: Caribbean Commission, Institute of Inter-American Affairs (IIAA), PASB.

Second Inter-American Meeting on Livestock Production, Baurú, Brazil (8–15 December 1952): Argentina, Brazil, Chile, Colombia, Costa Rica, Dominican Republic, Ecuador, El Salvador, France, Haiti, Netherlands, Nicaragua, Panama, Paraguay, Peru, UK, USA, Uruguay, Venezuela. Observer: PASB.

Page 183

Latin American Training Center on Production, Distribution, and Utilization of Milk, San José, Costa Rica (9 August–5 September 1953): Chile, Costa Rica, Ecuador, El Salvador, Haiti, Honduras, Nicaragua, Panama.

Page 184

Latin American Seminar on Land Problems, Campinas, Brazil (25 May–26 June 1953): Bolivia, Brazil, Chile, Colombia, Costa Rica, Cuba, Dominican Republic, Ecuador, El Salvador, Haiti, Honduras, Mexico, Paraguay, Uruguay, USA. Observers: ECLA, the Holy See, Inter-Governmental Committee for

European Migration, International Bank for Reconstruction and Development (IBRD), ILO, Organization of American States (OAS), UN, UNESCO.

Center on Land Problems in Asia and the Far East, Bangkok, Thailand (22 November–11 December 1954): Burma, Cambodia, India, Indonesia, Japan, Laos, Malaya, Nepal, Pakistan, Philippine Republic, Thailand, Viet Nam.

Page 186

Central American Seminar on Agricultural Credit, Guatemala City, Guatemala (15 September–15 October 1952): Brazil, Costa Rica, Chile, Cuba, El Salvador, Guatemala, Haiti, Honduras, Mexico, Nicaragua, Panama, Puerto Rico, USA. Observers: Caribbean Commission, Central American Coffee Federation–Mexico–the Caribbean, ECLA, IBRD, ILO, International Monetary Fund, Organization of American States.

Page 187

Panel of Experts on Supervised Credit, Asunción, Paraguay (3–17 December 1953): Brazil, Costa Rica, Honduras, Paraguay, Peru, USA, Venezuela.

Page 188

Technical Meeting on Agricultural Extension, Turrialba, Costa Rica (23 August–3 September 1949): Chile, Colombia, Costa Rica, Ecuador, El Salvador, Guatemala, Haiti, Honduras, Mexico, Netherlands, Nicaragua, Panama, UK, USA. Observers: Paraguay, Peru, Caribbean Commission, the Holy See, OAS, PASB, UN, UNESCO.

Training Center for Latin American Countries, Agricultural Extension, Turrialba, Costa Rica (3–23 February 1951): Bolivia, Costa Rica, El Salvador, Guadeloupe-French Antilles, Haiti, Honduras, Nicaragua, Panama, Peru, Puerto Rico, Uruguay, Venezuela.

Second Latin American Extension Training Center, San José, Costa Rica (6–25 April 1952): Chile, Costa Rica, El Salvador, Guadeloupe, Guatemala, Haiti, Honduras, Nicaragua, Puerto Rico, Uruguay, Venezuela.

Andean Agricultural Extension Training Center, Lima, Peru (15 May–8 August 1953): Bolivia, Chile, Colombia, Paraguay, Peru.

Regional Agricultural Extension Training Center for Latin America, Lima, Peru (10 July–2 October 1954): Bolivia, Colombia, Chile, Honduras, Paraguay, Peru, Venezuela.

Caribbean Agricultural Extension Development Center, Kingston, Jamaica (5–10 August 1954): Dominican Republic, Haiti, France (Martinique), Netherlands (Surinam), UK (St. Lucia, Trinidad, British Guiana, Jamaica), USA (Puerto Rico). Agencies: Foreign Operations Administration, Caribbean Commission, Inter-American Institute of Agricultural Sciences (Northern Zone), United Nations (Trusteeship Dept.), UNESCO (Division of Fundamental and Adult Education), the Holy See, Development and Welfare Organization (Barbados), Jamaica Agricultural Society, Jamaica Social Welfare Commission.

APPENDIX 261

Page 191

Second Latin American Fisheries Training Center, Mexico City, Mexico (4 October–10 December 1954): Brazil, Colombia, Costa Rica, El Salvador, Guatemala, Haiti, Honduras, Mexico, Nicaragua, Panama, Puerto Rico, Uruguay.

Conference on Nutrition Problems in Latin America, Montevideo, Uruguay (18–28 July 1948): Argentina, Bolivia, Brazil, Chile, Colombia, Cuba, Dominican Republic, Ecuador, France, Guatemala, Mexico, Nicaragua, Panama, Paraguay, Peru, UK, USA, Uruguay, Venezuela. Observers: American International Institute for the Protection of Childhood, ECLA, ILO, Inter-American Cooperative Service of Public Health, Inter-American Council of Trade and Production, Inter-American Institute of Agricultural Sciences, League of Red Cross Societies, Military Sanitation Service in Uruguay, PASB, Pan American Union, UNICEF.

Page 192

Second Conference on Nutrition Problems in Latin America, Rio de Janeiro, Brazil (5–13 June 1950): Bolivia, Brazil, Chile, Colombia, Costa Rica, Dominican Republic, Ecuador, El Salvador, France, Mexico, Netherlands, Nicaragua, Paraguay, Peru, UK, USA, Uruguay, Venezuela. Observers: Argentina, ECLA, Inter-American Indian Institute, Inter-American Institute for the Protection of Childhood, ILO, International Refugee Organization, League of Red Cross Societies, UN, UNESCO, UNICEF, WHO.

Third Conference on Nutrition Problems in Latin America, Caracas, Venezuela (19–28 October 1953): Argentina, Brazil, Colombia, Dominican Republic, Ecuador, France, Haiti, Netherlands, Panama, Peru, UK, USA, Venezuela. Observers: the Holy See, Inter-American Institute for Child Welfare, International Union for Child Welfare, Red Cross, UN, UNESCO.

Page 193

Conference on Home Economics and Education in Nutrition, Port-of-Spain, Trinidad (30 June–5 July 1952): Dominican Republic, French Caribbean Departments, Netherlands and Territories, UK and Territories, USA and Territories. Observers: Associated Country Women of the World, the Holy See, Inter-American Institute of Agricultural Sciences, OAS, UN, WHO, Women's Missionary of the United Church of Canada, Young Women's Christian Association, five organizations from Trinidad and two from Puerto Rico.

Page 194

Technical Meeting on Cooperatives in the Caribbean, Port-of-Spain, Trinidad (22–27 January 1951): Barbados, British Guiana, Dominican Republic, France, Guadeloupe, Jamaica, Martinique, Netherlands, Puerto Rico, Surinam, Trinidad and Tobago, UK, USA. Observers: Colonial Development and Welfare Association, the Holy See, IFAP, ILO.

CHAPTER 11. EUROPE

Page 220

First International Meeting on Fisheries Statistics, Copenhagen, Denmark (26–30 May 1952): Belgium, Canada, Costa Rica, Denmark, Egypt, Faroe Islands, Finland, France, Germany, Italy, Netherlands, Norway, Sweden, UK, USA. Observers: International Commission for the Northwest Atlantic Fisheries, International Council for the Exploration of the Sea.

International Fishing Boat Congress, Paris, France (12–16 October 1953): Argentina, Belgium, Canada, Denmark, Finland, France, Germany, Iceland, Ireland, Italy, Indonesia, Malaya, Netherlands, Norway, Portugal, Spain, Sweden, Switzerland, UK, USA, Uruguay, Viet Nam, Yugoslavia. Observers: International Commission for the Northwest Atlantic Fisheries, ILO, World Meteorological Organization.

International Fishing Boat Congress, Miami, Florida (16–20 November 1953): Argentina, Barbados, Bermuda, Brazil, Canada, Chile, Cuba, Denmark, Finland, France, Germany, Martinique, Mexico, Netherlands, UK, USA, Venezuela, Virgin Islands. Observer: UN Korean Reconstruction Agency.

Page 221

International Timber Conference, Marianske Lazne, Czechoslovakia (28 April–10 May 1947): Belgium, Brazil, Canada, Chile, Czechoslovakia, Denmark, Egypt, France, Greece, Hungary, Italy, Luxembourg, Mexico, Netherlands, Norway, Poland, Switzerland, Syria, UK, USA, Yugoslavia. Observers: Austria, Bulgaria, Finland, Rumania, Sweden, Emergency Economic Committee for Europe, European Coal Organization, IBRD, International Federation of Building and Wood Workers, International Trade Organization (Preparatory Commission), UN, World Federation of Trade Unions.

European Forestry Commission (1953): Austria, Belgium, Canada, Denmark, Finland, France, Germany, Greece, Iceland, Ireland, Israel, Italy, Luxembourg, Netherlands, Norway, Portugal, Spain, Sweden, Switzerland, Turkey, UK, USA, Yugoslavia.

Timber Committee of the Economic Commission for Europe (1953): Albania, Austria, Belgium, Czechoslovakia, Denmark, Finland, France, Germany (Western Zone), Italy, Netherlands, Norway, Poland, Rumania, Sweden, Switzerland, UK, USA, USSR, Yugoslavia. Observer: Canada.

Page 223

Seventh FAO Hybrid Maize Meeting, Belgrade, Yugoslavia (8–13 February 1954): Algeria, Austria, Belgian Congo, Belgium, Egypt, France, Germany, Israel, Italy, Lebanon, Morocco, Netherlands, Portugal, Sweden, Switzerland, Turkey, UK, Yugoslavia. Observers: European Confederation of Agriculture, Foreign Operations Administration (USA), French Agricultural Mission in Lebanon, International Seed Trade Federation.

APPENDIX

Page 224

First Session of the European Commission for the Control of Foot-and-Mouth Disease, Rome, Italy (27–30 July 1954): Countries ratifying Constitution: Denmark, Ireland, the Netherlands, Norway, UK, Yugoslavia. Observers: Austria, Belgium, Finland, France, Hungary, Italy, Rumania, Spain, Sweden, Turkey, USSR, International Office of Epizootics, Organization for European Economic Cooperation, European Confederation of Agriculture, Foreign Operations Administration.

Page 225

International Meeting on the Olive Fly, Florence, Italy (16–21 March 1953): Algeria, France, Greece, Israel, Italy, Morocco, Spain, Portugal, Yugoslavia. Observers: Egypt, Libya, Consiglio Nazionale delle Ricerche (Italy), Fédération Internationale de l'Oléiculture, Mutual Security Agency, Organisation Européenne pour la Protection des Plantes, Union Internationale des Sciences Biologiques, World Federation of United Nations Associations.

Meeting on Agricultural Extension, Brussels and The Hague, Netherlands (August 1949): Austria, Belgium, Czechoslovakia, Denmark, Finland, France, Bizone Germany, Greece, Ireland, Italy, Luxembourg, Netherlands, Switzerland, UK, Yugoslavia. Observers: the Holy See, IFAP, ILO, Institute for International Collaboration in Agriculture and Forestry in Prague, OEEC.

Countries in which FAO experts made extension surveys (1950): Belgium, Denmark, France, Greece, Ireland, Italy, Norway, Portugal, Sweden, Netherlands, Switzerland, UK, Western Germany. (Later, Finland.)

International Training Center on Agricultural Extension Methods, Wageningen, Netherlands (13 July–8 August 1953): Argentina, Austria, Belgium, Burma, Denmark, Egypt, Finland, France, Germany, Gold Coast, Iran, Iraq, Italy, Lebanon, Libya, Luxembourg, Netherlands, Nigeria, Pakistan, Rhodesia, Sierra Leone, Surinam, Sweden, Switzerland, Syria, Turkey, Uganda, UK, USA, Yugoslavia.

Page 226

Regional Agricultural Extension Training Center for European and Mediterranean Countries, Wageningen, Netherlands (12 July–7 August 1954).

Sixth Meeting of the European Committee on Agriculture, Rome, Italy (14–18 June 1954): Austria, Belgium, Denmark, Finland, France, Germany, Greece, Iceland, Ireland, Italy, Luxembourg, Netherlands, Norway, Portugal, Spain, Sweden, Switzerland, Turkey, UK, Yugoslavia. Observers: European Association for Animal Production, European Confederation of Agriculture, the Holy See, International Commission of Agricultural Industries, International Dairy Federation, IFAP, International Institute for Refrigeration, ILO, International Permanent Bureau of Analytical Chemistry, OEEC, World Assembly of Youth, World Federation of United Nations Associations.

Some Source Material

Aamodt, Olaf S. *Report of Observations on Technical Assistance Program in Algeria, Egypt, Lebanon, Iraq, Iran, and Turkey* (Washington, D.C.: USDA,* July 1953). 10 pp. Mimeo.

Agricultural Economics, Bureau of. *Farm Costs and Returns, 1951, with Comparisons* (Washington, D.C.: USDA, 1952). 27 pp.

──── *Generalized Types of Farming in the United States* (Washington, D.C.: Agri. Inf. Bulletin No. 3, USDA, Feb. 1950). 35 pp.

──── *Hog-Dairy Farms, Organization, Costs and Returns, 1952* (Material furnished personally by BAE, USDA. Nov. 1952).

──── *Rural Life in the United States* (New York: Alfred A. Knopf, 1949). 549 pp.

Allahabad Agricultural Institute (New York: The Board of Founders, Inc., no date). 32 pp.

American Friends Service Committee. *The Story of the Committee, 1917-1952* (Philadelphia: April 1952).

Andrews, Stanley. *Point 4 around the World* (Washington, D.C.: US Dept. of State, Jan. 1953). Processed pictorial chart and short statement.

Armstrong, O. K. "When Good Neighbors Get Together," *Nation's Business* (Sept. 1950).

Atwater, Helen. *Home Economics Research in the U.S. Department of Agriculture* (Jan. 1943). Typed ms.

Atwater, W. O. *The Chemical Composition of American Food Materials* (Washington, D.C.: Office of Experiment Stations Bulletin 28, USDA, Rev. ed. 1940).

Ballou, Robert O., ed. *World Bible* (New York: The Viking Press, 1950).

Bliss, R. K., comp. and ed. *The Spirit and Philosophy of Extension Work* (Washington, D.C.: Graduate School, USDA, and Epsilon Sigma Phi, 1952). 393 pp.

Bock, Edwin A. *Fifty Years of Technical Assistance* (Chicago: Public Administration Clearing House, 1954). 65 pp.

* Abbreviation for the United States Department of Agriculture.

Some Source Material

Bonné, Alfred. "Land and Population in the Middle East," *The Middle East Journal*, Vol. V (Winter 1951), pp. 39-56.

Brodell, A. P., and Ewing, J. A. *Use of Tractor Power, Animal Power, and Hand Methods in Crop Production* (Washington, D.C.: USDA, FM-69, July 1948). 32 pp.

Burnet, E., and Aykroyd, W. R. "Nutrition and Public Health," *Quarterly Bulletin* of the Health Organization, League of Nations, Geneva. Vol. IV, No. 2. (June 1935), pp. 327-474.

Cardon, P. V. "Progress in Agriculture during the Last Fifty Years." Speech at Sesquicentennial Celebration, Univ. of Georgia, Athens. April 30, 1951. 21 pp. (Mimeo. doc. USDA).

Catholic Encyclopedia. "Reductions of Paraguay" (New York: Robert Appleton Co., 1911), pp. 688-700.

Central Office of Information. *Progress in Asia. The Colombo Plan in Action* (London: H. M. Stationery Office, 1953). 36 pp.

Chandrasekhar, S. "Demographic Disarmament of India," *Population Bulletin*, Vol. VIII, No. 5 (Nov. 1952), p. 44.

Coker, R. E. *This Great and Wide Sea* (Chapel Hill: Univ. of North Carolina Press, rev. ed. 1949). 325 pp.

Colombo Plan Technical Cooperative Scheme. *Report for 1952 by the Council for Technical Cooperation* (London: H. M. Stationery Office, Feb. 1953). 16 pp.

Colvin, Carl. *Report on Central American Seminar on Agricultural Credit* (Washington, D.C.: USDA, 1952). Mimeo.

Commonwealth Consultative Committee. *The Colombo Plan for Cooperative Economic Development in South and South-East Asia* (London: H. M. Stationery Office, 1952). 75 pp.

Congress of the United States. *Act for International Development. Title IV.* Public Law 535-81st Congress, 2nd Session. Chapter 220. H. R. 7797. Approved 5 June 1950.

Cooke, Hedley V. *Challenge and Response in the Middle East* (New York: Harper & Brothers, 1952).

Cressey, George B. *Asia's Lands and Peoples* (New York: McGraw-Hill Book Co., Inc., 2d ed. 1951). 597 pp.

Davis, Joe F., and Strickler, Paul E. *Electricity on Farms in the Eastern Livestock Area of Iowa* (Washington, D.C.: USDA in co-operation with Iowa Agricultural Experiment Station, Ames. *USDA Cir. No. 852.* Sept. 1950). 88 pp.

Dodd, L. P. *The Marshall Plan—A Program of International Cooperation* (Washington, D.C., Economic Cooperation Administration, no date). 63 pp.

Economic Cooperation Administration. *The Marshall Plan—A Handbook of the Economic Cooperation Administration* (Washington, D.C., no date). 18 pp.

Eisenhower, Dwight D. *The Chance for Peace* (Washington, D.C.: Dept. of State Pub. 5042, April 1953). 10 pp.

Escuela Agricola Panamericana. *Monthly News Letter.* Tegucigalpa, Honduras.

Federal Security Agency. *Proceedings of the National Nutrition Conference for Defense.* (Washington, D.C., 1942). 254 pp.

Fish and Wildlife Service. *Hydrography, Productivity, Fishing, Commercial Trials, Artificial Bait, Larval Studies, Racial Studies, Translations.* (San Diego, Calif.: Resumé for Tuna Industry Advisory Committee Meeting. U.S. Dept. of Interior, April 1953). 24 pp.

Fisher, W. B. *The Middle East; A Physical, Social, and Regional Geography* (New York: E. P. Dutton and Co., Inc., 2d ed. 1952).

Ford Foundation. *Financial Statements as of December 31, 1951.* New York. 7 pp.

────── *Annual Report, 1952* (New York, Dec. 31, 1952). 70 pp.

Foreign Agricultural Relations, Office of. *Teamwork in World Agriculture* (Washington, D.C.: *Agri. Inf. Bulletin* 21, USDA, 1950). 21 pp.

Galarza, Mae. "Gold Dust for the Land," *Co-op Grain Quarterly* (Winter 1952), pp. 61-65.

Glesinger, Egon. *The Coming Age of Wood.* (New York: Simon and Schuster, Inc., 1949). 279 pp.

Goodwin, Dorothy C., and Johnstone, Paul H. "A Brief Chronology of American Agricultural History," *Farmers in a Changing World. 1940 Yearbook of Agriculture* (Washington, D.C.: USDA, 1940), pp. 1184-1196.

Habib-Ayrout, Henry, S. J. *The Fellaheen.* (Cairo: R. Schindler, no date).

Hambidge, Gove. *Your Meals and Your Money* (New York and London: McGraw-Hill Book Co., Inc., 1934). 190 pp.

Harding, T. Swann. "Science and Agricultural Policy," *Farmers in a Changing World. 1940 Yearbook of Agriculture* (Washington, D.C.: USDA, 1940), pp. 1081-1110.

Harrar, J. G. *Mexican Agricultural Program* (New York: The Rockefeller Foundation, 1950). 36 pp.

Hatch, D. Spencer. *Up from Poverty in Rural India* (Calcutta: Oxford University Press, rev. ed. 1938). 208 pp.

────── *Further Upward in Rural India* (Bombay: Oxford University Press, 1938). 200 pp.

Heald, Frederick Deforest. *Manual of Plant Diseases* (New York: McGraw-Hill Book Co., Inc., 2d ed. 1933). 953 pp.

Huberman, M. A. "Forests in Ferment," *American Forests*, Vol. 55, No. 2 (Feb.–May 1949).

Human Nutrition and Home Economics, Bureau of. *Rural Family Living Charts.* (Washington, D.C.: USDA, Oct. 1952). 78 pp.

Hunnicutt, Benjamin H., and Reid, William Watkins. *The Story of Agricultural Missions* (New York: Missionary Education Movement of the United States and Canada, 1931). 180 pp.

Hussein, Ahmed. *Rural Social Welfare Centres in Egypt* (Cairo: Ministry of Social Affairs, 1951). 27 pp.
India, Government of, Planning Commission. *The Progress of the Plan* (New Delhi: Govt. of India Press, 1954). 137 pp.
India News. Washington, D.C.
Indiagram. No. 331. (Washington, D.C., Nov. 16, 1953).
Inter-American Institute of Agricultural Sciences. *Brief Statement of Its Main Accomplishments 1944-1952* (Turrialba, Costa Rica, March 1953). 6 pp. Mimeo.
International Bank for Reconstruction and Development. *Sixth Annual Report, 1950-51* (Washington, D.C., Sept. 1951). 70 pp.
────── *The Economic Development of British Guiana* (Baltimore: The Johns Hopkins Press, 1953). 366 pp.
────── *The Economic Development of Ceylon* (Baltimore: The Johns Hopkins Press, 1953). 829 pp.
────── *The Agricultural Economy of Chile* (Washington, D.C., Dec. 1952). 353 pp. Processed.
────── *The Economic Development of Jamaica* (Baltimore: The Johns Hopkins Press, 1952). 288 pp.
────── *The Economic Development of Mexico* (Baltimore: The Johns Hopkins Press, 1953). 392 pp.
────── *The Economic Development of Nicaragua* (Baltimore: The Johns Hopkins Press, 1953). 424 pp.
────── *Surinam—Recommendations for a Ten-Year Development Program* (Baltimore: The Johns Hopkins Press, 1952). 271 pp.
────── *The Agricultural Development of Uruguay* (Washington, D.C., 1951). 231 pp. Processed.
Issawi, Charles. "Population and Wealth in Egypt," *The Milbank Memorial Fund Quarterly*, Vol. XXVII, No. 1 (Jan. 1949), pp. 98-113.
James, Preston E. *Latin America* (New York: The Odyssey Press, rev. ed. 1950). 848 pp.
Johnstone, Paul H. "Old Ideals versus New Ideas in Farm Life," *Farmers in a Changing World. 1940 Yearbook of Agriculture* (Washington, D.C.: USDA, 1940), pp. 111-170.
Kuhn, Ferdinand. "500,000 Villages Hold the Key to India's Future," *The Washington Post* (Jan. 31, 1954).
Kuo, Leslie T. C. *A Brief Account of Important International Conferences on Food Problems since the First World War* (April 1943). 13 pp. Processed.
League of Nations. *The Problem of Nutrition.* Vol. I. *Interim Report of the Mixed Committee on the Problem of Nutrition.* 98 pp.; Vol. II. *Report on the Physiological Bases of Nutrition.* 27 pp.; Vol. III. *Nutrition in Various Countries.* 271 pp.; Vol. IV. *Report on Statistics of Food Production, Consumption, and Prices* (Geneva, June 1936).
────── *Nutrition. Final Report of the Mixed Committee of the League of*

Nations on the Relation of Nutrition to Health, Agriculture, and Economic Policy (Geneva, Aug. 1937). 327 pp.

Malenbaum, Wilfred. "The Colombo Plan. New Promise for Asia," *US Dept. of State Bulletin* (Sept. 22, 1952), pp. 441-448.

Mattison, Beatrice McCown. "Rural Social Centers in Egypt," *The Middle East Journal,* Vol. V (Autumn 1951), pp. 461-480.

McCollum, E. V., and Simmonds, Nina. *The Newer Knowledge of Nutrition* (New York: The Macmillan Company, 1929). 594 pp.

McDougall, F. L. "International Aspects of Postwar Food and Agriculture," *Annals of the American Academy of Political and Social Science,* Vol. 225 (Jan. 1943).

────── *Draft Memorandum on a United Nations Program for Freedom from Want of Food* [Prepared in collaboration with a group of economists and medical scientists; known as the McDougall Memorandum] (Washington, D.C., Oct. 1942). 31 pp. Mimeo.

Metcalf, John E. *The Agricultural Economy of Indonesia* (Washington, D.C.: USDA Monograph No. 15, July 1952). 100 pp.

Ministry of Social Affairs. *Social Welfare in Egypt* (Cairo, Oct. 1950). 173 pp.

────── *The Fellah Department* (Cairo, 1950). 43 pp.

Moomaw, Ira W. *The Farmer Speaks* (Calcutta: Oxford University Press, 1949). 199 pp.

────── *Education and Village Improvement* (Calcutta: Oxford University Press, 2d ed. 1947). 188 pp.

National Catholic Rural Life Conference. *Christianity and the Land* (Des Moines, 1951). 30 pp.

────── *The Conclusions of Manizales* (Des Moines, May 1953). 29 pp.

National Research Council. *Recommended Dietary Allowances* (Washington, D.C.: Reprint and Circular Series No. 129, rev. 1953).

Organization for European Economic Cooperation. *Fish Marketing in OEEC Countries* (Paris, Nov. 1951). 247 pp.

Orr, John Boyd. *Food, Health, and Income* (London: Macmillan and Co., Ltd., 2d ed. 1937).

────── "The Mineral Elements in Animal Nutrition," *Journal of the Society of Chemical Industry,* Vol. 44, No. 40 (1925). Quoted in H. C. Sherman, *Chemistry of Food and Nutrition* (New York: The Macmillan Company, 3d ed. 1931).

──────, and Scherbatoff, Helen. *Minerals in Pastures and Their Relation to Animal Nutrition* (London, 1929). 150 pp.

Production and Marketing Adm. *The Fifth Plate* (Washington, D.C.: USDA, PA-191, Dec. 1951). 42 pp.

────── *To Keep Your Plate Full* (Washington, D.C.: USDA, Sept. 1952). 53 pp.

Raper, Arthur F., and Martha J. *Guide to Agriculture, U.S.A.* (Washington, D.C.: USDA Info. Bulletin No. 30, 1951). 82 pp.

Reuss, L. A., Wooten, H. H., and Marschner, F. J. *Inventory of Major Land Uses in the United States* (Washington, D.C.: USDA, MP No. 663, 1948). 89 pp.
Rowe, C. O. "Point IV Showing Results in Latin America," *Journal of Commerce* (April 14, 1953). Institute of Inter-American Affairs, Building a Better Hemisphere Series No. 22. Wash., D.C. 8 pp.
Samuel, Viscount. "World Population and Resources," *Parliamentary Debates (Hansard)*. Vol. 187, No. 63 (London: H. M. Stationery Office, 28 April 1954), cols. 108-123.
Schultz, Theodore W. *The Supply of Food in Relation to Economic Development* (Chicago: Univ. of Chicago Office of Agricultural Economics Research Paper No. 5219, 1952). 12 pp. Processed.
Schurz, William Lytle. *Latin America. A Descriptive Survey* (New York: E. P. Dutton and Co., Inc., 1949). 386 pp.
Sherman, H. C., and Smith, S. L. *The Vitamins* (New York: The Chemical Catalog Co., Inc., 2d ed. 1931). 575 pp.
Stanley, Louise. "From Tradition to Science," *Food and Life. 1939 Yearbook of Agriculture* (Washington, D.C., 1939), pp. 97-99.
Statistical Office of the United Nations. *National and Per Capita Incomes, Seventy Countries, 1949* (New York: Statistical Papers, Series E, No. 1, Oct. 1950). 29 pp.
Stiebeling, Hazel K., and Munsell, Hazel E. *Food Supply and Pellagra Incidence in 73 South Carolina Farm Families* (Washington, D.C.: USDA Tech. Bulletin 333, 1932). 36 pp.
Stiebeling, Hazel K., and Phipard, E. F. *Diets of Families of Employed Wage Earners and Clerical Workers in Cities* (Washington, D.C.: USDA Cir. 507, 1932). 141 pp.
Stiebeling, Hazel K., and Ward, M. M. *Diets at Four Levels of Nutritive Content and Cost* (Washington, D.C.: USDA Cir. 296, 1933).
Sturtevant, A. H. Speech at California Institute of Technology. (Quoted in *The Washington Post and Times Herald*, June 24, 1954.)
Tannous, Afif I. "Egypt—Ancient and Agrarian," *Foreign Agriculture*. Vol. XIII, No. 9 (Sept. 1949), pp. 202-207.
———— *Extension Work among the Arab Fellahin* (Washington, D.C.: Dept. of State, Foreign Service Institute, 1951).
———— "Land Ownership in the Middle East," *Foreign Agriculture*. Vol. XIV, No. 12 (Dec. 1950), pp. 263-269.
Technical Assistance Board. *Contributions of Countries which Participated in the Technical Assistance Conference* (15 June 1950). Processed Doc. TAB/INF/R.3.
Tolley, Howard R. "Population and Food Supply," *Freedom from Want* (Waltham, Mass.: Chronica Botanica Co., 1948), pp. 217-224.
Truman, Harry S. *Address by the President of the United States before the*

Fourth Session of the FAO Conference, 24 Nov. 1948. (Washington, D.C., Nov. 29, 1948.) Mimeo. Doc. C48/PV/6.

——— *Inaugural Address* (Washington, D.C., 20 Jan. 1949).

——— "State of the Union Message to Congress," 7 Jan. 1953. (Quoted in *The New York Times,* Jan. 8, 1953.)

United Fruit Company. *The Story of the Escuela Agricola Panamericana* (printed in the USA, no date). 36 pp.

United Nations. *Daily Report.* Vol. IX, No. 72 (16 April 1953), pp. 7-8.

——— *Demographic Yearbook 1953* (New York, 1953). 441 pp.

——— *The Determinants and Consequences of Population Trends* (New York, 1953). 404 pp.

——— *Measures for the Economic Development of Under-Developed Countries* (New York, May 1951). 108 pp.

——— *Mission to Haiti* (Lake Success, July 1949). 327 pp.

——— *Statistical Yearbook 1952* (New York, 1952). 554 pp.

——— *Technical Assistance for Economic Development* (Lake Success, May 1949). 328 pp.

United Nations Educational, Scientific, and Cultural Organization. "Science and You," *UNESCO Features,* No. 85 (Nov. 28, 1952), pp. 19-21.

United States Delegation to the Seventh Session of the FAO Conference. *Statement on ETAP* (Nov. 1953). 4 pp. US Del/19, mimeo.

US Department of Agriculture. *Agricultural Statistics 1951* (Washington, D.C.). 742 pp.

——— *Plant Diseases. The Yearbook of Agriculture, 1953* (Washington, D.C.). 940 pp.

——— *Research and Related Services in the United States Department of Agriculture* (Washington, D.C.: Rept. for the Committee on Agriculture of the House of Representatives, 81st Cong., 2nd Session, Dec. 1950). 3 vols.

US Department of State. *United Nations Conference on Food and Agriculture: Final Act and Section Reports* (Washington, D.C., 1943). 61 pp.

——— *Outline of Point Four Organization, Policy, and Operations* (Feb. 14, 1952). 5 pp. Mimeo.

Van Veen, A. G. "Fish Preservation in Southeast Asia," *Advances in Food Research,* Vol. IV (1953), pp. 209-231.

Walters, F. P. *A History of the League of Nations* (London-New York-Toronto: Oxford University Press, 1952). Two vols. 833 pp.

White, John W. "We're Building a Better Hemisphere," *Collier's* (Jan. 27, 1951).

Willkie, Wendell. *One World* (New York: Simon and Schuster, Inc., 1943).

Woodbridge, George. *The History of the United Nations Relief and Rehabilitation Administration* (New York: Columbia University Press, 1950). 3 vols. Prepared by special staff under direction of George Woodbridge.

SOME SOURCE MATERIAL 271

World Health Organization. *WHO Newsletter*, Vol. V, No. 10 (Nov. 1952). Geneva.

FAO DOCUMENTS AND PUBLICATIONS USED AS SOURCE MATERIAL

General

Five Technical Reports on Food and Agriculture. (Interim Commission.) (Washington, D.C., 20 Aug. 1945). 313 pp.
Reports to the Governments of the United Nations by the Interim Commission on Food and Agriculture (Washington, D.C.: *First*—1 Aug. 1944. 55 pp. *Second*—16 July 1945. 3 pp. *Third*—25 April 1945. 47 pp.).
The Work of FAO. (Interim Commission) (Washington, D.C., 1 Aug. 1945). 57 pp.
Hambidge, Gove. "The Coming War against Want." Speech at Town Hall, New York. 18 Sept. 1945. Mimeo.
First Annual Report of the Director-General (Washington, D.C., 1946). 46 pp.
Second Annual Report of the Director-General (Washington, D.C., 1947). 34 pp.
Work of FAO 1947/48 (Washington, D.C., Sept. 1948). 90 pp.
Work of FAO 1948/49 (Washington, D.C., Oct. 1949). 104 pp.
Work of FAO 1949/50 (Washington, D.C., Oct. 1950). 89 pp.
Work of FAO 1950/51 (Rome, Sept. 1951). 67 pp.
Work of FAO 1951/52 (Rome, Oct. 1952). 32 pp.
Work of FAO 1952/53 (Rome, Oct. 1953). 46 pp.
Progress Report on the Work of FAO 1953/54. (Rome, July 1954). 60 pp. Mimeo.
Activities of FAO under the Expanded Technical Assistance Program 1950-52 (Rome, 1952). 76 pp.
Activities of FAO under the Expanded Technical Assistance Program 1952/53 (Rome, Oct. 1953). 88 pp.
Report of the First Session of the Conference (Washington, D.C., Jan. 1946). 89 pp.
Proceedings of the First Session of the Conference (Washington, D.C., Jan. 1946). 259 pp.
Report of the Second Session of the Conference (Washington, D.C., Dec. 1946). 70 pp.
Proceedings of the Second Session of the Conference (Washington, D.C., 1947). 198 pp.
Report of the Third Session of the Conference (Washington, D.C., 1947). 82 pp.
Proceedings of the Third Session of the Conference (Washington, D.C., 1948). 279 pp.
Report of the Special Session of the Conference (Washington, D.C., 1948). 6 pp.

Report of the Fourth Session of the Conference (Washington, D.C., March 1949). 100 pp.

Report of the Fifth Session of the Conference (Washington, D.C., March 1950). 92 pp.

Report of the Sixth Session of the Conference (Rome, March 1952). 214 pp.

Report of the Seventh Session of the Conference (Rome, March 1954). 256 pp.

Report of the Council of FAO. Sixth Session (Washington, D.C., 1949). 28 pp.

Report of the Special Meeting on Urgent Food Problems (Washington, D.C., 1946). 40 pp.

World Food Survey (Washington, D.C., July 1946). 39 pp.

Second World Food Survey (Rome, Nov. 1952). 59 pp.

Proposals for a World Food Board (Washington, D.C., July 1946). 12 pp.

Report of the Preparatory Commission on World Food Proposals (Washington, D.C., 1947). 84 pp.

Report on World Commodity Problems (Washington, D.C., Nov. 1949). 73 pp. Processed Doc. C49/10.

Report of the Rice Study Group (Washington, D.C., July 1947). 58 pp.

Report of the Rice Meeting (Washington, D.C., June 1948). 48 pp.

International Rice Commission: Report of the First Session (Bangkok, March 1949). 51 pp. *Report of the Second Session* (Bangkok, Feb. 1950). 46 pp. *Report of the Third Session* (Bangkok, May 1952). 76 pp.

Report of the FAO Mission for Greece (Washington, D.C., 1947). 188 pp.

Report of the FAO Mission for Siam (Washington, D.C., 1948). 126 pp.

Report of the FAO Fisheries Mission for Thailand (Washington, D.C., Dec. 1949). 73 pp.

Report of the FAO Mission for Poland (Washington, D.C., 1948). 160 pp.

Report of the FAO Oilseed Mission for Venezuela (Washington, D.C., 1949). 84 pp.

Agriculture in the Near East. Development and Outlook (Rome, Nov. 1953). 78 pp.

Agriculture in Asia and the Far East. Development and Outlook (Rome, Oct. 1953). 163 pp.

Agriculture in Latin America. Its Development and Outlook (Washington, D.C., Feb. 1951). 169 pp.

Prospects for Agricultural Development in Latin America (Rome, 1953). 146 pp.

Pawley, W. H., et al. *Possibilities of Increasing the Supply of Food and Agricultural Products by Exploitation of New Areas and Increasing Yields* (Rome, August 1954). 27 pp. Mimeo.

Agriculture

Phillips, R. W., Peebles, T. F., Cummings, W. H., Passerini, L. *FAO Advisory Assistance to Member Countries under the UNRRA-Transfer Fund*. Dev. Paper No. 24 (Rome, Feb. 1953). 54 pp.

Some Source Material

The Desert Locust. Fact Sheet No. X-2 (Rome, May 1952). 8 pp. Mimeo.
Summary Reports of Meetings of FAO Technical Advisory Committee on Desert Locust Control (Rome: *First,* March 1952; *Second,* November 1952; *Third,* April 1953).
Report of the FAO Desert Locust Control Meeting (Rome, Nov. 1953). 20 pp.
Logothetis, C. "The Migratory Locust in South America," *FAO Plant Protection Bulletin,* Vol. I, No. 3 (Dec. 1952), pp. 33-35.
Wheat Improvement in the Near East (Rome, 21 Dec. 1951). 3 pp. Mimeo. FAO/51/12/4728.
Near East Wheat Breeding Conference. Summary Report (Rome, July 1952). 8 pp. Mimeo. FAO/52/7/4115.
Summary Reports of Meetings on Wheat and Barley Breeding in the Near East (Rome: *Second,* May 1953, 14 pp., Mimeo. FAO/53/5/3498; *Third,* May 1954, 17 pp., Mimeo. FAO/54/5/2943).
Reports of Meetings of the Working Party on Mediterranean Pasture and Fodder Development (Rome: *First,* July 1952, 29 pp., Mimeo. FAO/52/6/3760; *Second,* July 1953, 46 pp., Mimeo. FAO/53/8/6207).
Carroll, Thomas F. *Report on the Latin American Seminar on Land Problems.* FAO Report No. 205 (Rome, Nov. 1953). 97 pp.
Report of the FAO Special Meeting on the Control of Foot-and-Mouth Disease in the Near East (Rome, April 1953). 29 pp. Mimeo. FAO/53/5/3424.
Report of the FAO Near East Meeting on Animal Health (Rome, July 1953). Mimeo. FAO/53/7/6088.
Rinderpest Vaccines—Their Production and Use in the Field (Washington, D.C., March 1949). 71 pp.
Rinderpest Conference for Asia and the Far East (Bangkok, June 1949). Mimeo.
Lee, Douglas H. K. *Manual of Field Studies on the Heat Tolerance of Domestic Animals* (Rome, Dec. 1953). 161 pp.
Improving Livestock under Tropical and Subtropical Conditions. Dev. Paper No. 6 (Washington, D.C., July 1950). 55 pp.
Report of the Inter-American Meeting on Livestock Production. Dev. Paper No. 8 (Washington, D.C., Dec. 1950). 95 pp.
Report of the Second Inter-American Meeting on Livestock Production (Rome, June 1953). 138 pp.
Hall, H. T. B. *Report on the Latin American Training Center on Production, Distribution, and Utilization of Milk.* FAO Report No. 225 (Rome, Jan. 1954). 15 pp.
The Development of Agricultural Extension or Advisory Services in the Near East (Rome, Nov. 1952). 22 pp. Mimeo. FAO 52/11/7708.
Wilson, M. L. *The Cultural Approach in Extension Work* (Rome, 1952). 12 pp. Mimeo. FAO/52/12/8236.
Najjar, Halim, and Maunder, A. H. *Report on the Near East Regional Exten-*

sion Development Center. FAO Report No. 114 (Rome, April 1953). 333 pp.

Educational Approaches to Rural Welfare (Washington, D.C., no date). 49 pp.

Labarthe, Enrique, and Paulling, John R. *Report on the Andean Agricultural Extension Training Center.* FAO Report No. 208 (Rome, Nov. 1953). 7 pp.

Rowat, Robert. *Report on the International Training Center on Agricultural Extension Methods.* FAO Report No. 234 (Rome, Jan. 1954). 15 pp.

Cheesman, W. J. W. *Report on the FAO/ILO Near East Cooperatives Training Center.* FAO Report No. 11 (Rome, April 1953). 6 pp.

Report of Technical Meeting on Cooperatives in Asia and the Far East (Washington, D.C., 1949). 21 pp.

Survey of Rural Cooperatives in Countries in South East Asia (Bangkok, 1949). 269 pp.

Report of the FAO/ILO Technical Meeting on Cooperatives in Asia and the Far East (Rome, June 1954). 26 pp.

Technical Meeting on Cooperatives in the Caribbean (Washington, D.C., 1951). 24 pp.

Seminario Centroamericano de Credito Agricola (Guatemala City, 1952). 353 pp.

Reports of Meetings of the Working Party on Rice Breeding. (Rome: *First,* included in report of second session of International Rice Commission; *Second,* Dev. Paper No. 14, Dec. 1951, 82 pp.; *Third,* Dev. Paper No. 30, Feb. 1953, 48 pp.; *Fourth,* Dev. Paper No. 40, Feb. 1954, 32 pp.)

Reports of Meetings of the Working Party on Fertilizers. (Rome: *First,* Dev. Paper No. 11, Oct. 1951, 18 pp.; *Second,* Dev. Paper No. 37, Aug. 1953, 46 pp.; *Third,* Dev. Paper No. 39, Dec. 1953, 44 pp.)

Vermaat, J. G. *Report on International Training Center on Soil Fertility.* FAO Report No. 113 (Rome, April 1953). 12 pp.

Land Utilization in Tropical Areas of Asia and the Far East. Dev. Paper No. 17 (Rome, Jan. 1952). 10 pp.

Dion, H. G. *Agriculture in the Altiplano of Bolivia.* Dev. Paper No. 4 (Washington, D.C., May 1950). 33 pp.

Report of the Seventh FAO Hybrid Maize Meeting (Rome, March 1954). 93 pp. Mimeo. FAO/54/4/2232.

Co-operative Hybrid Maize Tests in European and Mediterranean Countries: 1949. Dev. Paper No. 7 (Washington, D.C., Oct. 1950). 33 pp. *1950.* Dev. Paper No. 31 (Rome, Dec. 1952). 43 pp. *1951.* Dev. Paper No. 35 (Rome, Sept. 1953). 145 pp. *1952.* Dev. Paper No. 42 (Rome, March 1954). 179 pp.

Economics and Statistics

Yearbook of Food and Agricultural Statistics—Production, 1953. Vol. VII, Part 1 (Rome, 1954). 334 pp.

Some Source Material

Per Caput Fiber Consumption Levels. Commodity Series Bulletin No. 25 (Rome, March 1954). 50 pp.
The State of Food and Agriculture: 1953. Part I—Review and Outlook (Rome, Aug. 1953). 125 pp.
The State of Food and Agriculture: 1954 (Rome, August 1954). 157 pp.
"Rice: Bangkok Meeting," *Monthly Bulletin of Agricultural Economics and Statistics.* Vol. II, No. 2 (Feb. 1953), pp. 13-14.
Rice. Commodity Reports, Rice No. 4 (Rome, Dec. 1953). 33 pp.
Report on the Asian Center on Agricultural and Allied Projects. Technical Assistance Adm. of UN. Series A, No. 1 (Lahore, March 1951). 38 pp.
Formulation and Economic Appraisal of Development Projects. Main course lectures at Asian Center on Agricultural and Allied Projects. TAA. (Lahore, 1951.) Two vols. 473 pp.
European Agriculture: A Statement of Problems (Geneva, 1954). 83 pp. Joint FAO/ECE study.

Fisheries

Yearbook of Fisheries Statistics, 1950-51 (Rome, April 1953). 296 pp.
Indo-Pacific Fisheries Council: Proceedings of Third Meeting (Madras, 1951). 227 pp.
——— *Proceedings of Fourth Meeting* (Quezon City, Nov. 1952). 99 pp.
Schuster, W. H. *Fish Culture in Brackish Water Ponds of Java.* IPFC Special Publication No. 1 (Madras: Diocesan Press, 1952). 143 pp.
——— *Report on Fishculture Seminar.* FAO Report No. 46 (Rome, Oct. 1952). 8 pp.
Present Status and Prospects of the Fishery Industry in Latin America (Rome, 1953). Mimeo. FAO/53/4/2527.
Herring and Allied Species 1920-48. A Commodity Study (Washington, D.C., May 1949). 66 pp. First Progress Report.
The Technology of Herring Utilization (Bergen: A.s John Griegs Boktrykkeri, 1953). 405 pp.
General Fisheries Council for the Mediterranean: Proceedings and Technical Papers of the Inaugural Meeting (Rome, 1952). 99 pp. *Summary Report of the Second Meeting* (Rome, Nov. 1953). Mimeo. P.53/CGPM/22.

Forestry

Yearbook of Forest Products Statistics 1953 (Rome, 1953). 153 pp.
Report of the Near East Forestry Conference (Jerusalem: Greek Convent Press, Feb. 1953). 32 pp.
Report of the Inaugural Session of the Forestry and Forest Products Commission (Bangkok: Tiranasar Press, 1950). 26 pp.
Report of the Forestry and Timber Utilization Conference for Asia and the Far East (Mysore: Government Branch Press, 1949). 13 pp.

Flemmich, C. O. "Report on the First Timber Grading School," *Malayan Forester*, Vol. XV, No. 2, Reprint No. 88 (April 1952). 15 pp.

Keith, H. G. *Report on the Far Eastern Mechanical Logging Training Center.* FAO Report No. 183 (Rome, Oct. 1953). 88 pp.

Possibilities for the Development of the Pulp and Paper Industry in Latin America (New York, 1954). 142 pp. Joint FAO/ECLA study.

Report of the Latin American Conference on Forestry and Forest Products (Rio de Janeiro, June 1948). 45 pp.

Report of the International Timber Conference (Washington, D.C., June 1947). 57 pp.

European Timber Trends and Prospects (Geneva, 1953). 315 pp. Joint FAO/ECE study.

European Timber Trends and Prospects—Note by the Director-General (Rome, 30 Oct. 1953). 31 pp. Mimeo. C53/14.

Nutrition and Home Economics

Calorie Requirements (Washington, D.C., June 1950). 65 pp.

Tsongas, A. G. *Nutrition Work in Greece* (Rome, 1951). 67 pp.

Brock, J. F., and Autret, M. *Kwashiorkor in Africa.* Nutrition Studies No. 8 (Rome, March 1952). 78 pp.

——— Letter to the Editor of *The Lancet.* (Typed copy shown to author.) [1954.]

Report on the Third Session of the Joint FAO/WHO Expert Committee on Nutrition. Nutrition Meetings Report No. 7 (Rome, Dec. 1953). 30 pp.

Nutrition Problems of Rice-Eating Countries in Asia. Report of First Meeting of Nutrition Committee for South and East Asia (Washington, D.C., June 1948). 24 pp.

Report of the Second Meeting of the Nutrition Committee for South and East Asia (Rome, Nov. 1953). 37 pp.

Rice and Rice Diets—A Nutritional Survey (Washington, D.C., Sept. 1948). 72 pp.

Nutrition Conference (Montevideo, July 1948). 315 pp.

Report of the Second Conference on Nutrition Problems in Latin America (Washington, D.C., Aug. 1950). 34 pp.

Report of the Third Conference on Nutrition Problems in Latin America (Rome, June 1954). 60 pp.

Report of the Conference on Home Economics and Education in Nutrition (Port-of-Spain, 1952). 16 pp. Processed.

Report on the Seminar on School Feeding in Central America and Panama. FAO Report No. 238 (Rome, Jan. 1954). 30 pp.

Legislation

"Egypt Legislative Decree No. 178 on Agrarian Reform—9 September 1952," *Food and Agricultural Legislation*, Vol. I, No. 2 (Rome, 1952). 10 pp.

Some Source Material

Periodicals

Director-General's Newsletter (Rome). Monthly. Processed.
FAO Memo (Rome and each regional office). Monthly.
Fisheries Bulletin (Rome). Quarterly.
Food and Agricultural Legislation (Rome). Quarterly.
Information Bulletin of the General Fisheries Council for the Mediterranean (Rome). Mimeo.
International Rice Commission Newsletter (Bangkok). Quarterly.
Locust Control Progress Reports (Rome). Mimeo.
Monthly Bulletin of Agricultural Economics and Statistics (Rome).
Plant Protection Bulletin (Rome). Monthly.
Unasylva (Rome). Quarterly.
World Fisheries Abstracts (Rome). Bimonthly.

Index

Aberdeen, Scotland, 44, 46
Absentee ownership. *See* land tenure
Abu Libda, 3-17, 18, 20, 27, 28
Act for International Development, USA, 95
Addis Ababa, Ethiopia, 139
Afghanistan, 114-117
   annual per caput income, 34, 246
Africa
   composition of diets, 31
   food supplies, 30
   kwashiorkor, 108-109
   missionaries, work by, 90, 91
   statistics training institute, 112: participants, 255
   See also Near East
Agricultural co-operatives. *See* co-operatives
Agricultural credit. *See* credit, agricultural
Agricultural Economics and Statistics, Monthly Bulletin of, 113
Agricultural Missions, Inc., 92
Agricultural wages, Egypt, 6, 17
Agri-horticultural Society for India, 91
Ahura Mazda, 121
Aleppo, Syria, 120, 121
Alexandria, Egypt, 6, 10, 12
Algeria, Moroccan locust control, 103, 189
Algiers, Algeria, 106
All-India Conference of the Family Planning Association, 34
All India Women's Council, 168
Allahabad Agricultural Institute, 91
Allahabad Christian College, 91
Allegri, Ernesto, 126
Allison, J. L., 124
Allocation of food, IEFC, 63, 64
Altiplano of Bolivia, 205
Amazon Valley, 195-196
American Arabian Oil Company, 129
American Farm Bureau Federation, 22
American Farm School, Greece, 91
American International Association, 93, 187
American Society of Newspaper Editors, 97

Ames, W. A., 202
Amines, 41
Amino acids, 42
Amman, Jordan, 111, 254
Amoebic dysentery, 14
Amparai, Ceylon, 170
Amsterdam, Netherlands, 217
Anderson, C. M., 137
Andrén, Thyra, 140
Animals. *See* dairy, hides and skins, livestock, livestock disease, poultry, sheep production, water buffalo
Animals, laboratory, 42
Ankara, Turkey, 161, 258
Annals of the American Academy of Political and Social Science, 48
Anti-Locust Research Center, 102
Appalachian Mountains, 28
Appraisal of the World Food Situation for 1946-47, 63
Arab States fundamental education center, 135
Arabian peninsula, locust outbreak, 102
Arable land. *See* land, arable
Archibald, E. S., 140
Archimedes' screw, 11
Argentina, 183. *See also* Buenos Aires
Artibonite River Valley, Haiti, 212
Artificial insemination. *See* livestock
Asia. *See* Far East and Near East
Asir Tihama, Saudi Arabia, 130
Assyria, 120
Astor, Lord, 46
Asunción, Paraguay, 187, 260
Aswan Dam, 7, 15, 134
Atomic science, 52, 98
Atwater, Helen, 41
Atwater, W. O., 40
Austin, Ambassador, 83
Australia
   assistance to Ceylon, 170
   contribution to FAO budget, 53
   food supplies, 30, 243
   land, arable, 32, 244
   life expectancy, 34
   mortality, infant, 34, 246
   textiles used, 34, 244

Austria, 228-229
  FAO-UNRRA projects, 73, 74
Autret, Marcel, 108
Aykroyd, W. R., 45, 61

Babylonia, 120
Baghdad, Iraq, 112
  Faculty of Medicine, 127
Bagoong, 218
Baguio, Philippines, 146, 255
Bailie, Joseph, 92
Bain, R. V. S., 174, 175
Bajpai, Sir Girja, 52, 60
Baluchistan, Pakistan, 118-119
Bandung, Java, 146
Bangalore, India, 146, 159, 257
Bangkok, Thailand, 78, 113, 146, 151, 154, 163, 255, 256, 260
Barbados, 213-214
Bareilly, India, 165
Barley breeding
  Iran, 123
  Near East Regional program, 104
Barreto, Lirica, 211
Barton family, USA, 18-27, 216
Barton, G. S. H., 229
Basra, Iraq, 124
Baurú, Brazil, 181, 182, 259
Bazaars, Egypt, 6
Becker, Gunther, 209
Bedan, 142
Bedouins, 123
Beehives, Egypt, 14
Beirut, Lebanon, 110, 112, 159, 254, 255, 257
El-Bekr, Abdul-Jabbar, 128
Belgian Congo, 90
  kwashiorkor, 109
Belgrade, Yugoslavia, 223, 262
Bell, William C., 91
Bender, W. H., 131
Bender Cassim, Somalia, 142
Bennett, Henry G., 96
Bergen, Norway, 217, 219
Beriberi, 41, 149
Berkeley, California, USA, 186
Berseem clover, 9, 10
Bertone, Eugene, 114, 202
Bilateral technical co-operation programs.
  See name of country or agency
Bilharzia, 14
Bisara, 9
Black, A. G., 234
Blom, Erik, 233
Bloudane, Syria, 159, 257
Blue Nile, 7, 136
Bock, Edwin A., 95
Boerma, A. H., 61

Bogotá, Colombia, 205, 224, 255
Bolivia, 205
Bombay Milk Scheme, 166-167
Bombay State, mechanization of fishing boats, 153
Bongo, 202
Borneo, Indonesia, 176
Botke, F. O., 167
Bottemanne, C. J., 198
Bottomley, N. M., 233
Boudreau, Frank G., 45, 48
Boyd-Orr, Lord, 44, 45, 46, 48, 70
  actions during Director-Generalship, 61-78
  Nobel Peace Prize, 70
  Quebec Conference speech, 59-60
  resignation as Director-General, 70, 79
  World Food Board proposals, 66-67
Brahmaputra River, 119
Brant, J. W., 171
Brantjes, J. M. J., 197
Brazil, 194-198
  American International Association, work of, 93
  contribution to FAO budget, 53
  forestry, 195-196
  land, arable, 32, 244
  land use, 196-197
  livestock, 183, 197-198
  See also Baurú, Campinas, Rio de Janeiro
Bread
  bakery improvement, Chile, 201
  Egypt, 8
  Near East, 103
British Colonial Office, 151
British Guiana, 214-215
British Ministry of Food, 62
Broadley, Sir Herbert, 61, 68
Brock, J. F., 108
Brodie, Jessie, 127
Brol, Nicolás, 186
Brown, A. L., 208
Bruce, Viscount Stanley M., 45, 46, 70
  chairman, Council of FAO, 70
  World Food Council proposals, 68
Brucellosis. *See* livestock disease
Brussels, Netherlands, 75, 225, 263
Buchanan, R. E., 64
Buck, R. L., 125
Budget of FAO, 53, 249
Buenos Aires, Argentina, 159, 180, 190, 193
Buffer funds, for development projects, 160
Buffer stocks. *See* food reserves
Burdette, R. F., 200
Burdon, David, 123, 127

INDEX

Burkenroad, M. D., 211
Burma, 145, 174-175. *See also* Rangoon
Burnet, Etienne, 45
Burns, L. Vinton, 212
Byrd, Donald, 142

Cadastral Surveys and Records of Rights in Land, 184
Cafeterias, India, 168
Cairo, Egypt, 6, 12, 78, 105, 109, 112, 133, 159, 161, 253, 254, 257, 258
California, University of, 186
Calories
   energy value of foods, 31
   FAO expert committee on, 30
   minimum subsistence levels, 30
Cambodia, 178
   fisheries products, 219
   shifting cultivation, 156
Camel thorn, 124, 129
Camels, use in Egypt, 10
Cameron, D. Roy, 133
Campbell, J. G., 174
Campinas, Brazil, 185, 259
Canada
   annual per caput income, 34, 246
   assistance to Pakistan, 120
   composition of diets, 31
   contribution to FAO budget, 53
   food supplies, 30, 243
   land, arable, 32, 244
   rinderpest vaccine research, 73
   wood pulp and pulp products used, 32
   See also Colombo Plan, Quebec
Capps, W. J., 205
Caracas, Venezuela, 109, 192, 261
Caraçu cattle, 183
Cardon, P. V., 72, 81
Carey, William, 91
Caribbean
   co-operatives, 194: participants in technical meeting, 261
   extension, agricultural, 188: participants in development center, 260
   home economics and nutrition, 193: participants in conference, 261
Caribbean Commission, 193, 194
Carlson, T. C., 128
Carobs, 132
Carocci-Buzi, Vittorio, 125
Carroll, H. T., 197, 203
Carslaw, R. M., 200
Case, Brayton, 92
Cassabia, 10
Casseres, W. G., 195
Castel Gandolfo, 92
Catacamas, Honduras, 208

Catalogues of Wheat and Rice Genetic Stocks, 75
Catholic Church
   international meetings on agriculture and rural life, 92
   technical co-operation work, 90-93
   See also Holy See
Cattle. *See* livestock
Caudri, L. W. D., 123
Census of agriculture. *See* world census of agriculture
Census methods, 113
Center for foot-and-mouth disease, Latin America, 182
Central America
   credit, agricultural, 186: participants in seminar, 260
   extension, agricultural, 188: participants in meetings, 260
   foot-and-mouth disease, 182
   grain storage, 76
   integration program, 194
   locust control, 189
   nutrition surveys, 192
Central Committee for Technical Assistance, Sweden, 97
Central Rice Research Institute, Cuttack, India, 147
Central Tractor Organization, India, 165
Cereals, potential production, 36. *See also* barley, corn, rice, wheat
Ceylon, 145, 168-171
   land, arable, 32, 244
   See also Colombo, Kandy, Nuwara Eliya
Chaldaea, 120
Chamoun, Alfred, 110
"Chance for Peace, The," speech by Dwight D. Eisenhower, 97-98
Chandresekhar, S., 34
Chanos (milkfish), 154
Chapingo, Mexico, 188
Charcoal-making, Iran, 125
Cheesman, W. J. W., 111
Chenopodium, 205
Chien, Tien-Ho, 78
Children, in Egypt, 3, 11, 14
Children's Fund. *See* United Nations Children's Fund
Chile, 198-201
   livestock feeding and milk production, 183
   See also Santiago, Valparaiso
China, 145
   contribution to FAO budget, 53
   Cornell University, work by, 93
   FAO-UNRRA projects, 73, 74
   missionaries, work by, 90, 92

China (*Continued*)
  rinderpest, extent and control, 73, 151
  withdrawal from FAO, 74
Chinese Farm Economy, 92
Christian Rural Fellowship, 92
Christiansborg Castle, 67
Chuharkana, Pakistan, 118-119
City-country relations in USA agriculture, 22, 25, 27
Clark, Noble, 61, 77
Clark, W. S., 91
Clements, F. W., 109
Clothing, 31-32
Coal and Steel Community, Europe, 228
Cocoa production, Liberia, 144
Coffee
  Ethiopia, production and processing, 138
  pulp, as livestock feed, 183
Coimbatore, India, 148, 256
College of Catering and Nutrition, India, 168
Colleges and universities, USA, technical co-operation activities, 93, 96
Colombia, 92, 205-206. *See also* Bogotá, Manizales
Colombo, Ceylon, 96
Colombo Plan for Co-operative Economic Development in South and Southeast Asia, 96
  assistance to Ceylon, 170, 171; International Rice Commission program, 148; Pakistan, 120
Colonial powers, technical co-operation, 90
Colonization
  Brazil, 196-197
  Ceylon, 169-170
  Honduras, 208
  Israel, 131
Combined Food Board, 62, 63
Commissão de Valorisacão de Amazonia, 195
Commission of Churches on International Affairs, Protestant, 92-93
Commission for Technical Cooperation in Africa South of the Sahara, 108
Committee on Commodity Problems, 72, 73, 135: membership, 251
Committee to Study World Commodity Problems, 71: membership, 250
Commodity proposals
  Committee on Commodity Problems, FAO, 72: membership, 251
  International Commodity Clearing House, 71
  World Food Board, 66
  See also surpluses.

Commonwealth Colombo Plan. *See* Colombo Plan
Communal Land Tenure, 184
Composition of diets, various countries, 31, 243
Condliffe, John B., 71
Condliffe Committee: membership, 250
  proposals of, 71
Conference of FAO (governing body), 54
  first session, 59-60: participants, 249
  second session, action on World Food Board proposals, 66, 67-68
  fifth session, action on ICCH proposals, 72
  sixth session, action to increase food production, 85: land tenure, 184
  seventh session, food situation, 85-86: European timber trends study, 222
Conference on Food and Agriculture. *See* Hot Springs Conference
Conference of Ministers of Agriculture of Central America and Mexico, 189
Constitution of FAO, 52, 53, 59
  Article 1, 248
Consultative Committee of the Colombo Plan, 96: membership, 253
Consultative Subcommittee on Surplus Disposal, 72, 73: membership, 251
Contributions to FAO, scale of, 53, 249
Cooke, Hedley V., 16
Co-operatives
  Afghanistan, karakul sheep, 115
  Asia and the Far East meetings, 161-162: participants, 258
  Caribbean meeting and training institute, 194: participants, 261
  Egypt, 17
  Greece, 231
  India, 162
  Iran, 124
  Iraq, 124-125
  Mexico, 207
  Near East training institute, 110-111: participants, 254
  Syria, 124
  Thailand, 173
Coordinator of Inter-American Affairs, Office of the, 94
Copenhagen, Denmark, 67, 75, 220, 262
Copenhagen Conference. *See* FAO Conference, second session
Cormorants, 190
Corn
  in Egyptian diet, 5, 8
  yields, Egypt and USA, 9
Corn, hybrid
  European program: development, value, cost, 222-223; FAO-UNRRA work,

INDEX

Corn, hybrid (*Continued*)
  European program (*Continued*)
    75; participants in breeders' meeting, 262
  Mexican program, 93
Cornell University, work in China, 92, 93
Cortes, 207
Costa Rica, 76, 183, 211. *See also* San José, Turrialba
Cotton
  Afghanistan, 116
  Egypt (yields), 9
  Ethiopia, 139
  Iran, 124
  Iraq, 124
  Syria, 123
  USA (yields), 9
  Yugoslavia, 235
Council of FAO, 68-70: membership, 70, 250
Country projects and programs of FAO
  Europe, 228-237
  Far East, 163-178
  Latin America, 194-215
  Near East and Africa, 114-144
  See also name of country
Credit, agricultural, 57, 187
  Central America, seminar, 186: handbook, 186-187, participants, 260
  Honduras, 208-209
  Indonesia, 176
  Iran, 124
  Iraq, 124-125
  Latin America, surveys and meetings, 186-187: manual, 187, participants, 260
  Nicaragua, 211
  Syria, 124
  USA (international meeting), 186
Crédito Agrícola Supervisado para la América Latina, 187
Criollos, 157
Crop production. *See name of crop*
Crossley, E. L., 133
Cuba, textiles used, 32, 244
Cummings, Ralph W., 213
Cummings, W. H., 78, 172
Cuttack, India, 147, 148, 256
Cuzco, Peru, 204
Cyprus, 107. *See also* Nicosia, Prodhromos
Czechoslovakia
  FAO-UNRRA projects, 73, 74
  withdrawal from FAO, 74
  See also Marianske-Lazne

Dairy farming, USA, 18-27
Dairy programs
  Greece, 231

Dairy programs (*Continued*)
  Iran, 122
  Nepal, 177-178
  Nicaragua, 210
  Yugoslavia, 236
Dairy technology meeting, 75
Damascus, Syria, 107, 121, 253
Danbom, E. A., 171
Danube-Tisa-Danube irrigation canal, Yugoslavia, 236
Dates
  Iraq, 124
  Saudi Arabia, 127-129
Datta, S., 151
Daubney, R. L., 166
de Barros, Henrique, 197
de Castro, Josué, elected FAO Council chairman, 70
de Coulon, Jacques, 197
Deficiency disease. *See* nutritional disease
Dehra Dun, forestry school, India, 168, 174
de la Warr, Lord, 46
Denmark
  annual per caput income, 34, 246
  land, arable and grazing, 32, 244
  See also Copenhagen
Depression, effect on USA agriculture, 22, 23, 44
Desert locusts. *See* locusts
de Sousa, João Gonçalves, 185
Determinants and Consequences of Population Trends, The, 35-36
Deyoe, Carroll, 121, 122
Dickinson, W. W., 116
Diet
  balancing rice diets, 149
  different levels of cost, 43
  Egyptian fellaheen, 8-9
  Far East, use of fish products, 218-219
  farm family in USA, 24
Dion, H. G., 205
Director-General of FAO, 59
  election of first, 60; second, 79; third, 81
Disarmament, relation to economic development, 97
Disease, livestock. *See* livestock disease
Disease, nutritional. *See* nutritional disease
Djakarta, Indonesia, 154
Dodd, Norris E.
  actions during Director-Generalship, 80-81
  annual report, 1951, 87
  election as Director-General, 79
  International Commodity Clearing House proposals, 71

Dodd, Norris E. (*Continued*)
  resignation as Director-General, 81
  statement on World Food Board proposals, 67
Dols, M. J., 135
Dominican Republic, 213
Doornberg, Gustaaf E., 144
Drainage, 57
  Egypt, 15
  Pakistan, 118
  Yugoslavia, 235-236
  See also irrigation
Dry farming, Ceylon, 169
Dung cakes, 4, 111
Dunn, Paul M., 200
Dura, 9
Duroc Jersey hogs, 19
Dutch East Indies, 175
Dutch Guiana (Surinam), 214-215

East African High Commission, 103
East Pakistan, 119-120
Economic Commission for Europe, UN, 228
  Timber Committee, 221, 222: membership, 262
Economic Commission for Latin America, UN, 194
  agricultural credit survey, 186
  fertilizers survey, 193
Economic Cooperation Administration, 95, 96, 253
Economic development, 56, 57, 58
  training institutes on economic development projects—Arab countries, Latin America, Mediterranean, 161: participants, 258
Economic and Social Council, UN, 66, 69, 87
  Expanded Technical Assistance Program, resolution, 83
  pulp and paper surveys, co-operation in, 181
Economics, agricultural
  Chile, 200
  Europe, 227-228
  Far East, 159-161
  Honduras, 208
  Israel, 132-133
  Jordan, 127
  publications of FAO, 228: *Monthly Bulletin of Agricultural Economics and Statistics*, 113
  Thailand, 174
  Turkey, 234
Ecuador, 201-203
  grain storage, 76
  See also Quito

Edgar, G., 175
Education
  agricultural, USA, 21, 22
  Egypt, 13, 14
  See also fundamental education centers
Edwards, J. P., 163
Eggs
  in foot-and-mouth disease vaccine production, 224
  in rinderpest vaccine production, 150, 151
  See also poultry
Egypt, 3-17, 133-136
  ancient civilization, 6
  Arab States fundamental education center, 135
  co-operatives, 17
  crop production, 9
  diet of fellaheen, 5, 8, 9
  diseases, 14
  economic progress, 16
  education, 13, 28
  fly problem, 15
  houses, description, 3-4
  inheritance customs, 15
  irrigation, 7, 11, 15, 134
  land, arable, 32, 244
  land tenure, 3, 5, 6, 16-17: land reform decree, 241-242
  life expectancy, 15
  milk mission, FAO, 135-136
  mortality, infant, 9, 34, 246
  Nile River, 6-7, 10, 15
  rice production methods, 133-134
  skim milk, dried, 135-136
  Social Affairs, Ministry of, 14
  textiles used, 32, 244
  tools, 9, 10
  village, description of, 3-4
  water, use of, 10-12
  welfare centers, 13-15
  wheat breeding (regional project), 105
  See also Cairo
Eijkman, 41
Eisenhower, Dwight D., 97-98
El Salvador, 209-210
  grain storage, 76
  livestock feeding, 183
Electricity on USA farms, 24
Elizalde, Joaquin, 146
Emergency Economic Committee for Europe, 62
Emergency food reserve proposals, 72
Emsbo, Paul, 210
Energy (food), needs of human beings, 40
Energy (mechanical), 33, 245

INDEX

England, 34. *See also* United Kingdom, London, Reading, Weybridge
Escuela Agricola Panamericana, 93
Ethiopia, 7, 15, 136-140
  annual per caput income, 34, 246
  FAO-UNRRA projects, 73-74
  Oklahoma Agricultural and Mechanical College (USA), work in, 93
  Sweden, work in, 97
Euphrates River, 120
Europe, 216-237: regional projects, 217-228, country projects, 228-237
  agricultural research, 226-227
  background for FAO work, 216-217
  Coal and Steel Community, 228
  corn, hybrid, program, 75, 222-223: participants in meeting, 262
  economic studies, 227-228
  extension, agricultural and home economics, 225-226: countries surveyed, 263, participants in meetings and training institutes, 263
  fall webworm, 225
  fisheries, 217-220
    Fishing Boat Congress, 220: participants, 262
    General Fisheries Council for the Mediterranean, 219
    international statistics meeting, 220: participants, 262
  Food and Agricultural Programs and Outlook, Regional Meeting on, 159: participants, 257
  food supplies, prewar, 30
  foot-and-mouth disease, 223-225: membership of European Commission for the Control of Foot-and-Mouth Disease, 263
  forestry, 78, 220-222
    European Forestry Commission, 221-222: membership, 262
    Marianske-Lazne timber conference, 221: participants, 262
    Study of European Timber Trends and Prospects, 221-222
    Timber Committee (ECE), 221-222: membership, 262
  Green Pool, 228
  Land and Water Use and Conservation, Working Party on, 227
  livestock feeding, 226
  mountain peasants, problems of, 227
  olive-fly control, 225: participants in meeting, 263
  postwar food shortage, 63
  Southern and Eastern Europe, conditions and needs, 84-85

Europe (*Continued*)
  statistical training institutes, 112-113: participants, 254
European Agriculture: A Statement of Problems, 227
European Association for Animal Production, 226
European Commission for the Control of Foot-and-Mouth Disease, 224-225: membership, 263
European Committee on Agriculture, milk-butterfat recording, 226
European Confederation of Agriculture, 227
European Forestry Commission, 221-222
European Timber Trends and Prospects, Study of, 221-222
Ewert, W. F., 200
Executive Committee, FAO, 60, 68: membership, 249
Expanded Technical Assistance Program
  allocation of funds, 84
  briefing of experts by FAO, 89
  contributions for first financial period, 251-252
  co-ordination among agencies, 88-89
  ECOSOC resolution, 83
  operation of program, 87
  principles of the program, 88
  proposal by Harry S. Truman, 83
  relation to regular program in FAO, 88
  responsibilities of recipient countries, 88
  See also technical cooperation
Experiment stations, 21, 40, 124
Extension, agricultural and home economics
  Arab States fundamental education center, 135
  Brazil, 197
  Caribbean discussion meeting, 188: participants, 260
  Central American meetings and training institutes, 188: participants, 260
  Ceylon, 171
  Europe, meetings and surveys, 75, 225-226: participants, 262
  Haiti, 212
  Indonesia, 176
  international training institutes, 225-226: participants, 263
  Iran, 124
  Iraq, 124
  Latin America, meetings and training institutes, 187-188: participants, 260
  Liberia, 144
  Mexico, 207

Extension (*Continued*)
  Near East, development meeting, 109-110: participants, 254
  Peru, 204
  relation to supervised agricultural credit, 187
  Saudi Arabia, 129, 130
  Thailand, 174
  USA, 21, 57

Faiss, Wolfgang, 116
Fall webworm, Europe, 225; Austria, 229; Yugoslavia, 235
Family Planning Association of India, 34
Fanjul G., J. Roberto, 186
FAO, selection of name, 53-54
FAO Council. *See* Council of FAO
FAO-UNRRA agricultural advisory projects, 73-76
FAO-WHO Joint Expert Committee on Nutrition, 108: membership, 254
Far East, 145-178: regional projects, 145-163, country projects, 163-178
  composition of diets, 31
  conditions and needs, 84-85
  co-operatives, 161-162: participants in meetings, 258
  economic development projects, training institute on, 161: participants, 258
  fisheries, 151-155
    fish culture training institutes, 154
    Indo-Pacific Fisheries Council, 152, 154: membership, 256
    marketing, 154: participants in training institute, 256
    mechanization, 153-154
    statistics training institute, 154: participants, 256
  Food and Agricultural Programs and Outlook, Regional Meetings on, 159-161: participants, 257
  food shortage, postwar, 63
  food supplies, 30, 31, 159
  forestry, 162-163
    Commission for Asia and the Pacific, 163: membership, 258
    mechanical logging training institute, 163: participants, 259
    pulp and paper surveys, 181
    timber grading school, 162-163: participants, 258
  grain storage, 76
  land problems center, 184: participants, 260
  land utilization, 155-157: participants in meeting, 256

Far East (*Continued*)
  livestock production, 157-158: participants in meeting, 257
  regional office, FAO, 78, 172
  rice, 145-149
    International Rice Commission, 146-148: membership, 146
    rice breeding training institute, 148: participants, 256
    rice meeting (Baguio), 145-146: participants, 255
    rice study group, 145: participants, 255
    soil fertility training institute, 148: participants, 256
  rinderpest, 149-151
    Asia and Far East meeting, 151: participants, 256
    vaccine production training institute, 151: participants, 256
  shifting cultivation, 155-156
  statistical training institutes, 112-113: participants, 254-255
  See also International Rice Commission
Farm life, USA, 18-27, 28, 29
Farmers, percentage of population in various countries, 33, 245
Farmers' Union (USA), 22
Farouky, S. T., 133, 170
Fass, 9
Feddan, 15, 17, 241
Feeding livestock. *See* livestock
Fellaheen, The, 15, 90
Fellaheen of Egypt, life of, 3-17
Feluccas, 10
Fenugreek, 8
Fertilizers
  Egypt, 10
  guano, 190
  International Rice Commission, working party on, 146, 148: participants in training institute, 256
  Latin American survey, 193
  USA, 24
Fezzan, Libya, 140
Fiat Panis, 62
Fifty Years of Technical Assistance, 95
Finland, 229-231
Finn, D. B., 61
Finnish Agricultural Organization Committee, 230
Firestone Rubber Company, 143
Fish
  as protein food, 152
  flour, supplement to diet, 201
  hake, 200-201
  herring, 219
  potential production, 36

INDEX 287

Fish (*Continued*)
  processing in Asia, 218-219
  supplies in Equatorial belt, 152
  See also fisheries and fish culture
Fish culture
  Dominican Republic, 213
  Far East, 154
  Haiti, 212
  India, 167-168
  Israel, 133
  Java, 154
  Thailand, 173
  Yugoslavia, 237
  See also fisheries
Fisheries
  Brazil, 198
  Chile, 200-201
  Ecuador, 202-203
  Europe, 217-220
    General Fisheries Council for the Mediterranean, 219
    herring processing and marketing, 219
    Interim Committee on Fish Handling and Processing, 218
  Far East, 151-155
    Indo-Pacific Fisheries Council, 152, 154-155: membership, 256
    marketing institute for Far East, 154: participants, 256
    measures for development, 152, 153
  Finland, 230
  India, 154, 167
  Iran, 126
  Iraq, 126
  Israel, 133
  Latin America, 190-191
    report on present status and prospects of fisheries, 190
    training institutes, 190-191: participants, 191, 261
  Liberia, 143
  Libya, 141
  Panama, 211
  Saudi Arabia, 130
  Somalia, 142
  Yugoslavia, 237
  See also fish, fish culture, fishing boats, fisheries statistics
Fisheries statistics
  Indo-Pacific training institute, 154: participants, 256
  international meeting, Denmark, 220: participants, 262
  publications by FAO, 220
Fishermen, need for training, 153-154
Fishing boats
  important characteristics, 220

Fishing boats (*Continued*)
  International Fishing Boat Congress, 220: participants, 262
  mechanization
    Ceylon, 171-172
    Far East, 153-154
    India, 167
    Israel, 133
    Somalia, 142
  need for research and testing, 220
FitzGerald, Dennis A., 63
Flax, Ethiopia, 139
Florence, Italy, 75, 225, 263
Flores, Edmundo, 185
Food and Agricultural Programs and Outlook, Regional Meetings on, 159-161: participants, 257-258
Food composition, 39-40
Food consumption
  United Kingdom, 44
  United States of America, 44
  in various countries, 31, 243
Food, Health, and Income, 44
Food and Nutrition Board, USA, 43, 45, 48
Food and population, 34-35
Food preservation
  fish products, Far East, 218
  India, 168
  Yugoslavia, 236
Food, relation to health, 40, 41, 42, 43, 46
Food reserves (buffer stocks), 50, 68, 72
Food situation. *See* world food situation
Food Stamp Plan, USA, 23
Food supplies
  postwar, 30, 31
  prewar, 30
  See also World Food Survey
Foot-and-mouth disease. *See* livestock disease
Ford Foundation, 91, 93, 164
Foreign Assistance Act, USA, 95
Foreign Operations Administration, USA, 94, 96, 120
Forestry
  Austria, 228-229
  Brazil, 195-196
  Burma, 174-175
  Ceylon, 171
  Chile, 200
  Colombia, 206
  Ethiopia, 140
  Europe, 78, 220-222
    Forestry Commission, 221-222: membership, 262
    Marianske-Lazne timber conference, 221: participants, 262

Forestry (*Continued*)
  Study of European Timber Trends and Prospects, 221-222
  Far East, 162-163
    Commission for Asia and the Pacific, 163: membership, 258
    mechanical logging training institute, 163: participants, 259
    Mysore meeting, 163: participants, 258
    timber grading school, 162-163: participants, 258
  forest grazing, 106, 111, 125. *See also* grassland
  Guatemala, 209
  Haiti, 212-213
  Honduras, 209
  Iceland, 232
  inclusion in FAO charter, 111
  India, 168
  Indonesia, 176
  International Chestnut Commission, 222
  International Poplar Commission, 222
  Iran, 125-126
  Iraq, 126
  Israel, 133
  Latin America, 78, 179-180
    Forestry and Forest Products Commission, 179-180
    pulp and paper surveys, 180-181: countries surveyed, 259
    Teresopolis conference, 179: participants, 259
  Libya, 141
  Mediterranean forestry subcommission, 222
  Mexico, 207
  Near East, 111-112: participants in conference, 254
  Paraguay, 204
  Syria, 126
  Thailand, 173
  Yugoslavia, 237
Foulon, L. A., 197
4-H Clubs, 21, 25
France, contribution to FAO budget, 53
  See also Marseilles and Paris
Fraser-Brunner, A. F., 142
Freedom from want, 54, 55
Freeze-drying rinderpest vaccine, 150
Freezing and refrigeration of food, meeting, 75
French, J. J., 204
Frenkel, H. S., 224
Fridthjof, John, 201
Fritzle, Carl, 206
Fronda, F. N., 174

Functions of FAO, 53, 248
Fundamental education centers
  Arab States, Egypt, 135
  Ceylon, 171
  Haiti, 212
  Latin America, Mexico, 207
  Liberia, 144
  Thailand, 174
Funk, Casimir, 41

Gachot, René, 195
Gal Oya River Valley, 170
Galapagos Islands, 202
Gallant, M. N., 195
Gambia meeting on protein malnutrition, 108-109
Gamoosa. See water buffalo
Ganges River, 119
Garden of Eden, 120
Garum, 219
General Assembly, UN, 62, 87
General Fisheries Council for the Mediterranean, 219
Geneva, Switzerland, 46, 70, 73
Geneva Conference. *See* Conference of FAO, third session
Germany, 47
Gilfillan, Donald W., 201
Goats, use in rinderpest vaccine production, 150-151
Goiter, 39, 192
Gonzalez, Carlos, 203
Gopalaswami, R. A., 163
Gounelle, Hugues, 127
Grahame, Cunningham, 90
Grain storage, 75, 76
Grasshoppers. *See* locusts
Grassland
  Brazil, 183
  British Guiana, 214-215
  Chile, 200
  conservation functions, 105-106
  India, 166
  Iran, 122
  Israel, 132
  Mediterranean program, 105-106: training institute, 106
    Working Party on Mediterranean Pasture and Fodder Development, 106
  Mexico, 207-208
  Near East program, 106
  Nicaragua, 183
  pasture management training institute, Argentina, 183
  Syria, 122
  Yugoslavia, 236
  See also land, grazing

INDEX 289

Grazing land. *See* grassland and land, grazing
Greece, 64-66, 231
  American Farm School, 91
  FAO mission, 62, 64-66: membership, 250
  FAO-UNRRA projects, 73, 74
  nutrition work, 65-66
  See also Salonika
Green Pool, Europe, 228
Gregory, T. S., 233
Griffiths, D. T., 207
Grijns, 41
Grosse Isle, rinderpest vaccine research, 73, 151
Gualberto, Virgilio, 179
Guano, 13, 190
Guarani Indians, Paraguay, 90
Guatemala, 209
  grain storage, 76
  See also Guatemala City
Guatemala City, 186, 192, 260
Guayaquil, Ecuador, 202, 203

Haakon, King of Norway, 96
Habib-Ayrout, Father Henry, 15, 90
Hague, The, Netherlands, 75, 217, 225, 263
Haidari, Darwish, 52, 124
Haifa Institute of Technology, 132
Haig, E. F. G., 124
Haile Selassie, Emperor of Ethiopia, 136
Haiti, 211-213
  grain storage, 76
Hama, Syria, 123
Hammon, J. B., 197
Handbook on Sampling Techniques, 113
Hansen, J. C., 165
Hardy, Evan, 169
Hare, H. R., 125
Harris, F. S., 64
Hartmann, Robert, 116
Hatch, Spencer, 92
Hatch Act, USA, 21
Haugesund, Norway, 217
Headquarters, FAO, transfer to Rome, 79-80
Health centers, Egypt, 14-15
Health Committee, League of Nations, 45
Health Section, League of Nations, 45
Heat tolerance of animals, 157-158
Hefnawy, M. T., 78, 89, 133
Helsinki, Finland, 231
Hemisphere Solidarity Conference, 94
Hemorrhagic septicemia, vaccine development, 174
Herring, 217-219

Hides and skins
  Afghanistan, 115
  Ethiopia, 137
  India, 167
  Libya, 141
Higginbottom, Sam, 91
Hilary, Sir Edmund, 177
Hiloue, Abdul Hannan, 111
Himalaya Mountains, 177
Hindu Kush Mountains, 115
Hiroshima, Japan, 52
Hirst, Henry, 171
History of the League of Nations, 44, 46
Hoek, F. H., 167
Hofstede, A. E., 133
Hofuf, Saudi Arabia, 129
Hog-dairy farm, USA, 18-27
Hogan, T. T., 143
Hogg, Peter, 214
Holy See, The
  consultative status with FAO, 92-93
  international meetings on agriculture and rural life, 92
  See also Catholic Church
Home economics
  Barbados, 214
  Caribbean conference, surveys, workshop, 193: participants, 261
  Egypt, 135
  Ethiopia, 140
  extension, 187, 225-226
  Iraq, 126-127
  Israel, 133
  Latin America, 191-193
  Mexico, 207
  Near East and Africa, 109
  Syria, 126-127
  Yugoslavia, 237
Homestead Act, USA, 21
Honduras, 208-209
  Escuela Agricola Panamericana, 93
  grain storage, 76
  locust outbreak, 189
Hong Kong, 153, 154, 256
Hookworm, 14
Hot Springs, Virginia, USA, 49, 247
Hot Springs Conference, 49, 50, 51: participants, 247
House, Charles and Ann, 91
House, John Henry, 91
Houses
  Egypt, 3-4
  Syria, 126
Houthuis, N. J. J., 122
Hsia, Tsong-Kiu, 116
Huber, Alfred, 168
Hungary, FAO-UNRRA projects, 73

Huri, 142
Hybrid corn. *See* corn, hybrid
Hydroelectric power, Aswan Dam, 15

Ibadan, Nigeria, 255
Iceland, 231-233
   mortality, infant, 34
Imperial Agricultural College, Japan, 91
Imperial Ethiopian College of Agricultural and Mechanical Arts, 138
Implements. *See* tools.
Improvement of Agricultural Extension Services in European Countries, 226
Incentives to increase agricultural production, 160-161
Income, annual per caput, in various countries, 34, 246
India, 93, 145, 163-168
   Agri-horticultural Society, 91
   All-India Conference of Family Planning Association, 34
   contribution to FAO budget, 53
   fish-spawn industry, 154
   Five-Year Plan, 164
   mortality, infant, 34, 246
   Institute of Population Studies, 34
   key village plan, 158, 166
   life expectancy, 34
   missionaries, work by, 91
   Norway, work by, 96-97
   Planning Commission, 164
   rice, work with International Rice Commission, 145, 147, 148
   rinderpest vaccine research, 150, 166
   See also Bangalore, Bombay, Coimbatore, Cuttack, Dehra Dun, Izatnagar, Lucknow, New Delhi, Trivandrum
Indian Society of Agricultural Statistics, 113
Indica rice, 147
Indochina, 145
Indo-Pacific Fisheries Council, 78, 152-155: members, 256
   technical discussions, 154
Indonesia, 145, 175-177
   annual per caput income, 34, 246
   fish culture, Java, 154
   textiles used, 32, 244
   See also Bandung, Djakarta, Java
Indus River, 117, 118
Industrial development
   need for, 58
   relation to agricultural development, 160
Industry, relation to agriculture, USA, 20, 26-27

Infant mortality. *See* mortality, infant
Infestation of stored grains, 75
Inheritance customs, Egypt, 15
Insect control
   cotton pests, Syria, 123
   fall webworm: Austria, 229, Europe, 225, Yugoslavia, 235
   locusts: Central America, 188-190, Near East, 102-103
   olive-fly, 225
Insein, Burma, 175
Insfran Guerreros, G., 209, 211
Institute of Geography and Statistics, Brazil, 195
Institute of Inter-American Affairs, 94, 187, 188
Institute of Nutrition for Central America and Panama, 192
Inter-American Anti-Locust Committee, 190
Inter-American Institute of Agricultural Sciences, 94, 181
   extension training, 187-188
   pasture management training institute, 183
Inter-relationship between Agrarian Reform and Agricultural Development, 184
Interim Commission on Food and Agriculture, 51-59
   membership, 51-52, 247
   panels, 52, 247-248
   report on *The Work of FAO,* 54-59
   reports to governments, 54
   technical reports, 54
International Association of Agricultural Missions, 92
International Bank for Reconstruction and Development, 66
   aid to Thailand, 172
   IBRD-FAO missions
     British Guiana, 214
     Chile, 199
     Nicaragua, 210
     Surinam, 214-215
     Syria, 121
     Turkey, 233-234
     Uruguay, 203
International Chestnut Commission, 222
International Committee of Coordination for Locust Control, 189
International Commodity Clearing House, 71-72
International Council for the Exploration of the Sea, 218
International Emergency Food Committee, 63

INDEX 291

International Emergency Food Council, 63-64: membership, 250
International Institute of Agriculture, 54, 78, 82
International Labour Organisation, 110, 135, 162, 184, 207
International Office of Epizootics, 182, 224
International Poplar Commission, 222
International Rice Commission, 70, 145-149
  fertilizers
    training institute on soil fertility, 148: participants, 256
    working party on, 146, 148
  membership, 146
  rice breeding
    hybridization, 147-148
    training institute, 148: participants, 256
    working party on, 146-148
  See also rice
International Trade Organization (proposed), 66, 69, 72
International Wheat Council, 69
Investment, in agricultural expansion, 160
Iowa, hog-dairy farm, 18-27
Iowa State College Press, 113
Iran, Iraq, Syria, 120-127
  crop production, 123-124
  forestry, 125-126
  livestock production, 122
  Utah State Agricultural College, work by, 93
Iraq, Iran, Syria, 120-127
  co-operatives, 124-125
  date processing, 124
  extension, agricultural, 124
  forestry, 126
  home economics, 126-127
  machinery, 125
  research, agricultural, 124
  water supplies, 123
  wood pulp and pulp products, 32
  See also Baghdad
Irrigation
  Brazil, 197
  Ecuador, 201
  Egypt, 7, 11, 15, 134
  India, 164-165
  Iran, 123
  Iraq, 123
  Pakistan, East, 119-120
  Pakistan, West, 117-119
  relation to economic development, 57
  Saudi Arabia, 129-130
  Syria, 123
  Thailand, 77

Irrigation (*Continued*)
  Yugoslavia, 235-236
Israel, 131-133
Istanbul, Turkey, 105, 253
Italy
  FAO-UNRRA projects, 73, 74
  land, arable, 32, 244
  rice yields, 9
  See also Florence, Milan, Rome
Izatnagar, India, 151, 256

Jamaica, 109, 188, 192, 213-214
  livestock breeding and milk production, 183
  See also Kingston
Jamaica-Hope, breed of dairy cattle, 183
James, Preston, 203
Japan, 145
  fisheries, 151
  land, arable, 32, 244
  missionaries, work by, 91
  rice yields, 9
  source of silkworm eggs and mulberry trees, 116
  wood pulp and pulp products, 32
  See also Hiroshima, Sapporo, Tokyo
Japonica rice, 147
Java, 109, 176
Jedda, Saudi Arabia, 128, 129, 130
Jenkins, Merle T., 223
Jensen, E. A., 231
Jepsen, Aage, 133
Jerusalem, Israel, 133
Jesuits, early work in Paraguay, 90
Jezireh, Syria, 125
Jhansi, India, 165
Jimma Agricultural College, Ethiopia, 138
Johnson, W. Fred, 130
Joint FAO-WHO Expert Committee on Nutrition, 108: membership, 254
Jones, J. M., 202
Jones, Judge Marvin H., 50
Joosten, H. J. L., 208
Jordan, 127. See also Amman
Jorgensen, R. L., 122

Ka, the, 6
Kabul, Afghanistan, 116
Kanagasundram, K., 155
Kandy, Ceylon, 258
Kano, S. I., 175
Kapi, 218
Karachi, Pakistan, 117
Karakul sheep. See livestock and sheep
Karst area, Yugoslavia, 236
Karunakar, P. D., 148
Kashmir, 117, 118

Kasikit, Luang Suwan, 173
Katmandu, Nepal, 177
Keh, Kintson, 116
Keith, H. G., 163
Kellogg, C. E., 105
Kelton, I. W., 175
Kenya, 7, 151
    rinderpest vaccine research, 150
    See also Nairobi
Kepong, Malaya, 162, 163, 258
Key village plan, India, 158, 166
Khairpur State, Pakistan, 118
Khamsin, 12
Kharegat, Sir Pheroz, 78
El-Kharj farm, Saudi Arabia, 129
Khartoum, Sudan, 7
Khoury-Schmitz, Mona, 133, 135
Khyber Pass, 114
Kimmel, D. E., 144
Kingston, Jamaica, 260
Klauss, D. W., 131
Kolb, J. H., 197
Konnerup, Nels, 137, 205
Kopf, Kenneth, 124
Korea, 178
Kotok, E. I., 200
Kristensen, M. O., 167
Kuala Lumpur, Malaya, 163
Kuhn, Ferdinand, 164
Kunduz, Afghanistan, 116
Kushr, 9
Kushtia, Pakistan, 120
Kwashiorkor. *See* nutritional disease

Labarthe, Enrique, 188
Labor efficiency, USA agriculture, 20, 21, 23, 24, 26, 27
LaGrande, Florence M., 202
LaGuardia, Fiorello H., 67
Lahore, Pakistan, 161, 258
Lambert, W. V., 124
Lancaster, J. E., 174
Land, arable, in various countries, 15, 32, 244
Land, grazing
    Denmark, 32
    Mexico, 32
    See also grassland
Land reform. *See* land tenure
Land resources, in various countries, 244
Land settlement. *See* colonization
Land tenure, 57, 85, 183-186
    Egypt, 3, 5, 6, 15, 16-17: land reform decree, 241-242
    FAO Conference action, 184
    International Conference on Land Problems, USA, 184
    Latin America, 185

Land tenure (*Continued*)
    meeting of UN agencies, 184
    regional seminars, FAO
        Far East, 184: participants, 260
        Latin America, 184-186: participants, 259
        Near East (proposed), 184
    reports by FAO, 184
Land Utilization in China, 92
Land utilization in the tropics, meeting on, 155-156: participants, 256-257
    See also shifting cultivation
Land and Water Use and Conservation, European Working Party on, 227
Latakia, Syria, 126
Lateef, N. A., 130
Latifundia, 185
Latimer, Hugh, 46
Latin America, 179-215: regional projects, 179-194, country projects, 194-215
    composition of diets, 31
    credit, agricultural, meetings, 186-187: participants, 260
    economic development projects, training institute, 161, 193: participants, 258
    extension services and training of workers, 187-188: participants in meetings, 260
    fertilizer survey, 193
    fisheries, 190-191: participants in training centers, 191, 261
    Food and Agricultural Programs and Outlook, Regional Meetings on, 193-194: participants, 257
    food supplies, prewar, 30
    forestry, 78, 179-180
        participants in Teresopolis conference, 259
        pulp and paper surveys, 181: countries surveyed, 259
        research and training institute, 180
    grain storage, 76, 193
    home economics, 191-193
    land tenure, 183-186
        participants in seminar, 259
    livestock disease, 182-183
    livestock production, 181-183
        Latin American Livestock Commission (proposed), 181
        meetings, summary of discussion, 182-183: participants, 259
    locust control, 188-190
    milk production, distribution, and utilization training institute, 183: participants, 259
missionaries, work of, 90

INDEX 293

Latin America (*Continued*)
  national nutrition committees meeting, 46
  nutrition, 108, 109, 191-193
    regional nutrition conferences, 191-192: participants, 261
  pasture management training institute, 183
  regional offices, FAO, 78, 195, 200, 207
  statistical training institutes, 112-113: participants, 254, 255
Latin American Catholic Conference on Rural Life Problems, 92
Lavoisier, 40
League of Nations, 39
  food, agriculture, and nutrition work, 44-47, 48
  Mixed Committee on the Problem of Nutrition, 46
Lee, D. H. K., 157
Legislation, agricultural, USA, 22, 23
Leloup, Marcel, 61
Lepkovsky, Samuel, 132
LeRiche, J. E., 115
Libda, 14
Liberia, 142-144
Libya, 140-141
Life expectancy
  Egypt, 15
  in various countries, 34
Ligutti, Monsignor Luigi, 92, 103
Lima, Peru, 180, 188, 260
Lin, S. Y., 212, 213
Lind, 39
Ling, S. W., 173
Linville, Francis, 73
Livestock
  artificial insemination
    meeting in Milan, 75
    India, 158, 166
    Luxembourg, 233
  breeding
    Brazil, 183
    Jamaica, 183
    Nepal, 178
    in tropics, meeting on, 157: participants, 257
  criollos, 157
  feeding
    Afghanistan, 115
    Brazil, 183
    Chile, 183
    El Salvador, 183
    Europe, 226: meeting in Zurich, 75
    in tropics, 158
  heat tolerance, 157-158
  potential production, 36

Livestock (*Continued*)
  production
    Brazil, 197-198
    Burma, 175
    Ceylon, 171
    Chile, 199
    Colombia, 206
    Ecuador, 201
    European Association for Animal Production, 226
    Far East, 157-158
    India, 166-167
    Iran, 122
    Israel, 132, 133
    Latin America, meetings, 181-183: participants, 259
    Syria, 122
    Uruguay, 203
  See also dairy, hides and skins, livestock disease, poultry, sheep
Livestock disease
  Brazil, 197-198
  Brucellosis, 19, 197
  Burma, 175
  Ceylon, 171
  contagious bovine pleuropneumonia, Portugal, 233
  Ethiopia, 137
  foot-and-mouth disease
    Austria, 229
    avianized (egg) vaccine, 224
    Brazil, 183
    Colombia, 205-206, 224
    European program, 223-225: membership of European Commission for Control of Foot-and-Mouth Disease, 263
    Frenkel method of vaccine production, 224
    Greece, 231
    Latin America, 182
    Mexico-USA, 94
    Near East, 107: participants in special meeting, 253
    Organization of American States and Pan-American Sanitary Bureau, work of, 182
    Syria, 107
    Turkey, 234
  hemorrhagic septicemia, Thailand, 174
  Honduras, 209
  India, 166
  Iran, 122
  Iraq, 122
  meeting on animal health, London, 151
  meeting on control of animal diseases, Warsaw, 75

Livestock disease (*Continued*)
  Near East Meeting on Animal Health, 107: participants, 253-254
  Nicaragua, 210
  rinderpest, 73, 149-151
    Asia and Far East conference, 151: participants, 256
    China, 73, 151
    Ethiopia, 74, 137
    India, 166
    Nairobi conference, 151: participants, 256
    Thailand, 77
    vaccine production methods, 150
  Syria, 122
  Thailand, 174
  virus vaccine manufacture training institute, 151: participants, 256
  Yugoslavia, 236
  See also poultry, sheep production
Lloyd, William, 173
Locusts
  Anti-Locust Research Center, 102
  Arabian peninsula, outbreak, 102
  British Desert Locust Control, 102, 103
  Central American control program, 189
  control methods, 103
  Honduras outbreak, 189
  Inter-American Anti-Locust Committee, South America, 190
  Latin American control program, 188-190
  life cycle, 188-190
  Moroccan, in Algeria, 103, 189
  Near East control program, 102-103
  South American control program, 189-190
  swarm behavior, 102
  Technical Advisory Committee on Desert Locust Control, FAO, 102-103
Logging
  demonstration center, Brazil, 196
  India, 168
  See also forestry
London, England, 45, 62, 102
Louwes, S. L., 61, 78
Lovald, R. A., 200
Lowdermilk, Walter G., 131
Lubin, David, Memorial Library, 78
Lucknow, India, 158, 161, 165, 168, 256, 258
Luxembourg, 233

Mabee, Oliver S., 133, 135
MacArthur, J. A. B., 122
McDougall, F. L., 45, 46, 48, 49, 54, 61, 62, 63, 75, 82
Mace, Brice, 231

McGill Terrace, 52
McGrath, K. P., 195
Machinery, agricultural, 57
  Ceylon, 170
  India, 165-166
  Iraq, 125
  rice production and processing, 148: Thailand, 172
  USA, 20, 21, 22, 23, 24
  Yugoslavia, 236
MacPherson, D. A., 115
MacRae, Ian D., 166
Macy, Josiah, Jr., Foundation, **192**
Madison, Wisconsin, USA, 184
Madura, 176
Maize. *See* corn
Malaya, 145, 153, 178. *See also* Kepong and Kuala Lumpur
Maliepaard, C. H., 127
Malthus, Thomas Robert, 34, 35
Mam, 218
Managua, Nicaragua, 189, 210
Manizales, Colombia, 92
Manson, P. W., 132
Manual of Field Studies on the Heat Tolerance of Domestic Animals, 157-158
Marbial Valley, Haiti, 212
Marianske-Lazne, Czechoslovakia, 221
Marketing
  Chile, 200
  fish marketing, Europe, 217-219
  fish marketing institute, Far East, 154: participants, 256
  Israel, 133
  Yugoslavia, 236-237
Markley, K. S., 78
Marriage of health and agriculture, 45
Marseilles, France, 109, 254
Marshall, Gen. George C., 95
Marshall Plan, 65, 95
Maryknoll Order, work in Latin America, 90
Maternity clinic, Egypt, 14
Mecca, Saudi Arabia, 4, 128
Mechanical logging training institute, 163: participants, 259
Mechanization of agriculture. *See* machinery, agricultural
Mechanization of fishing boats. *See* fishing boats
Medellin, Colombia, 206
Medina, Saudi Arabia, 128
Mediterranean
  economic development projects, training institute, 161: participants, 258
  forestry subcommission, 222
  General Fisheries Council for the Mediterranean, 219

INDEX
295

Mediterranean (*Continued*)
  grassland program and conference, 105-106
  olive-fly control, 225: participants in meeting, 263
  See also Near East and Africa
Mehta, V. L., 161
Membership of FAO, 54, 88
Mesopotamia, 120
Mexico, 191, 206-208
  Agriculture, Department of, 93
  corn, hybrid, 93
  Corn Commission, 93
  foot-and-mouth disease, 94
  grain storage, 76
  grassland, 32, 207-208
  life expectancy, 34
  mortality, infant, 34, 246
  Rockefeller Foundation, work by, 93
  Statistics, Bureau of, 112
  See also Chapingo, Mexico City, Tapachula
Mexico City, 78, 112, 207, 254, 261
Miami, Florida, USA, 220, 262
Midrisha, Israel, 132
Miedler, K. A., 175
Milam, Ava B., 126, 127
Milan, Italy, 75, 226
Miles, Wayne, 132, 200
Milford, Utah, USA, 115
Milk
  Brazil, 183
  Ceylon, 171
  Costa Rica, 211
  Greece, 231
  Honduras, 209
  India, 166-167
  Iran, 122
  Jamaica, 183
  Mexico, 208
  milk-butterfat recording, 226
  mission to Egypt, 135-136
  Nicaragua, 211
  production, handling, processing, training institute, 183: participants, 259
  production in various countries, 183
  skim milk, dried
    Bombay Milk Scheme, 166-167
    Egypt, 135-136
Milkfish (*Chanos*), 154
Minerals in nutrition, 39, 41, 42
Minifundia, 185
Missionaries, technical co-operation work, 90-93
Mistikawy, A. E. M., 123
Mixed Committee on the Problem of Nutrition, League of Nations, 46
Modernization of agriculture, USA, 20-27

Moggio, Ethiopia, 139
Montevideo, Uruguay, 159, 191, 193, 194, 257, 261
Monthly Bulletin of Agricultural Economics and Statistics, 113
Moomaw, Ira W., 92
Morales Agacino, E., 189
Morrill Land-Grant College Act, USA, 21
Morrison, H. M., 210
Mortality, infant
  Egypt, 9, 15
  in various countries, 34, 246
Mott, John R., 92
Mt. Annapurna, 177
Mt. Everest, 177, 178
Mountain peasants, problems of, 227
Murcia Camacho, Efraim, 144
Murphy, R. S., 131
Mutual Security Act, USA, 96
Mutual Security Agency, USA, 96, 225
Mysore, India, 163, 258

Nadig, Grace K., 133, 135
Nagle, J. C., 224
Nairobi, Kenya, 151, 256
Nam-pla, 218
Nanking, University of, 92
Napier, George, 133
National Agricultural School, Mexico, 188
National Catholic Rural Life Conference, 92
National FAO Committees, 78
National Grange, USA, 22
National Nutrition Committees, 46, 127
National Research Council, USA, 43
Neale, John R., 188
Near East and Africa, 101-144: regional projects, 101-113, country projects, 114-144
  Arab States fundamental education center, 135
  bread, 103
  composition of diets, 31
  conditions and needs, 84-85
  co-operatives, 110-111: participants in training institute, 254
  economic development projects, training institute, 161: participants, 258
  extension, agricultural, 109-110: participants in development meeting, 254
  Food and Agriculture Programs and Outlook, Regional Meetings on, 159: participants, 257
  food supplies, prewar, 30
  Ford Foundation, 93
  forestry, 111-112: **participants in conference, 254**

Near East and Africa (*Continued*)
  forestry (*Continued*)
    pulp and paper surveys, 181
  grain storage, 76
  grassland program, 105-106
  home economics, 109
  land problems seminar (proposed), 184
  livestock disease
    animal health meeting, 107: participants, 253
    foot-and-mouth disease, 107: participants in special meeting, 253
    Near East Commission for Animal Health (proposed), 107
    rinderpest, 150-151: participants in Nairobi meeting, 256
  locust control program, 102-103
  nutrition, 109: participants in training institute, 254
  regional office, FAO, 78, 133
  statistics, agricultural, 112-113: participants in training institutes, 254, 255
  wheat and barley breeding, 103-105: participants in meetings, 253
Near East Foundation, 93
Near East Relief, 93
Negev, Israel, 132
Nehru, Jawaharlal, 164
Nepal, 177-178
  Switzerland, work by, 97
Netherlands
  mortality, infant, 34, 246
  See also Amsterdam, Brussels, The Hague, Wageningen
New Delhi, India, 96, 112, 254
New Zealand
  food supplies, prewar, 30
  Ceylon, assistance to, 170
Newton, H. W., 167
Nicaragua, 210-211
  grain storage, 76
  grassland, 183
  See also Managua
Nicosia, Cyprus, 110, 254
Nigeria, 124
  rinderpest vaccine research, 150
  See also Ibadan
Nile River, 3-6, 7, 10, 11, 12
  Aswan Dam, 7, 15, 134
  engineering works on, 15
Norag, 4, 5
Norkey, Tenzing, 177
Norway
  technical co-operation program, 96-97
  See also Bergen
Nuoc-mam, 218

Nutrition
  Caribbean, 193: participants in meeting, 261
  committee on calories, FAO, 30
  Costa Rica, 211
  Egypt, 9
  Greece, 65-66
  groups of foods in diet, 43
  importance to health and life, 42-43
  Indonesia, 176
  Institute of Nutrition for Central America and Panama, 192
  Iraq, 126-127
  Joint FAO-WHO Expert Committee on Nutrition, 108: membership, 254
  laboratory animals in research, 42
  Latin America, 191-193: participants in regional conferences, 261
  League of Nations work, 44-48
  minerals, 39, 41, 42
  Near East and Africa, 109: participants in training institutes, 254
  Nicaragua, 211
  Nutrition Committee for South and East Asia, FAO, 146, 148
  Nutrition Conference for Defense, USA, 47
  Nutrition and Public Health, 45
  Peru, 204
  Physiological Bases of Nutrition, The, 45
  Portugal, 233
  recommended allowances, Food and Nutrition Board, USA, 43
  requirements for good nutrition, 31
  research and development, 39-44
  status in UK and USA, 44
  Syria, 126-127
  Thailand, 174
  vitamins. *See* vitamins
  See also nutritional disease
Nutritional disease, 39, 41
  beriberi, 41, 149
  goiter, 39, 192
  kwashiorkor, Africa, 108-109
  polyneuritis, 41
  protein malnutrition
    Latin America, 108, 109, 192
    South and East Asia, meeting, 109
  rickets, 39, 41
  scurvy, 39, 41
  xerophthalmia, 41
Nuwara Eliya, Ceylon, 155, 256

Ogilvie, H. W., 142
Oklahoma Agricultural and Mechanical College, 93

INDEX

Olive-fly, Europe and Mediterranean, 225: participants in meeting, 263
Olive oil production, Greece, 65
One World, 52
Organization of American States, 94
  foot-and-mouth disease work, 182
Organization for European Economic Co-operation, 95, 106, 217, 228
Orr, John Boyd. *See* Boyd-Orr, Lord
Osorio-Tafall, B. F., 200
Otavalo, Ecuador, 202
Ozark Mountains, 28

Padec, 218
Pakistan, 117-120
  East Pakistan, 119-120
  Ford Foundation, work by, 93
  Sweden, work by, 97
  West Pakistan, 117-119
  See also Lahore
Pan, C. L., 133, 134
Panama, 211
  grain storage, 76
  See also Panama City
Panama City, 182
Pan-American Sanitary Bureau, foot-and-mouth disease work, 182
Pan-American School of Agriculture, Honduras, 93
Pan-American Union, 94
Paper. *See* pulp and paper
Paraguary, 203-204. *See also* Asunción
Paraná pine, Brazil, 196
Paraná River, Jesuit colonies on, 90
Parasites, internal, Egypt, 14
Paris, France, 71, 112, 220, 225, 254, 262
Pasto, Tuure, 114, 212
Pasture. *See* grassland and land, grazing
Pasture and Fodder Development, Mediterranean Working Party on, 106
Patis, 218
Patterson, Albion, 204
Patzcuaro, Mexico, 207
Pearson, L. B., 51, 59, 60
Pekelharing, 41
Penteado, Eurico, 52
Péres de Rivera, Señora Aida, 194
Persia. *See* Iran
Persian lamb. *See* sheep (karakul)
Peru, 13, 204
  fisheries resources, 190
  See also Lima
Peters, L. A. H., 63
Petersen, A. T., 125
Philippine Republic, 163, 178, 259. *See also* Baguio
Phoenicia, 120

Physiological Bases of Nutrition, The, 45
Plankton, as food, 154
Planning, agricultural. *See* economics, agricultural
Plant
  breeders, lists maintained by FAO, 75
  breeding
    corn, hybrid, Europe, 75, 222-223
    rice, Far East, 147-148
    wheat and barley, Near East, 104-105
  protection
    Iran, 124
    Iraq, 124
    Syria, 123
    Yugoslavia, 235
    See also insect control
  See also specific crops
Point Four proposals, 83, 95
Poland
  FAO mission to, 77: membership, 251
  FAO-UNRRA projects, 73, 75
  withdrawal from FAO, 77
  See also Warsaw
Popenoe, Wilson, 93, 187
Population in agriculture, 33, 245
  Thailand, 33
  USA, 20, 21, 22, 23, 26, 33
Population control, 35-36
Port-of-Spain, Trinidad, 193, 194, 261
Portugal, 233
Potentials of world food production, study by FAO, 36
Poultry
  Ceylon, 171
  Thailand, 173-174
Poverty, of farmers, 30
Pra-hoc, 218
Preparatory Commission on World Food Proposals, 68-70, 145: membership, 250
Prodhromos, Cyprus, 253
Proteins, 42
  loss in rice during processing, 148
Protein malnutrition. *See* nutritional disease
Protestant Commission of Churches on International Affairs, consultative status with FAO, 92-93
Pryor, L. D., 126
Publications of FAO, 75, 78, 86, 113, 157, 184, 220, 221
Puerto Rico, 194
Puerto Rico, University of, 193
Pulp and paper
  needs and possibilities for increased production, 180-181
  products used in various countries, 32

Pulp and paper (*Continued*)
　surveys by FAO, 181: countries surveyed, 259
Punjab, Pakistan, 90, 118-119

Quebec, Ontario, Canada, 59
Quebec Conference. *See* Conference of FAO, first session
Queen Aliya College for Women, Baghdad, 127
Quinoa, 205
Quito, Ecuador, 112, 159, 193, 201, 255, 257

Rabbits, use in rinderpest vaccine production, 150-151
Ramiah, K., 147, 148
Range land. *See* grassland and land, grazing
Rangoon, Burma, 146, 175
Rationing of food in wartime, 47, 48
Razmilic, R. V., 115
Reading, England, 75
Reclamation
　Ceylon, 169-170
　India, 164
　Pakistan, 118
　See also irrigation
Reductions, Paraguay, 90
Reerink, H. V., 170
Regional Meetings on Food and Agriculture Programs and Outlook, 159: participants, 257-258
　Far East, 159-161
　Latin America, 193-194
Regional offices of FAO, 78, 133, 172, 195, 200, 207
Regional projects and programs of FAO
　background, 101
　Europe, 217-228
　Far East, 145-163
　Latin America, 179-194
　Near East and Africa, 101-113
Reisner, George, 171
Reisner, John H., 92
Relation of Nutrition to Health, Agriculture, and Economic Policy, 46
Religious groups, technical co-operation work, 90-93
Research, agricultural
　Europe, 226-227
　Iraq, 124
　Israel, 132
　Syria, 124
Resident representatives, TAB, 87
Respiration calorimeter, 40
Ridley, Nicholas, 46
Rigsdagen, Denmark, 67

Rice
　balancing rice diets, 149
　economic aspects of, 146
　exporters, prewar, 145
　fortified, 149
　hybridization, 147-148
　importers, prewar, 145
　long-stemmed, 119
　machinery for production, processing, 148
　marketing, Thailand, 77, 172
　nutritive values, loss of, 148-149
　parboiled, 149
　polished, nutritional deficiencies, 41
　Preparatory Commission recommendations on, 70
　processing and storage, Liberia, 143
　production, postwar, 84-85
　production methods, Egypt, 133-134
　production, processing, and storage, Thailand, 77, 172-173
　undermilling, 148-149
　varieties, 147
　yields, Egypt, Italy, Japan, USA, 9
　See also International Rice Commission
Rice Meeting, 145-146: participants, 255
Rice Study Group, 78, 145: participants, 255
Rinderpest. *See* livestock disease
Rio de Janeiro, Brazil, 78, 94, 112, 179, 182, 192, 194, 255, 261
Robb, Elda, 133
Robb, R. L., 207
Robinson, H. C., 124
Rochac, Alfonso, 186
Rocher, Marc, 209
Rockefeller, Nelson A., 93, 94
Rockefeller Foundation, 93
Rodriguez, Ezequiel, 191
Roe, R. J., 107
Rogers, L. J., 196
Rome, Italy, 35, 78, 79, 80, 106, 159, 217, 257, 263
Roosevelt, Eleanor, 49
Roosevelt, Franklin D., 49, 111
Ross, Mary, 133, 135
Rossi-Doria, Manlio, 196
Royal Agricultural Society of England, 91
Rubber processing, Thailand, 173

Saari, Eino A., 204
Salonika, Greece, 91, 231
Samn, 9
Sampling Techniques, Handbook on, 113
San José, Costa Rica, 112, 188, 255, 259, 260
San Salvador, El Salvador, 189
Sandvig, E. D., 200

INDEX

Santiago, Chile, 78, 161, 180, 200, 258
Sapporo, Japan, 91
Saqia, 11
Saudi Arabia, 127-131. *See also* Mecca
Savage, D. A., 207
Sawmilling
  demonstration center, Brazil, 196
  See also forestry
Scattergood, Leslie W., 211
Schmid, G., 230
School feeding
  Costa Rica, 211
  Nicaragua, 211
  Portugal, 233
Schools, rural, USA, 22
Schulthess, W. G., 177-178
Schuster, W. H., 155
Schweigger, E. C. A., 202
Schweng, L. D., 127
Schwerdtfeger, F., 209
Schyns, P. J., 175
Scott-Robertson, G., 61
Seaweed, as animal feed, 183
Second World Food Survey, 30
Seed distribution, FAO, 75, 139-140
Selective expansion of agricultural production, 86
Semple, A. T., 115
Seravalli Céspedes, Francisco, 189
Sericulture
  Afghanistan, 116
  Burma, 175
Servicios, 94, 188
Shaduf, 11
Shamma, 139
Sharecroppers, USA, 28
Sheep production
  Afghanistan, karakul, 114-115
  Brazil, 197-198
  Ecuador, 201-202
  Ethiopia, 137
  Iceland, 232-233
  India, 167
  Libya, 141
  Turkey, 234
  Uruguay, 203
Sherpas, 177-178
Shifting cultivation
  Cambodia, 156
  dangers and control methods, 156
  Liberia, 143
  Southeast Asia, 155-156
  Thailand, 77
Silk culture. *See* sericulture
Silva, J. A., Jr., 201
Sind, Pakistan, 118
Sindibis, center in Egypt, 135
Singapore, 153, 159, 163, 257, 258

Singh, Sardar Datar, 158
Sirs-al-Layyan, Egypt, 135
Sismanidis, Mrs. Aristotelis, 65. *See also* Tsongas, Andromache
Sithiporn Kridakara, Prince, 146
Slaughterhouse improvement
  Ecuador, 203
  Iran, 122
  Pakistan, 117
Smith-Hughes Act, USA, 21
Smith-Lever Act, USA, 21
Society of Friends, 92
Soil conservation
  Israel, 131-132
  meeting, Florence, 75
  Yugoslavia, 236
Soil fertility training institute, IRC, 148
Soil management and use, 58
Somalia, 142
Sommerauer, Willi, 116
Sorensen, S. B., 166
Soya milk, experiments in Indonesia, 176
Special Meeting on Urgent Food Problems, 63: participants, 250
Spice Isles, 175
Sponges, burned, for goiter, 39
Staff of FAO, 61, 79
Staffe, A. I., 206
Stanley, Louise, 39
State of Food and Agriculture, 86
Statistics
  census methods, 113
  Chile, 200
  Colombia, 206
  Finland, 231
  Iran, 125
  Iraq, 125
  Liberia, 144
  Near East, 112-113
  Panama, 211
  Production and Price Statistics Seminar, 112: participants, 255
  Regional Sampling Demonstration Center for Far East, 113: participants, 255
  regional statistical officers, 113
  sampling technique for census taking, 113
  Syria, 125
  training institutes, 112: participants, 254, 255
  world census of agriculture, 113
Stem rust. *See* wheat
Stewart, W. Lyle, 232
Stiebeling, Hazel K., 43, 44
Strachey, John, 68
Sturtevant, A. H., 98
Subsistence farming, USA, 28, 29

Sudan, 7, 15
Sugar cane, Ceylon, 170
Sukhatme, P. V., 113
Sukswasti, Mom Chao Suebsukswasti, 163
Supervised agricultural credit. *See* credit, agricultural
Surinam (Dutch Guiana), 214-215
Surpluses
  during depression, USA, 22, 23
  FAO Conference comment, 85-86
  postwar, 31
  problem of, 56
  proposals for handling
    Consultative Sub-Committee on Surplus Disposal, 72-73, 251
    International Commodity Clearing House, 71-72
    Preparatory Commission on World Food Proposals, 69
    Special Meeting on Urgent Food Problems, 63
    Working Party on Surplus Disposal, 72, 251
    World Food Board, 66-68
  See also commodity proposals
Swain, E. H., 140
Sweden
  Ethiopia and Pakistan, work in, 97
  wood pulp and pulp products, 32
Switzerland, 227
  Nepal, work in, 97, 177
  wartime food production and rationing, 48
  See also Geneva, Zurich
Sylvain, Pierre, 138
Syria, Iran, Iraq, 120-127
  foot-and-mouth disease, 107
  forestry, 126
  grassland, 122
  nutrition and home economics, 126-127
  plant protection, 123
  water supplies, 123
  See also Bloudane, Damascus
Syrian University, 127

Taeuber, Conrad, 112
Taft, A. C., 230
Tal, Shimon, 212
Talkalore, India, 165
Tambaks, 154
Tambour, 11
Tamesis, Florencio, 163
Tang, P. C., 211
Tanganyika, 7
Tannous, Afif I., 64
Tapachula, Mexico, 189
Taylor, R. F., 232
Tea production and processing, Iran, 124

Teakwood, Thailand, 173
Technical assistance. *See* technical co-operation
Technical Assistance Board, 87, 194
Technical Assistance Committee, 87
Technical Assistance Conference, 84
Technical Assistance for Economic Development, 83
Technical co-operation
  beginnings in FAO, 82
  British Commonwealth program, 96
  Colombo Plan for Co-operative Economic Development in South and Southeast Asia, 96
  formulation of projects, 86
  governmental agencies, 94-97
  growth of the idea, 97-98
  history of early work, 89-98
  Norway, 96-97
  proposals for, 48-49
  religious groups, 90-93
  Sweden, 97
  Switzerland, 97
  USA colleges and universities, 93, 96
  USA government, 94-96; aid to: Burma, 175; El Salvador, 210; Greece, 65, 231; Haiti, 212; India, 93, 164, 167; Iran, 121; Iraq, 121; Israel, 133; Latin America, 94; Liberia, 143; Pakistan, 120; Turkey, 234; Paraguay, 204; Thailand, 172
Technical Cooperation Administration, USA, 94, 96
Tegucigalpa, Honduras, 93, 209
Tenant farmers, USA, 28
Tengku Ya'acob Ibni al-Marhum Sultan Abdul Hamid Halim Shah, 162
Teresopolis, Brazil, 179, 259
Textiles, used in various countries, 31, 32, 244
Thailand, 76-77, 145, 172-174
  annual per caput income, 34, 246
  energy, mechanical, 33, 245
  FAO mission to, 76, 172: membership, 251
  population in agriculture, 33, 245
  rinderpest, 77, 151
  textiles used, 32, 244
  wood pulp and pulp products, 32
  See also Bangkok
Thiamine. *See* vitamins
Thompson, E. F., 212
Threshing, in Egypt, 4, 5
Tibet, 118, 119
Tigris River, 120
Tilapia, in fish culture, 173, 212
Timber Committee, ECE, 221: membership, 262

INDEX

Timber grading school, 162-163: participants, 258
Timmer, W. J., 197
Tingo Maria Experiment Station, Peru, 204
Tobato, Seiichi, 146
Tokyo, Japan, 146
Tolley, Howard, 61, 112
Tools, agricultural, 33
　Afghanistan, 116
　Egypt, 9, 10
　Ethiopia, 138-139
　relation to economic development, 57
　USA, 20, 21
Trabzon, Turkey, 235
Tractors. See machinery, agricultural
Training institutes. See subject of institute
Trassi, 218
Traub, E., 205
Tripolitania, Libya, 140
Trivandrum, India, 78, 145, 255
Truman, Harry S., 52, 95
　FAO Conference speech, 82
　point four proposals, 83
Tsongas, Andromache, 65, 231, 234
Tukuls, 136
Turkey, 105, 106, 233-235. See also Ankara, Istanbul
Turrialba, Costa Rica, 94, 181, 188, 259, 260
Turrialba Institute, 94, 181, 183, 187-188
Tuwaiq Mountains, 130

Uganda, 7
Uhart, Edmond, 125
Union of Soviet Socialist Republics, 53, 59
United Fruit Company, 93
United Kingdom, 59, 90
　contribution to FAO budget, 53
　nutrition in war, 48
　status of nutrition, 44
　See also England, London, Reading, Weybridge
United Nations, 62, 184
　Arab States Fundamental Education Center, co-operation in, 135
　Bolivia, assistance to, 205
　Caribbean home economics program, 193
　El Salvador, mixed UN mission, 210
　Haiti, mission to, 211-212
　Peru, work in, 204
　population trends study, 35
　pulp and paper surveys, co-operation in, 181
　Technical Assistance Conference, 84

United Nations (*Continued*)
　Technical Assistance for Economic Development, 83
　See also Economic and Social Council, Economic Commissions, General Assembly
United Nations Children's Fund
　Costa Rica, co-operative milk project, 211
　El Salvador, co-operation in UN mission, 210
　Greece, assistance on milk plants, 231
　Honduras, milk-conservation plan, 209
　Iran, assistance on milk plant, 122
　kwashiorkor, co-operation in treatment of, 108
　Mexico, milk-conservation plan, 208
　Nicaragua, school feeding, 211
United Nations Educational, Scientific, and Cultural Organization, 181, 184
　fundamental education centers
　　Ceylon, 171
　　Egypt (Arab States), 135
　　Haiti, 212
　　Liberia, 144
　　Mexico (Latin America), 207
　　Thailand, 174
United Nations Korean Relief Administration, 178
United Nations Relief and Rehabilitation Administration, 62
　agricultural advisory projects transferred to FAO, 73-76
　technical co-operation aspects of program, 95
United Nations Relief and Works Agency, 110
United Nations Statistical Office, 112
United Nations Technical Assistance Administration, 115, 194
United States of America
　advances in agriculture during war, 24
　Agriculture, Department of, 21, 48, 53, 62, 94
　annual per caput income, 34, 246
　bilateral programs in various countries. See technical co-operation, USA
　Census, Bureau of the, 112
　city-country relations in agriculture, 22, 25, 27
　community activities, farm family, 25
　composition of diets, 31
　contribution to FAO budget, 53
　credit, agricultural, international meeting on, 186
　diet, farm family, 24
　energy, mechanical, 33
　European postwar co-operation, 228

United States of America (*Continued*)
  Expanded Technical Assistance Program pledge, 84
  farm life, 18, 19, 24, 25, 29
  farm organizations, 22
  food supplies, prewar, 30
  government services to agriculture, 21, 23
  industry, relation to agriculture, 20, 25, 26
  labor efficiency in agriculture, 20, 21, 23, 24, 26, 27
  land, arable, 32, 244
  land problems, international conference on, 184
  legislation, agricultural, 22, 23
  life expectancy, 34
  machinery, agricultural, 20, 21, 22, 23, 24, 26
  modernization of agriculture, 20-27
  mortality, infant, 34, 246
  nutrition status, 44
  population in agriculture, 20, 21, 22, 23, 26, 33
  rationing, 48
  rinderpest vaccine research, 73
  surpluses, during depression, 22, 23
  textiles, 32
  tools, agricultural, 20
  types of farms, 28
  typical farm, hog-dairy, 18-27
  wood pulp and pulp products, 32
  yields, corn, cotton, rice, wheat, 9
  See also technical co-operation, USA, and Washington
Upward, G. R., 167
Uruguay, 203
  milk production, 183
  See also Montevideo
Utah State Agricultural College, 93
Uttar Pradesh, India, 165-166
Uvarov, B. P., 102, 103

Vaccines
  foot-and-mouth disease, 183, 224
  hemorrhagic septicemia, 174
  rinderpest, 149-151
  virus vaccine manufacture training institute, 151: participants, 256
  See also livestock disease
Valenzuela, Professor, 200
Valiente, A. F., 197
Valparaiso, Chile, 191, 201
van Blommestein, W. J., 120
van Dillewijn, C., 170
Van Pel, Hubertus and Jan, 143
van der Heyden, W. F. L., 167
van der Plas, C. L., 131
van der Ploeg, J., 176
Varossieau, W. W., 126
Veiga, João Soares, 181
Veillet-Lavallée, Marc, 61
Venezuela, 206
  American International Association work, 93
  FAO oilseed mission to, 78: membership, 251
  grain storage, 76
  See also Caracas
Vera Cruz, Mexico, 208
Veterinary education, Finland, 230-231
Veterinary laboratory techniques, meeting, 75
Veterinary work. *See* livestock
Viale delle Terme di Caracalla, Rome, 80
Village development, India, 164
Viña del Mar, Chile, 191
Visser, J. W. B., 176
Vitamins, 39, 41
  B_1 (thiamine), loss in rice during processing, 148
Volos, Greece, 231
von Bottenburg, M., 126, 206
von Monroy, J. A., 175

Wadi Jizan, Saudi Arabia, 130
Wageningen, Netherlands, 225, 226, 263
Wahlen, F. T., 48, 61
Wakeley, Raymond E., 197
Walker, R. H., 76
Wall, Duncan, 61
Walters, F. P., 44, 46, 47
Ward, Gordon, 173
Warsaw, Poland, 75
Washington, D.C., USA, 52, 63, 68, 71, 72, 73, 78, 79
Water use, Egypt, 10-12, 134
Water buffalo, 3, 8, 73, 157
Water conservation, Israel, 131-132
Weaving, Ecuador, 202
Weisl, Frank, 61
Welfare centers, Egypt, 13-15
Weybridge, England, 75
Wheat
  breeding
    Iran, 123-124
    Near East program (including barley), 103-105: participants in meetings, 253
  production
    Brazil, 197
    Near East, 104
  stem rust control, 104-105
  threshing, Egypt, 4
  yields, Egypt, USA, 9
White Fathers of Africa, 90

INDEX

White Nile, 7
Whyte, R. O., 166
Wilder, Russell, 62
Williams, Milo, 118
Willkie, Wendell, 52
Wilson, M. L., 110
Wisconsin, University of, 184
Wood and wood products. *See* forestry
Wood pulp and pulp products, used in various countries, 32
Wool. *See* sheep production
Work of FAO, 54-59
Working Party on Disposal of Agricultural Surpluses, 72: participants, 251
World census of agriculture, 78, 113
World Council of Churches, 93
World food and agriculture situation, review by Council and Conference of FAO, 69
World Food Board, 66-68
World Food Council, 68-70
World Food Proposals, Preparatory Commission on, 68
World food situation, 61-63, 85-86, 87
  action by FAO Conference, 85-86
  appraisal, 61-63
  Director-General's observations (1949), 84-85
World Food Survey (first), 30, 62: membership of working groups, 249
World Food Survey, Second, 30

World Health Organization
  co-operation in: Arab States fundamental education center, 135; fundamental education center, Mexico, 207; kwashiorkor work, 108
  El Salvador, work with UN mission, 210
  protein malnutrition, meeting, 192
  WHO-FAO Joint Expert Committee on Nutrition, 108: membership, 254
World Monetary and Economic Conference, 45
World Population Conference, 35
World war against want, 86
World's Pulp and Paper Resources and Prospects, 181

Xerophthalmia, 41

Yak, 178
Yarmouk River Valley development, Jordan, 127
Yesilköy Plant Breeding Station, Istanbul, 105
Yugoslavia, 235-237
  FAO-UNRRA projects, 73
  See also Belgrade

Zamorano, Honduras, 93
Zebu Cattle of India and Pakistan, 157
Ziener, P. B., 167
Zoroastrianism, 121
Zurich, Switzerland, 75, 226